PENGUIN BOOKS

GEORGE AND ROBERT STEPHENSON

L. T. C. Rolt was born at Chester in 1910. After his education at Cheltenham College he embarked on an engineering career, until he decided to turn to writing. From childhood he was fascinated by the history of engineers and engineering, and his writing reflected this interest. His first book, *Narrow Boat*, published in 1944, describes a journey along the English canals during the twelve years that he lived afloat. His subsequent biographies of famous engineers, like his writings on railways and motor cars, show his concern to give the story of the Industrial Revolution an imaginative and literary shape.

He was a founder member of the Vintage Sports Car Club and was also co-founder and first Honorary Secretary of the Inland Waterways Association. He founded the Talyllyn Railway Preservation Society, of which he was Vice-President for many years, and he was a member of the Science Museum Advisory Council and Vice-President of the Newcomen Society for the study of the history of engineering and technology. He was a Fellow of the Royal Society of Literature, in 1965 was awarded an Honorary M.A. degree by the University of Newcastle and in 1973 received an Honorary M.Sc. from Bath University. Mr Rolt died in 1974.

Among his many publications, he has written biographies of *Isambard Kingdom Brunel* and *Thomas Telford* (both published in Penguins), and two volumes of autobiography, *Landscape with Machines* and *Landscape with Canals*.

L. T. C. ROLT

George and
Robert Stephenson

The Railway Revolution

With drawings and maps
by KENNETH LINDLEY

PENGUIN BOOKS

PENGUIN BOOKS

Published by the Penguin Group
27 Wrights Lane, London w8 5TZ, England
Viking Penguin Inc., 40 West 23rd Street, New York, New York 10010, USA
Penguin Books Australia Ltd, Ringwood, Victoria, Australia
Penguin Books Canada Ltd, 2801 John Street, Markham, Ontario, Canada L3R 1B4
Penguin Books (NZ) Ltd, 182–190 Wairau Road, Auckland 10, New Zealand

Penguin Books Ltd, Registered Offices: Harmondsworth, Middlesex, England

First published by Longman 1960
Published in Pelican Books 1978
Reprinted in Penguin Books 1984, 1988

Made and printed in Great Britain by
Hazell Watson & Viney Limited
Member of BPCC plc
Aylesbury Bucks
Set in Monotype Bembo

God! shall we ever honour what we are,
And see one moment ere the age expire,
The vision of man shouting and erect,
Whirled by the shrieking steeds of flood and fire?

Or must Fate act the same grey farce again,
And wait, till one, amid Time's wrecks and scars,
Speaks to a ruin here, "What poet-race
Shot such cyclopean arches at the stars?"

G. K. CHESTERTON

PREFACE

GEORGE STEPHENSON is the most famous engineer who ever lived. This is a sweeping statement, but its truth can be proved by asking any school boy, or disinterested adult for that matter, to name one celebrated engineer. Nine times out of ten the answer will be Stephenson. The tenth may give the name of James Watt, thanks very largely to the story of the boiling kettle which, like the legend of Alfred and the cakes, has become a part of English folk-lore. Yet in spite of this, compared with Stephenson, Watt is an also ran in popular memory.

The reason why George Stephenson is remembered while the names of engineers of equal or greater ability are forgotten is a simple one. He is popularly regarded as the author of the railway and the steam locomotive. No other invention had such an over-whelming effect upon society as this first form of mechanical trans-port, nor has anything usurped its place in the affections of subsequent generations. From the outset the spectacle of a railway train in full cry excited wonder and admiration not unmixed with awe. Contemporaries of George Stephenson grew to manhood in a world which had never known any tractive power other than horses, yet they lived to see express trains travelling at mile-a-minute speeds. We have since conquered the road and the air with newer forms of power and can travel faster than sound, but no subsequent development has equalled in significance or in sheer impact upon the imagination this first mighty stride which took man from a secure and settled environment hallowed by centuries into a new, exciting, yet disturbing world which at once opened up limitless possibilities. The railway train was the harbinger of this brave new world. The rhythmical thunder of iron tyres on rails, the powerful heart-beats of the exhaust, the precise, majestic movement of side rods and great driving wheels, the flicker of furnace light on flying steam, these things brought to the Victorians a new romantic poetry of motion. It is arguable that engineers have not succeeded in producing any such romantic poetry since. The spectacle of any small boy on any station platform, eagerly watching the passage of an express train while a jet plane screams unheeded across the sky, makes it easy to understand why George Stephenson's pride of place is so perennially secure.

For many of us who are no longer young railways have become one of the most poignant and evocative memorials of a vanished world. It was a world distinguished by extremes of wealth and poverty which today offend our social conscience; yet it was also a world in which men looked forward to a millenium of peace and prosperity untroubled by the fear of disaster upon a cosmic scale. Perhaps it is more than a coincidence that, as Canon Roger Lloyd pointed out not long ago, the railway is one of the very few major inventions which fallen man has been unable to turn to any destructive purpose. For all its power and majesty, the steam locomotive has always remained a docile beast of burden and, unlike the motor car or the aeroplane, it has never become an engine of war. It was the sound of a distant train which prompted Siegfried Sassoon to write:

> That somehow its habitual travelling comforts me,
> Making my world seem safer, homelier, sure to be
> The same tomorrow and the same, one hopes, next year,
> 'There's peacetime in that train.'

Of what other manifestation of man's technical ingenuity could the same be said?

It is not too much to say that the railway engineers, and in particular the two Stephensons, created the Victorian Age. Their iron roads were the vital arteries by which it lived and grew so precociously. Whereas the fretful roar of the internal combustion engine sets the pace of our civilization, the world which finally passed away in 1914 spun to the rhythm of wheels on rails and the measured, less hectic pulse of steam power. That pulse sounds slow and labouring today because, like the clip-clop of hooves in an Edwardian street, it is doomed soon to die. Yet the railways are with us still and we should see them and value them for what they are, the greatest achievement of the 19th century. They represent a colossal outpouring of creative energy unmatched by any other age; the embodiment of the pride, the hope and the aspiration of a pioneer generation expressed in the cyclopean masonry of arch and pier, and in the smoke-blackened architectural splendour of great stations. Such stations with their iron arcades and high vaulting of glass and slender roof rib are temples consecrated to an unquestioning faith in material progress.

If George Stephenson was not the author of all this, it was unquestionably his vision and his unshakable faith in the powers of the locomotive which brought it about. No one can say, then, that his fame is undeserved, even though the practical and inventive part he played may have been popularly exaggerated. The man who, above all others, helped to make George Stephenson's vision a reality was his only son, Robert Stephenson. By their contemporaries this fact was recognized and honoured, yet in the recollection of posterity the son plays second fiddle to the father and his achievements are often wrongly credited to the older man. For this, Samuel Smiles's famous biography of George Stephenson is partly responsible. He magnified at Robert's expense the contribution made by George, and although the former lived long enough to read Smiles's text, he was too modest a man to cavil at it. True, Robert Stephenson had his own biographer, J. C. Jeaffreson, but he was not so well served. Jeaffreson lacks the narrative gift of Smiles; his painstaking book is stiff and formal and never appealed to so wide a public as did *The Life of George Stephenson*.

These two books were written nearly a century ago, but they are still the standard works on their subjects. Having re-read them I came to the conclusion that if a fresh assessment of the Stephensons was to have any value and add anything to our understanding, it must deal with father and son together on a perfectly equal footing. It seemed to me that the association between them was so close that any attempt to concentrate upon one to the exclusion of the other must create a misleading and partial impression. Despite their close relationship, the characters of these two great men were very different and in many respects complementary to each other. An important point which neither Smiles nor Jeaffreson brings out is that it is doubtful whether either could have succeeded without the other. In the early stages of their fight to establish the steam-powered railway Robert Stephenson, self-doubting, diffident, easily discouraged, would not have got far without the unwavering faith, the tremendous drive and self-confidence of his father. On the other hand, George Stephenson's ambitions might never have been realized without the support of his son, whose engineering and administrative talent was undoubtedly far superior to his own. This is evident in the way his affairs went so sadly awry during Robert Stephenson's absence abroad.

Elsewhere in this book I have contrasted conventional Victorian portrait painting with what was seen by the candid eye of the early camera lens. The figures of the two Stephensons which emerge from the pages of Smiles and Jeaffreson closely resemble the works of their contemporary portrait painters. They conform to the ideal Victorian conception of what a great man should be: George Stephenson, the unlettered genius, a paragon of all the simple virtues; Robert Stephenson a model example of the devoted son. They are stiff, hieratic figures and there is scarcely a hint that the winds of ordinary human emotion, of jealousy, hostility, rivalry or bitterness, ever swayed their lofty pedestals or ruffled a dignity and poise so assured. False idealization of this kind ultimately defeats its own object. In this case it led inevitably to the fashionable literary exercise of debunking the Victorians, but happily the great engineers escaped the attention of such iconoclasts, whose silly pastime is now out of date. Because a great man is shown to be a creature of flesh and blood with all the faults and failings that man is heir to, it does not necessarily make him any less great. Surely the fact that he succeeded in his purpose despite the handicap of his own faults may make him the greater. My own admiration for the two Stephensons is not lessened because I have tried to look at them with a candid eye. If as a result George Stephenson's pedestal is somewhat lower than it was, while that of Robert Stephenson stands proportionately higher, such a reversal of the popular estimate is not due to prejudice or to any perverse desire to differ from the majority verdict, but to an honest assessment based on a study of all the available facts. Even if Robert Stephenson had not been so modest a man, the son of a famous father always labours under the great handicap of reflected glory which tends to dazzle and confuse those who try to assess his own stature. If the father is not only famous but also the object of jealousy and hostility, as was George Stephenson, then the son's handicap is all the heavier. Robert Stephenson triumphantly overcame such difficulties to stand beside his father as a great man in his own right.

Robert Stephenson was an exact contemporary of his great rival, I. K. Brunel, and this fact inevitably invites comparisons. Some have been drawn in the pages which follow, but this summing up by F. R. Conder, an engineer who knew them both, may be more appropriately quoted here:

> The imperfections in the character of Mr. Brunel [writes Conder] were of the heroic order. He saw always clearly before him the *thing* to be done and the way to do it, although he might be deficient in the choice and the management of the human agency which was necessary to effect his designs. Mr. Stephenson, on the other hand, knew how to derive from his staff and his friends a support and an aid that carried him, at times, over real engineering difficulties with a flowing sheet. It may be that the perfection and success of each individual work was more the study and aim of Mr. Brunel, the return of benefit to the shareholders the more present idea to Mr. Stephenson. The former preferred the luxurious cabins of Atlantic steamers and the commodious sofas of the Broad Gauge carriages; the latter opened the way for parliamentary and workmen's trains.

This appraisal is just and apt. Although they were so frequently opposed to each other in their policies and so very different in character, the railway age was fortunate in having two such men as Robert Stephenson and Brunel in command during its formative years. For all pioneer work requires the caution, the conservatism and the patient thoroughness of a Stephenson no less than the sceptical, adventurous and daring genius of a Brunel. Solid achievement is always the product of these contrasting types of mind, and the fact that they often strike sparks from each other in the process is all to the good.

This book completes a trilogy of engineer biographies which was planned in 1953. The idea originated in a suggestion made to me by a publisher that I should write a life of Brunel, and it was for this reason only that the volume on Brunel appeared first. So far as the final result was concerned the fact that the trilogy would not appear in chronological sequence was of no account.

A criticism made of the two previous biographies in this trilogy is that I paid far too little attention to the general historical background, to the rapidly changing social, political and economic scene

in England during the lifetime of my subjects. Apart from the
practical consideration that such a 'Life and Times' treatment would
have made these biographies much longer than they are already and
therefore more expensive, I doubt that the addition of such a broad
landscape background would do much to enhance the portraits of
the men concerned. For those who want more general historical
information about the Industrial Revolution in England there is no
shortage of literature on the subject. Having read a great deal of this
admirable historical writing myself, it seemed to me that if the names
of the comparatively few leaders of the Revolution were mentioned
at all they appeared only as lay figures, mere pawns in a vast,
impersonal collective process of historical change. My object in
undertaking this biographical trilogy was not to add anything to this
general historical picture, but to attempt to correct its bias by trying
to breathe some life into a few of the most important of these
leaders and put them in the foreground where they properly belong.

It is easy for the modern historian, wise after the event, to say
that George Stephenson and his son accomplished what they did
merely because they happened to be born at the right moment in
history. We may judge now that this was so, that England was
economically and socially ripe for the railway revolution. But that
this was not evident to George Stephenson's contemporaries should
be obvious to anyone who reads this book. The railway revolution
only came about after Stephenson had fought his way through to
success against apathy, scepticism, ridicule and every kind of
opposition. The historian may reply that the world would have had
railways just the same if Stephenson had never been born. Maybe;
but only if some other engineer had come forward to play Stephenson's historic role by swimming resolutely against the current until
it turned in his favour.

One object of this trilogy, then, has been to assert the immense
importance of the parts played by a comparatively small number of
individuals in that momentous process of historical change which we
call the Industrial Revolution. That they were indeed a small
company may be judged from the frequency with which a few
names recur in the three books.

It seemed to me important to try to rescue these great men from
an inexcusable literary neglect. Soldier, sailor and statesman, poet

and painter, literary lion and social reformer, all have been paid their due, and sometimes more than their due, by the historian and the biographer. But not the great engineers who laid the foundations of the modern world. For this neglect the gulf between the Arts and Sciences is responsible. It has widened and deepened rapidly in the last hundred years. If it is not bridged, and bridged quickly, the future of our civilization will be dark indeed. If this biographical trilogy contributes a brick or two to such a bridge it will have served its purpose.

L.T.C.R.

ACKNOWLEDGEMENTS

Thanks are due to the following who either provided material to illustrate this book or granted reproduction permission:

The Radio Times Hulton Picture Library for Nos. 15, 16 and 18. *The Illustrated London News* for Nos. 2 and 3. The Director of the Science Museum, South Kensington, for permission to reproduce Nos. 4, 5, 6, 7, 9, 10, 11, 12, 13, 14 and 17. (Crown Copyright reserved.) With the help of Mr. C. R. Clinker, No. 1 is reproduced from the portrait engraving in *The Life of Robert Stephenson*, Vol. 1. No. 8 is reproduced from a print in the author's possession with the co-operation of Mr. C. Hamilton Ellis.

Thanks are also due to Miss D. E. Collins for permission to reproduce the last two verses of 'King's Cross Station' by G. K. Chesterton from *The Wild Knight and Other Poems*, published by Messrs. J. M. Dent & Sons Ltd.

CONTENTS

CONTENTS

PART I

The Kings of Liverpool
1784–1830

PART II

The Years of Power
1830–1836

PLATES

DRAWINGS AND MAPS IN THE TEXT

THE STEPHENSON FAMILY

ROBERT STEPHENSON — MABEL CARR

JAMES
b. 1779

Driver of the *Blucher*, the *Locomotion* and many other early Stephenson loco-motives. Died at Snibston, Leics.

GEORGE
1781–1848

Married first Frances Henderson by whom he had an only son

ELEANOR
b. 1784

Acted as George Stephen-son's housekeeper at Killing-worth after the death of his first wife. Later she married Stephen Liddell, who died after an accident while working for George Stephenson at Newcastle. George thereafter sup-ported the family.

ROBERT
b. 1788

Laid out the Hetton Colliery, Nantle and Bolton & Leigh railways under George Stephenson's direction. Finally became Manager of Pendleton Colliery, Lancs. He had one son.

JOHN
b. 1789

Was employed by George Stephenson at the Newcastle works and was killed in an accident there in 1831, leaving a large family, whom George Ste-phenson supported.

ANNE
b. 1792

Married John Nixon and emigrated to the U.S.A. She died at Pitts-burgh, leaving six children.

ROBERT
1803–1859

Who died without issue.

GEORGE ROBERT
1819–1905

On the death of his cousin, Robert Stephenson, in 1859, he inherited his interest in Robert Stephenson & Com-pany, Newcastle. His two sons, George and Robert, became joint Managing Directors of the Company.

PART ONE

The Years of Endeavour

1781–1830

CHAPTER ONE

Early Days at Killingworth

IT IS a pitch-dark winter's night in the year 1805. A bitter wind off the North Sea is whipping across the stone-walled uplands of Northumberland carrying with it the acrid, sulphurous fume of the pit banks. It is the hour after midnight and only two lights are visible, a flicker of furnace light from the winding house at West Moor pit and the feeble glimmer of a horn lantern bobbing along the rutted trackway leading past the huddle of miners' hovels called 'The Three Houses'. The lantern bearer is old Gilbert Lowerson the Killingworth 'knocker-up', for this desolate hour is what the pitmen call 'calling course' for the first shift at West Moor which is due down the pit at half-past one in the morning. A second shift will follow at half-past three.

Soon old Gilbert is knocking on the cottage doors with his stick. No need for him to carry one of those long poles crowned with a bunch of twigs or wires to rattle against the windows of upstairs bedrooms, for at West Moor in 1805 such luxuries were unknown. The single room of a 'back house' measuring twelve feet by ten was all the living space that a pitman and his wife were then allowed. Only when they had four or more children were they entitled to occupy a 'front house' in which a ladder-like stair led up from the little living room into a garret under the roof which extended the full width of the building.

As the knocker-up goes his relentless round the single windows of these crowded back-to-backs become faintly lit by tallow dip or rushlight or merely by the glow from the stirred embers of a banked up fire. Presently doors bang as men and boys, some no more than eight years old, emerge from their kennels into the icy darkness. Trappers and 'rolley' drivers, wood leaders, putters, hewers and on-setters dodging the stinking midden heaps, hob-nailed boots crunching the cat ice in the ruts of the cart-way as they all head towards that flicker of furnace light which marks the West Moor pit.

Once there the creaking 'whim' will lower them into the deeper darkness of the coal seams where, in galleries so low that a man is bent double, they must hack the precious coal from the working faces, break it and load it on to primitive sleds. These must be dragged by harnessed boys straining their way along on all fours to the pit bottom where the coal will be reloaded into wicker corves on 'rolleys' and drawn to the surface. In addition to the sheer physical hardship of the work there lurks in every narrow tunnel of this underground warren the constant threat of death—death from a sudden fall of roof; death from burns or suffocation following an explosion of gas—for West Moor is notorious for its 'blowers' of gas which the pitmen's naked lights or the underground furnace under the upcast shaft that ventilates the mine may all too easily ignite. Under such conditions these men and boys must labour for a shift of fifteen or sixteen hours without even a break for food—they must snatch a bite of their 'bait' when they can. This means that in the winter months they never see daylight except on pay Saturdays and Sundays. The short winter's day will have dawned and set and darkness will have fallen long before they come to the surface to breathe the raw northern air again and to stumble back over the frozen ruts to a home almost as cramped and airless as the pit.

So began and ended a typical day for those who worked for one of the wealthiest and most powerful commercial partnerships to emerge during the early years of Britain's industrial revolution—that of the celebrated Grand Allies. These Grand Allies were the Earl of Strathmore, Sir Thomas Liddell, later Lord Ravensworth, and Mr. Stuart Wortley, afterwards Lord Wharncliffe. The West Moor pit at Killingworth was only one of the many which they either owned or leased in the rich coalfields of Northumberland and Durham. The smoking chimneys of rapidly expanding London were the source of the wealth of the Grand Allies, for the great bulk of the coal they mined was shipped south by brigs from the Tyne and new shafts were constantly being sunk to the coal measures in the effort to keep pace with the demand.

To us, work in the collieries of the Grand Allies seems a black and almost inconceivable nightmare, yet to suppose that its effect was to make men mere abject or brutalized beasts of burden would be woefully to underestimate the splendid resilience of human nature; whereas nothing destroys a man more swiftly than soft living, hardship will temper him as surely as fire tempers a steel blade. This is certainly the lesson of Killingworth, for out of the squalor of its back-to-back terraces and the perilous dark of its mine galleries there were soon to emerge the men destined to free the steam engine and send it thundering across the world on iron rails. In 1805 it must have seemed that the future held nothing for these men but the same monotonous round of grinding toil which would ultimately hurry them, either diseased or maimed, to an early grave. Yet from West Moor, High Pit, Felling and other mines in the Tyne district would one day come those muscled men, hewers, blasters and tunnellers, who drove the first iron road from Stockton to Darlington and went on to build others: the Liverpool & Manchester, the London & Birmingham. Two of them, John Stevenson of Felling and Tommy Harding of West Moor lived to become prosperous railway contractors. On the winding engine of the Jimmy Pit at Killingworth two brothers, Henry and Thomas, worked with their father Joseph Cabery.[1] Henry, whose job was to brake the winding drum, was destined to engineer railways in Belgium and to receive a knighthood from the Belgian king, while young Thomas, whose humble task it was to hitch the 'rolleys' on to the winding rope, would one day be engineer of the York & North Midland. David Duncan, a boy at Dick's Pit, Killingworth, became an expert permanent-way engineer who left his name cast on the point levers of the Midland Railway, while a youthful brakesman named Thomas George—inexplicably called Tammy Grey by his mates—would drive Timothy Hackworth's *Sans Pareil* in the famous locomotive trials at Rainhill. As for Robert M'Cree, the little son of the Killingworth engine-wright, it was his destiny to drive the most celebrated locomotive in all railway history—none other than the *Rocket*.

But in 1805 all this was locked in the future and railways as we know them were as yet undreamed of, for the man who would not only change the lives of his work-mates but change the world had only lately moved to Killingworth from Willington Quay. He had taken the job of brakesman at West Moor pit and settled, with his

[1] In some contemporary sources the name is spelt Cabry.

ailing, pregnant wife Fanny and his infant son Robert, into a single-roomed 'cottage' at the Three Houses.

At the age of twenty-four, young George Stephenson was no stranger to that iron routine of the pit to which old Gilbert Lowerson summoned the men of Killingworth so remorselessly each morning. It was the only life he had ever known. When he was born, the second of six children, on 9 June 1781, his father, old Robert Stephenson, now engineman at the Blucher pit close by, was working as a fireman at Wylam Colliery at a wage of 12s. a week. Immediately after his marriage on 17 May 1778 to Mabel Carr,[1] the daughter of a dyer at Ovingham, Robert had worked at Walbottle colliery before he moved farther west along the Tyne valley to Wylam. There George was born and spent the first years of his life in the cottage known as Street House which still stands beside the railway line on the north bank of the river and is now cared for by the National Trust. That railway was then a wooden wagon-way, and as it passes within two yards of the cottage door George's first job was to keep his younger brothers and sisters, Robert, John, Eleanor and Ann, from getting under the feet of the horses which drew the loaded chaldron wagons along their primitive way. It is remarkable that George grew into such a wiry, muscular youth who excelled in weight lifting, wrestling, leaping and hammer throwing and who proved, in his celebrated fight with Ned Nelson, the battling pitman of Black Callerton, that he was a match for any man. For George does not appear to have inherited his strength from his parents. In the rich dialect of Tyneside his mother was called 'a delicat' boddie', while old Robert was described as 'like a peer o' deals nailed the-gither, an' a bit o' flesh i' th' inside; he war as queer as Dick's hatband—went thrice aboot an' wudn't tie'.

It is somehow typical of these strange years when a new England of smoke and steam and furnace flame was being forged out of a ferment of eager speculation and invention, that while the Stephenson family were coming into the world at Wylam the three eccentric brothers Martin were born at the neighbouring village of Ovingham. Jonathan Martin became a religious fanatic whose most celebrated feat was to set fire to York Minster after concealing himself among

---

[1] Mabel could not read or write and signed the register at Ovingham with an X. The christening of George Stephenson is recorded in the same register on 22 July 1781.

the organ pipes; his brother Willie wasted most of his life in attempting to solve the problem of perpetual motion and in pestering the King with letters in which he laid claim, on no grounds whatever, to George Stephenson's inventions. John Martin is the only one of this strange trio whose name has lived. The great tunnels, the cavernous mines, the smoke and the flame of the new industrial England inspired his strange genius to paint those weird apocalyptic scenes of hell, death and the last judgement which may yet prove prophetic of ultimate catastrophe. It is not without significance to reflect that George Stephenson, the father of railways, and John Martin, the painter of apocalypse, both played as children on the banks of the Tyne.

In those days of primitive coal-getting methods the life of a pit was often brief. When the more easily worked coal had been got the pit would be closed and the discharged men would be forced to migrate to some new and more promising 'winning' in the neighbourhood. Like their fellows, the Stephenson family had to 'follow the work' in this way. When George was eight years old Robert got a job as fireman at Dewley Burn Colliery and moved his family thither. Six years later, however, Dewley pit was closed and the family moved again to Jolly's Close near Newburn, where a new pit belonging to the Duke of Northumberland known as 'the Duke's Winnin' had just been opened up. This new venture, however, did not fulfil expectations and was soon closed, with the result that Robert had to move once more, this time to another new pit opened by the Walbottle Colliery owners at Water Row by the Wylam Wagonway, a little to the west of Newburn.

Meanwhile young George was growing up and making an increasing contribution to the family earnings. His first work was for the widow of a farmer at Dewley, herding cows, leading horses at plough and hoeing turnips, but the colliery soon drew him away from the land and he got himself a job as a wellor or picker of "bats and brasses" out of the coal at Dewley Burn pit for the wage of sixpence a day. Next he drove a gin horse for a spell at Black Callerton colliery, two miles away and then returned to Dewley Burn as assistant fireman to his father. When Dewley closed down, however, he did not follow his father to the Duke's Winning but obtained work as a fireman on his own account, first at the pit called

Mid Mill Winning and later, when this pit closed, at Throckley Bridge. Then, in 1798, George rejoined his father for a time in the new engine house at Water Row.

It is significant of the progress which George Stephenson had already made that at the age of seventeen he should have been put in charge of the new pumping engine at Water Row, whereas his father still remained in his old job of fireman and his brothers James and John were also doing less responsible work at Walbottle. George's youthful ability attracted the notice of the engineer to the Walbottle Colliery who had been responsible for erecting the Water Row pumping engine of which George had charge. This was none other than Robert Hawthorn, a man whose sons were later to found the famous Newcastle engineering firm which perpetuated his name, and who was at this time the most celebrated engine-wright on Tyneside. At this time, too, Stephenson formed a close friendship with a banksman at Water Row named William Locke. Locke later moved to Yorkshire, but the early friendship was not forgotten for Stephenson was later to take Locke's son Joseph as his apprentice and so set him on the road to fame as a railway engineer.

After a spell at Water Row and other Walbottle pits, Stephenson returned in 1801 to Black Callerton where, as a boy, he had driven a gin horse. This time he held the responsible job of brakesman at the Dolly Pit. This meant that he had charge of a 'whim' or winding engine which raised the loaded corves of coal to the surface and also brought the pitmen to and from the coal face. Such work called for considerable skill and judgement and therefore commanded a wage of from 17s 6d to £1 per week, which was high in those days. Added to this, George was earning money 'on the side' by making and repairing boots and shoes in his limited spare time, and in the light of these improved circumstances he began to look around for a wife.

His eye first lit upon Elizabeth Hindmarsh, the daughter of the largest farmer in Black Callerton parish. His advances met with immediate success and a series of romantic clandestine meetings took place in Hindmarsh's orchard until the farmer discovered what was afoot and sternly forbade the couple to meet again. Elizabeth tearfully declared that she would never take another man for husband

—a resolution which she kept, strangely enough—but George, by all accounts, took the reverse lightly and made no attempt to defy the angry father. Maybe the possibility of a dowry and not the personal charm of Miss Hindmarsh was the primary attraction.

The next object of George's affection was Anne Henderson, and this does seem to have been an affair of the heart on his side. Anne was the daughter of a small farmer at Capheaton. Her two elder sisters, Hannah and Frances, were servants in the house of Thomas Thompson of Black Callerton where George lodged, and it was in this way that he met her. Like her sisters, Anne was in domestic service so in this case there was no dowry to tempt him. It is said that George painstakingly fashioned a new pair of shoes for Anne as a token of his affection but that she very firmly rejected both the gift and the proposal that went with it. He took this second reverse very hard and forthwith switched his attentions to Anne's sister, Frances. A younger woman might have resented playing second fiddle to her sister in this way, but Fanny Henderson was twelve years older than Stephenson, village gossips were already calling her an old maid, and so she would be reluctant to turn down a belated offer of marriage, if only to prove the gossips wrong.

So it came about that George Stephenson and Frances Henderson were married at Newburn church on 28 November 1802. Thomas Thompson gave them a wedding breakfast at the Lough House where the bride had worked and the groom had lodged and then, when the festivities were over, the couple retired to the lodgings which Stephenson had taken in a cottage nearby. George did not remain much longer at Black Callerton, however, for Robert Hawthorn had not lost sight of him.

Hawthorn had just completed the erection of a winding engine at Willington Quay on the Tyne six miles below Newcastle. It was at this Quay that the Tyne collier brigs, returning from the Port of London, discharged their ballast into wagons, and Hawthorn's new engine was installed to draw these wagons up an inclined plane to the top of the huge mound known as the Ballast Hill. It was the first installation of its kind on the Tyne, and it was on Hawthorn's recommendation that George Stephenson was offered the job of brakesman there at an increased wage.

George accepted this offer with alacrity and secured a single upper room in a cottage on the Quay which the couple managed to furnish out of their savings. He set off upon the fifteen mile journey through Newcastle and Wallsend to Willington on a farm horse borrowed from a Mr. Burn of the Red House Farm, Wolsingham, his faithful Fanny riding pillion behind him. So the couple came to their first home where, a few months later, their only son, Robert Stephenson, was born on 16 October 1803.[1]

It was at Willington that George became a clock mender and cleaner as well as a cobbler in his spare time. As the Tynesider of that time set such store by clocks that even the poorest pitman's cottage could usually boast one, this new venture proved even more profitable than the shoe mending. It was at Willington also that he first made the acquaintance of another man whose name was destined to become famous in engineering history—William Fairbairn. Robert Stephenson's biographer, J. C. Jeaffreson, writing of these Willington days, says that it was here that George Stephenson's acquaintance with Robert Hawthorn 'first took the form of personal intimacy'. In view of the fact that he owed his advancement to the recognition of his ability by that great engine-wright, this is understandable. Yet Hawthorn's recommendation of Stephenson and this alleged friendship are difficult to reconcile with the terms of a letter which Stephenson was later to write from Killingworth to William Locke at Barnsley in which he said: "Hawthorn is still at Walbattle I daresay you will well remember he was a great enamy to me but much more so after you left. I left Walbattle Colliery soon also after you and has been verey prosperous in my concerns ever since. I am now far above Hawthorn's reach." It has been said in explanation that Hawthorn was a tyrannical master and that both Stephenson and Locke believed that he was concerned to keep them down because he was jealous of their ability. Yet this is no explanation at all. Stephenson must have been conceited indeed if he supposed that Hawthorn considered him as a serious rival when he came to Walbottle as a mere youth of seventeen. Moreover, had he done so he would scarcely have recommended him to take charge of the new engine at Willington.

[1] Curiously, both Robert and his father were throughout their lives uncertain whether the month of his birth was October, November or December. Robert first told Smiles November and then corrected this to December, but it is practically certain that October is correct.

The truth is that this is the first evidence of the flaws in George Stephenson's character which became increasingly evident as he rose to fame. He was a proud and jealous man who would acknowledge no peer and brook no contradiction in the field he made his own. He may have been generous to a fault in the way he enabled old associates to share in his success, but woe betide them if they became too successful themselves and claimed a share of the limelight which he enjoyed. Throughout his life he lost no opportunity of asserting that he had fought his way to success entirely single-handed against every kind of opposition from his fellows. Obviously no man born, however great his gifts, has ever achieved fame without some help from others, and in order to maintain his fiction Stephenson either ignored or disparaged those engineers who, like Hawthorn, helped him in his early days or who, like Richard Trevithick, laid the foundations upon which he built his railway empire.

Stephenson did not remain long at Willington. In the late autumn of 1804 he took the job of brakesman at the West Moor pit of the Grand Allies and moved his family to Killingworth. Whether this move was the result of some disagreement with Hawthorn we do not know; but if this was the case it was superficially healed again, for we are told that long after Stephenson moved to Killingworth he continued to meet Hawthorn at infrequent intervals in order to discuss the steam engine with him. If this be so, then one is forced to conclude that Stephenson concealed his dislike for Hawthorn in order to profit by his experience.

George had not been long at West Moor when fate dealt him a heavy double blow. On 13 July 1805 Fanny bore him a daughter who died three weeks later. Fanny's health had appeared to benefit from the move to Killingworth, but after the death of her child she sickened rapidly and died of consumption on 14 May of the following year at the age of thirty-seven. She was buried in the churchyard of Long Benton beside the infant daughter who was named after her.

Very shortly after this tragedy, George engaged a housekeeper to look after little Robert and set out on foot for Scotland. According to Smiles he had received an invitation from the owners of a spinning mill at Montrose to superintend the working of a Watt engine which they had recently installed. How these gentlemen came to hear of an obscure Northumbrian engineman and why they should have singled him out for the work Smiles does not explain. But that he went to the Montrose mill seems certain. He may simply have heard of the prospect of employment there on his way into Scotland, for the melancholy associations of the little cottage at Killingworth are explanation enough for his decision to cut loose and take to the road. The mill-owners at Montrose must have paid him well, for during the year he spent there he managed to save £28, the greatest sum of money he had ever had in hand.

Time and a change of scene having blunted the sharp edge of his sorrow, George Stephenson tramped back to Killingworth and was given his old job of brakesman at West Moor. He was concerned to find his little cottage locked and deserted but discovered to his relief that during his absence his housekeeper had married his younger brother, Robert, and had taken his little boy with her to her new home. There he had been well cared for, but George wanted the boy to live with him and this meant engaging a new housekeeper. This newcomer was not a success and she was soon succeeded by George's unmarried sister, Eleanor, an arrangement which proved completely satisfactory. No mother could have been kinder to the little boy than Eleanor, and throughout his life Robert Stephenson recalled his 'Aunt Nelly' with the greatest affection.

George discovered that during his absence in Scotland his father, old Robert, had been severely scalded and blinded by escaping steam in a boiler house accident. Unable to work, the old man had run up debts. These George promptly paid, and continued to help his father financially for the rest of his life. Soon after his return, too, George had the misfortune to be drawn for service in the militia, and as he was naturally unwilling to leave his sister and son there was nothing for it but to make the customary payment for a substitute. These two unexpected outgoings consumed all his hard won savings and this impoverishment, coupled with his bereavement, made him very depressed. "I knew not where I should have found my destiny and wept", he confessed when he recalled these dark days to Thomas Summerside years afterwards. His sister Anne had recently married and emigrated to America, a circumstance which prompted Stephenson to consider doing likewise. He discussed the idea with two Killingworth friends, John Blacklock and John Wigham, and they decided that with their combined skills it would be worth trying their luck in the new world. Had they done so, the history of nineteenth-century England might have been very different, but for some reason, perhaps no more than the passing of Stephenson's black mood, the idea was finally dropped.

Today a modern housing estate confronts Stephenson's old cottage at West Moor, but in his day its windows looked out across the trackway leading to the North Shields turnpike to a fine sweep of open country, a view unmarred by the chimneys and spoil banks of the Killingworth pits which were on the higher ground of the Moor behind the cottage. To the right, its chimney tops just visible above surrounding trees, lay Gosforth Hall, the home of the brothers Charles and Robert Brandling,[1] the colliery owners who would later champion Stephenson in the controversy with Sir Humphry Davy over the safety lamp. In the foreground, across the breadth of a small paddock, lay the buildings of Long Benton glebe farm which was tenanted by Anthony Wigham, by all accounts a better scholar than he was a farmer. His son John worked as an under-viewer for the Brandlings and it was he who planned to emigrate with Stephenson.

Jeaffreson maintains that Anthony Wigham gave George Stephenson lessons in mathematics and what was then termed 'natural philosophy' and that George subsequently rewarded his old master by putting him in charge of his stables at Tapton House, Chesterfield. If this is true, however, Anthony must have been a very old man by the time he came to Chesterfield. Thomas Summerside's personal recollection is probably the more trustworthy source here. He maintains that it was the son, John Wigham, who played the schoolmaster and that George later acknowledged his debt by finding him a job in the famous locomotive works at Forth Street, Newcastle.

In the light of subsequent events in his life, this question of George Stephenson's education—or the lack of it—is a very important one. How much book learning did he in fact acquire? As a child he received no education whatever and at the age of eighteen he could neither read nor write. He subsequently learned to do both, after a fashion, but he read with difficulty, while his handwriting was bad and his spelling likewise. Throughout his life his letters were

[1] Charles Brandling's other Christian name was John. He is confusingly referred to sometimes as John and sometimes as Charles in contemporary records.

written for him, at first by his son Robert and later by secretaries.[1]
Samuel Smiles, who made George Stephenson the great exemplar of
his doctrine of self-help, paints a sentimental portrait of the earnest
young engineman wrestling with mathematical problems by
furnace light in the night watches. He tells us that George attended
night schools, first at Walbottle and later in Newburn, where 'he
became well advanced in arithmetic'. Smiles also quotes a fellow
pupil at Newburn as saying that "he took to figures so wonderful".
On the other hand, Summerside, a lifelong admirer and associate of
George Stephenson, declares that it was John Wigham of Killingworth who deserves the credit for the little that George ever
mastered of the three Rs. "I remember", Summerside goes on to say,
"when very young being at George's house as a companion of
Robert when the latter produced the 'cyphering book' of his father,
the contents of which extended as far as the 'rule of five' from
Tinwell's Arithmetic. I dont think he went much beyond this in his
arithmetical education." These words of a man who was subsequently to serve Stephenson as a clerk surely carry an unmistakable
ring of truth.

Stephenson may well have attended night schools before he came
to Killingworth, as Smiles relates, but all reliable evidence indicates
that his brain totally lacked the capacity to store theoretical knowledge, even of the simplest kind. In compensation for this deficiency
he possessed remarkable powers of observation, great shrewdness
and, above all, such outstanding ability where anything mechanical
was concerned that it amounted to intuition. It was these gifts rather
than the efforts of teachers which enabled him to profit so greatly
from his varied experience of contemporary steam-power on Tyneside before ever he came to Killingworth. It was these gifts, too,
which carried him to fame by enabling him to assess accurately the
virtues and the defects of contemporary machines or to put an
unerring finger on the heart of some engineering problem which
baffled those with far greater theoretical knowledge. Because of this
almost uncanny ability, George Stephenson affected to despise
scholars and theorists and he would maintain his views against theirs,

[1] Where such letters are quoted elsewhere in this book, the phrase "George Stephenson
writes" should not be taken literally. A few almost indecipherable rough drafts appear to have
been written by him, but letters despatched were either written at his dictation or fair-copied
from such drafts.

right or wrong, with a stubbornness which could be pig-headed. Nevertheless, he did in fact feel his own complete lack of scholarship and formal engineering training very keenly, covering with a cloak of arrogance this sense of inferiority. These characteristics explain the difficulties, the conflicts and the jealousies which marked and marred his astonishing career. They also help us to understand the relationship which grew up between father and son and to assess more fairly the contribution which each of these two great men made to the development of the steam locomotive and the railway.

It seems clear that even in his early days at Killingworth, before he had had any opportunity to make his mark, confidence in his ability gave George Stephenson great ambitions. At the same time, recognizing his lack of knowledge and feeling himself cut off from the accumulated fund of experience and learning which others had set down in print, he determined to realize his ambition by means of a working partnership with his son in which Robert would supply what he lacked.

No parent ever displayed more interest or more intimate concern over his son's education; no crammer ever kept a boy's nose to his books more assiduously. Robert had been a weak and sickly baby; so much so that when he had been christened in the school house at Willington, those who were present, knowing his mother's consumptive tendencies, shook their heads and predicted an early death. He did, in fact, inherit his mother's lung weakness, but the sturdy Stephenson blood ran sufficiently strongly in his veins to overcome it and he grew into a tall, slim but wiry boy with deceptive reserves of strength, and full of energy, mischief and humour. Had this not been so he could not have withstood so intensive a training.

As soon as ever Robert's legs were strong enough to carry him there he was sent to Tommy Rutter's village school in Long Benton a mile and a half away. Yet childhood was sweetened for him by the constant kindness and sympathy of his Aunt Nelly who, somewhat to George's displeasure, would take him with her when she went gleaning in the harvest fields or on ever memorable visits to his lost mother's two sisters, Hannah, who had become the wife of an innkeeper at Ryle, and Anne who had married farmer Burn of the Red House, Wolsingham. Anne especially, regretting perhaps that she had once jilted his father, showered kindness on little Robert and filled him with buttered eggs and other fresh farm food.

As soon as he was strong enough, Robert began to help his father and could be seen staggering off to school under a load of blunted picks from the pit which he would leave at the blacksmith's to be drawn out and sharpened and to be collected on his return journey. George was certainly a hard task-master, yet Smiles assures us that Robert had a very deep affection for his father. Whether this is true or not, this much is certain; that throughout their long partnership Robert displayed towards his father a splendid loyalty which, though it must often have been sorely tried, only once wavered.

When Robert was twelve years old, his father took him away from the village school and sent him as a day boy to a private school in Percy Street, Newcastle, run by Dr. Bruce for the children of middle-class parents. This involved a walk of ten miles a day, which even his ambitious father realized was asking too much of the boy so he bought him a donkey or 'cuddy' as it would then be called on Tyneside. Dr. Bruce's establishment was considered a step above the Newcastle grammar school and the social status of most of his pupils was so far above that of Robert Stephenson that at first, until he won respect as he soon did, his harsh Northumbrian dialect and rough clothes made him the laughing-stock of the other boys. He was described by one who knew him at this time as 'a thin-framed, thin-faced, delicate boy with his face covered with freckles'. His dark eyes were unusually large and lustrous, and though he was much stronger than he looked he was fine-boned. These physical characteristics, combined with his quiet courtesy and good manners would have enabled him to pass as the son of a gentleman had not his speech and clothing betrayed him. As the years went by, Robert was to lose his dialect whereas success never tempered his father's speech, which was so broad as to be almost unintelligible to southerners.

When Robert's 'cuddy' had carried him back from school there was still much work ahead of him, for George Stephenson—'o'er strict' the neighbours considered—allowed his son little respite. Not only did he keep the boy hard at his home work, but he would question him minutely about his lessons and often get him to read long passages from books on science and invention which Robert had borrowed from the library of the Newcastle Philosophical and Literary Society of which he was a member. In this way George pursued his aim to use his son's brain to supplement his own deficiencies. Sometimes, however, the books and the mechanical drawings were bundled away and father and son would turn to some practical job; repairing a clock, maybe, or modifying the perpetual motion machine on which George wasted a great deal of misguided ingenuity. It was at this time, too, that the pair constructed the sundial which still stands above the doorway of the Killingworth cottage, witness to the progress which young Robert Stephenson had made. It was no mean feat to work out the exact latitude and longitude of Killingworth and then to calibrate and mount the sundial correctly.

It has been said that George Stephenson had to pinch and scrape and make great sacrifices in order to give his son such a good education, but this is not the case. On the contrary throughout the period (1815-1819) that Robert attended Dr. Bruce's school, George's affairs prospered to such an extent that he never earned less than £200 a year, whereas Jeaffreson tells us that Robert's school fees for the whole four years did not amount to more than £40. His home at West Moor, moreover, no longer consisted of a single room and a garret but had been rebuilt and extended until it became the roomy cottage which we see today.

At about the time that Robert left school his beloved Aunt Nelly got married and left the West Moor cottage. The domestic difficulty so caused made George Stephenson decide that his best solution would be to take another wife. Accordingly a few months later, at the end of March 1820, he brought as bride to his comfortable home Elizabeth Hindmarsh, the object of his first frustrated courtship who, true to her word, had remained unmarried. Farmer Hindmarsh who had once so summarily dismissed Stephenson the poor brakesman of Black Callerton now welcomed as a son-in-law the up and coming engineer.

From the moment George Stephenson was given a chance to display his powers as a mechanical engineer his fortunes never looked back. That opportunity came his way in 1811. In the previous year the Grand Allies had sunk the new High Pit, as it was called, at

Killingworth and an atmospheric pumping engine of John Smeaton's design[1] was installed at the pithead to keep the workings clear
of water. This the engine conspicuously failed to do. For months it
laboured, but despite the ministrations and advice of the best
engine-wrights in the neighbourhood, the new workings were
still drowned out. This was just the kind of problem to appeal to
George and one evening he took a walk up to the High Pit engine
house to see for himself.

It should here be explained that an atmospheric engine is so called
because it depends primarily for its power on the vacuum created
in the cylinder by the condensation of steam and only to a very
limited extent upon the expansion of steam which is admitted at a
very low pressure. When this low pressure steam, aided by the
weight of the descending pump rods at the other end of the beam,
has raised the piston to the top of its stroke, water is injected into
the cylinder to create a vacuum beneath the piston. The weight of
the atmosphere then drives the piston down again on its power
stroke.

With a shrewd eye informed by familiarity with many a Tyneside
pumping engine George Stephenson studied the layout of the
labouring engine. He decided that the valve which admitted the
injection water was of too small a bore, while the cistern which
supplied this water had been mounted too low down in the building
so that there was insufficient head. An inadequate jet of water into
the cylinder meant that it was not condensing the steam effectively
and so creating a very low vacuum. No wonder the engine lacked
power. George had reached this conclusion when his ruminations
were interrupted by the appearance in the engine house of Kit
Heppel, one of the pit sinkers. "Weel George", Kit called out
jokingly, "what do you mak' o' her?" "I could alter her, man, and
make her draw", came the confident reply. "In a week's time I
could send you to the bottom."

Stephenson's assurance so impressed Kit Heppel that he reported
it to Ralph Dodds, the head viewer, who decided that as everyone
else had tried their hand at the engine and failed he would give

[1] Engines of Smeaton's improved Newcomen type continued to be built in the North
long after the introduction of the Watt engine elsewhere. With coal so readily available, the
north country colliery owners preferred to forgo the superior economy of the Watt engine
rather than pay the dues demanded by Messrs. Boulton & Watt.

George a trial. George accepted Dodd's invitation on one condition—that he should be allowed to select the men to work under
him. He knew very well that the interference of a mere brakesman
would be resented by the regular Killingworth engine-wrights and
that this, his first great opportunity, might well be ruined for him
by jealous men. "The men must either be all Whigs or all Tories"
was Stephenson's way of putting it, and, appreciating his point,
Dodds agreed.

With the help of the mates he recruited from West Moor George
set to work forthwith on the High Pit engine.[1] The injection water
tank was raised ten feet. The injection valve was almost doubled in
size and was set to shut off earlier. Although it was contrary to north-
country practice in engines of this type, Stephenson raised the
working steam pressure from five to ten pounds per square inch.
This meant that the engine would become to a greater degree
double-acting, that is to say it would rely more on steam pressure
and less on the weight of the descending pump rods to complete its
cycle. This caused much head-shaking among the wiseacres, whose
doubts appeared to be confirmed when the engine was first started.
The ponderous beam swung to such a tune that it struck its stops
and shook the engine house to its foundations—"came bounce into
the house" was George's picturesque way of putting it. "She'll
knock the house down", shouted Dodds in alarm, "she was better
as she was." But George smiled and shook his head for he realized
that with the pit shaft practically filled with water there was as yet
almost no load on the beam. Sure enough, as the level fell at each
mighty stroke of the pump, so the engine settled down into its even
stride. By ten o'clock that night the water level in the pit was lower
than it had ever been before and the little crowd of enginemen who
had come to mock at the expected failure of Stephenson's efforts
melted away to their beds in a somewhat chastened mood. All that
night, all the following day and throughout a second night the High
Pit engine laboured tirelessly and by the afternoon of the next day
the pit had been pumped dry so that the men could go to the

---

[1] Edward Corderoy, an ardent Lord's Day Observer, gave a lecture on the life of George
Stephenson in 1857 in which he claimed that Stephenson did himself "immense mischief" by
undertaking "this unnecessary work" on the Sabbath. "How different might have been the
railway system of Great Britain", he exclaimed, "if George Stephenson had resolved to keep
the Sabbath day holy! Is it not *monstrous* that we are told of the *necessity* for Sunday trains?"

bottom as Stephenson had promised. A gratified Ralph Dodds made Stephenson a present of £10. It was a pitifully inadequate reward for the saviour of a drowned-out coal pit, but the reputation which Stephenson acquired as a result of his achievement was worth more to him than gold.

Early in the following year (1812) M'Cree, the Killingworth engine-wright, was accidentally killed and George Stephenson was appointed in his stead. Moreover, such was his reputation as a mechanic that he was henceforth placed in charge of all the machinery in the collieries of the Grand Allies at a salary of £100 a year. He was also presented with an Irish horse named 'Squire' to enable him to visit their more distant coal workings at Black Fell and Bracken Beds.

The fame of Stephenson's achievements in developing his safety lamp, in constructing his first locomotives and laying down his first colliery railways has tended to eclipse the great improvements which he made in the years following his 1812 appointment, not only at the collieries controlled by the Grand Allies, but at many other pits in the Tyneside field. He was able to do this because the Grand Allies thought so highly of him that they granted him complete freedom to work for other colliery proprietors provided he continued to keep their own plant in order. The £100 salary which they continued to pay him thus became merely a retaining fee to which Stephenson was able to add such earnings from other sources that he became a man of substance long before he left Killingworth. This freedom which the Grand Allies allowed him must be the explanation of the statement which Stephenson later made in his evidence before the Commons Committee on the Liverpool & Manchester Railway Bill in which he said that he left the employment of the Grand Allies in 1813 to become a civil engineer on his own account and mentions the names of Dodds and Robert Weatherburn as his partners. In the same statement he claims that besides superintending the Grand Allies collieries at Killingworth, Mount Moor, South Moor, Derwent Brook and Burraton, his activities extended to the Newbottle and Hetton pits and to the colliery owned by Lord Stewart. He goes on to claim that he was responsible for building a total of thirty-nine stationary engines during this period, of which some were high-pressure engines. The largest engine built by him, he stated, was of 200hp. He must here have been referring to the Friar's Goose Pumping Engine constructed by Messrs. Losh, Wilson & Bell at the Woodside Pit of the Tyne Main Colliery. One of the largest engines of its day, Friar's Goose had a 6ft cylinder and a 9ft stroke and it drew water from a depth of fifty fathoms at the rate of 1,000 gallons a minute. It began work in July 1823 and soon became famous throughout Northumberland.

Less spectacular but of much greater significance in the history of coal mining were the improvements which Stephenson made in coal handling methods both at the pithead and below ground by introducing trams and rails in conjunction with stationary haulage engines. Under his influence a network of tram rails spread from the Killingworth pitheads to the coal stacks and waste heaps in place of the old primitive horsedrawn sleds with their loaded corves. It was of these that Summerside wrote in old age: "As I have looked at railways now, where passengers and goods have been conveyed for the last forty years, I have considered the rails with the switches, crossings &c, at those pits above and below the pattern or origin of modern railways, with improvements, as we see them now."

George Stephenson installed three underground rope haulage engines at Killingworth which became known to the pitmen as the 'Geordie', 'Jimmy' and 'Bobby' engines after George and his two brothers, James and Robert. On much of this underground engineering work George was assisted by his son, for when he left school young Robert was apprenticed to his father's friend Nicholas Wood. Born in 1795, Wood was fourteen years younger than George Stephenson. He came to Killingworth in April 1811 to learn the profession of viewer under Ralph Dodds, whom he succeeded as head viewer.

These three underground engines at Killingworth wonderfully lightened and speeded up the work of the pit but they brought with them an added risk of fire. The brick-lined flues from the boilers which supplied these engines were carried up to the surface through the coal measures and there was always a risk that the surrounding coal would ignite if the flues become overheated. One such fire in 1819 is referred to by George Stephenson in a letter to Joseph Cabery, who had temporarily left Killingworth and was working at Newton Colliery near Parkgate on the Dee estuary. We must remember that 1819 was a year of trade depression, when the agitation for parliamentary reform was renewed and was savagely repressed by a frightened government. It was the year of the notorious Peterloo Massacre and the iniquitous Six Acts which virtually set at nought the rights of the subject. Stephenson's letter to Cabery not only gives us a first-hand glimpse of his doings at this time, but it also gives a graphic and humorous description of the impact of this sombre national situation on local affairs. It is therefore worth quoting in full:

The soot in the Geordy flues caught fire beside the damper [George writes] and set the coal on fire nearly all the way to the Jimmy. We got it under last night. I will find work for you and Thomas when you return. I intend setting you both with my Bro. Robert in erecting the Large Engine at Tyne Main Colliery [Friar's Goose]. It will very likely be 15 or 16 months finishing. Burraton engine is started and works very well.

I'm sorry to inform you I have become a soldier. We send a dozen every day to Mr. Brandling's to learn exercise and I do assure you we can handle the sword pretty well. Mr. Wood makes an excellent soldier but I hope we shall never be called to action as I think if any of us be wounded it will be in the *Back*. Three hours drill daily and plenty to eat and drink at Gosforth Ho. The Reformers have also been learning their exercises. I do assure you they have alarmed the Gents in our county, especially our worthy masters. Ld Strathmore's cavalry having marched through Winlaton lately, the day following the Reformers of that place marched their cavalry through in imitation of the Noble Lord's. It consisted of 72 asses with hardy nailers for their riders.

The letter ends with a postscript by Robert Stephenson addressed to Thomas Cabery in which he again refers to the fire. "Dear Thomas," he writes, "My father has almost wrought me to death in the flues, but he himself has been two or three times dropt with the choak damp . . . I took care not to go so far, but where I was I think I would not have been long in making a joint of meat ready."

Although George Stephenson always made quite clear to inquirers about his early life that he had never been a coal miner, his work at Killingworth frequently took him below ground, sometimes in circumstances of great personal danger. He therefore knew at first

hand the perils of fire, explosion and suffocation which hourly
threatened the lives of those who toiled for such long hours in those
dark galleries. Quite apart from the physical hazard, Stephenson was
well aware of the cost of the fire danger in terms of coal output. He
had seen valuable seams of coal sealed off either because a fire had
broken out which could not be overcome or because they were
too gaseous to be worked. He had seen miners, not daring to light
their candles, groping about their work by the ghostly luminescence
of rotten fish or by the intermittent glimmer of sparks struck by an
attendant boy with flint and steel. It was experience such as this which
led George Stephenson to develop his famous 'Geordie' safety lamp,
a work which, more than any other—the improvement of the
locomotive not excepted—ensured that his name would be remembered with affection by generations of miners in his native Northumberland.

CHAPTER TWO

The Safety-lamp Controversy

WEST MOOR colliery had the reputation of being one of the most dangerous pits in the country. In 1806 and again in 1809 serious blasts occurred with the combined loss of twenty-two lives. After one fatal blast George Stephenson himself recruited and led to the pit bottom the small party of volunteers who risked their lives to build a wall which effectively sealed off the affected workings. In this way the fire which had followed the blast was contained and extinguished for lack of oxygen before more harm could be done.

The spectacle of workmates in the prime of life suddenly struck down by death in one of its most horrible forms and of the abject misery or lamentation of the wives and mothers who clustered about the pithead challenged Stephenson's ingenuity to right so terrible a wrong. But before his speculations could take tangible shape the problem of the lighting of mines had become a national issue. In 1812 not only Tyneside but the whole country was shocked by the news of a terrible explosion at the Brandlings' Felling Pit, near Gateshead in which ninety men and boys were either burnt to death or suffocated by choke damp.

The first man to offer a solution was Dr. Clanny of Sunderland who produced a safety lamp in 1813. Although it apparently found favour for a time in some local pits, this Clanny lamp was too unwieldy to be an effective answer to the problem because air had to be fed to the lamp through a water container by means of hand bellows. A committee of coal owners therefore appealed for assistance to one of the foremost scientists of the day—Sir Humphry Davy. Davy responded by visiting the Tyne coalfield in August 1815 by which time George Stephenson was already actively pursuing his own experiments.

So it came about that these two men, the one a famous scientist and the other an unknown and ill-educated mechanic, set out almost simultaneously to seek the same goal by completely different routes. Whereas Sir Humphry applied scientific theory and conducted his experiments under safe, controlled conditions in the laboratory of the Royal Institution, Stephenson, the practical man, literally groped his way to success through the gaseous darkness of Bob's Pit at Killingworth by a process of trial and error which might have cost him his life.

Inevitably, this situation led to a dispute over priority of invention. More than this, even the nature of Stephenson's experiments and the amount of personal risk which they involved have been hotly argued by subsequent writers, with the effect that the whole story of this important episode in Stephenson's life has become fogged by conflicting statements. Because of the light which it sheds upon Stephenson's character and courage, and in justice to his memory, it is worth re-examining accounts of this bygone drama in some detail in an attempt to arrive at the truth.

The first account of Stephenson's experiments is that given by Samuel Smiles in his biography. He tells us that Stephenson's starting point was to study the behaviour of a flame when exposed to carburetted hydrogen gas. This he did by holding a lighted candle up to a 'blower' in the pit, greatly to the consternation of the pitmen. Noticing that the gas tended to burn round the base of the flame and not at the top he conceived the notion that if the velocity of the draught of air to the flame could be increased it would not then ignite inflammable gas. It was in accordance with this theory that his first lamp was made. His friend Nicholas Wood, now the Killingworth head viewer, helped him to sketch it out. Air was supplied to the flame of the lamp through a single tube and it had a tall glass chimney. Matthews, a tinman of Middle Street, Newcastle, constructed the body of the lamp and the chimney was specially made by the Northumberland Glass House.

Smiles then goes on to describe the memorable evening of 21 October 1815 when this precious lamp arrived at Killingworth and was at once put to the test in the pit. Young Robert was sent hotfoot to fetch Wood and John Moody, the under viewer, so that they might witness the experiment. This was to take place in the foulest gallery of Bob's Pit at a point far in bye where gas was escaping through a fissure in the roof with a clearly audible hissing sound. In order to ensure that there should be an explosive concentration of gas at this place, Stephenson had had a screen of deal boarding thrown across the gallery, and, before making the experiment, he asked Moody to go to the spot and express his opinion on the state of the air. Moody declared that if a light was brought into the place there would inevitably be an explosion and such was his conviction that neither he nor Nicholas Wood dared accompany Stephenson. Both men waited apprehensively at a safe distance while Stephenson strode forward into the dark gallery, lighted lamp in hand. After an interval of tense expectancy they heard the hollow echo of Stephenson's voice calling to them as he groped his way back—the lamp had not fired the gas, it had gone out.

Not long after Smiles had published this dramatic account of the affair it was emphatically repudiated by Robert Stephenson's biographer, J. C. Jeaffreson. "The time has now come for the final sweeping away of a fiction", he declared, and having summarized the Smiles' version he then continues: "Wilfully and deliberately to encounter extreme peril, with the full knowledge that it is needless, is the part of a fool—not of a hero. Whatever may be George Stephenson's claim to be regarded as the latter he certainly had nothing in common with the former. The important experiment, which has been so greatly misrepresented, was made on a certain insulated quantity of gas, and under circumstances that precluded the possibility of serious disaster."

This forceful piece of debunking has been accepted by subsequent writers, not merely because Smiles's tendency to magnify the achievements of his heroes is well known, but because it rests upon the seemingly unimpeachable evidence of Nicholas Wood himself. In a statement made many years after the event Wood said: "The box, or cabin, in which the lamp was tried was not of such dimensions as would, if an explosion had taken place, have produced the effect described; as only a small quantity of gas was required, and we had had sufficient experience not to employ more gas than was necessary; at most, an explosion might have burnt the hands of the operator, but would not extend a few feet from the blower." In other words, Wood is directly contradicting Smiles by maintaining that the purpose of the wooden screen which Stephenson erected

was not to ensure a dangerous concentration of gas but to make
the experiment safe by reducing the volume present.

Such a first-hand statement as this seems irrefutable, but truth
will out eventually and we now have evidence to show that whatever Wood may have said afterwards about the safety of the classic
experiment he was by no means so sure about it at the time. The
Brandling brothers of Gosforth Hall who, as already mentioned,
were Stephenson's influential and most active champions in the
safety-lamp controversy, had the good sense to take signed statements from those concerned when the dispute with Sir Humphry
Davy arose in 1816. These important documents remained in the
possession of the Brandling family until 1944, when they were
acquired by Colonel S. John Thompson, D.S.O., and presented by
him to the Institution of Mechanical Engineers.

Subsequent literary squabblings are silenced when we turn these
yellowing papers and come upon John Moody's own signed
statement dated from Killingworth Colliery, 23 December 1816.
It reads as follows:

I, John Moody do hereby certify whom it may [concern] that on the
21st of October [1815] at 6 o'clock that evening I accompany'd Mr.
Stephenson and Mr. Wood down the A Pit at Killingworth Colliery in
purpose to try Mr. Stephenson's first safety lamp at a Blower. But when
we came near the Blower it was making so much more gas than usual
that I told Mr. Stephenson and Mr. Wood if the lamp should deceive
him we should be severely burnt, but Mr. Stephenson would insist
upon the tryal which was very much against my desire. So Mr. Wood
and I went out of the way at a distance and left Mr. Stephenson to
himself, but we soon heard that the lamp had answer'd his expectation
with safety. Since that times I have been many times with Mr. Stephenson and Mr. Wood trying his different lamps. I likewise recollect Mr.
Stephenson trying many experiments at Blowers long before we had
any lamp.

(Signed) JOHN MOODY
Under Viewer.

In a similar signed statement, Stephenson's friend and tutor John
Wigham confirms the experiments—with a lighted candle at
blowers—which preceded the testing of the first lamp. Finally there
is Stephenson's own account of the first trial of the lamp, written at

his dictation by Robert: "When we came within a certain distance of the blower it was making such a great noise", he says, "that my companions made a full stop and the under viewer told me that if the lamp should deceive me we should very likely be burned to death." He then describes how he left them and went forward alone, but that there was so much gas present that it fired within the chimney of the lamp and extinguished it before he was able to reach the blower. Having rejoined Wood and Moody he resolved to try the lamp again.

I got my lamp trim'd again and desir'd my companions to accompany me to the blower the second time, but they would not altho' they did not leave me so far as before. When I approached towards the blower the second time I carried my lamp very slow and steady to observe the alteration of the flame in the lamp. As I went along I observed the flame increasing in size and change its colour to a kind of blue. I went a little further; the flame then went out. I then told my companions the effect [and] in a short time my companions became more bold so that they went up with me and seed the gas burn within the lamp.

The most subtle literary art could not improve upon this. In this simple, factual account of one of the most dramatic episodes in the history of invention, a semi-literate engineer achieves a masterpiece by understatement. Moreover, corroborated as it is by John Moody's own version, its truth is surely beyond dispute. Why, then, when both the Stephensons were dead and could not answer him, did Nicholas Wood seek to belittle the whole affair? Unlike Moody, Wood actively and financially assisted Stephenson in his development of the safety lamp, so it may well be that in retrospect he felt ashamed of his own timidity and lack of confidence in its success. He was Stephenson's partner in the venture whereas Moody, with no knowledge of the ideas behind the lamp but with a much greater practical experience of firedamp in pits than either of his companions, could lag behind with a clear conscience and freely admit that he had done so. As for Jeaffreson's charge of fool-hardiness, which Stephenson must face if we accept his own story of the affair, this surely overlooks two things. First, Stephenson's supreme confidence in the rightness of his ideas: that his lamp could fail and destroy him would scarcely occur to him. Secondly, as a practical man with a long experience of pits and pitmen, Stephenson knew very well that no safe 'controlled' experiment could ever convince the men on the job.

Stephenson's own statement tells us more particularly what the lamp used in this first experiment was like and how it was improved. The oil reservoir was three inches in diameter by three inches high and through it passed a single air tube half an inch in diameter. The glass chimney was nine inches high with a narrow top "something like a wine decanter". Its fault, he decided, was that it went out much too easily 'when in sharp motion' owing to the design of the chimney and the air feed. He therefore had a second lamp made by Matthews of Newcastle in which three air tubes of smaller diameter took the place of the single one and the chimney was a plain cylinder. This was an improvement, but it was still too apt to go out. Many experiments were made with this lamp not only in the pit but also in Stephenson's cottage at West Moor, using a bladder of gas and a crude apparatus, Robert and Nicholas Wood acting as assistants. "We had two or three blows up in making the experiments" said Stephenson in later years, and went on to recall how on one occasion, as a result of a mistake on Wood's part, the whole apparatus was blown to pieces.

In the course of these experiments Stephenson's original notion of increasing the draught through his lamp developed into a conviction that the gas could not ignite if it was passed through tubes of sufficiently small diameter. This was purely the result of practical experiment and observation: he had no idea why it should be so. Proceeding on these lines another lamp was designed in which many tubes took the place of the three previously used. Before this third lamp was actually made, however, the thought struck him that it was not the *length* of the air tubes which mattered but their small diameter. In other words he could dispense with the tubes altogether and instead admit air to the lamp through small holes.

A remarkable thing which does not seem to have struck previous writers was the extraordinary speed with which George Stephenson developed his invention, especially when we remember that he had a job to do and could only work on the lamp in his spare time. The first lamp had been tested on 21 October 1815, the second on 4 November, while on 20 November Stephenson went to Newcastle to order the third. He explained his requirements to the tinsmith over a pint of beer in the 'Newcastle Arms' and Robert Stephenson was able, years after, to show Smiles the crude, beer-stained sketch which his father had made on that occasion. In this final version the lamp and its cylindrical glass chimney was completely surrounded by metal plate perforated with small holes. Even the top of the chimney was fitted with a perforated metal cap. This final version was quickly made and tried out in the pit at Killingworth on 30 November, proving itself a great improvement on its two predecessors.

While all this had been going on at Killingworth, Sir Humphry Davy had not been idle. On 9 November he announced the successful outcome of his experiments to the Royal Society in his historic paper: *On the Fire-Damp of Coal Mines and on Methods of lighting the Mine so as to prevent its explosion.* The practical result of Sir Humphry's work was a lamp on exactly the same principle as Stephenson's. Instead of perforated metal plate, Sir Humphry used wire gauze and he dispensed altogether with the glass chimney, but at a quick glance the two lamps were almost identical.

Sir Humphry's invention was greeted with great acclaim by his scientific colleagues and by the committee which had solicited his help. The friends of Sir Humphry and certain colliery owners in Northumberland and Durham resolved to express their gratitude by raising a subscription, and in due course he was presented with the sum of £2,000 for 'his invention of *the* safety lamp'. Their attention had been drawn to Stephenson's work, but they contented themselves by voting him a purse of a hundred guineas as a kind of consolation prize for what they regarded as the clumsy efforts of an uneducated man. This cavalier treatment of Stephenson and the bland assumption that Davy was alone entitled to credit for the invention angered Stephenson's supporters, who were by no means uninfluential including as they did the Brandlings of Gosforth, William Losh and the formidable Grand Allies. An advertisement of a subscription to reward Stephenson more suitably appeared over their names in the local press and at the same time Charles Brandling obtained the statements which have already been quoted. Brandling also asked Stephenson to prepare a statement for the press, the original draft of which in Robert Stephenson's hand is preserved among the Brandling papers. In this he rightly claims that his lamp, though similar in principle to Davy's, was the first in practical application. But he also points out that true priority was due to Dr. Clanny although his lamp was different in principle.

These proceedings culminated in a public dinner at the Newcastle Assembly Rooms with Charles Brandling in the chair, at which Stephenson was presented with an inscribed silver tankard and the balance of the sum of £1,000 which had been raised. In acknowledging this, Stephenson had to make his first public speech, and this he found a fearful ordeal beside which the perils of the West Moor pits were as nothing. He laboriously set down beforehand what he was going to say and the result, which has been preserved, is so ill spelt and lacking in punctuation that its effective delivery is difficult to conceive. "If thou could but ha' seen ma meeting so many gentlemen at the 'Sembly Rooms, thou maught ha' lit a canle at me face", he confessed afterwards to his sister-in-law, Grace Henderson. "Noo thou'll be for having a bra' ruffle to tha shirt, and then thou'll be looking doon on a' th'own frien's", she teased him. "No, Jane," he insisted seriously, "thou'll nivar see no change in ma."

It had been better for Sir Humphry Davy's reputation if he had maintained a dignified silence and allowed the argument between his own and George Stephenson's supporters to exhaust itself. As it was, the petulant arrogance of his reaction has left an indelible stain upon his reputation. It appeared to him inconceivable that an obscure, uneducated working man could possibly have forestalled him. The man must be an impostor, and that anyone should support so absurd a claim was an insult to his scientific reputation. The meeting to reward Stephenson had taken place on 1 November 1817. Ten days later Davy despatched a letter to each of Stephenson's prominent supporters. That addressed to William Losh is a typical specimen:

Sir,
Having seen your name in the papers connected with an opinion which every Man of Science in the Kingdom knows to be false in substance as it is absurd in expression, I wish to know if it is used with your consent.
The Public Scientific Bodies to which I belong must take Cognizance

of this indirect attack on my Scientific fame, my honour and varacity [*sic*]. I wish to know my enemies on this occasion, not from any feeling of fear, but because I would not connect the names of honourable men who may have been led into this business from mistaken ideas of benevolence with those of other persons whose conduct with respect to my exertions in *this cause* will, I think, awaken public indignation.

I am, Sir, Your Obd^t Humble Servant,

H. DAVY.

To this Losh rightly replied with a stinging snub:

Your letter which I have just received is written in a style of authority, to say the least of it, very unusual in the correspondence of gentlemen. My name was undoubtedly inserted as a Member of that Committee, the objects of which appear to have given you so much offence, with my perfect approbation.

Satisfied as I am with my conduct on this subject I must say that I am wholly indifferent as to the cognizance which may be taken of it by the 'Public Scientific Bodies' to which you belong.

Notwithstanding my sense of the great benefits which you have conferred upon the public, I consider myself at perfect liberty to testify my esteem for the genius and merits of any other person in whatever way I think best.

Equally devastating in its frigid courtesy was the Earl of Strathmore's reply to a similar letter from Davy. "It is not without some degree of surprise that I have just received a letter from you on the subject of what passed at a meeting lately held at Newcastle . . ." writes the Earl. He continues:

I beg leave to inform you that George Stephenson is, and has been for many years, employed at Killingworth and other Collieries in which I am concerned, and that no other Safety Lamp but that of his Invention ever has been used in any of them. . . . The men who work in them are perfectly satisfied with those lamps and no explosion has taken place in any of our collieries since their introduction.

Is it to be wondered at that I should be anxious to reward a very deserving, unassuming Man, who has to his employers always proved himself a faithful servant and whose abilities, if they had been aided by the advantage of education, would probably have rendered him conspicuous in the annals of Science.

No man can more highly appreciate your merits than I do . . . but at the same time I can never allow any meritorious Individual to be cried down because he happens to be placed in an obscure situation— on the contrary, that very circumstance will operate in me as an additional stimulus to endeavour to protect him against all overbearing efforts.

This last letter possesses an added value in that it reveals how very high George Stephenson's reputation stood at this date in the esteem of the powerful Grand Allies. Sir Humphry Davy could have had no idea what formidable champions of Stephenson he was provoking by his ill-conceived attacks and their onslaught drove him into sullen silence. And yet, fourteen years later, Sir Humphry Davy's biographer, Dr. Paris, could still write: "It will hereafter be scarcely believed that an invention so eminently scientific, and which could never have been derived but from the sterling treasury of science, should have been claimed on behalf of an engine-wright of Killingworth, of the name of Stephenson—a person not even possessing a knowledge of the elements of chemistry."

This passage is typical of the superior attitude adopted by the scientific theorists of the day with whom Stephenson was soon to cross swords again in the greater battle over the locomotive railway. Confronted by the undoubted facts of the creation of the 'Geordie' safety lamp, the scientific fraternity were forced to argue that Stephenson must have been aware of the nature of Davy's experiments and so attempted to forestall him. To this aspersion Stephenson's supporters replied with a counter allegation. A friend of George Stephenson's named Captain Robson, a sailor who had swallowed the anchor and bought a farm at Killingworth, always stoutly maintained that Davy had been fully informed about Stephenson's experiments. He claimed that Stephenson had explained them to him at his house in the presence of Dr. Burnet, the colliery doctor, and that Burnet had then foolishly passed the information on to John Buddle,[1] the colliery engineer who was Davy's chief representative and agent in the north.

In the circumstances, allegations of this kind on both sides became almost inevitable, but it is pretty safe to assume that they were

---

[1] John Buddle (1773-1843) was the most celebrated mining engineer of the day, becoming known on the Tyne as 'The King of the Coal Trade'. His name was associated with the Chapman locomotive —see p. 46.

unfounded and that Stephenson and Davy did in fact reach the same goal quite independently. It is greatly to the credit of Stephenson that, unlike his rival, he maintained a dignified silence throughout the whole controversy, resting his case upon the simple, factual statement which he made at Brandling's request.

As to the respective merits of the 'Geordie' and 'Davy' lamps, opinions in the Tyne and Durham coalfields were divided for years after, some pits preferring one and some the other. The Davy lamp was favoured because it gave slightly more light, but the collieries of the Grand Allies and all the more gaseous pits remained faithful to the 'Geordie', the men insisting that it was the safer lamp. When Stephenson's lamp began to be produced in quantity, he adopted Davy's wire gauze in place of the perforated plate, but he insisted upon retaining the glass chimney within. The wisdom of this insistence was conclusively proved by a disaster in January 1825 at Charles Brandling's Gosforth Colliery at Middleton near Leeds where the top of a Davy lamp became red-hot, causing an explosion in which twenty-four men and boys lost their lives. Again, there was an occasion at the Oaks Colliery at Barnsley, where both types of lamp were in use, when a sudden strong influx of gas caused the Davy lamps to become red-hot whereas all the 'Geordie' lamps went out. Fortunately in this case there was no explosion.

These episodes convincingly vindicated the preference of the men of Killingworth for the lamp which had been bred in their own mine as a result of practical experience. Thomas Summerside's father, Robert, who was overman and manager of the Bob's Pit where Stephenson made his experiments, was unstinting in his praise for the Geordie lamp and declared that after its introduction there were no more blasts in this notoriously dangerous mine. Later, when he removed to the Spring Well Colliery where seventy lives had previously been lost in explosions, Robert Summerside boasted of the same proud record after introducing the Stephenson lamp. There can be no more satisfying reward for an inventor than the saving of human life and suffering upon such a scale as this, and if the name of George Stephenson had never become associated with railways it would have deserved immortality for this achievement alone.

CHAPTER THREE

The Birth of the Locomotive

IN THIS year, 1960, it is evident that the newer powers of the electric motor and the diesel engine are, between them, going to banish steam from the railways of the world as surely and as swiftly as the steamship swept the sailing ship from the seas. In basic principle the steam locomotive has changed very little in the hundred years that have passed since Robert Stephenson died, and for this reason a whole generation now regards its faithful servant as the archaic survivor of a bygone age. To the uninitiated, the engineer who can pack the greatest concentration of horsepower into the smallest streamlined container is necessarily the most progressive, a smooth exterior concealing the watch-like complexity of the highly stressed machinery within, even if it cannot suppress the ear-shattering commotion of its efforts. By contrast, the simplicity of the steam locomotive which is its supreme virtue is now dismissed as mere crudity. Yet no mechanical product of the industrial revolution has given us such long and reliable service or succeeded in capturing the imagination of so many generations of men. Its passing will be mourned as widely as that of the tall sailing ship.

That doyen of a famous firm of locomotive builders, the late Colonel Kitson Clark, was the author of the fairest and finest tribute ever paid to the steam locomotive. "In my judgement", he wrote, "there is nothing so serviceable or so valuable to mankind as the steam locomotive . . ." It is, he continues, "A machine easy to make, easy to run, easy to repair, never weary from its birth in mint condition to the days that saw it worn, dirty and old; wasteful as nature and as inefficient as man, very human in characteristic, far from ideally economic in action but, like our race, ever in a stage of development, master in emergencies, its possibilities of improvement inexhaustible."

The mechanical simplicity of the steam locomotive contrasts

with the complexity of its early history. Ask any schoolboy who invented it and almost invariably he will answer 'George Stephenson', a reply which is patently untrue. In fact, the origins of the steam locomotive as we know it have been the subject of so much bitter dispute between the champions of rival claimants as to make the controversy over the invention of the safety lamp seem a very mild affair indeed. Unless he walks with great circumspection the student of early locomotive history is likely to become completely lost in a labyrinth of contradictory facts, conflicting claims and allegedly original drawings and illustrations which, more often than not, turn out to be conjectural. Indeed, it is doubtful whether any other major invention has been the subject of so much heated argument. Why should this be? The answer is to be found in the origins of the still current popular belief that George Stephenson was the father of the steam locomotive and, indeed, of the railway.

There is no doubt at all that George and Robert Stephenson were together responsible for introducing the locomotive and the railway as a practicable means of long-distance transport for passengers and goods. Their success and the undying fame which they earned thereby was due to their own ability and foresight and to George Stephenson's unshakable faith in the potentiality of the steam locomotive. It was also due to the fact that, unlike other great pioneers such as Richard Trevithick, the Stephensons had the good fortune to be born at precisely the right moment in history and not before. The canals of Brindley, Telford and Rennie had produced a wave of industrial expansion so powerful that these narrow waterways could no longer contain it. Consequently the Stephensons found an economic and commercial climate in England that was ripe for railway development and they found a rapidly developing technology capable of executing their ideas in a workmanlike manner. But no great invention has ever been brought to its definitive form by the unaided efforts of one man, and the steam locomotive is no exception. The fact must be faced that George Stephenson himself was largely responsible for initiating the legend that he was its sole parent. During the years of his fame he was frequently called upon to make public speeches, having quite overcome that bashfulness which afflicted him on the occasion of the safety lamp presentation in his early days. In these speeches he would invariably recall his early struggles and paint a graphic picture of his battle to establish the steam locomotive with every man's hand against him. To do him justice, Stephenson never boasted about, still less exaggerated, the practical part he had played in the development of locomotive design, but on the other hand he never acknowledged the efforts of those other engineers, predecessors or contemporaries, whose work, in the technical sense of the word, contributed at least as much as he did to the ultimate practical success of the locomotive railway.

As a result of this sin of omission on Stephenson's part, it is not surprising that contemporary speakers and writers should magnify his personal contribution and eulogize him as the Father of locomotives and railways. Dr. Dionysius Lardner, the scientific popularizer of the day, bestowed the title of "Father of the Locomotive" on George Stephenson as early as 1836, while Samuel Smiles and other writers carried on the tradition until George Stephenson and the locomotive, like Watt and his kettle, became a part of English folklore.

Not unnaturally, the friends and descendants of other pioneer locomotive engineers resented this undue concentration of limelight upon Stephenson and so the great argument began. Francis Trevithick threw down the gauntlet in the form of a massive two volume biography of his father, Richard Trevithick; Oswald Dodd Hedley entered the lists to champion his father William Hedley with his *Who Invented the Locomotive?*; while for years John Wesley Hackworth crusaded in the press on behalf of his father, Timothy Hackworth. As late as 1923 a descendant, Robert Young, discharged a belated broadside in defence of Hackworth in his *Timothy Hackworth and the Locomotive*. Matthew Murray and Blenkinsop, too, had their spokesmen.

These instances of family loyalty may be admired, but unfortunately nobody smarting under a sense of injustice can possibly write an accurate, unbiased account of past events, so it is small wonder that the total effect of these efforts is confusing instead of enlightening. On the popular Stephenson legend they made no impact at all. The most they achieved was to raise doubts in the minds of a few as to whether George and Robert Stephenson were really entitled to claim any credit at all. Such a total reversal of popular belief is, needless to say, quite unjustified.

There were two stages in the development of the locomotive

around which the battle of rival claimants raged with particular heat. One was: Who first determined that the friction between smooth wheel and smooth rail would be sufficient to enable the locomotive to draw an economic load? The other was: Who first realized that the boiler fire would be quickened and steam-raising improved by turning the exhaust steam from the cylinders into the chimney and, if necessary, contracting the outlet to sharpen the blast? Both these developments were credited to Stephenson and both were fiercely challenged. That such arguments went on with undiminished vigour long after the deaths of the two Stephensons is revealed by a drawing entitled 'The Battle of the Blast Pipe' which a local cartoonist produced during the Railway Jubilee celebrations at Darlington in 1875. George Stephenson, Samuel Smiles and John Wesley Hackworth may be distinguished among the group of top-hatted, frock-coated Victorian worthies engaged in belabouring each other unmercifully with their umbrellas.

The dust raised by these controversies has settled now, and for this the present-day biographer of George Stephenson must be duly thankful. But it has not, unfortunately, been blown away; rather does it lie in a thick layer over the facts. All the conflicting accounts of the disputants, however, do reveal a common error by avoiding which it may be possible, even at this distance of time, to blow the dust away and arrive at some closer approximation to the truth. This error is that of applying to the past the critical standards of the present; of failing to appreciate the totally different conditions which confronted engineers at the time when the locomotive was born from those which prevailed a mere twenty or thirty years later. Had the nineteenth-century writers on the steam locomotive considered matters coolly and tried to think themselves back into the past, they might have realized that an engineer's failure to apply such (to them) familiar principles as the blast pipe or the smooth wheel does not necessarily imply ignorance of such principles. It may well be that contemporary conditions made their application impracticable. Had this been appreciated, far less printer's ink might have been wasted upon fruitless argument.

There can be no doubt at all that if any one man is entitled to be called the inventor of the steam locomotive it is that great Cornishman Richard Trevithick. The low-pressure condensing beam

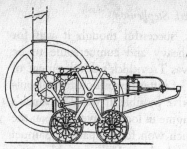

Trevithick's Gateshead Locomotive,
1805.

Blenkinsop/Murray Rack Locomotive,
1812.

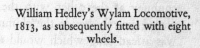

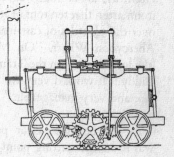

William Hedley's Wylam Locomotive,
1813, as subsequently fitted with eight
wheels.

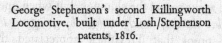

George Stephenson's second Killingworth
Locomotive, built under Losh/Stephenson
patents, 1816.

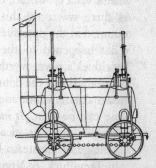

THE BIRTH OF THE LOCOMOTIVE

engine developed by James Watt, successful though it was for
stationary purposes, was far too heavy and cumbersome to be
adapted to the locomotive and it was Trevithick's development of
his high-pressure engine in the face of bitter opposition from Boulton & Watt that made the locomotive possible. It was Trevithick's
embodiment of his high-pressure engine in locomotive form on the
Pen-y-Daren tramway in 1804 which won for his patron, Samuel
Homfray, the famous wager laid by Anthony Hill, a neighbouring
ironmaster, that ten tons of iron could not be hauled by steam power
over the 9½ miles of cast-iron plate tramway from Pen-y-Daren to
Abercynon Wharf. "On Monday [13 February 1804] we put it
[the locomotive] on the Tram Road", wrote Trevithick to his friend
Giddy. "It work'd very well, and ran up hill and down with great
ease and very manageable." From that moment locomotive history
in Britain began.

As will be made clear presently, the Pen-y-Daren locomotive
was to be the starting point of locomotive development on Tyneside, so some consideration of it is essential. It had a return flue
boiler; that is to say, the cylindrical boiler contained a single large
U-shaped firetube, the furnace being at one end of this tube and the
chimney at the other with the effect that the furnace door was
placed directly beside the chimney. In the tube above the furnace
was a lead plug which would melt if the water in the boiler fell
dangerously low, a simple device which has been used in every
locomotive from that day to this. A single cylinder was recessed
horizontally into the boiler above the firedoor and this drove the
wheels via a crosshead, twin connecting rods and a train of gearing.
As there was only this one cylinder, the crankshaft, which was
mounted at the opposite end of the boiler, carried a large fly-wheel.
What happened to the exhaust steam may best be described in
Trevithick's own words: "The steam is delevered [sic] in to the
Chimney above the damper, and when the damper is shut the steam
then makes its appearance at the top of the chimney, but when open
none can be seen. *It makes the draft much stronger by going up the
chimney.*" Here is clear proof that Trevithick appreciated the
advantage of the steam blast.

In Trevithick & Vivian's Patent Specification of 26 March 1802,
which covered the application of the high-pressure steam engine

The Birth of the Locomotive

to road and rail vehicles, the following provision occurs: "The periphery of the carriage wheels is sometimes made uneven by projecting heads of nails, or bolts or cross grooves, of fittings to railroads, and, in cases of hard pull, a lever, bolt, or claw is caused to project through the rim of the wheels, so as to take hold of the ground. . . ." Later writers, when dealing with the smooth-wheel controversy made great play with this quotation as proof of the fact that Trevithick did not appreciate the sufficiency for propulsion of the friction between smooth wheel and smooth rail. But they failed to point out that Trevithick's patent was intended to cover road as well as railway locomotives and they also suppressed the words immediately following those quoted which read: ". . . but, in general, the ordinary structure or figure of the external surface of the wheel is found to answer the intended purpose". The Pen-y-Daren locomotive did in fact have smooth flangeless wheels for working on its flanged cast-iron plateway.

It seems certain that Trevithick realized that smooth wheels could give sufficient traction on rails *provided* that there was a reasonable adhesive weight upon them. That was the rub, for his locomotive was far too heavy for a tramway built for horse haulage. It broke the fragile cast-iron tramplates wholesale, and having won the wager for Homfray and drawn a test load of twenty-five tons it was converted into a stationary engine. But its fame spread and very soon reached the Tyne, probably through the agency of the Crawshay family who had iron works at Cyfarthfa in South Wales and in Gateshead. The effect of this was that Christopher Blackett, the owner of the Wylam Colliery, ordered a locomotive of Trevithick type in 1804. Some subsequent writers maintained that this engine was built for Trevithick at Coalbrookdale or Bridgnorth and shipped by him to the Tyne; others that it had nothing whatever to do with Trevithick but was built under the superintendence of John Steel, a millwright employed by Trevithick who had worked for him at Pen-y-Daren and who copied his design. It is now accepted, however, that the engine was built at John Whinfield's foundry, Pipewell Gate, Gateshead with John Steel's assistance and with the full knowledge of Trevithick. Possibly some of the smaller parts may have been supplied from the south. An authentic original drawing of this locomotive has survived, and if the conjectural drawing of the Pen-y-Daren engine is correct, the two differed only in the layout of cylinder, connecting rods and crankshaft which was transposed. In the South Wales engine, the intrepid fireman must have been constantly menaced by the piston rod, sweeping to and fro over his head like the business end of some gigantic trombone. In the Newcastle engine he had to contend with crankshaft, flywheel and gears instead, the cylinder being at the opposite end of the boiler.

The Gateshead locomotive was completed in 1805 and a distinguished company gathered to see her run on a temporary way laid down at the foundry. But Blackett never took delivery and, like the Pen-y-Daren engine, it was taken off its wheels and used to drive cupola bellows in the foundry. An old employee of Whinfield's, writing in 1858, spoke of 'some disagreement between him [Blackett] and my master' and the reason for this is plain. Blackett refused to accept the engine because it was much heavier than he had expected and he knew it would be useless on the Wylam road.

The Wylam wagonway, which ran past George Stephenson's birthplace, was at this time of the usual double-rail type which had been in use on Tyneside for many years. This would consist of oak rails mounted on cross sleepers at three-foot spacing, the latter covered with cinders between the rails to protect them from the horses' feet. The running surface of the oak rails would be protected by a renewable strip of beechwood, hence the term 'double rail' to distinguish it from the still more primitive type which lacked even this refinement. It is obvious that if Trevithick's first locomotive had smashed the cast-iron Pen-y-Daren tramplates, his second would speedily have reduced the Wylam wagonway to matchwood.

Trevithick does not appear to have been unduly concerned by this failure. He was at this time intent on promoting the sales of his high-pressure engine and upon adapting it to a great variety of duties, of which locomotion was only one. He accepted the fact that the advantage of his tram engine over horse haulage was not so great as to induce colliery owners to embark upon the costly reconstruction of their wagonways to bear its weight and he therefore wisely concentrated upon other applications of his engine.

So matters rested for seven years, but amongst the resourceful engine-wrights of Tyneside the seed had been sown. Debates continued, and not infrequently they took place in the little parlour of George Stephenson's cottage at West Moor, Killingworth. Here might be found young Nicholas Wood, Robert Hawthorn, or John Steel—the man who had actually helped to build the Trevithick locomotives but who was also 'one of them'. The son of a brakesman on the Pontop wagonway, when still a boy Steel had lost a leg on this wagonway and had then been apprenticed by the Pontop proprietors to the Winfield Foundry, where he met Trevithick. More rarely there came to the West Moor cottage a still more significant visitor—none other than Richard Trevithick himself. Between 1805 and 1808 the great Cornishman visited Newcastle on several occasions, but that he should seek out an obscure brakesman in his cottage some miles from the city seems highly unlikely. Yet many years later Trevithick would declare that he had many a time dandled the infant Robert Stephenson upon his knee, a fact which suggests that he had already discerned George Stephenson's ability and knew him for a man of mark before he had achieved even local fame.

At this distance of time we are apt to forget what an immense advance Trevithick's high-pressure engine was over the low-pressure engine of Watt. For the first time in history it offered men mechanical power in a reasonably compact and portable form and its challenge to the ingenuity of resourceful engine-wrights like George Stephenson was as great as that of the Otto four-stroke gas engine to Gottlieb Daimler eighty years later. The eager discussions by cottage firesides or in candlelit taprooms may be readily imagined, but unfortunately the most ingenious mechanic needs a lot of money before he can translate his dreams into reality, and for the present no money was forthcoming from the only men who could provide it—the colliery owners.

It was not the arguments of their engine-wrights but the war with Napoleon which finally induced Charles Brandling of Gosforth, Christopher Blackett of Wylam, and the Grand Allies to loosen their purse-strings. An effect of the war was an enormous increase in the cost of the fuel upon which their transport systems depended— horse fodder—and it was this which forced them to consider more seriously the claims of an iron horse using a fuel which they produced themselves.

Charles Brandling was the first to make a move. In the seventeenth century his ancestor, Ralph Brandling, had acquired by marriage the Middleton estate near Leeds, and in 1758-9 his father, Charles Brandling, had laid down a wooden wagonway of Tyneside pattern to carry the coal from the Middleton collieries to Leeds. The Brandling family left the management of the Middleton estate in the hands of a succession of Agents and at the time with which we are here concerned the Agent was a Leeds man, John Blenkinsop. In 1811, Blenkinsop patented a system of rack propulsion for locomotives and at the same time Brandling authorized the building of an engine on this system by Matthew Murray of Messrs. Fenton, Murray & Wood, the Round Foundry, Holbeck, Leeds. While this was under construction the old wooden tramway was relaid with cast-iron edge rails, one line having the rack teeth cast on the external face.

The Blenkinsop/Murray locomotive was given its first test run on 24 June 1812. Its boiler had a single straight flue instead of the return flue used by Trevithick and the two vertical cylinders were recessed in the top of the boiler barrel. By means of cross-heads and long connecting rods, these drove twin crankshafts mounted under the frame and these in turn were coupled by spur gears to the central shaft upon which the single rack wheel was mounted on the left side. Trevithick had used a similar vertical cylinder mounting on his Camborne road locomotive of 1801, and on the majority of his stationary engines. His locomotive patent also covered the use of two cylinders, but the Blenkinsop engine appears to have been the first to embody them. It is significant, however, that £30 was paid to Trevithick for the use of his patent. Needless to say, the use of two cylinders was far more satisfactory and dispensed with the need for the large flywheel, despite which the Trevithick engines were said to progress by fits and starts. Murray did not turn the steam from the cylinders into the chimney but exhausted it to atmosphere, at first through a straight pipe and later through some form of silencer. Matthew Murray, the practical engineer, protested against the unscientific and lop-sided arrangement of one rack wheel, but his advocacy of rack wheels and rails on each side was unsuccessful, probably on economy grounds. The alternative of a single central rack and pinion was out of the question because the space between the running rails had to be kept clear as a horse path.

On 12 August 1812 the first Blenkinsop/Murray locomotive *Prince Regent* and her sister *Salamanca* began regular work on the Middleton tramway. They were later (1813) joined by two more, of which one was initially sent to the Tyne where it worked for a short trial period on part of the Kenton & Coxlodge tramway before being returned to Leeds. As this trial was made within three miles of West Moor, we may be sure it did not escape the shrewd eye of George Stephenson.

In 1825, when the great locomotive debate began, Thomas Gray of Nottingham, one of the first railway advocates and the author of *Observations on a General Iron Railway*, wrote to the *Gentleman's Magazine* as follows: "The man who can *now hesitate* to recommend steam engines instead of horse-power must be pitied for his ignorance or despised for his obstinacy ... after the demonstration of their utility proved by Mr. Blenkinsop these fourteen years." From this it is fair to assume that the engines at Middleton gave reasonably reliable service over a number of years, in which case they were the first in the world to do so. Blenkinsop's own claim was that one engine did the work of sixteen horses by drawing a load of ninety-four tons on the level at a speed of $3\frac{1}{2}$ m.p.h. As originally built, steam admission to the cylinders was controlled by four-way semi-rotary plug valves of the type introduced by Trevithick,[1] but later they were most probably fitted with Matthew Murray's great contribution to locomotive development, the slide valve which he patented in June 1802.

Smiles and other writers would later point to Blenkinsop's rack as clear evidence that he did not realize the practicability of simple adhesion. In fact it was a solution to the problem of the hour, which was to produce a locomotive light enough not to punish a primitive permanent way yet possessing a sufficiently high tractive effort to appeal to colliery owners as an effective substitute for horses. In this he succeeded. Where speed was of no consequence a haulage capacity

[1] Like most engineers of the day, Murray mistrusted Trevithick's high-pressure engine and for this reason 'played safe' by following Trevithick's design minutely.

of ninety-four tons with a five-ton locomotive was no small achievement.

Two other locomotive pioneers tackled the same problem in different ways at about the same time as Blenkinsop. One of them, William Brunton of the Butterley Ironworks, need not concern us since his extraordinary machine had no influence on George Stephenson's work.[1] His locomotive was propelled by two feet actuated by the piston rods via a complicated system of levers. The other pioneer was William Chapman of Murton House, Durham. A well-known civil engineer of the day and a close associate of John Buddle, his contribution to the locomotive was undeservedly ignored when the argument between rival claimants to fame broke out. With his brother Edward of Willington Ropery, Chapman applied in 1812 for a patent on a locomotive designed to haul itself along upon a chain cable laid between the rails. Locomotive historians sometimes admit as much in passing, adding that the first four-wheeled engine built to Chapman's design was tried at Heaton Colliery in 1813 and proved a costly failure. But they fail to mention that Chapman's patent also offered a solution to the weight problem, which is of much greater significance than his chain-haulage plan.

The rail-destroying tendency of the locomotives so far mentioned was greatly enhanced by the fact that they were completely unsprung. In some cases the method of drive prohibited any relative movement between axles and frame, but in any event industry at this time could not produce leaf springs of sufficient strength to carry a five-ton locomotive. Chapman solved this problem of weight by distribution, mounting his locomotive on what we now call bogies.[2] In 1934 there was discovered in Derby an early Butterley Company drawing of a six wheeled chain-haulage engine having a leading four wheeled bogie, and on 3 January 1815 there appeared in the *Tyne Mercury* an account of the trial of yet another Chapman locomotive which took place on the 4-ft. gauge Lambton wagonway on 24 December 1814. It is clear from the Press report that this

---

[1] On 31 July 1815, while being tried out on "The Earl of Durham's Railway", the boiler of Brunton's locomotive exploded, killing both enginemen instantly and injuring many spectators, some fatally. This was the first serious railway disaster.

[2] In 1825, Chapman looked forward to "long carriages resting on eight wheels and containing the means of providing the passengers with breakfast, dinner, etc., whilst the carriages are moving." This was a prophetic vision indeed in 1825.

engine was mounted on two four wheeled bogies and that the chain-haulage system was now retained only as a means of auxiliary assistance on steep gradients. Under favourable conditions the drive was transmitted to the carrying wheels through gearing so arranged as to allow the bogies a limited amount of movement. "The engine", we are told, "was mounted upon eight wheels, by means of which the weight is so far reduced as to avoid the great expense of relaying ways with stronger rails, which in many instances has been done to obtain the vast annual saving between the use of locomotive engines and horses.

"The cast-iron rails of Mr. Lambton's way were only calculated to carry waggons of three tons weight, inclusive of their loading, and the locomotive, with its water, was nearly six tons; so that upon four wheels this way could not have borne it." The reporter recorded that there was considerable slipping when the engine was starting its load from rest, but that once it had got moving it drew eighteen loaded coal waggons weighing fifty-four tons up a gradient of 1 in 115 at just under 4 m.p.h. It can fairly be claimed for Chapman not only that he was the father of the bogie but also that he built the parent of all articulated locomotives.

At this juncture the Wylam wagonway, now relaid as a cast iron plate tramway, comes into the story once again. In 1813 William Hedley, Christopher Blackett's viewer at Wylam colliery, constructed a four-wheeled frame, the wheels of which could be cranked by men, and with this he carried out experiments to determine the tractive power of smooth wheels on smooth rails. Disregarding Trevithick's achievement at Pen-y-Daren nine years before, Hedley's champions claimed that as a result of these experiments he established a new and epoch-making principle while Blenkinsop, Brunton and Chapman were blundering about in the dark.

Following these experiments, Hedley constructed his first successful locomotive at Wylam, the celebrated 'Wylam Dilly'. This had four smooth flangeless wheels suitable for running on the 5-ft. gauge Wylam plateway. Like the Trevithick engines, Hedley's boiler had a return flue, but instead of being recessed into it the two vertical cylinders were mounted upon each side of the boiler at the end farthest from the chimney and furnace door. The connecting rods to a single central crankshaft, which drove the wheels by spur gears, were actuated by longitudinal beams and Watt parallel motion. The exhaust steam first entered a receiver which acted as a silencer before passing up the chimney. 'Wylam Dilly' and her successors of similar design proved successful in practice, except that in four-wheeled form they were too heavy for the cast iron plateway. They were therefore subsequently converted into eight-wheeled engines in which form they ran until some date between 1825 and 1830, when the Wylam line was again relaid, this time with wrought iron edge rails. They then reverted to four flanged wheels. For years Hedley has been given the credit for the conversion to eight wheels, but it now seems almost certain that Chapman bogies were used.

While Hedley was experimenting and building his locomotives at Wylam colliery, Timothy Hackworth was foreman blacksmith there. In the light of Hackworth's subsequent achievements, his champions later awarded him and not Hedley the major share of the credit. Furthermore, in order to establish priority, Hackworth's biographer, Robert Young, unaccountably set the date of commencement of the Wylam experiments back to 1811. No doubt Hackworth did make a contribution to the achievement, but so also would Jonathan Foster the chief engine-wright at Wylam, and this is no reason for denying William Hedley the major share of the credit as the presiding mind. To seek to transfer credit from designers to executants, however able, is to introduce an element of futile argument which can only reduce the history of invention to nonsense.

Not only had George Stephenson seen the Blenkinsop and Chapman engines at work on the Coxlodge and Lambton ways but he was very friendly with Jonathan Foster and with him he had frequent opportunities to inspect progress at Wylam. He must have realized that his own long-awaited chance to enter the locomotive lists and so give years of eager speculation a practical shape was not far off. For it was safe to assume that where Charles Brandling and Christopher Blackett had led, the far more powerful Grand Allies must sooner or later follow. That great chance came towards the end of 1813 when Sir Thomas Liddell ordered Stephenson to supervise the construction of a locomotive for the Killingworth wagonway in the West Moor colliery workshops. The result was the *Blucher* and in after-years Thomas Summerside recalled how, on 25 July 1814, he joined the great throng of spectators who watched it make its first journey, lumbering slowly past Stephenson's cottage at West Moor.

It was in a lecture to the Literary and Philosophical Society of Newcastle in December 1836 that Dr. Lardner delivered his eulogy of George Stephenson in the course of which he referred to him as 'the Father of the locomotive'. This was at once challenged by William Hedley in a statement from Shield Row, dated 10 December, which was inserted for three weeks in all the local newspapers. Later, Hedley's supporters would make great play with the fact that it was never challenged. That it was not is certainly strange because it contains some curious inconsistencies. Having correctly quoted 25 July 1814 as the date when the *Blucher* first took the rails, Hedley continues: "Long before this period the use of horses on the Wylam Railroad was superseded by the locomotive engines, and a large annual sum in the course of being saved to the colliery from the reduced charge in conveying the coals." "I", he continues, "am the individual who established the principle of locomotion by the friction or adhesion of the wheels upon the rails. . . . I trust you will see the propriety in your future lectures of not designating Mr. Stephenson the 'Father of the Locomotive Engine'." Earlier in his long statement, however, Hedley summarized the previous history of the locomotive pioneers, with dates, bringing the story down to the trial of Brunton's 'walking engine', which he says took place in May 1813. He then gives an account of his own experiments as though following on from these earlier efforts, but, significantly, without quoting any dates. Finally, however, he does state that his patent was taken out on 13 March 1813. It is, in fact, quite certain that Hedley's significant contribution to locomotive history, such as it was, was made during 1813 and this being the case his claim that locomotives had superseded horses on the Wylam line 'long before' Stephenson first steamed the *Blucher* at Killingworth in July 1814 is, to say the least of it, misleading. Its only justification rests upon the story that one—some writers say two—single-cylinder locomotives of Trevithick type were built and tried out on the wagonway over the three years preceding 1813. Smiles states that the first of these engines was built by Thomas Waters of Gateshead and was a complete failure, and that the second was of the Blenkinsop rack type and was built at Wylam. "Its weight was found too great for the road, and the cast iron plates were constantly breaking", writes Smiles. "It was also very apt to get off the rack rail and then it stood still. . . . At length it became so cranky that the horses were usually sent out after it to drag it when it gave up." According to Smiles it was this further failure which induced Hedley to make the experiments which resulted in the first 'Wylam Dilly'. This, the first successful Wylam locomotive, cannot have preceded the *Blucher* by more than fifteen months, and probably less.

Another important point must be made here. By putting a smooth-wheeled engine on a flanged plateway, Hedley was doing no more than Trevithick had done at Pen-y-Daren nine years before. The Killingworth railway, on the other hand, was laid with cast iron edge rails so that the *Blucher* had flanged wheels. The area of contact between wheel and edge rail was so much less than that obtaining on a plateway, that the feasibility of adhesive working on edge rails must have been judged extremely doubtful, if not impossible, until Stephenson's *Blucher* proved the contrary on that memorable July day in 1814. In this respect, if in no other, George Stephenson had set in motion the first locomotive of modern type.

With this significant exception it cannot be said that the *Blucher* represented any advance on its predecessors. Of the locomotives built so far, those of Blenkinsop and Murray's design had performed more useful work than any, and it was probably for this reason that Stephenson followed them very closely, the only important difference being that the crankshafts on the frame were geared to the two axles instead of to a central rack wheel shaft. The arrangement of guided cross-heads used by Blenkinsop and now by Stephenson was certainly simpler than the beams and parallel motion favoured at Wylam, which were a cumbersome adaptation of contemporary stationary-engine practice. In one respect, however, the Wylam engines were superior; in their boilers they remained faithful to the Trevithick return flue which almost doubled the heating surface. Stephenson followed Blenkinsop in using the single straight flue, and clung to it for many years for no very obvious reason. With the limited means available in a colliery workshop at that time, a return-flue boiler was a much more difficult thing to make, and one can only assume that Stephenson decided to sacrifice the advantage of increased heating surface for the sake of ease of construction and maintenance. To suggest, as some of his critics did, that for years he failed to appreciate the obvious advantage of the return flue is an insult to his intelligence.

At first, the *Blucher* exhausted the steam from her two cylinders straight to atmosphere like the Blenkinsop & Murray engines, but as she was always chronically short of steam, Stephenson decided to try the effect of turning the exhaust into the chimney through an upturned pipe with a restricted orifice. It was Smiles's description of this experiment which really sparked off the great blast-pipe controversy. Ignoring the fact that Trevithick had done the same thing years before and had not failed to observe its effect, Smiles grossly exaggerated the significance of Stephenson's experiment, hailing it as one of the great moments in the history of invention. He describes it as 'a simple but beautiful expedient' which at once transformed the *Blucher* and ensured the future success of the locomotive. Critics of Samuel Smiles and champions of other engineers, especially of Timothy Hackworth, poured scorn on Smiles and so, indirectly, discredited Stephenson. They pointed to the undoubted fact that in later Stephenson engines the exhaust steam was merely turned into the chimney in order to dispose of it, the pipes being of unrestricted size and laid out in such a way that they did not constitute a blast pipe at all and so could have little effect upon the fire. To them this was conclusive proof that for years George Stephenson failed to understand the principle of the blast pipe and therefore could not have tried it out on the *Blucher*.

Both sides in this argument were equally wrong. Had either possessed as much practical grasp of steam boilers as an illiterate engineman or fireman, the protracted wrangle over the blast pipe could never have occurred. For they appear to have based their arguments on the modern type of multitubular locomotive boiler, the prototype of which did not appear until 1829. In order to draw gas at high temperature through many small diameter tubes and so reap the full advantage of a greatly increased heating surface, it was absolutely essential to use a vigorous steam blast to obtain a high vacuum in the smoke box. But, in the case of the primitive single-flue boiler such as Stephenson used in the *Blucher* and her successors, or even in the return-flue Wylam boiler, the effect of a steam blast of the same strength would be to 'tear the fire', in other words to throw most of it out of the chimney. Moreover, with such a limited heating surface available and therefore such a high heat-loss in any event, such a fierce draught would produce only a very limited gain in steam-raising capacity. This is exactly what Stephenson found when he experimented with the blast pipe on the *Blucher*. Her steaming powers were certainly improved to some extent, but fuel consumption increased so greatly that Stephenson decided that the proper approach to the problem was to eliminate the fierce blast and endeavour to improve the steam-raising power of the boiler by modifying the flues. Another consideration which weighed heavily with him was the great noise made by the experimental blast pipe. This terrified the horses with which his locomotives had to share the wagonways, while both the noise and the cinder-throwing brought complaints from lineside property owners.

The foregoing is not mere conjecture; it is corroborated by one who participated in all George Stephenson's early locomotive experiments—Nicholas Wood. In his famous *Treatise on Rail Roads* of 1825, Wood wrote:

> When the engines were first made, the steam escaped into the atmosphere and made comparatively little noise; it was found difficult then to produce steam in sufficient quantity to keep the engine constantly working; or, rather, to obtain an adequate rapidity of current in the chimney to give sufficient intensity to the fire. To effect a greater rapidity to increase the draught of the chimney, Mr. Stephenson thought that by causing the steam to escape into the chimney through a pipe with its end turned upwards, the velocity of the current would be accelerated and such was the effect; but, in remedying one evil, another has been produced, which, though objectionable in some places was not considered as objectionable on a private Rail-road; the tube through the boiler having been increased there is now no longer any occasion for the action of the steam to assist the motion of the heated air in the chimney. The steam thrown in this manner into the chimney acts as a trumpet, and certainly makes a very disagreeable noise; nothing, however, is more easy to remedy, and the very act of remedying the defect will also be the means of economizing the fuel.

This statement makes it perfectly clear that Stephenson tried a steam blast but, finding it unsuited to the flue boiler, discarded it and, instead, improved steam-raising by increasing the diameter, and therefore the heating surface, of the boiler flue. Wood's book was readily available to Samuel Smiles and all who later joined in the great 'Battle of the Blast Pipe', so it seems quite extraordinary that they either never read this passage or, if they did, that they did not understand it. The simple fact was that the *Blucher* and her successors down to the time of the *Rocket* were chronically deficient in steam-raising power owing to the type of boiler used, and that no blast pipe, no alteration in the proportions of the flues, could do more than mitigate this fatal defect. Such locomotives were incapable of sustained hard work and even on the short hauls demanded of them on the first colliery lines they would frequently come to a standstill through shortage of steam.

George Stephenson's elder brother James was the first driver of the *Blucher*, and his fireman Thomas Ward related an incident typical of those early days. They were hauling a train of twelve loaded chaldron wagons weighing thirty-six tons and were passing James Stephenson's home by the 'Swalley Pit' where the railway crossed the turnpike, when the *Blucher* laboured practically to a standstill, her train blocking the road. Glimpsing his wife through the cottage window, James bawled "Come away Jinnie and put your shoulder to her", at which summons the buxom Jinnie duly downed tools and pushed with such good effect that the train cleared the crossing and rumbled on its way towards the staithes. Evidently James had a wife that any engineman might envy, for Thomas Summerside tells us that Jinnie Stephenson used to get up regularly at 4 a.m. to light up the fire in the *Blucher*.

The few anecdotes such as this which have survived are reminiscent of the struggles of the first motoring pioneers with horseless carriages which were just as underpowered and temperamental. They also help us to understand why the great majority of men at this time, engineers included, refused to take the locomotive seriously. To perceive the giant's power latent in a machine so crude, so hesitant and breathless, and to labour stubbornly in the face of every kind of odds both mechanical and human until that power was loosed upon the world, this was the historic role of George Stephenson. He might not possess the inventive genius of Trevithick, from whose pioneer work his own locomotives and those of his contemporaries all stemmed; in the immediate future he might make no greater practical contribution to the development of the loco- motive than did Timothy Hackworth: yet he alone possessed the vision to see far beyond the Tyneside colliery lines to a day when England would be ruled with iron rails and the steam from his locomotives would fly across counties where mechanical power was still unknown. "I will do something in coming time which will astonish all England", Stephenson once said to old Robert Summer- side at Killingworth, and he was true to his word.

The most obvious mechanical defect of the *Blucher* was the method of transmitting the power to the wheels through spur gears. In this respect Stephenson had followed contemporary practice but he was very dissatisfied with the result. As each cylinder alternately gave a power impulse to one or other of the two crankshafts the interconnecting gear wheels protested vigorously, making, in Nicholas Wood's words 'a great noise' very offensive to Stephen- son's ear. He therefore asked himself whether the method of transmitting the power to the wheels could not be simplified, and his answer was to couple the connecting rods directly to crank-pins on the wheels. Trevithick's original model had been direct coupled, while conjectural drawings of his Camborne road locomotive show a similar arrangement, though it is doubtful whether it could ever have worked on a single-cylinder engine with no flywheel. Stephen- son was therefore the first to use this simple form of transmission successfully on a full-scale locomotive.

In order to adopt this arrangement, Stephenson had to make other alterations. The two vertical cylinders had now to be widely spaced in the boiler barrel to bring them over the axle centres, while some new method of coupling the axles had to be evolved. Ralph Dodds helped Stephenson to take out a patent for these improvements in February 1815, and in this specification two methods of wheel-coupling were proposed. One was to use cranked axles and a single coupling-rod between the frames, and the other was to use sprockets on the axles and chain-drive. He had already tried a similar chain-drive on the *Blucher* to connect the leading wheels of the tender (or "convoy carriage" as it was then called) with the rear axle of the locomotive, with the object of obtaining extra adhesion, but had found it unnecessary. In practice, the forging

of satisfactory cranked axles was found to be beyond the capacity
of the Killingworth blacksmiths, and so the next Stephenson locomotives to appear, the *Wellington* and the *My Lord* had chain-
coupling. It is strange, so obvious does it now seem to us, that the
simpler method of connecting the wheels by outside coupling-rods
did not supersede this chain-drive for several years.

Like Chapman before him, Stephenson also applied his mind to
the problem of making the locomotive easier on the road so that it
would be less likely to break the brittle cast-iron rails. He was
undoubtedly aware of the Chapman bogie and therefore sought a
different solution which would not infringe Chapman's patent. The
result was the so-called 'steam spring'. This consisted of a piston
which was rigidly attached to the axle and worked in a vertical
cylinder whose upper end was open to the boiler. It will be appreciated that by discarding the old system of spur-wheel drive, Stephenson also dispensed with the need for a massive wooden underframe
and made the boiler itself the backbone of the locomotive with only
a light wrought-iron frame below. Hence, his adoption of the 'steam
spring' meant that almost the whole weight of the engine, apart
from the wheels and axles, was carried by the steam pressure in the
boiler. The introduction of this form of suspension also meant that
there was now relative movement between the crossheads above the
boiler and the crank pins on the unsprung wheels, but this movement must have been small because it was apparently catered for
satisfactorily by using ball-and-socket joints at the ends of the
connecting rods.

Later critics of Stephenson dismissed these 'steam springs' as a
dismal failure. As this was before the days of piston rings, the
suspension pistons, like those used for propulsion, were packed with
hemp, so it must have been extremely difficult to keep them steam
tight. When the locomotive was working, one can imagine the
mist of leaking steam under the boiler or the steady drip of water
when it was lying cold in the shed. Nevertheless, the fact remains
that Stephenson's 'steam springs' continued in use on his locomotives
until laminated springs capable of bearing such a weight became
available.

No authentic complete drawing of the *Blucher* survives, but only
a detail showing the geared drive. The precise arrangement of the

cylinders and motion is therefore unknown. We do know, however, that her successors had slide valves and that these were actuated by two eccentrics, one on each axle. These eccentrics represented Nicholas Wood's most important contribution to locomotive development. They worked the valves by means of rods and bell-cranks, there being no valve gear in the modern sense of the term to enable the steam cut-off to be varied or the locomotive to be reversed from the foot-plate. In these first engines, reversing must have been a laborious business. The eccentrics were of the 'slip' type, that is to say their sheaves were loose on the axles and driven by an arm and pin, the latter engaging in a quadrant-shaped slot in the sheave. To reverse the engine it was necessary to manhandle the engine backwards (perhaps with the help of a horse if one was handy) until the driving pin reached the opposite end of the slot in the eccentric sheave, when the valve events would then be correct for reverse working. Simple slip-eccentrics working in exactly the same fashion may still be found on some children's toy steam engines.

The building of the *Blucher* had brought George Stephenson's name to the notice of an increasing number of influential men on Tyneside, among them William Losh, senior partner in the firm of Losh, Wilson & Bell of the Walker Ironworks, Newcastle, and the man who supported him in the safety-lamp controversy. So impressed was Losh with Stephenson's ability that early in 1815 he invited him to come to the Walker Ironworks for two days a week at a salary of £100 a year, the firm to receive a share of any profits arising from his inventions. Such store did the Grand Allies set by their engine-wright that they agreed to this arrangement without making any reduction in Stephenson's retaining fee. So it came about that when Stephenson patented the 'steam spring' in November 1816, William Losh's name appeared as co-patentee.

The 'steam spring' was not the only item covered by this patent. It also included an improved wheel using malleable iron instead of cast iron and, more important still, an improved type of cast-iron rail and chair. The cast-iron edge rails hitherto used had straight butt joints and the seat of the chairs in which they rested was flat. It had become usual to mount these chairs on stone-block sleepers bored and plugged with oak to receive the chair spikes. If one of these stone sleepers settled unequally and the chair canted as a result, this cant was transmitted to the rail. The effect of this was a very rough and uneven way, one rail being higher than its fellow at the joint. This not only played havoc with locomotives and wagons but resulted in many broken rails. The Losh and Stephenson cast-iron rails had half-lap joints, that is to say one rail overlapped its fellow at the joint, and the seating of their chairs was slightly curved instead of flat, the rail resting normally on the apex of the curve so that if the sleeper canted this was not transmitted to the rail. The improvement was so great that the whole of the Killingworth wagonway was relaid with these Losh/Stephenson rails.

The champions of William Hedley and Timothy Hackworth later alleged that all this early development work which Stephenson carried out with the assistance of Ralph Dodds, Nicholas Wood and William Losh represented no advance at all on practice at Wylam, where the unwieldy eight-wheeled geared 'dillies' were still lumbering to and fro on their plateway. Yet this is a case where results speak louder than words. For whereas no other colliery owners followed the example of Wylam, Stephenson stated in his evidence on the Liverpool & Manchester Bill that he had built sixteen of his patent locomotives by the time he finally left Killingworth. One of these engines went as far afield as Scotland, being built to the order of the Duke of Portland for use on his tramway between Kilmarnock and Troon. This was a six-wheeled engine, the centre pair of wheels not being chain-coupled but mounted, like the others, on steam springs.

The merit of Stephenson's patent rails was likewise proved by results, for Stephenson also stated in his evidence that he had laid down new railways at Burraton, Mount Moor, Spring Vale and Hetton, besides relaying and improving the Killingworth, Southmoor and Derwent Brook lines "and several others". This demand for Stephenson's locomotives and rails must have meant good business for Messrs. Losh, Wilson & Bell and doubtless for other Tyneside foundries as well. It also confounds Stephenson's critics and confirms the tribute of that pioneer advocate of railways, William James, who, after a tour of Tyneside railways in 1821, wrote: "The Locomotive engine of Mr. Stephenson is superior beyond all comparison to all the other Engines I have ever seen—

Next to the immortal Watt I consider Mr. Stephenson's Merit in the invention of this Engine.''

William James wrote these words in the course of a letter to an unknown colleague of Edward Pease, the Quaker industrialist of Darlington, who was at this time concerned in promoting a railway between that town and Stockton. Such was the reputation which George Stephenson had now won in the north, that a meeting between him and Pease became inevitable, with consequences which would win for both men national fame.

CHAPTER FOUR

The Stockton & Darlington Railway

WHILE THE Tyne coalfield was expanding, thanks to its relatively easy access to water transport, farther south the Auckland coalfield was seriously handicapped by the long overland haul to Stockton on the navigable Tees. The story of local attempts to remedy this disadvantage and so enable local coal owners to compete with their more fortunate neighbours on Tyneside goes back thirteen years before the birth of George Stephenson—to 1768 when James Brindley's son-in-law Robert Whitworth, assisted by George Dixon, surveyed a line of canal from Stockton through Darlington to Winston Bridge, near Barnard Castle, with branches to Yarm, Croft and Piercebridge. In the following year, Brindley himself went over the line and confirmed Whitworth's estimated cost of £64,000. Nothing was done, and similar schemes advanced by Ralph Dodd in 1796 and George Atkinson in 1800 likewise came to nothing. The first practical improvement to be made was the construction, between 1808 and 1810, of a new navigable cut to improve the Tees navigation at Portrack, near Stockton.

Among those who played a prominent part in this enterprise were Leonard Raisbeck, Recorder of Stockton and solicitor to the Tees Navigation Company, and the Quaker brothers Edward and Joseph Pease, woollen merchants and bankers of Darlington.

At a dinner which was held at Stockton Town Hall on 18 September 1810 to celebrate the completion of the new cut, the question of opening up a direct line of communication with the Auckland coalfield was not unnaturally raised again. It is significant of the changing times, however, that on this occasion the canal advocates found themselves arguing against a new faction headed by Edward Pease, who expressed themselves strongly in favour of a horse tramway. Both sides agreed that something should be done and a

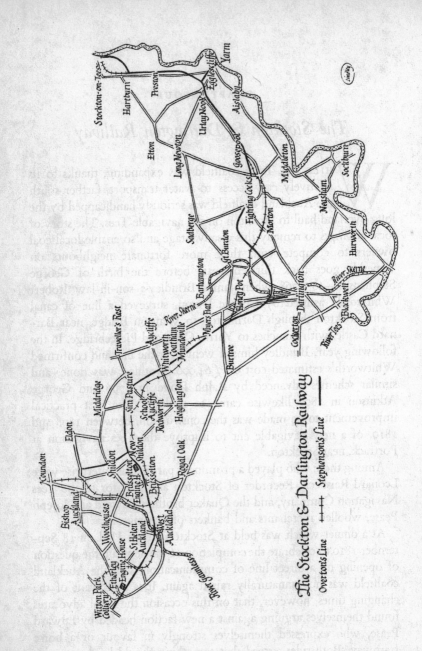

The Stockton & Darlington Railway

Stephenson's Line ▬▬▬

Overton's Line ▬▬▬▬

Stations shown: Stockton-on-Tees, Hartburn, Preston, Eaglescliffe, Yarm, Elton, Long Newton, Urlay Nook, Aislaby, Goosepool, Middleton, Sockburn, Sadberge, Fighting Cocks, Morton, Neasham, Gt. Burdon, Hurworth, Farthampton, River Skerne, Blackwell, River Skerne, Darlington, Cockerton, Goney Pot, Myers Flat, Burtree, River Tees, River Skerne, Travellers' Rest, Aycliffe, Whitworth, Coatham Mundeville, Heighington, Middridge, Sim Pasture, School Aycliffe, Redworth, Royal Oak, Eldon, Shildon, New Shildon, Brussetton Enginc H., Brusselton, Coundon, West Auckland, Bishop Auckland, Woodhouses, St Helen Auckland, Witton Park Colliery, Etherley, Enginc House, River Gaunless committee was set up to investigate the matter. On 13 January 1812 this committee organized a public meeting at the King's Head, Darlington, where it was decided to employ no less a person than John Rennie to make a fresh survey and report. For some unknown reason it took Rennie three years to deliver a report, which simply recommended a canal on substantially the same route which had been proposed by Brindley and Whitworth nearly fifty years earlier. Shortly before Rennie presented this belated document the whole county of Durham suffered a crippling financial blow when the local Hollingsworth banking organization failed. "We lost twelve millions sterling by the failure of the Country Banks in this neighbourhood in 1815", wrote a member of the Stockton & Darlington committee three years later. In view of the magnitude of this disaster it is not surprising that Rennie's report was pigeon-holed.

It was in 1818 that the next move was made, when the committee proposed that Rennie should carry out a further survey, for a railway this time, in association with Robert Stevenson of Edinburgh. Robert Stevenson, grandfather of Robert Louis Stevenson, was a civil engineer of distinction, but the choice seems an odd one, so remote was his field of operations from the matter in hand. He is chiefly remembered as Engineer to the Board of Northern Lights and builder of the Bell Rock lighthouse. A letter dated 26 December 1818, from John Rennie left the committee in no doubt as to his opinion of the proposed collaboration.

"I have been accustomed," he wrote, "to think for myself in the numerous Publick Works in which I have been engaged, many of them of infinitely greater magnitude and importance than the Darlington Railway. If the subscribers to this scheme have not sufficient confidence in me to be guided by my advice I must decline all further concern with it." In matters of this kind Rennie was notoriously prickly and in this case he was undoubtedly influenced by the fact that he had been Consultant for the Bell Rock lighthouse and that the credit for that work had subsequently been disputed between him and Stevenson. Not unnaturally, Rennie's hot-tempered reply marked the end of his connection with the Stockton & Darlington scheme and he did not live to learn how wrong he had been to belittle its importance.

Meanwhile, during the summer of 1818, a Mr. George Leather

had been surveying a canal route at the expense of "a public-spirited inhabitant of Stockton" named Christopher Tennant. George Leather subsequently announced a plan for a direct line of canal from the Tees at Stockton to the coalfield, which ignored Darlington and Yarm altogether yet won considerable support from the canal party. This roused the railway advocates in Darlington and Yarm to instant counter-action. They consisted of Edward Pease, Thomas Meynell, Benjamin Flounders, Richard Miles, Cuthbert Wigham and Jonathan Backhouse and they were not without influential supporters in Stockton, notably Leonard Raisbeck. Backhouse, the Quaker banker of Darlington, in a letter to Miles on the subject of the canal prospectus wrote: "the calculations are erroneous; I cannot conceive that the public will be gulled by them".

This formidable alliance decided to appoint an engineer forthwith to carry out a survey for a line of railway. Thomas Meynell, the Chairman of this new railway committee, had a land steward named Jeremiah Cairns who strongly recommended as engineer a relative of his, George Overton of Lanthelly, near Brecon. It was agreed that Overton should be asked to make the survey and report, but Meynell wrote to Richard Miles, the Committee Secretary, suggesting that he should issue the invitation privately because "some of the Gents feel a delicacy in appearing to employ any Engineer but Mr. Rennie". This was in August 1818, a few months before Rennie finally left the stage. Overton accepted this somewhat furtive invitation and came north to Darlington bringing with him as his assistant surveyor David Davies of Llangattock, Crickhowell.

In this same year a small pamphlet was published in Durham entitled *Observations on the proposed Rail-way or Tram-road from Stockton to the Collieries by way of Darlington*. In a surviving copy of this work an unknown hand has written in the margin of the page which records Overton's appointment these words: "This was an unfortunate appointment; he was wholly incompetent." This was unfair to George Overton. At first thought it may seem very strange that, with such a wealth of pioneer railway talent available on nearby Tyneside, the Stockton & Darlington promoters should have gone to remote Breconshire for their engineer. Yet in fact, although wooden wagonways had been used on Tyneside since the seventeenth century, South Wales was the cradle of the cast-iron tramway

and George Overton was an engineer who had had a longer experience of the construction and operation of such tramways than any
man living. Between 1799 and 1802, when the youthful George
Stephenson was still an obscure engineman and before rumours of
iron ways and locomotives had reached Tyneside, George Overton
had built the Pen-y-Daren tramway on which Trevithick's locomotive made its first epic journey. Overton's assistant, Davies, was
also a man with railway experience. He had surveyed the Swansea
Canal tramroad in 1810 and the Brecon & Abergavenny Canal
tramroad which Overton built in 1813-14.

Rennie had never been popular with the railway party at Darlington because he was known to favour canals, but in George Overton
the committee had found a staunch advocate of railways. "Railways
are now generally adopted and the cutting of canals nearly dis-
continued", he wrote at the time of his appointment, and went on
to list tramways totalling nearly one hundred miles which had been
constructed in South Wales. Of the Brecon canal he said: "About
five years ago I constructed a tramroad which leads into it, and upon
which is conveyed not more than one-third of what passes upon the
canal. The road was completed in one year since which time I have
guaranteed the proprietors seven per cent. The canal was ten years
in completing and has never averaged one per cent per annum!"
Overton also pointed out that where the gradient was with the load,
as would be the case between the Auckland coalfield and Stockton,
the railway would show to best advantage because on the alternative, a heavily locked canal, the boats would take just as long to
lock down as to lock up.

Such comments must have been music to the ears of the Stockton
& Darlington Committee, while they evidently caused the advocates of the rival canal scheme to have second thoughts. They
quickly switched to a plan for a railway on a similar course, missing
Darlington and Yarm. After discussions with the Darlington
Committee, however, they consented to drop their scheme, having
reached agreement over the tolls to be charged on the new tramway.[1]
With this hurdle surmounted, Overton and Davies went ahead
with their survey and plans so rapidly that by March 1819 the

---

[1] This direct line was afterwards built under the name of the Clarence Railway and caused
the Stockton & Darlington Company some concern.

committee were ready to apply for parliamentary powers. Their greatest difficulty now was to overcome the opposition from local landowners. Great efforts were made in this direction, but two of the most influential, Lord Eldon and Lord Darlington of Raby Castle, proved implacable. It was largely due to their influence that when the Stockton & Darlington Bill came up for its second reading in May it was lost by the narrow margin of thirteen votes.

Edward Pease and his colleagues were undeterred by this defeat and George Overton was at once ordered to make a fresh survey including deviations to placate the opposing landlords. This appears to have exasperated Overton, who had evidently not encountered such difficulties when laying out his lines in Wales. He was also understandably nettled by the fact that the Committee had again sought the advice of Robert Stevenson. However, after some negotiation, Overton was at length prevailed upon to make a fresh survey, which he completed by the end of August 1820. Another Bill was promoted before the end of the year but was delayed by the illness and death of the King. It was presented early in the following year and by the end of March it had, in the words of Leonard Raisbeck, 'passed the Committee in high stile'. Again the fight was hard, but this time it was successful and the Stockton & Darlington Railway Act received the Royal Assent on 19 April 1821.

This far distant day was a memorable one in railway history for it was also the occasion of the first momentous meeting between George Stephenson and Edward Pease at the latter's house in Northgate, Darlington. Neither man could then have known that the Bill was passed. An extraordinary variety of conflicting accounts of this historic meeting have been given, interspersed with fantastic local legends. The fable that at the Bulmer Stone, near Pease's house, Stephenson and Nicholas Wood, who accompanied him, removed their boots and approached the house barefoot as a mark of respect is only surpassed by the variant which maintains that they walked barefoot from Durham and put their boots *on* at the Bulmer Stone. A popular version of the story is that the decision to make the journey from Killingworth was made spontaneously by Stephenson without making any appointment with Pease beforehand. He had heard of the railway project and decided to try his luck by applying for a job. According to this account 'the two strange men' were shown into the back kitchen, having walked all the way from Killingworth, only to be told that Edward Pease would not see them. They were on the point of leaving when Pease had second thoughts and came down to the kitchen to talk to them.

As to the interview itself, we are told that Nicholas Wood acted as spokesman for the humble engine-wright who, in rough clothes and with a knotted handkerchief round his throat, stood in awed and uncouth silence before Pease. To dismiss such picturesque nonsense, which would have us believe that Stephenson leapt from humble obscurity to fame in one bound, is not to undervalue the importance of the encounter as a great landmark in Stephenson's career. By the time he met Pease there was nothing uncouth about Stephenson other than his broad Northumbrian speech. So far from being a poor and obscure engine-wright he already enjoyed a wide reputation in the north as an engineer and possessed considerable financial means. In addition to his income from the Grand Allies and from Losh, Wilson & Bell, since 1819 he had been drawing a salary as engineer to the Hetton Colliery Company and was doubtless drawing profits from his other railway undertakings as well. In December 1820 he had become part owner of the Willow Bridge Colliery, he and his partner Thomas Mason each subscribing £700 to the venture. In the same year, Stephenson made a loan of £1,300 at five per cent to a landowner near Darlington. The man whom Nicholas Wood introduced to Pease was therefore no tongue-tied, horny-handed hobble-dehoy from the pit-bank but a tall, powerfully built, commanding figure to whom success had already brought dignity and assurance.

Shortly after the death of Robert Stephenson, Nicholas Wood delivered a memorial address in the course of which he gave a first-hand account of the historic visit to Darlington. This would have effectually disposed of the legends had it been more widely noticed by subsequent writers. "The incident is given by Smiles not quite correctly", says Wood. "The fact is, we rode on horseback from Killingworth to Newcastle, a distance of five miles, travelled from thence by coach, thirty-two miles, to Stockton, then walked along the proposed line of railway, twelve miles, from Stockton to Darlington. We had then the interview with Mr. Pease, by appointment, and afterwards walked eighteen long miles to Durham, within three miles of which I broke down, but was obliged to proceed, the beds being all engaged at the 'Travellers' Rest'." Apparently this failure of the younger man to stay the course on this marathon walk much amused Stephenson, for Wood says that whenever they met in subsequent years, Stephenson seldom failed to twit him about it.

Wood's statement makes it clear that the meeting took place by prior engagement and it is indeed extremely unlikely that the two busy men would otherwise have embarked on such a journey. On whose initiative the meeting was arranged is not known, but it is most probable that Edward Pease was the instigator. Stephenson already had so much work on hand and his financial position was so sound that there is no reason why he should be so eager to solicit employment. On the other hand, the Stockton & Darlington Committee, as was the habit of both railway and canal promoters at this period, seem to have sought the advice of every engineer whom they thought might prove helpful, the effect being to bewilder themselves and to cause a great deal of professional jealousy among their numerous consultants. As Stephenson was already the most celebrated railway engineer in the north, the surprising thing is that he had not been approached before.

Stephenson obviously made a deep impression on the shrewd Quaker, for after their momentous interview Pease said: "There was such an honest sensible look about George Stephenson, and he seemed so modest and unpretending, and he spoke in the strong Northumberland dialect." Moreover, although histories of the Stockton & Darlington Railway record no further move until after a general meeting of the Company had been held in July, in fact, Edward Pease, on his own initiative, reached a verbal agreement with Stephenson there and then and confirmed it to him in writing the very next day when he had received the news from London that the Act had passed. This letter has not survived, but the following reply to it from George Stephenson, which was preserved in the Pease family archives, is confirmation enough:

Killingworth Colliery,
April 28th, 1821.

Edwd Pease, Esq.
Sir,—
    I have been favored with your Letter of the 20 Inst. and am glad to learn that the Bill has passed for the Darlington Rail Way.

I am much obliged by the favourable sentiments you express towards me, and shall be happy if I can be of service in carrying into execution your Plans.

From the nature of my engagements here and in the neighbourhood I could not devote the whole of my time to your Rail Way, but I am willing to undertake to survey and mark out the best line of way within the limits prescribed by the Act of Parliament and also to assist the Committee with plans and estimates and in letting to the different contractors such work as they might judge it advisable to do by Contract, and also to superintend the execution of the work. And I am induced to recommend the whole being done by Contract under the Superintendence of competent persons appointed by the Committee.

Were I to contract for the whole line of road it would be necessary for me to do so at an advanced price upon the Sub Contractors, and it would also be necessary for the Committee to have some person to superintend my undertaking. This would be attended with an extra expense and the Committee would derive no advantage to compensate for it.

If you wish it I will wait upon you at Darlington at an early opportunity when I can enter into more particulars as to remuneration, etc. etc.—

I remain yours

respectfully,

GEORGE STEPHENSON.

We know from an account of charges which Stephenson later submitted that he did in fact 'wait upon' Pease again on 22 May and that he spent the following three days "looking over the Country" at a charge of two guineas a day.

From the moment that George Stephenson met Edward Pease the name of George Overton was no more heard in Darlington. Presumably he returned to Wales a sad and disgruntled man. Overton had made it clear to his employers that in using the term 'Rail Way' he intended a horse tramway or plateway whereas to to Stephenson a railway meant steam traction on edge rails. This was the great significance of Stephenson's historic first visit to Darlington. He expressed his faith in the future of the steam locomotive with such conviction that Pease was completely won over, and succeeded in his turn in persuading his fellow proprietors that a line suitable for locomotives should be laid down. Consequently the first resolution passed at the July meeting read: "That in the best information this Meeting has been able to collect a Railway be adopted as preferable to a Tramway, and that Land sufficient for a double Railway be purchased as soon as the precise line is definitely settled." "If the railway be established and succeeds," declared Pease prophetically, "as it is to convey not only goods but passengers, we shall have the whole of Yorkshire and next the whole of the United Kingdom following with railways."

Such were the terms of reference upon which George Stephenson was asked to resurvey Overton's line. "We beg thee to take them into consideration", wrote Pease to Stephenson on 28 July, "and as soon as thou canst name thy charge for effecting all they contain which attaches to thee as Engineer, please drop me a line. . . ." After detailing the Company's resolutions he concludes: "It does not seem needful to add more than to request that so soon as Crops are off the ground, no time may be lost. . . . In making the survey it must be borne in mind that this is for a great public way and to remain as long as any Coal in the district remains, its construction must be solid, and as little machinery introduced as possible; in fact we wish thee to proceed in all thy levels, estimates and calculations with that care and economy which would influence thee if the whole work was thy own. . . ."

In his reply, Stephenson would not commit himself to a definite figure as to the cost of the survey but thought it would not amount to less than £140. He would, he said, require another surveyor to accompany him and the services of four men, two to hold the levelling staves and two chain men. He also asked Pease to "send a suitable person along with me who knows the different Gentlemen's grounds thro' which we should pass". He thought the survey would take five weeks at the least and added that his own fee would be two guineas a day plus expenses. He agreed to supply the Company with information on the comparative costs of different types of rail, on the expense of quarrying and preparing the stone-block sleepers and the cost of laying the permanent way. He was of opinion that suitable stone for sleepers might be got from 'the Quarry near the great Coal Road' and 'on the north side of Brusselton Hill near to the Roman Road' and urged that quarrying should begin at once so that blocks would have a chance to weather before being used. "I think we should not well go on with the survey till after the corn harvest", he concluded in a postscript. On 27 September, Stephenson attended a meeting of the Managing Committee at Darlington, where his terms were accepted and John Dixon appointed as the 'suitable person' with local knowledge to accompany him. This John Dixon was the grandson of George Dixon who had assisted Whitworth in his canal survey of 1768, and he would figure prominently in the Stephenson story from this time forward.

It was early in October that Stephenson was ordered to proceed with the survey immediately. At this time Robert Stephenson, now aged eighteen, had not yet completed his three years apprenticeship under Nicholas Wood at Killingworth. Robert often had to accompany Wood underground, and this work was not only affecting his health but it also exposed him to considerable danger. While the Stockton & Darlington negotiations were going on, an incident had occurred at West Moor which might have cost Robert his life. He had gone down the pit with Wood and John Moody who wished to inspect a certain level and, finding the feeble light of their 'Geordie' lamp inadequate, proposed lighting a candle. "If you go she'll fire on you", cautioned Robert Summerside, who was then managing overman, but Moody dismissed the warning with an impatient "Nought o' the sort". Old Summerside took Robert by the arm. "Thou shannot go in but shalt sit wi' me i' th' air course" he insisted. Meanwhile Wood and Moody went forward with their candle and, sure enough, a blast followed. "I well remember this", wrote Thomas Summerside, "for I was in the pit at the time and we escaped with our lives in our hands. As it fortunately happened, the fire knocked herself out, and Moody and Wood only were burnt." "Your father saved my Robert's life on that occasion" was Stephenson's comment to Summerside many years after.

This episode and Robert's ill health made Stephenson decide to ask Nicholas Wood to release his son from his apprenticeship so that he could assist him on his survey. Wood agreed and it was a red letter day for Robert when he travelled to Darlington with his father. It marked the end of his work at the colliery and the true beginning of his career as a railway engineer. The fact that Robert Stephenson's signature subsequently appeared on some of the railway plans has been dismissed by previous writers as a mere whim on the part of a proud father. "It is difficult to suppose", wrote J. S. Jeans in his Jubilee History of the Stockton & Darlington, "that at this early period his own knowledge enabled him to render more assistance to his father and to Mr. Dixon than any other very intelligent but inexperienced lad." This supposition is quite incorrect. Young though he was, Robert had evidently already acquired considerable experience, probably through helping his father to lay out the Hetton and other colliery lines. Not only did he act as assistant surveyor to his father but, as will presently appear, he later carried out survey work for the Company on his own account, and deputized for his father on Parliamentary business.

The survey was greatly favoured by perfect weather, and as the trio of railway engineers with their escort of stave-bearers and chain-leaders tramped through the stubble fields in the golden October sunshine Robert's health speedily improved. After confinement in the West Moor pits, the fresh air and exercise and the pauses for refreshment at wayside inns must have been the best tonic in the world. Added to this, the knowledge that they were pioneering a unique enterprise infected the little party with tremendous enthusiasm and high spirits, for while coal transport was still the primary object in view, the railway the Stephensons were now projecting was to be a public one far more ambitious in extent and scale than the private colliery lines of Tyneside. Joseph Pease, Junior, later recalled how he once encountered the Stephensons while they were working on the survey, and how George and his "slight, spare bronzed boy" were arguing over their problems at the tops of their voices in an almost unintelligible Northumbrian brogue.

Thanks to the good weather, the survey was completed much more rapidly than George Stephenson had forecast. According to the account which he subsequently submitted to the Company it was begun on 14 October and completed on the last day of that month. For this his charge was £140, plus an additional sum of £13 10s for surveying the Black Boy and Evenwood branch lines.

George Stephenson's plans, estimate and report were presented to the Company on 18 January 1822. It would be tedious to deal in any great detail with Stephenson's lengthy report, though his description of the proposed route is studded with evocative place names such as Brussleton Bank, Sims Pasture (later shortened to Simpasture), Stand Alone, Myers Flat, Honeypot Lane and Fighting Cocks, some of which would become familiar to all railway historians.

The chief physical obstacles on the course of the railway were the two hill ridges of Etherley and Brussleton lying to the north-west and south-east of the valley of the River Gaunless where the village of St Helens Auckland is situated. Witton Park Colliery, the western extremity of the line, lay in the valley of the Wear beyond the Etherley ridge. George Overton had recommended a devious route from Witton Park passing to the north of the Etherley ridge and a single short and steep inclined plane to lift the line out of the Gaunless valley on to Brussleton hill. From this point eastward his line was designed for horse haulage. Stephenson favoured a more direct route using four inclined planes to surmount the two hill-ridges, three of these inclines to be worked by two winding engines installed on the summit of each hill. He eased the gradient of Overton's Brussleton plane, which he considered dangerously steep, and carried his fourth inclined plane from Brussleton Top down to New Shildon. The Etherley East plane was to be self-acting. Apart from these inclines, Stephenson designed this westernmost portion of the railway to be used by horses only, but from New Shildon eastwards he laid out the whole of the rest of the line with an eye to locomotive working. With this end in view he eased the sharp curves with which Overton's line abounded and was at pains to secure an even falling gradient all the way to Stockton. He was also concerned to save expense in forming the cuttings and embankments—"cuts and batteries" as they were then called. He pointed out that in building the embankments called for on Overton's line, spoil would have had to be carted by road a considerable distance, whereas he had arranged his levels so that his embankments could be built from the spoil excavated from neighbouring cuttings and transported in tipping wagons on temporary ways. By a southward deviation near Aycliffe he not only avoided a tunnel which Overton had proposed at that place, but also shortened the length of the branch line to Darlington by nearly three miles. Altogether his route was shorter by four miles than Overton's, while his estimate of the cost was £60,987 13s. 3d. as compared with Overton's figure of £77,341 18s. 8d.[1]

[1] These figures are quoted from the original document as transcribed in the *Northern Echo*

Edward Pease and his companions were evidently not disposed to
waste any time, for only four days after the date of Stephenson's
report it was accepted at a meeting of the proprietors held at the
Company's new office at High Row, Darlington. Some of Stephenson's improvements upon George Overton's line went far beyond
the limit of deviation of one hundred yards on either side which the
Company's Act permitted. Undaunted by this, however, the
meeting ordered that work should begin immediately on those
sections of the line which lay within the present statutory limits,
and they appointed George Stephenson engineer at a salary of £600
per annum including all expenses and the salaries paid to his assistants. He had made it clear that he could not devote his whole time
to the railway, but the Company stipulated that he should spend at
least one week in each month on the works. Two resident engineers
were appointed under Stephenson, John Dixon for the section from
Stockton to Heighington Lane (the site of the present Heighington
Station) and Thomas Storey, a Northumbrian mining engineer
recommended by Stephenson, for the western half from Heighington to Witton Park. On Stephenson's advice the line was split for
tender purposes into small contract lots of only one mile each and
contractors were advised that sections could be examined at the
Company's offices at Darlington or on application to Robert
Stephenson at Killingworth Colliery.

Meanwhile the vital question of the type of rail which should be
used had been the subject of great debate. As this would be the
greatest single item of expenditure, apart from the earthworks, it
was of the utmost importance that the best choice should be made
and a special sub-committee was set up to examine existing railways

Railway Centenary Supplement. A copy of the Report in the Stockton & Darlington
Records gives the following figures:

	Old			New		
Main Line	73,434	1	2	58,419	17	9
Darlington Br.	2,609	9	0	1,269	7	0
Yarm Br.	—			1,298	8	6
Evenwood Br.	3,738	1	0	3,650	0	0
Total	£79,781	11	2	£64,637	13	3

Yet again Priestley quotes the following:

Overton: £84,000
Stephenson: £74,300

and tram roads, to obtain tenders and to make recommendations. The outcome of these deliberations had very important consequences for the two Stephensons.

While the Stockton & Darlington Railway was being brought to birth a technical development of immense significance had taken place. Until 1821 the only metal alternative to cast-iron rails had been simple square section wrought iron bars whose application was limited to light, narrow gauge tramways in mines as an alternative to wood. Early in this year, however, John Birkinshaw of Bedlington near Morpeth had perfected and patented a method of rolling true wrought iron rails of 'I' section in fifteen foot lengths. Although there was apparently some trouble at first due to these rails 'laminating' or splitting, all who saw them were at once impressed with their possibilities.

John Birkinshaw was an engineer in the Bedlington Ironworks owned by Michael Longridge, and the news of his invention soon reached George Stephenson who, on 28 June 1821, wrote to Robert Stevenson in Edinburgh as follows:

Sir,

With this you will receive three copies of a specification of a patent by John Birkinshaw of Bedlington, near Morpeth.

The hints were got from your Report on Railways, which you were so kind as to send me by favour of Mr. Cookson some time ago. Your reference to Tindal Fell Railway led the inventor to make some experiments on malleable iron bars, the result of which convinced him of the superiority of the malleable over the cast iron—so much so, that he took out a patent.

Those rails are so much liked in this neighbourhood, that I think in a short time they will do away with the cast iron railways.

They make a fine line for our engines, as there are so few joints compared with the other.

Bearing in mind that Robert Stevenson was at this time still advising the Stockton & Darlington Company, George then adds a piece of salesmanship: "I am confident a railway on which my engines can work is far superior to a *canal*. On a long and favourable railway I would stent my engines to travel 60 miles per day with from 40 to 60 tons of goods."

So enthusiastic was Stephenson about Birkinshaw's invention

that, disregarding his own pecuniary interest in the Stephenson & Losh cast-iron rails, he strongly recommended it to the Stockton & Darlington Committee. This disinterested action on his part, while it must have added considerably to his prestige at Darlington, greatly displeased William Losh and quickly brought to an end Stephenson's association with Messrs. Losh, Wilson & Bell. Soon it was Michael Longridge who occupied the place of the disgruntled William Losh in Stephenson's affairs, but this change of business connections had one grave disadvantage. While Longridge might be willing to supply Stephenson's enterprises with his admirable rails, his ironworks at Bedlington were not equipped to construct the locomotives and stationary engines of Stephenson's design which had hitherto been built by Losh, Wilson & Bell at the Walker Ironworks. As will be related presently, it was this situation which led directly to the founding of the famous firm of Robert Stephenson & Company in Newcastle.

On 29 December 1821 the Stockton & Darlington subcommittee on rails reported that the lowest tenders they had received were £12 10s. per ton for malleable rails as against £6 15s. for cast iron. As the weight per yard of wrought-iron rails was less than half that of cast-iron rails of equivalent strength, the cost per mile was approximately the same. The committee recommended that two-thirds of the single line of railway which had been decided upon should be laid with malleable rails and the rest with cast iron. When this report was considered by the managing committee they decided to go even further and lay the whole of the main running line with wrought iron rails, using cast iron only for the passing loops. Michael Longridge's tender for Birkinshaw rails of £15 per ton delivered Stockton was accepted. They were 15 feet long and weighed 28 lb. per yard. Curious to relate, it was the Neath Abbey Ironworks of South Wales who contracted for the cast rails and all the chairs. This would seem to indicate that the rupture between Stephenson and William Losh went very deep. It is evident that the cast-iron *v.* wrought-iron rail argument of 1821 roused just as strong feelings as did the locomotive *versus* fixed-engine debate or the gauge battle of later years. No less an engineer than William Jessop was one of the correspondents who wrote to warn Edward Pease against the wrought-iron rail, while Longridge advised Pease that he "was particularly anxious to have the rails manufactured at Bedlington under my own inspection as every effort is using to prejudice the Public against their adoption, and were your Rail-way to be made in an imperfect manner it might prove extremely injurious to me".

On the western section of the line locally-quarried stone-block sleepers were used as George Stephenson had suggested, but to save the long haul from the quarries wooden blocks were used on the section between Stockton and Darlington. The latter were supplied by sea from Holmes & Pushman, the Portsmouth ship-breakers at the price of sixpence each. It may be wondered why cross-sleepers were not used instead of blocks, but it must be remembered that in addition to locomotives a heavy horse-hauled traffic was anticipated. It would have been necessary to bury cross-sleepers completely, and, even so, experience on the old wooden cross-sleepered wagon ways of Tyneside had shown that it was difficult to maintain a smooth horse-path between the rails, and that the sleepers either rotted in the ground or became damaged by horses' hooves as the protective covering broke up.[1] Blocks, on the other hand, left a clear path between the rails although, as may be imagined, it was not easy to keep the rails to gauge. That gauge; Stephenson had decided, should be 4ft. 8in.,[2] the same as that of the Killingworth way.

It is a measure of the historic importance which the Company rightly attached to their undertaking that the Stockton & Darlington was the first railway in the world to engage an architect. He was Ignatius Bonomi of Durham, elder son of the celebrated eighteenth century architect, Joseph Bonomi. This first railway architect prepared the design of the handsome Skerne Bridge at Darlington, and when George Stephenson was called away to Liverpool in the spring of 1824 he instructed Bonomi to superintend its erection. This is the bridge which figures prominently in Dobbin's famous picture of the opening of the railway.

Few of the contract lots on the railway were taken up locally.

[1] On the Surrey Iron Railway side towing-paths were provided as on a canal. But this arrangement called for an extra width of way, had practical disadvantages, and was never favoured in the North.

[2] 4ft 8in was also to be the gauge of the Liverpool & Manchester according to the Minutes of that Company. When the additional half-inch of the present 'standard' gauge crept in is a minor railway mystery.

The majority of the contractors and the élite of the labour force were recruited by George and Robert Stephenson at Killingworth. They took from West Moor, says Summerside, the best blasters and tunnel makers, and among the army thus recruited were Stephenson's own brothers, James and John, besides many a workmate of his younger days. For these stalwart Tynesiders who forsook the darkness and the iron discipline of the pit to march on Darlington under the banners of Geordie and young Bob, it was the great moment of release, the turning point in their fortunes. For many of them it was a point of no return had they but known it, for the Stephenson star was now in the ascendant and would lead them, the architects of a new world, across the length and breadth of England.

On a line of such unprecedented length, Stephenson's small skilled corps could not do more than leaven the larger lump of local labour, and sections of the work which they took up had to be sub-contracted to local men, often with dire results. Here is a typical tale of woe sent to Edward Pease from a distracted Thomas Storey:

> When I arrived at home on Friday last I found J. Hastings [Stephenson's sub-contractor] has been making another break up of the wagons and carrying away walls by running them *amain* which might as easily been houses. The destruction of the Co's property by this sub-contractor has not been less than 50 or 60 £. He refuses to carry on the work any way but that of his own, deposits the earth where and how he pleases, and runs the risk of lives and Property by wilfully running the waggons at improper speed both down the inclines and across the turnpike at Auckland. John Stephenson wishes to be clear of him and has therefore for that purpose given the cut up. . . .

Notwithstanding such vicissitudes, the work on the sections covered by the Act of 1821 was pressed forward resolutely, and at the beginning of May 1822 the Company announced that the first rail would be laid at St. John's Crossing, Stockton, on the 23rd of that month. The junketing which marked this occasion is a measure of the importance attached to the enterprise. Never since the battle of Waterloo, it was recorded, had Stockton witnessed such scenes of jubilation. A flag flew from every masthead on the Tees, bunting fluttered in the streets, church bells pealed and bands played. From Yarm came Thomas Meynell, the Chairman of the Company, accompanied by Benjamin Flounders and other proprietors in a carriage drawn by singing navvies and preceded by the Yarm town band. They were greeted by the Mayor of Stockton and the Recorder, Leonard Raisbeck. While the assembled bandsmen blew with a will and cannon were discharged, Meynell proceeded, without any preliminary oration, to lay several lengths of Birkinshaw rail. He was known to be a man of few words and on this occasion the accompanying uproar afforded him a good excuse for holding his tongue. His reticence also enabled certain enterprising youths of Stockton to earn a few dishonest pennies by selling blank, folded broadsheets entitled "A Full and Faithful Report of What Mr. Meynell Said at the Opening".

In the summer of this year, at George Stephenson's invitation, Edward Pease paid a visit to Killingworth to see the Stephenson locomotives at work and was greatly impressed. So also was Pease's cousin Thomas Richardson who accompanied him. A Quaker like his cousin, Richardson was the founder of the famous discount banking house of Overend, Gurney & Co. of Lombard Street, and a man of considerable influence in the City of London. When the Stockton & Darlington Company was launched, he had taken up £5,500 worth of stock, the largest single holding. There were also close ties between the Pease family and the Gurneys, Edward's son, Joseph Pease, Junior, having married the daughter of Joseph Gurney, the Norwich banker and uncle of Richardson's partner, Samuel Gurney. Without the aid of these powerful connections the pioneer venture might have foundered. Not only was the passage of the successive Stockton & Darlington Bills through Parliament smoothed by the great influence which these men wielded in London and Norfolk, but when, inevitably, the cost of the works exceeded Stephenson's estimate, Messrs. Overend, Gurney made a loan of £20,000 to the Company pending a new issue of stock.

It was particularly important that Stephenson should succeed in impressing Richardson with the powers of his locomotives, for in the new Bill which would authorize his deviations from Overton's original line it was intended to insert a clause permitting the Company to use locomotive haulage. This Bill came up in the spring of 1823 and George Stephenson paid his first visit to London to prove the estimate and accounts before a Committee of the Lords. This was no ordeal, for thanks to the railway's powerful friends it had a smooth passage and received the Royal Assent on 23 May. This established the historical importance of the line, for although it was not, as is sometimes claimed, the first public railway,[1] upon the passing of this second Act it became the first public line in the world to employ locomotives.

The third Stockton & Darlington Railway Act was passed almost exactly a year later, and its chief purpose was to authorize a branch line to Haggar Leases which, after much delay, was completed in May 1830. Its details need not concern us; its significance in this story is that George Stephenson played no part in it but delegated the responsibility entirely to his young son. Here is the account which Robert Stephenson subsequently submitted to the Company:

Rob. Stephenson:
· May, 1824.

To setting out, levelling & making Section of Haggar Leases Branch Railway	15	15	0
To 34 Days attendance in London when the above Branch was before Parliament	35	14	0
To Travelling Expenses and a Bill at the Imperial Hotel	20	0	0
	71	9	0

This account, ignored by earlier biographers, has lain in the Stockton & Darlington archives to record Robert Stephenson's début as a railway engineer on his own account, and to prove that at twenty-one he was not only capable of carrying out a survey unaided, but also possessed the self-confidence and ability required to shepherd the result of his work through Parliament. George Stephenson's ambition to make his son the brains of their partnership had speedily borne fruit. But, as we shall see, this was Robert Stephenson's last contribution to the Stockton & Darlington Railway for many years. In a matter of weeks he was on the high seas bound for the New World.

On 13 July 1823 George Stephenson was able to report that twenty-two miles of the line had been completed, that all the rails and chairs had been delivered, and that the railway should be

---

[1] The Surrey Iron Railway had this distinction.

completed by the following midsummer. The quarries at Etherley and Brussleton were producing all the stone required for sleepers and buildings, and to facilitate its delivery a temporary inclined plane had been built up to the Brussleton quarry. That winter, however, bad weather set in early and violent rains played havoc with the raw sides of cuttings and embankments. Years later at the age of seventy-seven, one of the navvies, Robert Metcalf of Darlington, recalled in illiterate but graphic style[1] that cruel winter when the railway pioneers fought against the elements. "It came on wet on friday night", he wrote, "and rained all day saturday/Myers flat battery was a 4 foot metal/on monday morning battery went down and blow pete earth mountain high/company men was many week levying/as we were going through codling cut there was a slide came down and broke both my legs and collar bone. . . ." There was difficulty, too, in carting ballast to the eastern section of the line through lanes which had become quagmires, and Stephenson reported in December that although only three miles of line had still to be constructed, seventeen miles were as yet unballasted. But he also reported that the river Gaunless had now been spanned by the iron bridge designed by him and cast by Burrell & Company of Newcastle, a section of which still stands in the Railway Museum at York. This was the first iron railway bridge.

Immediately after his rift with William Losh, Stephenson had entered into a partnership agreement with John and Isaac Burrell, ironfounders of Orchard Street and South Street, Newcastle. There is no evidence that they built any locomotives for Stephenson and it seems likely that, like Michael Longridge, they were not equipped to undertake such work. Consequently, when the Act authorizing the use of locomotives on the Stockton & Darlington Railway had been passed and Edward Pease's visit to Killingworth had convinced him of the merits of Stephenson's design, the vital question arose: Where should these locomotives be built? Stephenson's burning faith in the locomotive, though he had succeeded in communicating it to Pease and Richardson and other proprietors of the railway, was not widely shared. Even some of those who had played a part in bringing the locomotive to birth seem to have lost heart. Thus,

---

[1] Metcalf uses no punctuation. His original style is reproduced to preserve its flavour but with the appropriate pauses indicated for easier reading.

notwithstanding the limited success achieved by the Blenkinsop & Murray locomotives, Fenton, Murray & Wood of Leeds informed Pease in 1825 that "It does not suit with the present arrangement of our Business to take orders for High Pressure or Locomotive Engines. We have not made any this 8 years."

Faced with this apathy and doubt in the engineering industry, yet still convinced that the demand for locomotives would increase as railways spread, the two Stephensons, Edward Pease and Michael Longridge took the momentous decision in June 1823 to enter into partnership and open a locomotive works of their own. With the signing of their Agreement on the 23rd of that month, the firm of Robert Stephenson & Company, Forth Street Works, Newcastle, was founded. Although Thomas Richardson was a party to these deliberations, he did not become a partner until later. The initial capital was £4,000 divided into ten shares, of which Pease took up four and the other partners two each. Edward Pease also loaned Robert Stephenson some of the money for his shares, and years later, when Pease was eighty-one and the Company was yielding him handsome dividends, he wrote in his Diary: "Pecuniarily I have cause to admire how an effort to serve a worthy youth, Robert, the son of George Stephenson, by a loan of £500, at first without expectation of much remuneration, has turned to my great advantage. During the course of the year I have received £7,000 from the concern at Forth Street."

Under the Agreement, George Stephenson was to assign his Patents to the partnership in return for £300 compensation to be paid after three years, but the most significant thing about the document is clause 5 which reads: "The said *Robert Stephenson* shall be Managing Partner, and be paid a Salary of Two Hundred Pounds per annum upon condition that his Father George Stephenson furnish the Plans etc., which may be required, and take the general charge of the Manufactory as long as required by the Partners." Robert's biographer, Jeaffreson, goes further than this and states that he was required to "supervise the building operations, engage men, take orders, advise on contracts, draw plans, make estimates, keep the accounts, and in all matters, great or small, govern the young establishment on his own responsibility". This was a formidable undertaking indeed for a youth of twenty years, and it is clear evidence of his remarkable ability that such astute and experienced business men as Pease and Longridge should have placed so heavy a burden upon such young shoulders.[1]

Orders for the first two Stockton & Darlington locomotives, Nos. 1 and 2, *Locomotion* and *Hope*, were placed with the new Company on 16 September 1824 and for Nos. 3 and 4, *Black Diamond* and *Diligence*, on the last day of the September following. An order was also placed with the firm for the two stationary winding engines of 30 and 60 hp which were required for the Etherley and Brussleton inclines. We learn later that the latter cost the Company £4,000 whereas the average cost of a Stephenson locomotive at this time was £550.

Despite the setbacks of the preceding wet winter, George Stephenson was able to inform the Company at the beginning of September 1825 that the main line and the branch to Darlington had been completed and that they would be ready for public traffic on 26 September. He proposed that the 'Grand Opening' should take place on the following day. More momentous news followed on the 12th of the month when he wrote to Joseph Pease, Junior, from Newcastle: "I beg to inform you that the Improved Travelling Engine was tried here last night & fully answered my expectations. And if you will be kind enough to desire Pickersgill to send horses to take it away from here on Friday it shall be loaded on Thursday evening. I calculate the weight of the Engine between 5 and 6 tons." He added that he hoped to attend a first trial of the fixed engine at Etherley on the Friday.

The *Locomotion* was a four-wheeled engine which differed from the Stephenson design described in the last chapter in the following respects. The drive from the piston rods to the connecting rods was taken by means of half-beams and parallel motion instead of by the simple crossheads previously used, a more complex and, in some ways, a retrograde design. It was closer to Wylam practice, and it has been suggested that this change was due to the fact that Timothy Hackworth was employed at Forth Street while the engine was building. Others have attributed the change to John Kennedy (later

---

[1] During the short period which elapsed between the founding of this locomotive business and George Stephenson's removal to Liverpool, the Stephensons left the cottage at West Moor and occupied a house in Eldon Street, Newcastle.

of Bury, Curtis & Kennedy), but there is no proof that either of these men was at Forth Street at this time.

Two Prussian mining engineers[1] who visited the Stockton & Darlington Railway in April and May 1827 mention the 'four short pipes or supports' for the boiler with their flanges as used on the engines with steam springs, but they then state that these were bolted direct to a cast-iron frame to which the axle bearings were fixed, thus implying that the locomotive was unsprung. Whether *Locomotion* originally had steam-springs which were subsequently eliminated in this way, or was delivered unsprung is uncertain. The one positive improvement upon earlier engines was that the wheels were connected by outside coupling rods instead of by chain and sprockets.

Loaded upon a wagon, *Locomotion* was drawn by Pickersgill's straining team down the long, rough road from Newcastle to Heighington Lane (by some called Aycliffe Lane). Here she was carefully unloaded on to the metals where she would so soon make history. Let an eye-witness, old Robert Metcalf, now fully recovered from his accident in Codling Cut the previous winter, give his own graphic account of this memorable occasion.

> No. 1 came to heighton lane by road/ we had to get her on the way/ when we got her on the way we pump water into her/ we sent John taylor for a lantern and candle to acliffe/ when we done that I thought I would have my pipe/ it was a very warm day though it been back end of the year/ I took me pipe glass and let me pipe/ I thought to myself I would try to put fire to Jimmy ockam/ it blaaze away well the fire going rapidly/ lantern and candle was to no use so No. 1 fire was put to her on line by the pour of the sun.

How vividly these words recall this historic moment! Having got the engine on to the rails and filled her boiler, the little group of labourers sit or stand around the new-fangled machine in the hot September sunshine impatiently waiting for John Taylor to return with the candle lantern from Aycliffe so that they can put fire into her and make her show her paces. As Robert Metcalf lights up his pipe with his burning glass his eye falls on a spare wad of oakum

[1] Carl Von Oeynhausen and Heinrich Von Dechen. It was through the researches of J. G. H. Warren that their report on their visit was discovered in *Archiv Fur Bergbau Und Huttenwesen*, Vol. XIX, 1829.

packing for the feed pump which the fitters at Forth Street have thoughtfully sent along. There is no need to wait any longer for that slow-coach John who has probably stopped for a drink on the way. In a few moments Robert has kindled the dry oakum with his glass, thrust it flaming through the fire door and thrown in after it the pieces of kindling passed to him by eager hands. From the top of *Locomotion*'s tall chimney a blue drift of woodsmoke lifts lazily into the clear air. . . . There is surely some symbolic significance in this little piece of humble and quite spontaneous ritual by which the sun's heat kindled fire in the belly of the first locomotive in the world to move on a public line of railway.

Just in time for the opening there arrived at New Shildon, which was to be the headquarters of the Company's locomotive and engineering department, the *Experiment*, the first passenger railway coach. The body had been built locally on an unsprung frame supplied by Robert Stephenson & Co. It had longitudinal seats along the sides with a table between them, and for the benefit of the directors who would ride in it on the opening day these seats had been cushioned and the floor carpeted. On the eve of the opening, *Locomotion* was coupled to the *Experiment* and a trial trip was made from Shildon to Darlington. James Stephenson drove *Locomotion* with William Gowland as his fireman, while in the coach behind rode Edward Pease with his three sons, Edward, Joseph and Henry, Thomas Richardson, William Kitching and George Stephenson. It was as well that the Peases took this opportunity to become the first railway passengers, for old Edward's son Isaac died that night and for this reason no member of the Pease family was present at the opening ceremony.

The celebrations which had marked the laying of the first rails paled into insignificance beside the scenes which marked the ever memorable 27 September 1825. The Company rightly regarded the opening of the line as an event of national importance and had made every effort to ensure that it should be a day that nobody in the neighbourhood would ever be likely to forget. We may imagine the mingled feelings of eager anticipation and anxiety with which George Stephenson, the only begetter of all this, awaited the great day. If all went well it would be a day of triumph for him, a triumph which he sorely needed at this moment, for in his association **with** the Liverpool & Manchester Railway project, which had begun in the previous year, his reputation was temporarily under a cloud. He had recently been consulted about a railway from Canterbury to Whitstable, too, while here and elsewhere he sorely missed the help and support of his son Robert, who had gone abroad. His locomotive, the fixed engines at Etherley and Brussleton, and the long line of metals were all so new and untried. Only he knew how many things could go wrong, and he also knew now the fickleness of fame and fortune; knew how speedily an engineer's mistakes could turn fulsome praise to scorn. Were the great hempen ropes sound that lay coiled on their drums in those tall hill-top engine houses? And what of *Locomotion* sleeping in her shed at Shildon? Stephenson must have run over in his mind all the possible sources of trouble, gland and piston packings, connecting-rod bearings, the feed pump.

Long before dawn, on foot and in every kind of conveyance from carriage and four to donkey cart, thousands of people began to converge upon the railway from all the country round. The proceedings began modestly and at an early hour at the western end of the line, gradually building up throughout the day to their tremendous climax at Stockton. Between 7 and 8 a.m. ten loaded coal wagons from the Phoenix pit at Witton Park were led by horses to the foot of the Etherley inclined plane, where they were attached to the rope and hauled to the top of the ridge by the winding engine. They then rumbled down to the foot of the self-acting plane on the east side where fresh horses were waiting. Here, by the St. Helens Auckland turnpike, a wagon load of flour was coupled up and the horses then drew their train over the Gaunless iron bridge to the foot of Brussleton Bank. Here the sloping fields were black with the thousands of people who had assembled to see the working of the 60 hp engine. Mercifully there was no mishap, for as many as could obtain a precarious foothold clung to the ascending wagons as the beam engine in Brussleton tower swung into action, drawing them up at a steady eight miles an hour.

Waiting to receive the wagons at Shildon Lane End at the foot of Brussleton east bank stood *Locomotion* with steam up, coupled to the *Experiment* and twenty-one new coal wagons fitted with temporary seats. The whole long train was besieged by a dense, swaying and jostling mass of humanity, among whom the Company's small staff, distinguished by their blue sashes, struggled in vain to restore order. There was a panic stampede when *Locomotion*'s weight safety valve suddenly lifted and shot a roaring jet of steam into the sky, but when the crowds saw that her crew, George Stephenson himself and his brother James, remained quite unmoved by this terrifying occurrence, they realized that the iron monster was not going to explode and surged forward once more, so that it was with the utmost difficulty that the additional wagons were marshalled into the train.

The total seating capacity of the train was three hundred persons and the company had distributed that number of tickets among their shareholders, but these careful arrangements were all undone as the privileged ticket holders were overwhelmed by the struggling crowd of boarders. Exactly how many people managed to find a precarious perch on that train will never be known; some accounts say 400, some 550, and others 600 people were on board by the time George Stephenson eased his regulator open, chain couplings creaked taut and the 400ft-long train lumbered off on its historic journey, preceded by a single horseman and followed by a procession of twenty-four horse-drawn wagons crammed with less fortunate passengers.

The start was not auspicious. The train had not travelled more than a few hundred yards before one wagon, which had been reserved, with how much success we know not, for assistant engineers and surveyors, came off the road. *Locomotion* clanked to a halt and amid much shouting and commotion many willing hands lifted the wagon back on to the rails. Only a few yards farther on, however, the same wagon came off again and it was realized that one wheel had shifted on its axle. The lame duck was therefore shunted off at the first passing loop, injuring a bystander in the process. The long caravan then rumbled on its way as far as Simpasture where there was another involuntary stop. This time *Locomotion* was in trouble and George Stephenson was seen to clamber down and go into conference with his brother James beside the engine. There was more delay while the two brothers, part shrouded in hissing steam, performed some operation on their monster which was quite beyond the ken of the patient passengers. Then George Stephenson returned to his foot-plate, announcing that they had removed a piece of oakum packing which had fouled one of the valves of the feed pump and that all was now well. Once again the train got under way and completed the 8½ miles to the junction with the Darlington Branch nonstop, arriving there at 12 noon. This represented 65 minutes running time, equal to an average of 8 miles an hour, 55 minutes having been lost by the stoppages.

At the junction the train was greeted by the cheers of a waiting crowd of 12,000 who looked on in awed wonderment while some shunting operations were performed. Six of the coal wagons were detached for distribution to the poor of Darlington and two wagons were picked up, one containing more local worthies and the other the Yarm[1] town band. The next five miles towards Stockton were nearly level, the fall being only 57 ft, while the "immense" load behind *Locomotion* was estimated at between eighty and ninety tons. Nevertheless, she managed to cover this section at an average of four miles an hour with only one stop, at Goosepool, for water. Near Whiteley Springs, 2¾ miles from the terminus, the line ran beside the turnpike for some distance, and here there were scenes of wild excitement as the drivers of carriages and carts whipped up their horses to keep pace with the train, their occupants shouting, cheering and waving to the passengers, who gave back as good as they got.

Finally, pandemonium broke out when, at a quarter to four, three-quarters of an hour after scheduled time, the long train clanked over St. John's crossing and on to Stockton Quay, where crowds estimated at 40,000 had been patiently awaiting her arrival. As George Stephenson closed his regulator (no doubt with a heart-felt sigh of relief) and *Locomotion* came to a standstill, seven 18-lb cannon thundered a deafening thrice-repeated salute, the bands on the train and on the Quay struck up 'God Save the King', and church bells pealed amid the storm of cheering.

The guests of honour then threaded their way through the packed streets to the Town Hall for an official banquet which lasted until midnight, the last of the twenty-three toasts being drunk to George Stephenson. And so the long day drew to its successful end. The Stockton & Darlington Railway had been fittingly launched upon the world.

[1] The Branch to Yarm was not opened until 17 October.

CHAPTER FIVE

A Rift in the Partnership

THE TIME of the two Stephensons was by no means wholly occupied by the survey and construction of the Stockton & Darlington Railway. On the contrary the years 1821-1825 saw a great expansion of their activities and influence, and in reviewing this period the biographer is confronted by the one great mystery in the Stephenson story. He is bound to ask himself what motives could have induced Robert Stephenson, at a time when the prospects before the partnership of father and son seemed on the face of it so rosy, to accept in 1824 the appointment of engineer to the Colombian Mining Association which took him to South America for more than three unprofitable years. Previous writers make no mystery of the matter at all, dismissing it easily by saying that George Stephenson agreed to his son's appointment on the ground that the change might improve Robert's health—surely a slender and doubtful premise. As the following review of the events leading up to Robert's departure will show, this explanation simply will not hold, though what the real explanation was must be a matter of inference.

A eulogy on Stephenson's locomotive written by William James after his first visit to Killingworth in the spring of 1821 has already been quoted. More must now be said about William James because at this point he plays an important part in our story, only to leave it in somewhat peculiar circumstances three years later. Born at Henley-in-Arden, William James inherited a substantial fortune from his father and became a prosperous estate agent and colliery owner with an office, first in St. John's, Warwick, and later in New Boswell Court, Lincoln's Inn. The ramifications of his business interests were remarkable. He managed the Dew estates at Wellesbourne and the Clutton Mines in Somerset for Lord Warwick. He owned a number of collieries in the Midlands including those at

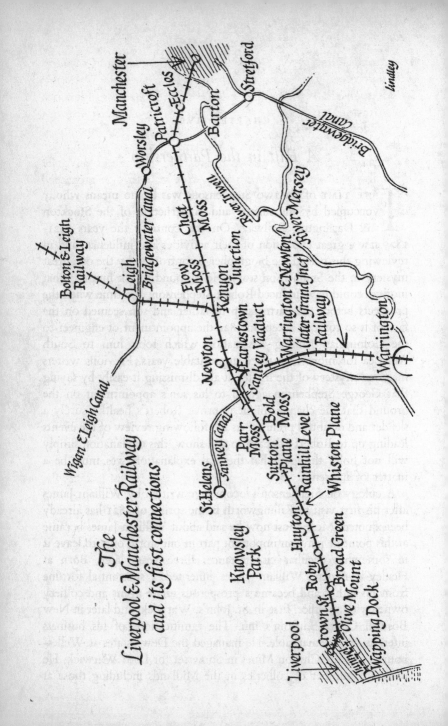

The
Liverpool & Manchester Railway
and its first connections

Bolton & Leigh Railway

Wigan & Leigh Canal

Bridgewater Canal

Leigh

Worsley

Patricroft

Eccles

Manchester

Stretford

Barton

Bridgewater Canal

Chat Moss

Flow Moss

Kenyon Junction

River Irwell

River Mersey

Warrington E Newton
(later Grand Junct)
Railway

Warrington

Newton

Earlestown

Sankey Viaduct

Bold Moss

Parr Moss

Sankey Canal

St Helens

Sutton Plane

Rainhill Level

Knowsley Park

Huyton

Whiston Plane

Broad Green

Roby

Olive Mount

Crown St

Liverpool

Wapping Dock

lindley

Goldenhill, Ocker Hill, Swadlincote and Wyken, near Coventry. He purchased large estates in Warwickshire and South Wales. He was responsible for enclosing wastelands in Hounslow, Isleworth and Dulwich and for surveying the turnpike road from Warwick to London. He superintended the Stratford-on-Avon Canal and is said to have spent £6000 on the improvement of the River Avon Navigation. In 1818, James became such an enthusiastic advocate for railway construction on a nation-wide scale that he proceeded in the next few years to devote a great deal of his resources to surveying and promoting railways at his own expense. Between 1819 and 1820 he surveyed a line to convey coal from the Midlands to London which he called the Central Junction Railway. A series of branch lines from the coalfields would be linked to a main route running via Oxford, Thame, Wendover, Amersham, Rickmansworth and Uxbridge to Paddington. The Stratford & Moreton Railway, of which James became Vice-Chairman, was the only part of this ambitious project to be actually constructed. As related elsewhere,[1] on Telford's recommendation this line was built as a horse tramway using cast-iron rails. This was clean contrary to William James's advocacy, for after his visit to the north in 1821 he became the convinced and most enthusiastic champion of Stephenson's Killingworth locomotives.

William James's admiration for George Stephenson and his work was unbounded and for some time after their meeting the two men were on terms of intimate friendship. A standard Killingworth type locomotive was depicted on the cover of a pamphlet publicizing his ideas which James produced in 1823, and Stephenson doubtless shrewdly appreciated the fact that in James he had found a disciple who could sell the idea of locomotive railways far more widely and with much greater eloquence than he could. This proved true, but the results were not fortunate for William James.

So impressed was James with what he saw at Killingworth that in September 1821 he made an agreement with Stephenson and Losh whereby he would endeavour to sell their patent locomotives in return for a fourth share of the profits. He also allowed them the right to adopt the water tubes which his son, W. H. James, introduced into his steam road-carriage boiler and which he afterwards patented.

[1] See this author's *Thomas Telford*, p. 157.

This agreement, of course, terminated when Stephenson and Losh fell out and there is no evidence that such water tubes were ever used in a Stephenson locomotive.

It has been said that William James's part in the development of railways has been greatly underestimated, but while there is some truth in this, there is little evidence to support some of the claims which have been made on his behalf. For instance, it has been said that James was responsible for bringing George Stephenson and Edward Pease together and that he, rather than either of the latter, deserves the title 'Father of Railways'. But it is clear that James's letter (quoted in chapter 3) was written immediately after his first visit to Killingworth and Bedlington, while it is dated 22 June 1821, two months after the historic meeting took place between Stephenson and Pease. On the other hand, while this claim cannot stand, it is true that George Stephenson might never have become associated with the Liverpool & Manchester Railway project had it not been for James.

One obvious cause of James's ultimate failure was that his enthusiasm carried him away, driving him to embark upon too many over-ambitious schemes at once. His Central Junction Railway project was ambitious enough in all conscience, for England was not yet ripe for a trunk line of this magnitude. Yet James talked of extending it still farther to Southampton and, not content with this, as he travelled about the country in search of technical data and support for his plans he would enthusiastically recommend railway construction wherever dissatisfaction existed over inadequate transport facilities. He found such a situation existing when he visited Liverpool in 1822 and at once set to work to exploit it.

The abuse by the Bridgewater Canal Company of the monopoly of goods transport between Liverpool and Manchester which they had enjoyed for fifty years had long been bitterly resented by merchants and manufacturers, particularly those in Liverpool. William Jessop had surveyed a line for a horse tramway between the two cities in 1797 and a further survey was made by Outram in the following year, but nothing came of this scheme to break the canal monopoly. William James went to Liverpool armed with a letter of introduction to a merchant of that city named Joseph

Sandars, one of the most vocal critics of the Canal Company, who lent a very willing ear to James's railway talk; so much so that he agreed to defray the expenses of a new survey.

James thereupon established himself in convenient headquarters at the Horse and Jockey inn at Newton-le-Willows and began his operations. What he undertook was no mere reconnaissance or 'flying survey', but a well organized detailed survey carried out by a team which consisted of his eldest son, W. H. James, Paul Padley, his brother-in-law and a qualified surveyor, George Hamilton, Hugh Greenshields and, last but not least, Robert Stephenson. The eastern half of the line surveyed by James and his party crossed Chat Moss and corresponded closely with that which was eventually adopted, but at the crossing of the Sankey valley (approximately the half-way point) the line veered away northwards up that valley to St. Helens, skirted the parks of Knowsley and Croxteth and then swung south into Liverpool, avoiding the high ground at Olive Mount and Edgehill.

With the memories of those idyllic days spent with his father on the Stockton & Darlington survey during the previous autumn, the work must have come as a rude and unpleasant surprise to young Robert Stephenson. For whereas in Durham he had experienced nothing but kindness from the local people, William James's party encountered the most determined and violent hostility. They found farmers and their men armed with guns and pitchforks guarding field gates, and on one occasion an unfortunate chainman was run through the back with a pitchfork before he could escape. Whenever they approached villages or towns they were followed by wild bands of women and children screaming abuse and hurling stones. In St. Helens especially, they went in peril of their lives. There, another of their chainmen was seized by a posse of pitmen who threatened to throw him down a mineshaft, while a local bruiser whom James had hired to carry their precious theodolite was routed in pitched battle and the instrument smashed to atoms. Only on the dreary wastes of Chat Moss were the little party left undisturbed, for local opinion held that only lunatics would think of building a railway across that great expanse of quaking bog and that if left to themselves the surveying party would doubtless drown themselves in it. William James was, in fact, almost lost on one occasion when attempting to find a firm stand for the theodolite and was recovered with difficulty, dripping black ooze from head to foot.

The indomitable spirit with which James met and defeated all these difficulties to carry his survey through to a successful conclusion on 4 October 1822 immensely impressed Robert Stephenson, and it was with expressions of great affection that the two men parted, James, with the help of Padley, to complete his plans for submission to the Railway Committee which Joseph Sandars had set up, and Robert Stephenson, at his father's suggestion, to spend a six months' term at Edinburgh University. On 15 November James wrote to George Stephenson from Newton-le-Willows announcing the completion of his work and outlining his proposals. He had decided that there should be one fixed haulage engine at the Liverpool end of the line but that the rest of the railway should be worked by locomotives. He went on to give particulars of the gradients and to ask Stephenson to send him figures showing the hauling capacity of his locomotives on such gradients. Stephenson duly complied.

Away in Edinburgh, Robert Stephenson was studying Natural Philosophy, Chemistry and Natural History, while during the winter he joined a small group of students who accompanied Professor Jamieson on a geological survey of the Scottish coast. Although all this must have made a welcome change after the rigours of the Liverpool & Manchester survey, it is doubtful whether he can really have derived much benefit from so short a term. That he was himself sceptical of the value of much of the teaching is revealed in a letter he addressed to Michael Longridge: "Natural historians", he writes, "spend a great deal of time in enquiring whether Adam was a black or white man. Now I really cannot see what better we should be if we could even determine this with satisfaction." The rest of the letter is in the same strain. Perhaps the most valuable outcome of this Edinburgh interlude was the friendship which Robert formed with a fellow student named George Parker Bidder, a man who subsequently became a close friend and associate of the two Stephensons, a distinguished engineer and, ultimately, President of the Institution of Civil Engineers.

Robert Stephenson left Edinburgh University in April 1823, and from June onwards he was fully occupied with the new locomotive business in Newcastle. At the beginning of September father and son set out upon a long business tour which took them to London, Bristol, Ireland and Shropshire. This was mainly concerned with the installation of stationary steam engines and boilers, work which continued to form a very important part of George Stephenson's work at this time, though it has naturally been overshadowed in history by his railway enterprises. They had heard rumours of a new high-pressure engine built by the American, Jacob Perkins, the pioneer of ultra high-pressure steam, and, scenting possible competition in this field, they paid Perkins a visit in London. The Stephensons were sceptical. "My father and he [Perkins] have had a severe scold", wrote Robert to Longridge. "Indeed the most of the birkies were embittered at my father's opinion of the engine. He one day stopped the engine by his hand, and when we called the next day Perkins had previously got the steam to such a pitch (equal 15 atmosphere) that it was impossible for one man to stop it, but by a little of my assistance, we succeeded in stopping it by laying hold on the flywheel. This engine", Robert adds with dry humour, "he formerly called it 8 or 10 horse-power, but now only a 4."

From London the Stephensons travelled to Bristol en route to Cork, but finding that the Cork steam packet had broken down they were forced to cross to Dublin and to travel thence to Cork by coach. Before setting out on this coach they were astonished to observe the guard arming himself with two blunderbusses, four cavalry pistols and a sword. "I can assure you my father's courage was daunted", wrote Robert, "though I don't suppose he will confess with it." But although the guard did his best by regaling them with stories of horrible murders, the journey proved quite uneventful. As a result of their visit to Macnay's Dripsey Paper Works at Cork, Michael Longridge received an order for a boiler. "I hope Mr. Birkinshaw will see the plates nicely cut, as we want it neatly finished", Robert adds. They then journeyed back to England, spending several days at Shifnal in Shropshire on some unspecified business before returning home.

Meanwhile in Liverpool Joseph Sandars and his fellow merchants were about to open a subscription list. But what of their engineer? The plans of 1822, despite all James's efforts were completed too late for submission to Parliament, and now, as the months of 1823 slipped by, things went from bad to worse for poor William James.

Owing to his single-minded preoccupation with his many railway schemes he had been neglecting his other ramified business interests, and had expended great sums of money for no return. No sooner had he realized the gravity of his position and determined to retrieve it than he was incapacitated by recurrent bouts of illness.

Robert Stephenson was very distressed by the news of his friend's ill-fortune, especially when he remembered James's enthusiasm and determination on the survey only six months before. Just before he left the north for London with his father he wrote to James on 29 August:

> It gives rise to feelings of true regret when I reflect on your situation; but yet a consolation springs up when I consider your persevering spirit will for ever bear you up in the arms of triumph, instances of which I have witnessed of too forcible a character to be easily effaced from my memory. It is these thoughts, and these alone, that could banish from my thoughts feelings of despair. . . . Can I ever forget the advice you have afforded me in your last letters? and what a heavenly inducement you pointed before me at the close, when you said that attention and obedience to my dear father would afford me music at midnight. Ah, and so it has already. My father and I set off for London on Monday next, the 1st, on our way to Cork. Our return will probably be about the time you wish me to be at Liverpool. If all be right, we may possibly call and see what is going on. That line is the finest project in England.

Notwithstanding his difficulties, William James contrived during 1823 to complete a survey of the Canterbury & Whitstable Railway which he first visited in April, and when that Company applied for parliamentary powers in November 1824 it was James's plans which were deposited. Also he continued to be active in the affairs of the Stratford & Moreton Railway, much of his correspondence being addressed from the Railway Office at Stratford-on-Avon. But he was apparently unable to meet the demands of the Liverpool & Manchester Railway Committee. They had resolved to promote a Bill in the forthcoming session, but before doing so they required James to resurvey their line with a view to reducing the formidable weight of opposition to the project.

It was early in 1824 that Thomas Richardson consulted George Stephenson on behalf of the Mexican Mining Company of which he was one of the leading promoters. The object of this Company was to re-open certain gold and silver mines which had been worked by the Spaniards before the Revolution. The idea that such mines might be re-opened and worked with profit had originally been cautiously expressed by Alexander von Humboldt after his famous voyage of exploration, but to eager speculators in the City of London the prospects were now presented in much more positive and glittering terms. It would appear that in April 1824 the Mexican plan was abandoned, possibly owing to some difficulty in obtaining concessions, and the whole project was switched to Colombia in South America, being re-styled the Colombian Mining Association. The belief was that with the aid of the steam power which they could now command, an El Dorado of wealth awaited British mining engineers in the new world. Earlier, in September 1814, the great Richard Trevithick had been lured away to Peru in pursuit of a similar will-o'-the-wisp by the Swiss, Francisco Uvillé, and little had been heard of him since.

The promoters relied upon George Stephenson's experience and advice in the selection of the miners, implements and machinery which it would be necessary to despatch on this venture, and it was suggested that because the Stockton & Darlington Railway and other commitments did not permit him to leave the country, young Robert should be released from his duties as managing partner of the Forth Street works to lead the expedition. George Stephenson and his partners, Longridge and Pease, were reluctant to agree to this. It was represented to them, however, that Robert would not be absent for more than twelve months, because as soon as he had seen the party securely established he would be free to return to England. The prospect of large orders for steam engines and other mining machinery was also dangled before the partners, who finally gave grudging consent to Robert Stephenson's release, Longridge agreeing to deputize during his absence.

Robert himself was anxious to go.

Let me beg of you not to say anything against my going out to America [he wrote to his father], for I have already ordered so many instruments that it would make me look extremely foolish to call off. Even if I had not ordered any instruments, it seems as if we were all working one against another. You must recollect I will only be away for a time; and in the meantime you would manage with the assistance of Mr. Longridge who, together with John Nicholson,[1] would take the whole of the business part off your hands. And only consider what an opening it is for me as an entry into business. . . .

To this argument, George Stephenson might reasonably have replied that to have been appointed managing partner of a new and promising engineering works in Newcastle at the age of twenty was surely a sufficiently promising entry into business. The fact was, however, that for reasons which we can only assume, Robert had determined to break with his father and his other partners.

In February and March, with the projected expedition in mind, Robert Stephenson and his uncle Robert visited Cornwall and presented a long report upon Cornish mining methods and organization. At the end of April, Robert went to London. His biographer Jeaffreson would have us believe that this visit was solely concerned with preparations for his departure abroad, which had now been agreed upon. We know, however, that he in fact visited London at the expense of the Stockton & Darlington Railway Company in order to see their 1824 Act through Parliament. We also know that he had not at this time finally agreed to go abroad, although he seems to have been none the less determined to leave the Newcastle partnership. This emerges from a very significant letter which was discovered, among others of lesser importance, in a house in Rochester Road, Coventry, in 1930. It is dated from Forth Street, Newcastle, 18 April 1824, and is addressed to William James at the Railway Office, Stratford-upon-Avon. In it Robert Stephenson states that he has been 'in treaty' with the Mexican Mining Company but has turned it down. This being so he asks James whether he can find him employment.

Such a request for employment addressed to a man who was already known to be in serious difficulties can only have been dictated by two things: a sense of loyalty to James and an acute dissatisfaction with the Newcastle partnership. Events now moved swiftly and dramatically. The Liverpool & Manchester Railway Committee decided to drop William James and to ask George Stephenson to re-survey their line in his stead.

---

[1] Referred to in subsequent correspondence as Thomas Nicholson.

I think it right to inform you [wrote Joseph Sandars to James on 25 May] that the Committee have engaged your friend Mr. G. Stephenson. We expect him here in a few days.

The subscription list for £30,000 is filled, and the Manchester gentlemen have conceded us the entire management. I very much regret that by delay and promises you have forfeited the confidence of the subscribers. I cannot help it. I fear now that you will only have the fame of being connected with the commencement of this undertaking. If you will send me down your plans and estimates I will do everything for you I can, and I believe I possess as much influence as any person. I am quite certain that the appointment of Stephenson will, under all circumstances, be agreeable to you. I believe you have recommended him yourself. If you consent to put your plans &c under my control and management your name shall be prominent in the proceedings and this, in such a mighty affair, will be of importance to you. You may rely upon my zeal for you in every point connected with your reputation.

Stephenson at once accepted the Liverpool Committee's invitation and on 9 June he wrote a letter of instruction to John Dixon, his resident engineer at Darlington, in which he said: "I shall be obliged to set off for Liverpool on Friday morning as I am so teased by the prospectors of the intended railway . . . to visit them. It will likely be a fortnight or 3 weeks before I can see you again. . . . Anything you may want from Forth Street in my absence, drop a line to Thos. Nicholson, the clerk in our office."

If we accept the fact that William James's circumstances prevented him from carrying out the wishes of the Liverpool Committee, then to invite in his stead a man whom James himself had recommended to them seems a perfectly proper and logical step to take. Yet Sandars's protestations of goodwill and continued support seem to betray some sense of guilt, while James himself was convinced that his friend Stephenson had betrayed him by persuading the Liverpool Committee to appoint him over James's head. There seems to be little doubt however that the Committee's invitation to Stephenson was quite unsolicited, and since we do not know the precise business arrangements existing between the three parties in the dispute, we cannot judge whether the invitation was ethical or not or whether, in the circumstances, Stephenson should have refused to accept it.

It would appear that James refused to deliver up his plans and estimates as Sandars requested and that in a last-minute attempt to retrieve the situation he wrote to his brother-in-law, Paul Padley, who had been his second in command on the survey, asking him to go to Liverpool on his behalf and proceed with the fresh survey. But he was too late. On 28 June Padley replied:

> I am sorry it was not in my power at this time to act according to your instructions by going into the country immediately. I am much obliged by your intention of giving me employment. I could not leave town for some days until my business in hand is finished, and in the next, believing that you had altogether relinquished the Manchester business, I have accepted an offer kindly made me by Mr. Geo. Stephenson (a few days since) of becoming one of his surveyors on that and other business and I should have joined them last Thursday had I been at liberty. I have written to him to say I will do so at the end of this week, and I am now awaiting his reply to say when and where, and I know you would not think me acting honourably to accept another offer while this is pending.

This letter came as another bitter blow to poor William James, and on 7 July he wrote to his son: "The reason why you have not heard from Padley is that he has made terms with George Stephenson, so he is lost to us forever. He knows my plans of which he and S. will now avail themselves. I confess I did not calculate upon such duplicity in either. Stephenson like P. and R. [Paul and Robert?] will now get so impenitent. . . ."

There remained yet heavier blows in store for William James. He lost his position as engineer to the Canterbury & Whitstable to George Stephenson ("I have not heard from Canterbury, therefore I conclude that Stephenson's intrigues still are predominant there", he wrote bitterly) and finally he was arrested in London for debt. William James's son, W. H. James, maintained until his death that the debt which led to his father's arrest and subsequent bankruptcy was feigned and was, like the loss of his railway business, all part of an elaborate plot. There is no evidence whatever to support this melodramatic notion. Though he may have been ill-used and betrayed by his friends in time of trouble, the main cause of William James's undoing was that his enthusiasm ran away with his business judgement and led him to bite off far more than he could chew.

Nevertheless, although it may have been a shrewd move on the part of George Stephenson to secure Paul Padley's services as soon as he heard of James's difficulties, it was certainly not an admirable one. Moreover, Stephenson was, as James had forecast, quite impenitent. Never once, when he achieved national renown, did he acknowledge his debt or pay any kind of tribute to his unfortunate predecessor. Like the other men, Ralph Dodds, William Losh, or George Overton, upon whose shoulders Stephenson climbed to fame, William James sank beneath his weight into an obscurity which, so far as he was concerned, was as dark as the peat bogs of Chat Moss. But by Robert Stephenson James was not forgotten. Years later when James was living in obscure and straitened circumstances and the two Stephensons were riding the crest of the railway wave, Robert[1] contributed to a subscription which was raised for James and put his name to the accompanying testimonial in which James was described as "the original projector and surveyor of the Manchester & Liverpool railroad and many other of the most important railroads of this kingdom . . . principally at his own cost." George Stephenson, on the other hand, did not contribute or sign and was, it is said, furious with Robert for having done so. Did the spectre of the impoverished James haunt the elder Stephenson?

If William James occasionally troubled George Stephenson's sleep, Robert's conscience remained perfectly clear, for his course of action, while it disconcerted his partners at Forth Street, ensured that he would no longer be a party to the Liverpool & Manchester scheme. Obviously William James rejected Robert's request for employment, but what James told him when he did so we may never know. Perhaps, realizing that his proud ship was already sinking under him, he warned his young friend not to join his crew. Be this as it may, Robert's immediate reaction to James's refusal was to sign an agreement with Messrs. Graham & Company, Agents for the Colombian Mining Association, to lead the proposed expedition to South America. So much his partners at Forth Street were told. What Robert did not tell them was that the term of this agreement was not one year but three.

---

[1] Robert Stephenson himself wrote in 1844: "I believe him [James] to have been the original progenitor of the Liverpool & Manchester Railway. He afterwards spent a great deal of both time and money in extending the introduction of railways."

At a time when the first small wave of railway promotion was just breaking over England, when construction of the Stockton & Darlington Railway was well under way, when the wheels of the new and promising engineering works in Newcastle were just beginning to revolve and the future had never looked more bright for the two Stephensons, what motives impelled Robert secretly to sign himself into exile for three years? It is unlikely that a positive answer to this question will ever be revealed. In the light of all the known facts it is probable that, in particular, Robert Stephenson was shocked by the way in which his father had supplanted William James and that, in general, he had grown so sick of his father's domination that he was prepared to resort to subterfuge and to go into exile rather than suffer it longer. On the face of it, George Stephenson's action in ensuring that his son's name and not his own should appear on the Stockton & Darlington plans and in the title of the new company at Newcastle appears magnanimous and self-effacing, the tribute of an indulgent father to his talented son. But true magnanimity of this kind is, alas, extremely rare, and it is to be feared that there were strings attached to these gifts which Robert was anxious to break. It should not be forgotten that from the day Robert learned to walk he had been made the tool of his father's ambition, his mind relentlessly forged by the most intensive education and training to become the precision instrument which his father's was not. Robert had played his part loyally, but now that he had grown to man's estate he had become conscious of the fact that education and training had given him powers which were in many respects superior to those of his father. What was more natural than that he should feel an urge to kick over the traces and exercise his great ability in freedom?

George Stephenson was much too shrewd a man to remain blind to the risk that he might lose the services of the partner whom he had been at such pains and expense to train for his own purposes. He alone realized how greatly he depended on Robert's filial loyalty. Seen in this light the events of 1822 and 1823 take on an added significance. If any circumstance made George Stephenson alive to the danger of Robert escaping from his control it must have been the close friendship formed between his son and William James during the 1822 Liverpool & Manchester survey, for it is clear that

Robert made no secret of his admiration and respect for James. George Stephenson need have had no fear that James would deliberately try to steal his son's allegiance. On the contrary, that strange letter which Robert wrote to James before leaving for Ireland suggests that in reply to Robert's expressions of dissatisfaction, James had strongly urged continuing loyalty to his father. But the inescapable inference is that by hustling Robert away from James's influence for that absurdly brief sojourn at Edinburgh University and then naming him as managing partner of Robert Stephenson & Company, George Stephenson was taking no chances. At the same time Robert, who was no fool, could scarcely fail to grasp the significance of these moves and to resent them.

On 8 June 1824 Robert Stephenson, his expedition companions and a load of baggage and equipment weighing over a ton, arrived in Liverpool from London in a specially chartered coach.

I never recollect in all my travels being so terrified on a coach [he wrote]. I expected every moment for many miles that we should be upset, and if such an accident had happened we must literally have been crushed to pieces. . . . The coach-top . . . was actually rent; all the springs, when we arrived at Liverpool, were destitute of any elasticity, one of them absolutely broken, and the body of the coach resting on the framework, so that, in fact, we rattled into this town more like a stage-waggon than a light coach.

Four days later, true to his promise to the Railway Committee, George Stephenson also arrived in Liverpool to superintend the new survey. "I found Mr. Sandars, Robert and Charles waiting for me at the coach office", he wrote to Longridge, "It gave me great pleasure to see Robert again before he sails. He expects to leave the country on Thursday next . . . the poor fellow is in good spirits about going abroad, and I must make the best of it." He describes how they dined in great style on successive nights with Sandars and Lister Ellis (another deputy chairman of the Railway Committee). "Magnificent fellows", he calls them and adds: "What changes one sees!—this day in the highest life, and the next in a cottage—one day turtle soup and champagne, and the next bread and milk, or anything that one can catch."

Whatever their private feelings may have been, the relations between father and son remained outwardly cordial until the time came for them to part on the quayside. Robert's biographer tells us that George Stephenson 'took an affecting leave of him' but, however this may be, the precise entry in Robert's log book of the voyage for this day betrays no trace of emotion or sadness in departure:

June 18, 1824—Set sail from Liverpool in the *Sir William Congreve* at three o'clock in the afternoon: wind from the south-east, sea smooth, day beautiful; temperature of the air towards evening in the shade, 58°. Made some experiments with 'Register Thermometer' to ascertain the temperature of the sea at various depths. . . .

With the exception of the Stockton & Darlington Railway, which was by this time well under way, little went right with George Stephenson's affairs from the moment he watched his son's ship cross the Mersey bar until the day he returned. To begin with, his partners soon discovered to their dismay that they had lost Robert Stephenson for three years. Michael Longridge was particularly disconcerted by this discovery for he had his own business to look after at Bedlington and had only consented reluctantly to hold a watching brief over the business affairs of Robert Stephenson & Company for twelve months. He certainly did not relish the prospect of taking Robert's place as managing partner for three years or more.

On 17 August he wrote:

My Dear Robert,

I wrote to you at Liverpool, but am uncertain whether you received my letter or not. In this letter I expressed my regret that you have signed an Agreement for *three years*[1] with Messrs. Graham & Coy.

When your father and your other Partners consented that you should go out to Colombia it was with the clear understanding that your engagement was only of a temporary nature and that as soon as you had informed yourself about the practicability of forming a Rail Way and had made your geological inquiries you should then return to England and make your report.

On no account would we ever have consented that you should become the *Agent of Messrs. Graham & Coy for* 3 *years.*

I have spoken to our friend Mr. Thomas Richardson upon the subject and he has promised me to use his influence with Mr. Powler so that

---

[1] The italics represent underlinings in the original.

you may be released as soon as you have satisfied yourself upon the subject for which you are gone out and I do hope you will be able to return to us in the course of the year 1825.

Longridge goes on to mention the Liverpool & Manchester and other railway projects and then continues: "I have little hesitation in saying that the mode of conveyance upon Rail Roads by Steam will soon become National. You will readily conceive what a vast source of Business to us this will prove if we do but rightly manage it. At present the Work presses too hard both upon your Father and myself and we therefore feel anxious for your return. . . ."

We will follow first the fortunes of Robert Stephenson & Company. The partners seem at the outset to have been undeterred by the loss of Robert Stephenson, for on the last day of 1824 they resolved to extend the works by building their own foundry. They had come to the conclusion that the existing arrangement whereby they were dependent on Messrs. John & Isaac Burrell for cylinders and other castings was unsatisfactory and that they should make their own. Additional capital was raised and borrowed, the foundry was built and eventually the Burrell foundry, which adjoined it, was also absorbed.

On the day that this decision was reached a second Company was formed by agreement between the same partners. This was to be known as George Stephenson & Son and it has sometimes been confused with the engine-building concern. It was, in fact, a completely separate undertaking formed to execute railway surveys and construction. This venture was obviously inspired by William James's grandiose schemes of railway development and it reveals how George Stephenson and his partners planned to step into that unfortunate man's shoes by securing a monopoly in this field. It also reveals that at this time the partners must still have been counting upon Robert Stephenson's early return, for his name figures prominently in the Agreement. Not only was he named among the share-holding partners, but as Chief Engineer with his father at a joint salary of £1,500 a year plus all expenses, the Company charging five guineas a day for their services. They would be responsible for all parliamentary business and have under their charge a team of assistant engineers, surveyors and apprentices. Michael Longridge was to take charge of the Company's Newcastle office, which was to adjoin that of Robert Stephenson & Company. The deployment of George Stephenson's forces on the various railway schemes which were then so optimistically thought to be in train, makes interesting reading because it includes a number of names which were later to become famous in railway history. Robert Stephenson was to take charge of a 'London & Northern Rail Road' with Joseph Locke, Robert Taylor and Elijah Galloway as his chief assistants. The 'Liverpool & Birmingham Rail Road' was to be the responsibility of John Dixon with William Allcard as second in command. The 'London & South Wales Road' would have Hugh Steel, Thomas Gooch and Paul Padley in charge, while Thomas Storey was nominated for the Liverpool & Manchester Railway. The salaries to be paid to these and other assistants and the rates to be charged for their services were all minutely set forth.

On 18 January 1825, Longridge sent a copy of this document to Edward Pease and explained:

> Some few of the persons are already engaged by Geo. and he proposes to engage the others at the salaries mentioned if he should be appointed engineer for those Rail-ways. From what I see and hear I am well satisfied that Geo. has an extraordinary field for the display of his peculiar Talents, and that if he manage well he may easily distance all his Competitors. We must however assist him much—Wood's Book must undergo a strict censorship before it is published—and I fear this will be a work of considerable delicacy, but it must be done.

The book in question was Nicholas Wood's *Treatise on Railroads* which was published that year, and it is doubtful whether this suggestion of muzzling the author in the interests of the Stephenson monopoly met with much success even if it was ever tried.

This early attempt to secure a monopoly of a new form of transport is reminiscent of Harry J. Lawson's plan to monopolize motorcar manufacture in Britain at the end of the century and, like the latter, it could not prevail. The steam railway and the motor car were no ordinary inventions; they brought about social revolutions and no one man or group of men can hope exclusively to control and exploit such momentous innovations. Although a number of George Stephenson's pupils and apprentices would subsequently achieve fame and fortune, they did so not as members of Stephenson's staff but on their own initiative and in circumstances which would, in at least one case, cause their old master considerable chagrin.

The most celebrated of Stephenson's pupils were Thomas Gooch, elder brother of Daniel, and, above all, Joseph Locke. Thomas Gooch was the son of John Gooch, described as an Iron Merchant of Bedlington and he was bound apprentice to Stephenson for a six years term in October 1823, two years 'making, building and fitting up steam engines' and four years as a civil engineer. Joseph Locke was the youngest son of George Stephenson's old workmate William Locke, whom he had first known as the banksman of the Water Row pit at Newburn. Joseph was born after his father's removal to Yorkshire, and according to his biographer, Joseph Devey, he joined George Stephenson 'towards the end of 1823' when he was nineteen. It is obvious from the letters which Locke wrote to Robert in South America that the two young men became close friends. According to an Agreement signed on 11 January 1825, Locke "Agrees to serve George Stephenson as an engineer and clerk for 2 years at a salary of £80 per annum", yet in the articles of George Stephenson & Son dated only a week later it is stated that he had been engaged for three years at £100 a year, a curious discrepancy.

George Stephenson failed to fulfil the hopes which Michael Longridge expressed in his letter to Pease. He did not 'manage well'. He made the same fatal mistake as William James by putting more irons into the fire than he could possibly keep hot. The grandiose schemes envisaged in the articles of George Stephenson & Son came to nothing and meanwhile the business of Robert Stephenson & Company languished for lack of effective technical direction. Apparently Thomas Richardson received an anonymous letter blaming poor Michael Longridge for the mismanagement of the Forth Street works, and Richardson passed it on to Longridge. The latter made his position clear in the following reply dated 7 March 1825:

> It is but seldom that I notice anonymous letters—and had our acquaintance been of longer standing I should have hardly deemed it requisite to have made an exception of the letter you have transmitted to me.
>
> I will intrude but a few minutes upon your time to state my reason for being concerned in Engine Building with G. & R. S.

George had rendered me very considerable service in giving an opinion favourable to Malleable Iron Rails, whilst *his own interest* lead him to recommend *Cast Iron*. It was not in my power to recompense the pecuniary loss he sustained, but I have ever since done what in me lay to forward his own interest and Robert's.

It was against my wish they commenced engine Builders, but after they had begun, considering it beneficial to the Bedlington Iron Co. and that Geo. and Robert would benefit from my habits of business, in which they were both deficient, I offered to take part with them. Most assuredly I never intended to have the slightest charge of the Manufactory, any further than attending the monthly meetings of the Partners. . . .

Circumstances, over which I had no control, have unfortunately for me thrown the responsibility upon my shoulders *for the present*; but I do hope that Robert's early return to England will soon relieve me, and in the meantime, if you or Mr. Pease can appoint a more suitable person it will much oblige.

As Richardson had been the agent of Robert Stephenson's departure, the unfortunate Longridge had every reason to feel aggrieved when criticism came from such a quarter.

Apparently by November 1825 the new foundry at Forth Street had been completed, for Joseph Locke then informed Robert in a letter that "the Manufactory is quite Metamorphosed into a place quite beyond your conception". But however impressive the firm might look, its situation was far from happy. Almost the only customer of any moment on the order book in 1825 was the Stockton & Darlington Railway Company and even in that quarter the position was not too rosy. As we have seen, apart from her outside coupling rods, *Locomotion* could scarcely be called an improvement on her predecessors and immediately after the opening day she broke a wheel and was out of action for several weeks before the firm could supply a replacement. Delivery of her sister engine *Hope* was late, and when she did arrive at the beginning of November 1825 she was found to be so defective that the Shildon engine-wrights had to work on her for a fortnight to make her fit for work and even then she performed very indifferently. Small wonder that the Forth Street works received bitter complaints of bad workmanship from the railway's Managing Committee.

J. G. H. Warren, the Company's historian, estimates that by the end of 1826 Robert Stephenson & Co. had executed £12,000 worth of orders, but it is evident that this did not amount to an adequate return on the capital expended. In June 1826, Longridge urged Pease to use his influence in the Stockton & Darlington Company to obtain settlement of an account because "R. S. and Co. are so distressingly in want of money". Two years later there was a similar request for early settlement "as we are rather pressed for cash at this time". From the letters he received during 1827 it must have become abundantly clear to Robert Stephenson that the firm which bore his name was in a very bad way.

> I want you very much [wrote Longridge on 2 February] and look forward with considerable anxiety to the period when I can welcome you back to 'canny Newcastle'. . . . Of your father I see but little as he spends nearly the whole of his time at Liverpool. He was so dissatisfied with Thomas Nicholson that I removed him back to Bedlington. Of course our Steam Engine Building Mfy and Foundery in Newcastle is left to its Fate or such assistance as I can occasionally render it. A man of the name of Harrison that your Father had placed there killed himself with drinking very speedily. Under these circumstances you cannot expect to receive large profits when you return. Mr. Pease is vastly out of humour about it but I will endeavour to pacify him until you get back when we must come to some arrangement respecting this place.

These gloomy tidings were endorsed by Locke towards the end of the same month: "I know not how the Manufactory goes on at Newcastle, I fear not so briskly as it has done. I believe Mr. Longridge wishes to decline the engine business until your return. Thos. Nicholson has left. . . . The present clerk Harris Dickinson is a very pushing young man whom I think you will like. . . ." Here Locke thought wrong, for after his return Robert Stephenson passed the following verdict on Dickinson: "He was active, intelligent, and what is usually termed a man of business—but the establishment would have been ruined by this time had that kind of management not been entirely altered."

In April, Edward Pease wrote to Robert in his characteristic style: "I can assure thee that your business in Newcastle, as well as thy father's engineering, have suffered very much from thy absence and unless thou soon return, the former will be given up as Mr.

Longridge is not able to give it that attention it requires and what *is* done is not done with credit to the house."

So much for the course of events at Newcastle. Turning now to Liverpool we find an equally gloomy picture. Like Robert before him, George Stephenson soon found that the Liverpool & Manchester Railway project was a vastly different proposition from the colliery lines of the north-east, the Stockton & Darlington not excepted. Not only did it call for engineering works of far greater magnitude, but the weight of opposition ranged against it was far more formidable than anything he had previously experienced or imagined. It goes without saying that the most determined of these opponents was Captain Bradshaw, the managing Trustee for the Bridgewater estates. A parley between Bradshaw and the railway promoters had been held at that same "Little White House" at Worsley where, years before, James Brindley and Francis, Duke of Bridgewater, had held the historic meetings which led to the building of the Bridgewater Canal. Then they had been pioneers concerned to defeat the opposition from the old Mersey & Irwell Navigation. Now it was the turn of the Bridgewater Canal, in the person of Bradshaw, to be on the defensive. He refused to be placated by offers of shares; his terms were all or nothing; either he would buy off the railway altogether or it would be war to the knife.

So it was that George Stephenson and his helpers soon found themselves in a hornet's nest made all the angrier for having been stirred up once already by William James's party. In November 1825 Stephenson wrote ruefully to Edward Pease:

> We have sad work with Lord Derby, Lord Sefton and Bradshaw the great Canal Proprietor whose grounds we go through with the projected railway. Their ground is blockaded on every side to prevent us getting on with the survey. Bradshaw fires guns through his ground in the course of the night to prevent the surveyors coming in the dark. We are to have a grand field day next week. The Liverpool Rly Co. are determined to force a survey through if possible. Lord Sefton says he will have 100 men to stop us. The Company thinks those great men have no right to stop our survey. It is the Farmers only who have a right to complain and by charging damages for trespass is all they can do.

Of his experiences on the Bridgewater estate, Stephenson later said in evidence:

I was threatened to be ducked in the pond if I proceeded, and of course we had a great deal of the survey to take by stealth at the time when the persons were at dinner; we could not get it by night, for we were watched day and night and guns were discharged over the grounds belonging to Captain Bradshaw to prevent us. I can state further, I was twice turned off the ground myself by his men; and they said if I did not go instantly they would carry me off to Worsley.

In addition to such difficulties as this, Stephenson was under constant pressure from the Committee to complete his plans and estimates as quickly as possible so that they could be deposited in time for the forthcoming session of Parliament. They had already missed one and were anxious not to miss another. Stephenson later admitted that, pressed by other concerns, he did not take the levels himself. Asked who did do the surveying he gave the names of Steel and Gillever. Hugh Steel appears in the articles of George Stephenson & Son as an apprentice working only for board and lodgings, and in 1827 Joseph Locke refers in a letter to 'the melancoly death of poor Hugh Steel'. The name of Gillever is wrapped in obscurity. Both were obviously quite incompetent, yet it was upon their levels that Stephenson made his estimates. It is seriously to be doubted whether Stephenson was a sufficiently competent surveyor to have produced a better set of levels himself.

In view of this combination of circumstances it is not surprising that the plans and estimates which were deposited with the Clerk of the Peace in accordance with statutory requirements would not stand examination by any qualified civil engineer. The Railway Committee were obviously uneasy, for at the eleventh hour they called in the canal engineer, William Cubitt, to make a hasty check, with the result that certain corrections were made so that the plans submitted to Parliament differed materially from those previously deposited. But they were still incorrect.

When the Stockton & Darlington Bill came before Parliament the canal companies had not woken up to the railway threat and the Bill had only met landowner opposition, but now they were roused and the whole weight of the powerful Bridgewater and Leeds & Liverpool Canal Companies was thrown against the Liverpool & Manchester scheme. Their own engineers, Francis Giles and his surveyor Alexander Comrie, and Thomas Telford's assistant H. R.

Palmer, had been engaged as expert opposition witnesses. The canal party was jubilant, for these engineers had themselves checked the levels against the deposited plans and discovered the errors. It was as a sheep to the slaughter that George Stephenson went to London in March 1825 to give his evidence on the Committee stage of the Bill. Captain Bradshaw's gunmen lurking in the Worsley coverts were as nothing to the merciless attack which was launched upon him by Mr. (later Baron) Alderson, the leading opposition Counsel. "I was not long in the witness box", George afterwards confessed, "before I began to wish for a hole to creep out at." No one could read through the minutes of his evidence without feeling pity for the wretched Stephenson as his skilled and implacable opponent drove him from one clumsy excuse or evasion to another until the sorry truth was revealed that not only were the plans hopelessly inaccurate but that his estimates were guesswork.

To mention only one of a number of errors, it had been stipulated that the railway should cross the Irwell at a height which would provide a minimum headroom of 16ft 6ins for navigation with the river at normal level, yet the plans showed a rail level only ten feet above the water and three feet below maximum flood level. Having established this damning fact, Alderson's relentless cross-examination continued by proving that Stephenson had estimated the cost of this Irwell bridge at £5,000 without any idea as to its dimensions or form. "So", he concluded scathingly, "you make a bridge, perhaps 14ft high, perhaps 20ft high, perhaps with 3 arches and perhaps with one, and then you boldly say that £5,000 is a proper estimate for it?" "I think so", answered Stephenson lamely, and, turning to the Committee, "I merely set out the line for other surveyors to follow." "Did you not survey the line of the road?" asked Alderson in tones of incredulity. "My Assistant did", replied Stephenson.

As Alderson had by now established that there were numerous errors in the levels of anything up to ten feet, he now sprung an obvious question. "What", he asked, "was the original base line on which all your levels are calculated as marked on the section?" "Near the Vauxhall Road in Liverpool" came the reply. "Whereabout?" pressed Alderson. "I think", answered the unhappy Stephenson, "about 150 yards from it, but I am not quite sure." Pursued further

by his merciless opponent it became obvious that he had no idea
how the base line had been determined.

The final passage of arms went like this:

"Then it is possible you may be out at other parts?"

"It may be, but I do not think so."

"You do not believe you are out on your levels?"

"I have made my estimate from the levels which I believe are
correct".

"Do you believe, aye or no, that your levels are correct?"

"I have heard it reported that they are not."

"Did you take the levels yourself?"

"They were taken for me."

"Other people have taken them for you and upon their estimate
you have made your estimate?"

"Yes."

When the time came for Alderson to deliver his summing up,
Stephenson's humiliation was complete.

This is the most absurd scheme that ever entered into the head of man
to conceive [thundered Alderson]. I think I may put it to them fairly
whether they ever before saw such an estimate. My learned friends
almost endeavoured to stop my examination. They wished me to put
in the plan, but I had rather have the exhibition of Mr. Stephenson in
that box. I say he never had a plan—I believe he never had one—I do
not believe he is capable of making one. . . . He is either ignorant or
something else which I will not mention.

Of the mistakes over the Irwell bridge he said:

It was the most ridiculous thing I ever heard stated by any man. I am
astonished that any man standing in that box would make such a statement without shrinking to nothing. . . . Did any ignorance ever arrive
at such a pitch as this? Was there ever any ignorance exhibited like this?
Is Mr. Stephenson to be the person upon whose faith this Committee
is to pass this Bill involving property to the extent of £400/500,000
when he is so ignorant of his profession as to propose to build a bridge
not sufficient to carry off the flood water of the river or to permit any
of the vessels to pass which of necessity must pass under it, and leave
his own Railroad liable to be several feet under water?

He makes schemes without seeing the difficulties, and when the
difficulties are pointed out, then he starts other schemes. He has produced five schemes all resulting in one estimate. . . .

And when did Mr. Cubitt make his survey to detect his mistakes? Long before; and Mr. Stephenson has the face to say that he only *heard* that his levels were not correct. Why, at that time he knew they were incorrect and that Mr. Cubitt had been sent down to ascertain to what extent they were so.

I never knew a person draw so much upon human credulity as Mr. Stephenson has proposed to do in the evidence he has given.

I am told they are going to throw Mr. Stephenson and his estimate overboard and to call upon Hon. Members to decide without his evidence. Now if they attempt that it will be the strangest thing that was ever attempted in the House of Commons.

Needless to add, the Bill was lost and the opposition was triumphant, but if they thought they had heard the last of George Stephenson they were woefully mistaken.

If Stephenson had really been the ignorant impostor that Alderson had made him out to be he would have walked out of the House of Commons into oblivion. Many a man of average stature could not have recovered from such a humiliating defeat, from such a deadly blow to his reputation. Yet if it be the mark of greatness never to admit defeat but to hold fast to the chosen purpose undismayed, then, despite all his faults and weaknesses, George Stephenson showed his greatness at this dark moment. His faith in himself and in the future of the locomotive railway which he was determined to establish never wavered. He knew that he had bungled the whole affair of the Liverpool & Manchester survey very badly, but although he had lacked the ability to counter their quicker wits, he knew that Alderson and the opposition engineers had talked a great deal more nonsense than he had done when they had poured scorn on the idea of locomotive traction and on the plan of crossing Chat Moss. Through his mistakes in detail he had given his adversaries a breathing space, but the grand conception remained. He was confident that he still held the trump card; that sooner or later he would play it and confound those who had scorned him.

It is a measure of the power of Stephenson's personality that notwithstanding a costly defeat for which he was so largely responsible, a majority of the Liverpool & Manchester Committee still possessed unshaken confidence in him. "I assure you", wrote John Moss, a deputy chairman, "I regret the loss of the Rail Road Bill as much on your account as for the mortification we all feel. No one can be more satisfied than I am that you deserved very different treatment than you met with from Mr. Alderson. Your talents are of a much more valuable nature than that of a witness in the House of Commons." "No doubt", wrote Locke to Robert Stephenson, "you would hear of the inaccuracy of the Manchester & Liverpool Levels which have affected the interest of your Father very much; we must endeavour by any future attention to regain that opinion which we have of late lost."

In reply to Moss, George Stephenson admitted that the memory of his experience in London still gave him 'great grief', but he then goes on confidently: "The Darlington Rly will be opened out in a short time. I wish I could get Alderson to be a longside of me on that day and could run his hounds into a corner more than he could do an engineer in the witness box."

The opening of the Stockton & Darlington undoubtedly gave a much needed fillip to George Stephenson's reputation. He also derived malicious satisfaction from the discovery that Benjamin Thompson's plans for the proposed Newcastle & Carlisle Railway, which he had been asked to investigate by the opposition, contained more errors than Francis Giles had found in his own. In reporting this to Robert Stephenson, Longridge concluded ruefully: "Robert, my faith in engineers is wonderfully shaken. I hope that when you return to us your accuracy will redeem their character."

Although their faith in George Stephenson as a practical railway engineer remained unshaken, the Liverpool Railway Committee decided that after the débâcle of 1825 their only hope of getting their Bill at a second attempt lay in obtaining the services of engineers of the highest standing to prepare a new set of plans and estimates. For this purpose the brothers George and John Rennie were engaged upon the recommendation of Lord Lowther and on 12 August 1825 the Rennies appointed a promising young engineer named Charles Blacker Vignoles to carry out the survey under their direction. He completed his work at the end of November in time for the next parliamentary session. While Stephenson had adopted William James's circuitous northern route via St. Helens and entering Liverpool through Bootle, the Rennies and Vignoles planned a more direct line into Liverpool at the expense of a deep cutting at Olive

Mount and a lengthy tunnel at Edgehill.[1] The new Bill passed the Commons in April by a majority of forty-seven, was opposed in the Upper House only by Lords Derby and Sefton and received the Royal Assent on 1 May.

At a meeting of the directors of the Company held on 5 June it was decided to retain George Rennie as consulting engineer and to invite either J. U. Rastrick or George Stephenson to act as 'operative engineer' under his general direction. In the meantime Charles Vignoles was ordered to stake out the line in return for a fee of four guineas a day. Unfortunately for the director's plans, the Rennie brothers inherited their father's attitude where fellow engineers were concerned. George Rennie attended the next Directors' meeting on 17 June and expressed himself forcibly. "He would not", the Minute Book records, "object to Mr. Jessop, Mr. Telford or any member of the Society of Engineers being consulted, but he would not be associated in any way with Rastrick or Stephenson." The meeting hurriedly adjourned for two days to consider this ultimatum. When it reassembled, Rennie's terms were rejected, it was resolved to invite Josias Jessop to act as Consultant in his stead and a sub-committee was appointed to treat with Rastrick and Stephenson. While these deliberations were going on, Vignoles was still, willy-nilly, acting engineer for the new Company.

At the next meeting in July, Joseph Sandars withdrew Rastrick's nomination. He had, he said, visited him in Warwickshire and had come to the conclusion that his terms would not be acceptable. George Stephenson was then appointed by unanimous resolution at a salary of £800 a year, it being agreed that he should spend nine months out of every twelve at Liverpool. He attended the next meeting and agreed to go over the whole line with Charles Vignoles.

As the directors should have realized, the position of Charles Vignoles was now a delicate one. To him had been delegated the difficult task of shepherding his plans and estimates through Parliament, and, unlike Stephenson, he had carried out this task with brilliant success. There can be little doubt that if the Company had given the Rennies a free hand they would have nominated him to act as 'operative engineer' and that Vignoles knew this. Yet now

1 This tunnel was to carry the line down to Wapping Dock and is not to be confused with the tunnel subsequently built when the railway was extended to Lime Street.

this talented and high-spirited young ex-soldier was expected to act as assistant to an uncouth Northumbrian who had previously failed so lamentably where he had succeeded. Yet having received no offer of other employment from the Rennies, Vignoles was apparently ready to swallow his pride and make the best of a bad bargain. He therefore presented Stephenson with a letter of introduction and recommendation from a friend of his, Edward Biddle. It did not, however, have the desired effect. "From Mr. S.'s subsequent expressions", wrote Vignoles to Biddle, "I found [the letter] gave him mortal offence, inasmuch as your friendly recommendations were construed by him as admitting me to be his *partner* instead of his *assistant*."

This was not a promising start and there was more trouble when George Stephenson and Josias Jessop, who had accepted the post of Consultant, were present together at a directors' meeting on 24 July. Stephenson's resentment of Jessop's overlordship was obvious and he expressed disagreement with every recommendation that Jessop made. Where Jessop advised deep cutting, Stephenson advocated inclined planes, and where Jessop recommended planes (at Olive Mount) Stephenson insisted doggedly upon cutting. Jessop advised the Company to let the whole line by single contract to a responsible contractor but Stephenson would have none of it, and in every case the directors let Stephenson have his way. Poor Jessop must have been left wondering why he had been appointed.

Joseph Locke, who had been surveying a proposed line from Leeds to Hull for Stephenson was now summoned by his master to take charge of the eastern end of the line including the 'impossible' section over Chat Moss where the work of cutting drains on either side of the line of way had already begun. In October, Josias Jessop died suddenly and was not replaced. One obstacle in the way of George Stephenson's plan to secure absolute engineering control over the undertaking was thus fortuitously removed, but there still remained Charles Vignoles at the western end.

The first shaft of the Edgehill Tunnel was sunk in September 1826 and in November 1826 Stephenson reported to the Directors that the pilot boring in the vicinity of this shaft was 13 ft. too far to the south of the true line and he maintained that on this account it threatened the foundations of certain houses in Great George

Square. Whatever the rights and wrongs of this matter may have been, Stephenson made Charles Vignoles the scapegoat of the affair and their relations became so strained that at the beginning of February, Vignoles resigned. With his departure, Stephenson had achieved his object. He at once transferred Joseph Locke to the western end of the line in place of Vignoles, summoned John Dixon from Darlington to succeed Locke on Chat Moss and appointed another pupil, William Allcard, to take charge of the central section. Thomas Gooch was also introduced as his chief clerk and draughtsman so that the whole railway was now completely under the control of George Stephenson and his subordinates. Vignoles accepted the situation frankly and philosophically.

> "I acknowledge [he afterwards wrote] having on many occasions differed with him (and that in common with almost all other engineers), because it appeared to me he did not look on the concern with a liberal and expanded view but with a microscopic eye; magnifying details and pursuing a petty system of parsimony very proper in a private colliery line or in a small undertaking but wholly inappliable to this national work. I also plead guilty to having neglected to court Mr. Stephenson's favours by crying down all other engineers, especially those in London for, though I highly respect his great natural talents, I would not shut my eyes to certain deficiencies.

Though the directors of the Company would not risk further trouble by taking Vignoles' part, they expressed to him their regret that 'the queer temper of Mr. Stephenson would not allow of his remaining in Liverpool' and paid all his expenses.

Unlike the unfortunate William James before him, Charles Vignoles does not pass out of this story into oblivion. Within weeks of his leaving Liverpool he was elected a member of the Institution of Civil Engineers and he lived, as a most distinguished railway engineer, to become President of that august body.

It is clear that Stephenson's sense of inferiority caused by his lack of formal education had been intensified to bitter resentment by the treatment he had received in London, and that he had stubbornly determined that no one remotely associated with those responsible for his humiliation should play any part in the Liverpool & Manchester project. He would show the world that he was fully capable of carrying it through without the aid of any smart book-learned engineers from London, and to make sure that no one should take from him the smallest share of credit he staffed the line with his own pupils.

Already he was making progress on the crossing of Chat Moss which those clever fellows in London had pronounced to be impossible. At first this work, begun in June 1826, had been discouraging. The sides of the drainage ditches had caved in as fast as they could be dug and a bewildered John Dixon had celebrated his arrival by sinking into the bog like William James, only to be rescued with difficulty by Joseph Locke. After this the engineers emulated the labourers by strapping boards to their feet before venturing on to the morass. The difficulty of the ditches was solved by placing in them lines of empty barrels with the ends knocked out, and when this had been done Stephenson's plan of floating his railway embankment across the Moss on a raft of brushwood and heather was put into operation. A vast tonnage of spoil was tipped only to be swallowed up, but Stephenson never lost heart and gradually a firm causeway began to stretch out into the Moss to confound the sceptics.

By March 1827, progress on Chat Moss was such that Locke was able to tell Robert Stephenson: "That shade which was unfortunately cast on the fame of your father has disappeared; and the place which he must often have reflected on with pain is now such a scene of operations as sheds lustre on his character and will, no doubt, immortalize his name. We are proceeding very briskly", he adds. "In the tunnel we are doing very well and I hope very correctly—at least I spare no pains in watching every part of it. I assure you I have had a busy time since I came here."

For the exiled Robert, such news must have done a great deal to offset the gloomy tidings he was receiving at the same time about the state of the factory in Newcastle. But the youthful Locke's optimistic letter may have conveyed a somewhat misleading impression, for the Edgehill tunnel and the Chat Moss crossing were the only works in progress at this time and, even there, more remained to be done than had been accomplished. On the intermediate section of the line it had not even been decided whether to construct the near-level road which the Rennies had proposed or whether to use inclined planes and haulage engines to save costly earthworks. Even

George Stephenson tended to favour inclined planes, and the question of motive power had not yet become the subject of protracted and sometimes heated debate at the Company's meetings. The future of the steam locomotive was, in fact, still very much in doubt. This then was the position which affairs had reached when Robert Stephenson at last announced his impending return to England in the summer of 1827. He, too, had had his adventures and misfortunes.

CHAPTER SIX

The Mines of Santa Ana

O N 23 JULY 1824 the *Sir William Congreve* had dropped anchor off La Guayra on the coast of the Caribbean in Venezuela and from her deck Robert Stephenson—to quote his log—'observed in silence the miserable appearance of the town'. It was the first of many disillusionments. He was very soon to discover that speculators in the City of London could launch grandiose schemes of overseas development without knowing anything about climate, terrain or other local conditions and without, apparently, taking any preliminary steps to find out.

Here Robert left the ship to sail on its way with the advance party of miners and their equipment to Cartagena whence they were to travel up the Magdalena River. Before himself proceeding to the Colombian Mines, Robert had been asked to report on the feasibility of building a breakwater and pier at La Guayra, and constructing a railway from that port to Caracas. Having inspected the havoc wrought by the heavy seas which had followed a hurricane the previous year, he came to the conclusion that a breakwater was out of the question, though he estimated that a new pier might be built for £6,000. As for the railway, having explored the deep valley leading to Caracas, hemmed in by mountains which he described as "six or eight times as large as Brusselton Hill", he reported that it would be too costly and that the tunnels and heavy earthworks required would be too liable to be damaged by the frequent earthquakes.

Having accomplished this first mission, Robert Stephenson, accompanied by Walker, the interpreter to the expedition, and one black servant, set out on muleback on the long and arduous journey through the foothills of the Merida Cordilleras to Santa Fé de Bogotá, the capital of Colombia. The little party went armed to the teeth, but they were unmolested and eventually arrived safely in

Bogotá on 19 January 1825, Robert having spent some time on the way prospecting and collecting mineral samples.

From Bogotá, Robert next proceeded to Honda, the upper navigable limit of the River Magdalena, which point his miners had already left on their twenty-four-mile journey through the town of Mariquita to the mines of Santa Ana which were to be the scene of their operations. He was disconcerted to find all the heavier equipment they had brought with them still lying on the river bank, and when he set out to follow them he soon appreciated the reason. The Colombian Mining Association had failed to discover that the so-called road from the river-head to their mines was in places no more than a precipitous path. No equipment could be carried to the mines except on the backs of mules. Robert at once despatched a message to London to this effect, but before it arrived a cargo of heavy machinery had been despatched which was fated to rust away on the river-bank at Honda, to the astonishment of the local peons.

Through desolate disused mine-workings Robert Stephenson rode into Mariquita to find it a ghost town. A mere 450 dispirited people haunted the ruins and the rubbish dumps to which earthquakes, revolution and the abandonment of the mines had reduced a once proud Spanish city with a population of 20,000. As his mule picked its delicate way through the debris of fallen palaces in the burning heat of the plain in which the lost city stood, Robert must have felt that he had indeed come to the end of the world. As for those who came to stare at the slim stranger with the bronzed face and the large dark eyes under the wide-brimmed sombrero, they may well have taken him for some young high-born Spaniard returned to the scene of his country's lost wealth.

Robert Stephenson and his small advance party made their headquarters in Mariquita until the main body of Cornish miners arrived from England. As Boulton & Watt had discovered years before when they began to introduce their engines into Cornwall, the Cornish miners were a wild and ungovernable clan recognizing no laws but their own. It was now Robert Stephenson's turn to make the same discovery. Bribed by high wages to leave their native heath, the Cornishmen celebrated their arrival in Honda with such an orgy of drinking and debauchery that Robert received a furious letter of protest from the Governor of the town. "Many of them . . .

are ungovernable," wrote Robert to Illingworth, the commercial manager of the Company in Bogotá; "I dread the management of them. They have already commenced to drink in the most out-rageous manner. Their behaviour in Honda has, I am afraid, incurred for ever the displeasure of the Governor, at all events so far as induces me to calculate upon his friendly co-operation in any of our future proceedings." With all speed Robert moved the whole party up to Santa Ana where, in a small village of only nine cottages, they would be out of temptation and unable to cause further trouble upon such a scale.

For the first six of the twelve miles that separated Mariquita from the silver mines of Santa Ana, La Manta, San Juan and El Christo de Laxas the way led across the scorching plain; then it became a narrow and precipitous mule-path climbing the eastern slopes of the Andes. At Santa Ana, Robert Stephenson lodged temporarily in a cottage lent to him by the local priest until he had built for himself his own bungalow of bamboo thatched with palm leaves. The view from the high shelf on which the little village stood was breathtaking. The ground fell away almost sheer to the depths of a ravine beyond which rose mountains, fold above fold, to the glittering snow-clad summits of the high Cordilleras. After the dust and intolerable heat of the ruined city in the plain, Santa Ana must have seemed a para-dise, for a cool breeze blew from the mountains and the temperature seldom exceeded 75° in the shade. On the rich soil grew great trees, cedars, tall palms where monkeys chattered, groves of bamboo and acacia, luxuriant tree-ferns and magnolia. And all this prodigality of green leaf and blossom was shot through with the jewelled plum-age of tropical birds, mocking birds and macaws, gaudy humming birds no larger than the brilliant butterflies with which they com-peted for nectar from the flowers. A stream, fed by the melting snows far above, fell into the ravine below through a succession of cascades and rocky pools where Stephenson disturbed the solemn pelicans to bathe.

Here Robert made his temporary home in the New World and here, belatedly, he received those letters from his friends Longridge and Locke upon which he depended for news from England. It must indeed have seemed a far cry from the mine galleries of Killing-worth, the stubble fields of Durham and the bleak waste of Chat

Moss. But the Cornish miners saw to it that his self-imposed exile was very far from idyllic. While they would have submitted readily enough to the discipline of such a master as Richard Trevithick, one of their own race and a man of herculean strength, the men in charge of the mine gangs bitterly resented taking orders from a slender young stranger who spoke an alien dialect. By Cornish custom these men were referred to by their gangs as 'Captains' and this title led both the Cornish and native labour into the mistaken belief, which the Captains themselves fostered, that they were in charge of the operations and that Robert Stephenson was merely a clerk sent out to pay them their wages.

It is somewhat ironical that the only physical peril that Robert had to face in South America threatened him from his own countrymen. One night the Captains, drunk as usual, suddenly invaded his bunga-low, shouting threats and calling to the 'clerk' to come out. Evidently they did not expect him to accept their challenge, for his sudden appearance, unarmed, from the inner room quite disconcerted them. Remarking that because he was sober and they were drunk a fight would be unfair, he ordered them to leave, and although they could easily have overpowered him they sheepishly did so. But for hours they lurked in the darkness of the trees outside defiantly shouting their slogan "One and all! One and all!" Next night, however, they returned in such force that Robert thought it more prudent to beat an unobserved retreat to a neighbouring cottage. "They plainly tell me", he wrote to Illingworth, "that I am obnoxi-ous to them, because I was not born in Cornwall; and although they are perfectly aware that I have visited some of the principal mines in that county, and examined the various processes on the spot, yet they tell me that it is impossible for a north-countryman to know anything about mining."

Gradually, however, Robert succeeded, with Illingworth's help, in establishing his authority. He had the happy idea of organizing sports in the evenings, in which he took part himself and so was able harmlessly to reveal the fact that, though slightly built, he was decep-tively strong. In their own favourite pastimes of quoits, wrestling and hammer-throwing the men of the west discovered that the wiry Northumbrian was more than a match for them and this, above all, enabled Stephenson to win their respect. But he could never stop them drinking. Of his total labour force of 160 Cornishmen not more than two-thirds were ever available at one time. The rest were dead drunk.

These labour difficulties were not his only troubles. The full and meticulous reports which he sent regularly to London appeared to be completely ignored, for the Company continued to send out consignments of heavy equipment to make scrap iron on the banks of the Magdalena. "What they have sent out", he told Longridge, "is a pretty good specimen of the ideas they have of the difficulties to be encountered in the conveyance of heavy materials. . . . I can say at once that a great number of the steam engines that were being made when I left may as well be made use of at home." While he was obstinately determined to honour the three-year agreement he had made in London, he now fully realized that the Company he represented was a wild-cat speculation and that the venture could not possibly succeed. All this made Robert very depressed and that he made no secret of his feelings in his letters home may be inferred from this reply from Joseph Locke: "I am very sorry to hear that you are not as comfortably situated as you could wish. I should have thought that the extent of country which you must by this have travelled over would have produced *some* objects to create pleasure and tend to dissipate the cloud of Melancoly which seems to settle over you. . . ." Locke, who at this time had just completed the survey from Leeds to Hull on which he had obviously enjoyed himself hugely, then continues: "Amid all the gay scenes which my *Wildness* led me into I still remember'd you, and the happiness I should have felt to have been with you. But, however, whilst surveying, what do you think I did? Only what others have done—fell in love! And (you may be sure) with one of the most enchanting creatures under heaven. My only regret is that we have finished surveying in that neighbourhood." To the lonely Robert in his palm-thatched hut in the Andes, such tidings must have been bitter-sweet indeed.

Meanwhile in Darlington, Francis Mewburn, solicitor to the Stockton & Darlington Railway, noted in his diary: "He [Robert Stephenson] has written home the most deplorable Accounts that can well be conceived of the difficulties he everywhere encounters and I prophesy that these mining speculators will share the fate of

Law's grand bubble." The precise lawyer returned to this entry at a later date and added: "My remarks have proved correct. Nearly all the speculations have entirely failed—1826."

Notwithstanding Mewburn's pronouncement, in 1826 there was apparently some attempt on the part of the Colombian Mining Association to induce Robert to remain abroad longer than the agreed term, for in March he wrote to Illingworth in Bogotá: "I will not be induced to stay beyond the contract term of three years unless my partners in England agree and unless I can be supplied with scientific books and instruments to equip a complete laboratory. Otherwise existence is insufferable." He must have realized that these stipulations were tantamount to a flat refusal.

The news from England about the state of the Newcastle works and the failure of the Liverpool & Manchester Bill can scarcely have raised Robert's spirits, but in connection with the latter he contented himself with the following dry comment to Longridge: "It is to be regretted that my father placed the conducting of the levelling under the care of young men without experience. Simple as the process of levelling may appear, it is one of those things that requires care and dexterity in its performance."

As the end of Robert's three-year term drew near the Company tried to persuade him to stay on at Santa Ana until a suitable engineer could be found to replace him, but he was adamant in his refusal to remain a day longer than his agreed period and it was finally arranged that Illingworth, the Bogotá agent, should take over from him temporarily, "The period of my departure from this place has at last really and truly arrived", wrote Robert to Longridge on 16 July 1827, "though not longer than a month or two ago I was despairing of being able to get away without incurring the displeasure of the Board of Directors. . . ." It had been, he went on, the news that the Newcastle factory might be abandoned if he did not promptly return to England which had induced him to notify the Company's office in Bogotá that he intended to leave 'with all convenient despatch'.

The one South American speculation about which Robert Stephenson did not feel completely disillusioned was the scheme to unite the Atlantic with the Pacific by cutting a canal through the Isthmus from Chagres to Panama. The idea evidently fired his imagination, for he wrote enthusiastically to Longridge on the subject and said that he planned to walk over the line himself before leaving for England via New York. But when he arrived at Cartagena the difficulties involved appeared too great and he reluctantly abandoned the plan.

At the inn at Cartagena whither he went to await ship to New York, Robert Stephenson had an extraordinary and ever memorable encounter. His curiosity was aroused by two fellow visitors whom he overheard speaking English together but, with typical English reserve, he was reluctant at first to approach them. He was particularly intrigued by one of the pair, a tall, gaunt shabbily-dressed figure wearing a wide-brimmed straw hat who seemed to be forever pacing restlessly to and fro. He made inquiries. 'The name is Trevithick', he was told, 'You may have heard it.' It was indeed Trevithick who, after years of almost incredible adventure and hardship in Peru and Costa Rica, had found his way with his companion, Gerard, to Cartagena. If anything was still needed to convince Robert Stephenson of the folly of the fond dreams of infinite wealth waiting to be grasped in the South American mines it was this chance meeting. For the man who had been greeted like a king on his arrival years before, the honoured friend of Simon Bolivar whose horse had been shod with silver by cheering Peruvians, was now a tattered castaway in Cartagena without the price of his passage home. Robert at once introduced himself. For a few moments Trevithick stared incredulously. "Is that Bobby?" he exclaimed at last, and then after another pause he turned to Gerard and added wistfully: "Why, I've nursed him many a time."

We have this account of the meeting from eye-witnesses who also tell us that the two men appeared to have little in common and treated each other with reserve. Their natures were, indeed, so different and the gap of years and experience so great that an immediate, intimate friendship was hardly likely to be struck. After his experiences at Santa Ana, Robert may well have felt that he had had enough of Cornishmen to last him a lifetime, but he gave Trevithick £50 to enable him to pay his passage back to England.

So it came about that the two great engineers left Cartagena for England, the younger man to find fame and fortune as a railway engineer and the older to die in poverty and obscurity. Trevithick obtained a passage direct to Falmouth, but Stephenson, accompanied by Gerard, chose to travel via New York. It was an eventful voyage. While their ship lay almost becalmed off the West Indies, they picked up two boatloads of starving survivors from ships lost in a recent hurricane. To Robert Stephenson's horror, one party of pitiable scarecrows, so weak that they had to be lifted aboard in rope cradles, had been keeping themselves alive by devouring the carcasses of two dead companions.

They were within one day's call from New York when it was the turn of their own ship to be caught in a hurricane. Driven helplessly towards the shore it struck rocks at midnight, and although the masts and sails were cut away the hull rapidly broke up. Everyone on board managed to get safely ashore, but practically all Robert Stephenson's baggage and his money were lost. Such was his dramatic introduction to the United States.

Robert, his biographer Jeaffreson tells us, 'found no difficulty in obtaining money in New York', though precisely how he accomplished this is not related. He evidently decided to see something of the country while he had the opportunity. With Gerard and three other Englishmen who had sailed from Cartagena on the same ship, he set off on a walking tour through New York State and over the Canadian border to Montreal, visiting the Niagara Falls en route. This was an ambitious trek to undertake, amounting as it did to a distance of 500 miles; but, notwithstanding the importance of his return to England, Robert was obviously determined to see as much as he could while they were about it. He was delighted with the hospitality the little party received from the country people all along their route. Small farmers and village store-keepers gave them bed and board and refused to accept any payment. But he did not form the same high opinion of the inhabitants of New York city for of them he wrote: "All outward appearances of things and persons were indicative of English manners and customs; but on closer investigation we soon discovered the characteristic impudence of the people. In many cases it was nothing short of disgusting". Yet he admitted that Canada was "far behind the States in everything. The people", he wrote, "want industry and enterprise. Every Englishman, however partial he may be, is obliged to confess the disadvantageous contrast. Whether the cause exists in the people or the system of government

I cannot say—perhaps it rests with both." When they returned to New York, Robert and his companions boarded the first-class packet *Pacific* bound for Liverpool.

George Stephenson had a house in Liverpool during the period he was superintending the building of the Liverpool & Manchester Railway. Consequently, when the *Pacific* docked there at the end of November 1827, father and son were soon reunited. They found each other greatly changed. At forty-six, George Stephenson was still in the prime of life, but while his health and strength were still unimpaired, his son saw that during his own absence his father's face had become lined and his hair had turned white. George saw before him a self-possessed and sophisticated young man of the world whose speech had completely lost the broad Northumbrian accent. If the South American adventure had not yielded the financial results which had been expected, Robert Stephenson had gained immeasurably thereby. He had won independence and self-confidence in a way he could never have done had he been content to remain tied to his father's leading strings. The partnership between them was now resumed with much of the old loyalty on Robert's side but, as George Stephenson must have realized, the basis of that partnership would never be the same as of old. The son who now stood before him would never again be the passive instrument of his will and it was upon terms of equality that the two Stephensons went forward to accomplish their mission.

CHAPTER SEVEN

The First Railwaymen

IN HIS EVIDENCE before the Committee which considered the ill-fated Liverpool & Manchester Bill of 1825, Nicholas Wood described a typical demonstration which he and George Stephenson staged in January of that year on the Killingworth railway before a party of engineers which included William Cubitt, J. U. Rastrick, William Brunton and Alexander Easton. One of Stephenson's locomotives, which he described as weighing $7\frac{1}{2}$ tons without tender and having 4ft driving wheels, was coupled to a train of twelve loaded coal-wagons weighing nearly 49 tons and run backwards and forwards over a 2,000-yard length of track on a gradient of 1 in 330. The highest speeds attained were 8 mph with the gradient and 7 mph against it, the average being $6\frac{2}{3}$ mph.

Ever since the Trevithick locomotive had run its brief course at Whinfield's Foundry in Gateshead in 1805, the Tyneside colliery lines had been the focal point of engineering interest and the stage for demonstrations of this kind. But from the moment the Stockton & Darlington Railway was opened to traffic in September 1825 the Tyneside lines ceased to be the chief centre of attraction. For over five years, until, that is, it was in its turn eclipsed by a successor, the Stockton & Darlington was, in the words of the Liverpool & Manchester Company's Treasurer, Henry Booth, "the great theatre of practical operations upon railways". The audience was international. Mention has already been made of the two Prussian engineers who visited the railway in 1827. Marc Seguin, the great French railway engineer was another visitor, while among those present at the opening ceremony was the American, William Strickland, who had been sent over as an observer by the Pennsylvania Society for the Promotion of Internal Improvement.

During the critical years of Robert Stephenson's self-imposed exile and George Stephenson's temporary eclipse, the future of railways and the fortunes of father and son alike depended absolutely on the success of steam traction on the Stockton & Darlington Railway. It is safe to say that of the many people who travelled from afar to watch the chief actress—the locomotive—play her part in this novel drama, only one in ten wished her a long run. The rest, those who had a professional or financial interest in canals or turn-pike trusts, hoped for, and indeed confidently forecast, her speedy failure. Rumours that the locomotives had not proved as economical as horses, and that the Company were about to abandon them, were circulated so assiduously that years afterwards writers of railway history would give them fresh currency. Yet the fact is that the Company did not abandon the locomotive and that the shrewd Quakers who presided over its affairs were much too hard-headed to persist in the use of an uneconomic machine merely out of loyalty to George Stephenson's theories.

On the opening of the railway, Thomas Storey, who, it will be recalled, was one of the two resident engineers under Stephenson, was appointed the Company's Chief Engineer, and his reports show that he was ordered to keep the most careful records of costs per ton-mile for haulage by the locomotives and the fixed-haulage engines. These figures reveal that notwithstanding all the faults of the early Stephenson locomotives and the fact that they suffered the additional handicap of having to work over a line continually cluttered by the horse-drawn traffic of 'bye traders', their superiority was evident from the outset. Here are Storey's figures for 1826, the first year of working:

	Cost per ton-mile
Locomotives	$\frac{22}{23}$ of a $\frac{1}{4}$d
Fixed Engines: Brussleton	$1\frac{3}{8}$d
Etherley	$1\frac{3}{16}$d

Storey calculated that his figure for locomotives represented a saving of 30% over horse haulage. This figure coincided closely with that of $\frac{1}{4}$d per ton per mile which he had earlier estimated on the following basis: "One Locomotive engine will perform 6 Stockton & Yarm journeys and 3 Darlington journeys each week at 45T each journey or 405T per week and at 50 weeks per annum is equal to 20,250T.

"The cost of one engine, to work it, uphold, coal consumption and watering and interest of capital is £373 2s per annum and will lead during that time 45T 7,100 miles which is equal to ¼d per ton per mile."

While Thomas Storey exercised general engineering superintendence over the railway, the responsibility for keeping the locomotives in service rested squarely on the shoulders of one man— Timothy Hackworth. He had been appointed in 1825 to take charge of the Company's Shildon shops on the recommendation of George Stephenson, and a better and more resourceful man for this exacting job it would have been hard to find. While Robert Stephenson & Co. was suffering from an almost total lack of competent technical direction due to the absence of Robert Stephenson and the preoccupation of his father with other concerns, it was left to Hackworth to uphold the honour of the steam locomotive. This he did most worthily. For the improvements which were made during this period, some of them of the first importance, the credit was undoubtedly his no matter whether they were carried out at Shildon or at Newcastle. The comparison between George Stephenson and Hackworth which has been drawn by the champions of the latter is invidious because it disregards the very different circumstances in which the two men were placed at this time. George Stephenson was too fully occupied in projecting roads for his locomotives to run upon to devote much time and thought to their improvement. On the other hand, it is no disparagement of Hackworth to say that when Stephenson recommended his appointment to Shildon he presented him with an absolutely unique opportunity. He became the world's first shedmaster and the improvements he made were the fruits of practical experience of locomotive running and maintenance such as no one else possessed or could possibly acquire at that time.

The spring safety-valve which Hackworth was the first to introduce was a typical product of this practical experience. In 1828 there were two boiler explosions. No. 2 *Hope* blew up at Simpasture in March and in July No. 1 *Locomotion* exploded while taking water at Aycliffe. Their drivers, John Gillespie and John Cree respectively, were killed. It did not take Hackworth long to discover the cause. Familiarity was breeding contempt. As the unsprung locomotives jolted over the rail joints the weight on the arm of the Stephenson

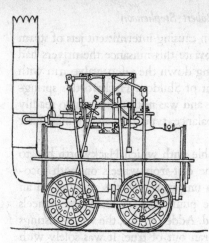

George Stephenson's *Locomotion*, the first locomotive to work on a public railway, 1825.

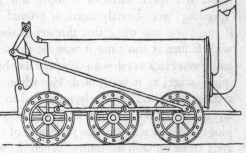

George Stephenson's *Experiment*, 1827/8. This drawing is based on the only known portrayal of this engine in J. U. Rastrick's note-book, a rough sketch which does not show boiler mountings and other details.

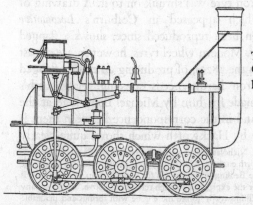

Timothy Hackworth's *Royal George*, 1828. The successful prototype of Hackworth's Shil-don locomotives.

STOCKTON & DARLINGTON RAILWAY MOTIVE POWER

safety-valve bobbed up and down causing intermittent jets of steam to escape from the valve. To obviate this nuisance the drivers had acquired the suicidal habit of tying down the safety valve arm with cord once they were out of sight of Shildon. Hackworth's spring-valve effectively put a stop to this and was not, moreover, so readily tampered with as the spring balance type of valve which later became so common.

By far the most frequent trouble with which Hackworth had to contend was the breakage of the cast-iron wheels on both loco-motives and rolling stock. With unsprung vehicles running on an unresilient stone-block road the punishment which these wheels sustained may be readily imagined. Added to this, the wheel-castings were often of poor quality and ran out of true. It was solely with the object of trying to reduce wheel failures that the company imposed a speed limit of 8 mph, but although drivers caught 'speeding' were heavily fined, it proved impossiole to enforce it. If there was one thing that threatened the locomotive experiment with failure at this time it was the perpetual breakage of wheels, and it was Hackworth who saved the day by designing the improved 'plug' wheel as it was called. His wheel was cast in two parts, a centre which was accurately machined to run true on the axle and an outer portion which was secured to it by wedge bolts and wooden plugs in such a way that the periphery of the wheel could be accur-ately trued up with the centre. When the wheel had been assembled in this way a wrought-iron tyre was shrunk on to it. A drawing of Hackworth's wheel which appeared in Colburn's *Locomotive Engineering* and has often been reproduced since, shows a flanged tyre such as is used today. Modern wheel tyres, however, are of cast steel and the difficulty, in the 1820s, of producing an endless flanged tyre out of wrought iron hardly needs stressing. Hackworth's improved wheels were made for him by Michael Longridge at the Bedlington Ironworks, and in the correspondence between them is a small marginal sketch[1] by Hackworth which shows quite clearly

[1] In the 1831 edition of his book, Nicholas Wood claims that he first fitted a set of wrought-iron 'rims' to one of the Killingworth engines and that they were so successful that Longridge installed a special set of rolls at the Bedlington ironworks for making them. If this is so it is difficult to understand the need for the explanatory sketch referred to above. The Company instructed Hackworth to go to Killingworth 'to see the engine with springs and malleable iron rims' which suggests that Wood may also have been the first to use satisfactory plate-springs.

that his tyres—or 'hoops' as they were then called—were plain rings like the tyres of a cart-wheel shrunk round the tread of the wheel outside the flange, the latter being a part of the wheel casting. Long-ridge was obviously impressed with the value of Hackworth's improved wheel for in reply to him he wrote: "My great fear for this description of Power was the great cost which the wheels had occasioned upon the Darlington Railway; but I now entertain hopes that this expense may be considerably reduced."

It is evident from the report of the two Prussian mining engineers that by 1827 an important change in the layout of the valve-gear had been made, though whether this was carried out at Hackworth's instigation cannot be known. The slip eccentrics were transferred from the axles to a short transverse shaft mounted above the boiler and between the cylinders. This shaft was rotated by cranks and long vertical connecting rods which were yoked to the centres of the outside coupling rods. The eccentric rods which operated the slide valves had hooked or 'gab' ends which dropped over driving pins on the eccentrics, and extension handles on these rods enabled the driver to lift them clear of these pins and so control by hand the admission of steam to the cylinders. This made the locomotives more controllable and did away with the laborious process of reversing mentioned in Chapter 3. To reverse his engine the driver now had only to disengage one eccentric rod and 'handle' the valve, since the slip eccentric ensured that the valve timing of the other cylinder would follow suit. Curiously enough the famous *Locomotion*, which survives at Darlington, is not fitted with this arrangement, but it is clear from a contemporary account of driving technique which will presently follow that her sisters must have been so fitted.

We now come back to the vexed question of the blast pipe. That George Stephenson fully appreciated the principle of the steam blast but was concerned to make his engines steam without a fierce blast in the interests of silence and economy has already been shown. The source of the legend that Hackworth 'discovered' the blast pipe can now be established with reasonable certainty. Like many another practical locomotive man since his day, Hackworth was not con-cerned with silence or with fuel economy; his aim was to make his engines steam and give maximum performance. There was plenty of cheap coal around at 3s. 9d. a ton, while, so far as Hackworth was concerned, if every horse could be frightened off the railway his life would be made very much easier. So, like the wily old driver who puts a 'Jimmy' in the blast pipe of a refractory locomotive when his shed foreman is not looking, Timothy Hackworth defied the cherished theories of George Stephenson and Nicholas Wood by closing up the exhaust steam outlet until the Stockton & Darlington locomotives vomited cinders and their tall stacks glowed red hot. Despite what were called 'networks' placed over these chimneys, a Mr. Marshall Fowler of Preston Hall complained so frequently of fire damage to his plantations that in dry seasons the Company had to station men along the lineside ready to beat out the fires. Hackworth's blast pipe certainly blasted, but it was not a revolutionary discovery; it was a desperate expedient which would eventually contribute to his defeat by the Stephensons at the Rainhill locomotive trials.

The driving, firing and maintenance of steam locomotives is much more than a job, it is a vocation. In the passage of years there has accumulated on the footplate and in the running shed a weight of custom and tradition that stamps the locomotive man as indefinably yet as unmistakably as ships and the sea leave their mark on the sailor. Soon, when the driver becomes a mere motorman and the shed fitter a garage mechanic, that tradition will die, so it is appropriate now that its source should be recorded. It began at Shildon shed on the Stockton & Darlington Railway. George Stephenson built the locomotives for the first public railway, but it was Timothy Hackworth and his men who had to keep their wheels turning. Let us salute them now, these first railwaymen, the pioneers. With unbelievably primitive machines and equipment and with no precedents whatever to guide them, they had to learn by bitter trial and error how to run a railway. In a few years, when railways began to spread across the world, the men trained in this first hard school at Shildon went with them, proud masters of the mysteries of a new power.

To find a precedent for the first Stockton & Darlington locomotives we can only look forward to the first 'horseless carriages' of the century's end. The trials and tribulations of the motoring pioneers are much closer in time to us and have been fully recorded, but although many books have been written about the first public railway none of them bring it to life, none of them tell us what it was really like to stand on the high, precarious footplate of a Stephenson locomotive, *Hope*, *Black Diamond* or *Diligence*, as she picked up her load at the foot of Brussleton plane and rumbled away towards Stockton.

Fortunately we can re-create such a scene with fair accuracy by combining the Traffic Manager's reports quoted by Tomlinson in his *History of the North Eastern Railway* with the recollections of a man who once drove *Locomotion* in the early days. The Traffic Manager was John Graham. He had come to the railway from Hetton Colliery, where he had risen to the position of Head Overlooker after ten years as a trapper and hewer. Like Hackworth, he was recommended to his new post by George Stephenson. The driver in question was his son, George Graham, and, like many another pioneer, his memories would have died with him had not Henry Oxtoby, a North Eastern Railway employee, had the good sense to take them down at the old man's dictation before it was too late.

Notwithstanding the alteration to the valve-gear, the Stephenson locomotive was still very hard to manage and George Graham maintained that only one man in three was capable of becoming a driver. Stopping a train was a work of art because there were no brakes on engine or tender and only crude wooden block brakes on the wagons which had to be held down. When, in his evidence on the first Liverpool & Manchester Bill, George Stephenson was asked how a locomotive and train was stopped, his replies were wondrously vague and evasive. Asked whether a man rode on each train to apply the brakes, he replied: "No, there was no man upon the train; there are a man and a boy to attend the engine, and by a communication with the last carriage they may be instantly disengaged". Pressed further to explain what he meant by this, Stephenson replied: "A rod runs on and stops them all." There is no evidence that this implied application of some crude form of continuous braking was ever seriously contemplated let alone fitted, and Stephenson was evidently relying upon Counsel's profound ignorance of railway matters to see him through. In fact, as George Graham explains, the only way of stopping was to reverse the engine and as there was no reversing gear, in order to do this the eccentric rods had to be lifted and the valves worked by hand. This involved four movements of the valve handles for each revolution of the driving wheels, so we may readily accept as an understatement George Graham's comment that this was "no easy matter when running at 12 miles an hour or more." It must indeed have called for a lightning-quick eye, remarkable dexterity and perfect timing. It must be remembered, too, that the driver's position was a precarious perch on a footboard *beside* the boiler and not with his fireman behind it.

There was only one driver, George Chicken by name, who was able to perform this operation in darkness without a light. He had perfected the trick of wedging his foot against the vertical connecting rod which rotated the eccentric shaft and in this way he was able to synchronize his movements correctly. When any of the other drivers wanted to stop after dark, retardation was delayed until the fireman provided the necessary illumination by holding aloft a blazing length of old hempen incline rope dipped in oil and ignited at the furnace door. Driver Chicken's heart evidently belied his name, for he was often reported for breaking wagon wheels by travelling too fast. He finished his career driving Edinburgh-Glasgow expresses on the North British Railway. It is, of course, possible that 'Chicken' was merely a Shildon nickname, for when driver Robert Pickering grumbled that he had tried four firemen, all of them useless, and was asked their names, he could only reply that he knew them as 'Badger', 'Bullet', 'Baggy' and 'Buck'. No doubt all four, like most of the men of Shildon, eventually made good. Graham recalled that one fireman, Joseph Bell, was driving on the South Eastern Railway until 1890, while another, Edward Corner, after a spell on the Great North of England Railway, also joined the South Eastern, finishing his career as shed foreman at Bricklayers Arms. Such recollections convey some idea of the far-reaching influence of the Shildon school.

The Shildon drivers engaged and paid their own firemen, provided their own fuel and oil and were paid by the Company at the rate of $\frac{1}{4}$d per ton per mile. There was thus a constant incentive to exceed the speed limit, especially if they were delayed by a breakdown or by other traffic. Chicken was therefore by no means the only driver to be reported and fined for 'speeding'. The record, apparently, was put up by driver Charles Tennison who covered the forty-mile journey from Shildon to Stockton and back, including stops, in $4\frac{1}{2}$ hours. For this feat he was instantly dismissed.

The locomotives had to stop several times en route to replenish the water barrels on their tenders, but it was driver George Sunter's boast that he could make the through trip without once stopping his train. His technique was to drop his fireman as they were approaching a watering place and order him to uncouple the leading wagon from his tender, which done he would open his regulator and make all speed to the water tank. This performance was so timed that Sunter had filled his water barrel and was moving slowly ahead once more by the time his train, lumbering slowly along on the falling grade with his fireman perched on the brake handle of the leading wagon, caught up with him.

The crude inside-bearings of the chaldron wagons were incapable of running a full journey from Shildon to Stockton without attention, and to cope with this without loss of time, Graham tells us, another hazardous expedient was practised. Having slowed down the train to walking pace, both driver and fireman would drop off the locomotive, one on each side, and proceed back along the train, attending to the bearings with brushes dipped in tins of oil. The only snag to this performance was that sometimes the train responded to the lubrication by rapid acceleration. "They would have to run to get on", said Graham, "but with a loaded train they would climb on the last wagon and go back over the coal."

With anecdotes such as these in mind, how easy it is to imagine the yarns that were spun and the arguments that must have been waged in the first of all 'footplate parliaments', the tap room of 'The Globe' at Shildon. It was the custom to pay the drivers on the Friday following the second Tuesday in each month, and over the saturnalia that marked these monthly pay nights it were best to draw a veil. On one such occasion Graham, arriving late, surprised the company endeavouring to cook their pocket watches in a frying pan over the tap-room fire. A few years later when Robert Stephenson & Co. built to Hackworth's design the first light four-coupled locomotive intended for passenger train working on the railway, Hackworth named it *The Globe*. It has always been assumed that the name referred to this engine's spherical copper steam dome, but no matter what Hackworth's intention may have been, we may be certain the name meant something else to the drivers.

If the events just described had taken place on a double line of railway exclusively reserved for locomotives they would have been quite enough to turn any Traffic Superintendent's hair white. Yet poor John Graham had far more to contend with than this. Not only was the line single and without signals or any other form of train control, but it was a public highway continually occupied not only by numerous 'bye traders' working horse-hauled coal trains but also by no fewer than six firms of coach proprietors who operated the *Experiment* and other horse-drawn passenger coaches to a daily timetable. The loaded horse-drawn coal trains ran by gravity where the gradient permitted, the horse riding in a special wagon coupled at the rear of the train which was called a dandy cart. The barrister, Thomas Shaw Brandreth, who subsequently produced the curious horse-propelled locomotive *Cycloped* at Rainhill, apparently claimed the credit for introducing the dandy cart, but in a letter to Timothy Hackworth dated 25 July 1828 George Stephenson wrote: "It appears that Brandreth has got my plan introduced for horses to ride, which, I suppose, he will set off as his own invention. It is more than two years since I explained this to Brandreth. Canterbury was the place where I meant to have put it to use but as that Company have now determined to work the line by steam power it will not be wanted."

It is clear from this letter that dandy carts were not used at the outset on the Stockton & Darlington, but when they were introduced we are told that the mileage covered by one horse in a week increased on an average from 174 to 240 miles. Leaving Shildon with a normal load of four loaded wagons, the horse rode in the dandy for three miles to the foot of Simpasture. Then it hauled the train over the Aycliffe level, mounted the dandy once more at Aycliffe Lane and coasted to the Darlington Junction. From this point there was a three-mile pull to Fighting Cocks, then a two-mile coast to Goosepool, then another two-mile pull to Urlay Nook, and finally a coast from Urlay Nook into Stockton. Returning with empty trains the horse had to pull all the way. So accustomed did the horses become to this procedure that the driver had only to unhook the traces and the horse would trot back to the end of the train and jump into the dandy without more ado. According to Tomlinson, dandy carts continued in use on the Throckley wagonway, near Newburn, until 1907.

As first built there were four passing-places to the mile on the Stockton & Darlington. Here the passenger coaches had the right of way, both locomotive and horse-drawn coal trains having to take to the loops to let them pass. Similarly, horse-drawn coal trains had to give way to locomotives. Midway between each passing loop a lineside post was erected, the rule being that when two trains met in mid section, the train which had passed the post had the right of way, the other being compelled to retreat until a passing loop was reached.

Conditions more difficult for locomotive working would be impossible to conceive. The Shildon drivers, not unnaturally, considered themselves the kings of the road and were, in the words of Robert Stephenson, "not the most manageable class of beings". On the other hand, the horse-leaders were a tough and truculent gang, not infrequently tipsy. Consequently a permanent state of war prevailed on the line which not infrequently reduced traffic movement to chaos. When the two rivals confronted each other head-on between passing loops it was often a case of the irresistible force meeting the immovable object. Here are a few examples from John Graham's reports to illustrate the sort of thing that went on.

Two horse-drivers refused to allow a steam train to pass them by entering the loops and forced it to follow them for four miles. On the same day another driver shunted some wagons so violently that his horse was pitched out of the dandy cart and fell down the Myers Flat embankment.

Three horse-drivers left their trains blocking the line at Spring Gardens while they went off to a neighbouring pub for a two-hour drinking session.

Ralph Hill met a locomotive train and absolutely refused to give way although the engine had passed the midway post. He was told not to bring his horse on the railway again and was summoned to appear before the magistrates.

One foggy morning, Thomas Sanderson, who was evidently suffering from a hangover, left his horse while it was hauling a train of empties and retired to the dandy cart behind to sleep it off.

He was rudely awakened when a locomotive ran into the rear of the dandy cart and was derailed. The line was blocked for two hours.

Two horse-drivers, William Ogle and George Hodgson, left Shildon in such a roaring state of drunkenness that Ogle continued to drive his horse at a gallop regardless of the fact that the dandy cart had jumped the rails and was tearing up the track. They forced another horse-driver whom they met to go back into a loop and overturned his empty wagons. Finally this precious pair met a steam train and, refusing to give way, tore up a rail, threatening to throw the engine off the line.

Such were the trials and tribulations which constantly beset the world's first railway Traffic Superintendent and handicapped the steam locomotive in its fight for recognition. To cope with this impossible situation the passing loops were progressively lengthened until by 1830 it was reported that there was a "gradual approxima-tion to a double line of railway." Soon afterwards the line was completely doubled and it must have been with profound relief that John Graham was able to report in April 1833 that on the main line all coal traffic was now being 'led' by locomotives.

It soon became evident that some improvement must be made to the Company's goods rolling-stock. Apart from the frequent breakage of wheels, the old unsprung chaldron wagons proved quite unsuitable for general merchandise, which was either damaged or flung out on to the lineside. Accordingly, on 27 November 1828 Robert Stephenson & Co. supplied to the Railway the first wagon to be fitted with springs and outside bearings in axle boxes. This was the prototype of the standard British goods wagon and two years later the same wagons were being supplied to the Liverpool & Manchester Railway. A similar design was used for the first pas-senger-coach frames, but in the introduction of steam-hauled passenger trains the Stockton & Darlington followed and did not lead.

Throughout these first critical years George Stephenson con-tinued to act as consulting engineer to the Company although he was not able to devote much time to the railway owing to his preoccupations elsewhere. He did, however, visit the line between July and September 1827 to make a preliminary survey for a proposed extension of the railway from Stockton over the Tees to a new terminus "in a close adjoining the River Tees, in the township of Leventhorpe or Middlesburgh" where it was proposed to make a new dock and erect coal staithes. This project was the result of the failure of the Tees Navigation Company to meet repeated requests from the railway proprietors for the improvement of the river up to Stockton.

On the basis of George Stephenson's report, which was received on 22 September, J. U. Rastrick carried out a detailed survey and estimates were then prepared by the Company's own engineer, Thomas Storey. The Act for the extension received the Royal Assent the following May, despite opposition from the Navigation Company and representatives of the town of Stockton, including such pioneer supporters of the Company as Leonard Raisbeck and the Chairman, Thomas Meynell of Yarm, both of whom resigned from the Board.

The only important engineering work involved on this extension was the bridge over the Tees where the Navigation Company had made things as awkward as possible by stipulating that the river should not be obstructed by piers. The Company engaged Captain Brown, the early exponent of suspension bridges, to design a bridge upon his plan, but the result was a complete failure. Quite unsuitable for the passage of locomotive-hauled coal trains, the bridge platform had to be shored up and locomotives forbidden to use it. A protracted wrangle with Captain Brown over payment was eventually submitted to Losh for arbitration. This unsatisfactory bridge has sometimes been attributed to the Stephensons, whereas in fact Robert Stephenson undertook its replacement in 1842. Years later, Robert would refer to his experience of the first Stockton bridge when he was contemplating the best design for his own great railway bridge over the Menai Straits. "Immediately on opening the suspension bridge for railway traffic," he wrote, "the undulations into which the roadway was thrown, by the inevitable unequal distribution of the weight of the train upon it, were such as to threaten the instant downfall of the whole structure." This Middlesbrough Extension was opened to traffic on 27 December 1830. The town of Middlesbrough grew from that event, while the river trade of Stockton gradually declined as had that of Bewdley on the Severn after the completion of Brindley's canal to Stourport.

There is no need to follow the fortunes of the Stockton & Darlington beyond the opening of the line to Middlesbrough, but before leaving the railway two very important additions to the Company's locomotive stock must be mentioned. These were the *Royal George* and the *Experiment* of 1827, the former designed and built by Timothy Hackworth at Shildon and the latter by George Stephenson at Newcastle.

Before this date the only addition to the four original Stephenson locomotives was an engine which the Company purchased second-hand on Hackworth's recommendation from Robert Wilson of Newcastle. Few details of this engine are known, but it proved a failure and the peculiar noises it made when working led the men at Shildon shed to name it the *Chitaprat*. Apparently it had a return-flue boiler of large dimensions, and Hackworth decided to make use of this to build a locomotive of his own design at Shildon. Two vertical cylinders were mounted above and upon either side of this boiler at the end opposite the chimney and firedoor. The locomotive was mounted on six coupled wheels, power being applied directly to the rear pair by short vertical connecting rods and crank-pins. A drawback to this arrangement was that this driving axle had to be unsprung and that the power impulses, acting vertically, must have been very hard on the track. The two leading coupled axles had compensated plate-springs. The controls were so arranged that the driver stood on a footplate behind the boiler instead of on that precarious perch beside it, but owing to the use of a return-flue boiler he was even further removed from his fireman, who was stationed at the chimney end. The boiler feed-pump was under the driver's control so that the water tender was at his end of the engine and the coal tender at the other. There was a Shildon legend to the effect that on an occasion of emergency a driver once took such an engine from Stockton to Shildon single-handed. He must have been a busy man and a remarkably athletic one.

This engine, the *Royal George*, began working in November 1827 in charge of driver William Gowland and at once proved a triumph for Hackworth. It was undoubtedly the most powerful locomotive in existence at that date and it became the prototype of a number of heavy coal engines produced for the railway by Hackworth at

Shildon. But the success of the *Royal George* has been used in conjunction with the rumoured failure of the earlier Stephenson engines to the disparagement of George Stephenson. It has been said that the *Royal George* was the first truly practical steam locomotive and that it was her performance alone which persuaded the Company not to abandon steam traction in favour of horses. This is quite untrue. It has already been shown that the Company had proved the superiority of locomotives over horses before the *Royal George* appeared, while comparative records made afterwards show that, allowing for their smaller size, the older Stephenson engines were giving as good an account of themselves as their larger sister. These champions of Timothy Hackworth have also been guilty of distorting the facts about Stephenson's *Experiment* and claiming that she was a failure.

The *Experiment* represented the first attempt to break away from the vertical cylinder convention which had held the field ever since the Blenkinsop & Murray rack engine had appeared. Instead, Stephenson returned to Trevithick practice by mounting the two cylinders horizontally in one end of the boiler. By means of levers with slotted links, the piston rods actuated a rocking shaft mounted in a massive cast-iron bracket above and behind the boiler barrel. On the overhung ends of this rocking shaft were two more levers which drove crank-pins on the leading driving wheels by means of very long inclined connecting rods. Because of the action of these levers and connecting rods the men of Shildon appropriately nicknamed the engine "Old Elbows". The boiler of *Experiment* was of the single flue type, but water tube fire-bars and an internal water drum were introduced to increase the heating surface, while George Stephenson also provided an exhaust steam feedwater heater.

According to Hackworth's biographer, Robert Young, the *Experiment* was Stephenson's unsuccessful reply to the challenge of the *Royal George*, but in fact the report of the two Prussian mining engineers describes the *Experiment* as they saw her, complete, in the Newcastle works early in 1827; some months, that is, before the *Royal George* made her first appearance. Precisely when the engine was sent to Shildon is not known. There is no record of her on the Stockton & Darlington before January 1828, and it is possible that she may have worked experimentally on the Killingworth Railway under Wood's supervision during 1827. As sent to Shildon, the locomotive was on four wheels, but the axle load was found to be too great for the track and in March a new six-wheeled frame was ordered from Robert Stephenson & Co. into which her machinery could be fitted. She then became a six wheels coupled engine like the *Royal George* but with this very important difference: the gentle inclination of the connecting rods on the *Experiment* made it practicable to use springs on the driving axle so that for the first time a locomotive was produced which was fully sprung on plate-springs.

Robert Young tells us that 'the engine was looked on as a general nuisance which got into everybody's way' and that she was driven by Michael Law 'one of the best drivers on the line, whose labours evoked the ironical sympathy of his companions'. Yet elsewhere in his book Young himself contradicts this impression of failure when he quotes the drivers' earnings for March 1828. As these wages were based on tonnage hauled, they form a guide to locomotive performance. In this month Gowland of the *Royal George* headed the list with £37 8s 11d but Law came next with £22 18s 1d. During the whole of this year, Gowland earned £344 19s 7d net and Law £269 15s 10d, but as the latter worked twenty-five days less—perhaps because *Experiment* was being rebuilt on her new frames—the difference in their average daily earnings was only 3s 7d, Law's being again the second highest figure. According to these records, therefore, George Stephenson's *Experiment* was very far from being an ignominious failure but ranked second in performance to the *Royal George*.

When Robert Stephenson established himself in Newcastle in 1828 these two locomotives, one in being and the other about to emerge from Shildon, represented the peak of locomotive development. But both, though more successful than their predecessors, were blind alleys of design and did not foreshadow the ultimate form which the locomotive would take. During Robert Stephenson's absence abroad Timothy Hackworth was undoubtedly the most successful and progressive locomotive engineer, but a close parallel may be drawn between his achievement and that of Carl Benz in the field of automobile engineering many years later. Both men, having evolved a reasonably successful and reliable machine, became conservative and clung to it too long, with the result that they were outpaced by other more progressive designers. With the exception of his *Globe*, Hackworth stuck to his *Royal George* design, which was well suited for working heavy coal traffic at slow speed but quite unsuitable for the task that the two Stephensons envisaged—the swift transport over long distances of both passengers and goods.[1] So it was that in 1828 the initiative passed from Hackworth back to the Stephensons, and it was from their works at Forth Street, Newcastle, that the true prototype of the modern locomotive very rapidly emerged.

[1] As late as 1846 a six-coupled goods locomotive with a return-flue boiler was built at Shildon by Hackworth.

CHAPTER EIGHT

The Battle for the Locomotive

ON HIS RETURN from South America, Robert Stephenson at once plunged back into railway affairs. With his father fully occupied on the Liverpool & Manchester, he took over responsibility for the Canterbury & Whitstable railway.[1] This and other business concerns involved much journeying to and fro, but he made his headquarters in Newcastle and it was here that he devoted the major share of his thought, his time and his energy to two closely related tasks: the revival of the sagging fortunes of the Newcastle works and the improvement of the steam locomotive. So well did he succeed that within a few years the name of Robert Stephenson & Company became famous throughout the world and for long retained that fame in the face of strenuous competition from other locomotive builders.

If those historic workshops at Forth Street which gave birth to the locomotive as we know it could be revisited, we should marvel at the quality of the workmanship produced there with the absolute minimum of equipment. One small steam engine with a sixteen-inch cylinder, which is still preserved, was enough to drive the few lathes, the planers and the drilling, punching and plate-shearing machines. Otherwise everything was done by hand. Wheels were driven on to their axles by sledge hammers and until 1837 there was not even a crane in the works. All heavy lifting was done by means of portable shear-legs and pulley blocks. Although wonders were performed with this primitive equipment, they involved taking

---

[1] Another minor railway undertaking with which George Stephenson was associated at this early period was the Nantlle Railway in North Wales which was authorized in May 1825. It ran from the Cloddfarlon Slate Quarries to Caernarvon quay, the gauge was 3ft 6ins and it was built for horse-haulage. George Stephenson sent his brother Robert and his assistant Gillespie (who later worked on the Leicester & Swannington) to North Wales to superintend, and letters from Robert to George at Liverpool are preserved in the Phillimore Collection (see bibliography). The elder Robert was also responsible for laying out the Bolton and Leigh line.

big risks and there were frequent accidents. It was a source of great grief to George Stephenson that in two such accidents both his brother John and his brother-in-law Stephen Liddell were fatally injured. He tried to make amends by supporting their widows and children out of his own income.

While locomotive development had so far been a monopoly of the North of England, engineers in the south, particularly in London, were pursuing a different goal—the steam road-carriage. In this way there grew up two quite different schools of design, both stemming originally from the genius of Richard Trevithick. Although in his single-minded championship of the railway locomotive George Stephenson scorned the efforts of the road-carriage builders, in fact their designs were in many respects more advanced. Less prejudiced than his father, Robert Stephenson had the good sense to realize this, with the result that the steam carriage had an important influence on locomotive development which is too little recognized. A close parallel may be drawn here between the road-carriage builders and the first aeronautical engineers. The absolute necessity of saving weight forced both to abandon precedents and evolve entirely original designs. By doing so they might fail, but their influence on contemporary engineering practice was wholly salutary. Just as aeronautical engineers hastened the motor car's escape from the horseless-carriage and road-locomotive conventions, so the work of the steam-carriage builders helped the makers of railway locomotives to escape once for all from that cumbersome stationary steam-engine tradition which had made Hedley's Wylam Dilly little more than a perambulating beam engine.

On New Year's Day 1828 Robert Stephenson despatched from Liverpool a letter to Longridge which is of the utmost importance because it sets forth the basis of the design policy which he was about to pursue at Newcastle.

Since I came down from London [he writes] I have been talking a great deal to my father about endeavouring to reduce the size and ugliness of our travelling-engines, by applying the engine either on the side of the boiler or beneath it entirely, somewhat similarly to Gurney's steam-coach. He has agreed to an alteration which I think will considerably reduce the quantity of machinery as well as the liability to mismanagement. Mr. Jos. Pease writes my father that in their present complicated state they cannot be managed by 'fools', therefore they must undergo some alteration or amendment. It is very true that the locomotive engine . . . may be shaken to pieces; but such accidents are in a great measure under the control of the enginemen, which are, by the by, not the most manageable class of beings. They perhaps want improvement as much as the engines. . . . There are three new steam-coaches going on with, all much on the same principle as Gurney's.

The *Experiment* had broken away from the vertical-cylinder convention only by means of a cumbrous rocking shaft and levers. It was Robert Stephenson's aim to combine the advantage of horizontal or inclined cylinders with that of direct drive to crank-pins on the wheels. The Liverpool & Manchester Railway Company very soon gave him the chance to try out his ideas, for at their meeting on 7 January 1828 the directors decided to order a loco-motive to assist in the construction of the line. This was at first referred to at Newcastle as 'the Liverpool Travelling-engine', but in April the railway company decided that their order had been premature and it was transferred by mutual agreement to the Bolton & Leigh Railway Company whose line was nearer completion. The engine was duly delivered, and when that railway was opened with due pomp on 8 August it drew a train of forty tons up an adverse gradient. The wife of the Chairman of the Company, Mrs. Hulton, attached a garland of flowers to the chimney of the locomotive and proclaimed: "No one can observe without admira-tion this beautiful engine, I therefore beg leave to name it after an object universally attractive—*The Lancashire Witch*."

Although Hackworth's *Royal George* has often been represented as upholding the honour of the locomotive alone until the appear-ance of the *Rocket*, in fact the *Lancashire Witch* was unquestionably more advanced. Within a few months of his return, Robert Stephen-son had robbed Hackworth of his brief leadership in design. The engine rested on four coupled wheels, the leaders being directly driven by two outside cylinders inclined at an angle of 45° above the rear axle. This inclination enabled both axles to be sprung, an immense advantage which was the chief aim of the design. The slide valves were driven by the usual slip eccentrics but in addition there was a rotary plug valve in the main steam pipe which was driven by bevel gears from the rear axle. This controlled the period of steam admission to the cylinders or, in locomotive parlance, it enabled the cut-off to be varied, which meant that the *Lancashire Witch* was the first locomotive in the world which could be worked expansively.

The success of the *Lancashire Witch* was such that Robert Stephenson designed and built at Newcastle during 1828-9 several locomotives, some on four and some on six coupled wheels, all with the same arrangement of inclined cylinders and sprung axles. One of these was sent to the United States to the order of Horatio Allen for the Delaware & Hudson Canal Company, and its cylinders are preserved in the Smithsonian Institution at Washington. Of the two six-wheeled engines built, one went to Samuel Homfray's Tredegar Ironworks and the other, the *Twin Sisters*, to the Liverpool & Manchester Railway where it assisted in the construction work.

While these locomotives were similar in their mechanical layout, the great diversity of their boilers shows that in this vital steam-raising department no truly satisfactory solution had been reached. As a locomotive engineer, the wisest thing George Stephenson ever said was in reply to Alderson during the ordeal of his long cross-examination on the Liverpool & Manchester Bill. When Alderson tried to pin him down on the horse-power of his engines he replied: "It is the size of the boiler that denotes the strength of the engine." If this sounds like a statement of the obvious, it should be explained that for half a century and more after Stephenson's death engineers would quote tractive-effort figures for locomotives with boilers quite incapable of sustaining such a performance. It is quite clear, then, that both Stephensons were fully alive to the vital importance of steaming capacity. The different types of boiler fitted to these engines represent their attempts to obtain freer steaming by increasing the heating surface in boilers of the 'straight through' type which they still greatly preferred to the return-flue boiler favoured by Hackworth. The *Twin Sisters* was so called because on this locomotive they tried the effect of twin vertical boilers with two smoke stacks. There is no need here to enter into any further technical detail because all these boilers proved to be blind alleys in design.

When the *Lancashire Witch* was first delivered, George Stephenson used the engine to make experiments on the effect of a forced draught through the fire by installing a large pair of bellows worked mechanically. This experiment was to be duly seized upon by the champions of Timothy Hackworth as proving that even at this late date Stephenson still did not appreciate the principle of the steam blast. Such an assertion assumes a quite incredible stupidity. What Hackworth's supporters do not reveal is that this, like other experiments made by the Stephensons at this time, was prompted by a clause in the Liverpool & Manchester Railway Act which laid down that all engines used on the line must consume their own smoke. When the same clause appeared in later railway Acts it was more honoured in the breach than in the observance, but at this time, when the locomotive was still on trial, it was taken very seriously. At Shildon, Timothy Hackworth had no legal restriction of this kind to worry about, though it may well have been the smoke and cinders which invariably heralded the approach of a Shildon locomotive that had caused this clause to be inserted in the Liverpool & Manchester Bill. For the Stephensons it meant re-designing their boilers to burn coke and making that much-derided experiment with the bellows which was obviously undertaken in the belief that by forcing more air below the fire there should be more complete combustion and therefore less smoke.

At this point we must leave the locomotive for a while to review progress on the Liverpool & Manchester Railway, where the time was fast approaching when the all-important question of motive power must be finally decided.

Notwithstanding the fact that George Stephenson had succeeded in getting the entire engineering responsibility for the railway under his control, the progress of construction was still marked by human as well as physical difficulties. It is evident that Stephenson continued to regard his assistant engineers—Dixon, Allcard and Locke—as employees of George Stephenson & Son and therefore exclusively under his orders. This being so they—and this applies to Locke especially—were often absent on other railway survey work on George Stephenson's instructions. As the Railway Directors had agreed in July 1826 to pay Locke a salary of £400 a year, they understandably reacted to this by insisting that he should work exclusively for the Liverpool & Manchester. In his reply (1829) Stephenson objected vigorously. He declared that he had stipulated when he was appointed that he should have absolute responsibility for the appointment and control of his assistants. Moreover, Stephenson went on, he had thought that this was clearly understood in the case of Vignoles where he had refused to employ him although urged by the Board to take him. He had then said that the Board could employ Vignoles themselves if they wished, but they had withdrawn him. Now, if the Board objected to Locke's absence, he, George Stephenson, would agree to Locke's permanent withdrawal.

Now in the absence of Locke, who was nominally in charge of the western section of the line, responsibility for the great tunnel at Edgehill fell directly upon George Stephenson. This tunnel, it will be remembered, had been the pretext for Vignoles' dismissal, but things were still going badly there. The vertical shafts were sunk as much as 20ft off the correct line with the result that cross tunnels had to be cut from the foot of these shafts to the true line. Moreover, it was said that the cutting of the pilot tunnel was so inaccurate that at one point the two approaching borings would have missed each other altogether if they had been allowed to proceed. There was also at least one serious fall in the tunnel due to inadequate centering. Remembering the circumstances of Vignoles dismissal and piqued by their chief engineer's intransigent attitude, the Board took the irregular step of ordering Locke directly to make a survey and report on the tunnel works. This placed the unfortunate Locke in a most delicate position, but he obeyed the Directors and produced a report which was, in all honesty, highly critical of the tunnel works. George Stephenson was furious, and although Joseph Locke continued for a time to work under Stephenson's direction, relations between master and pupil became strained. Whether George Stephenson had already carried out his threat to withdraw Locke permanently before the latter made his report is not clear, but it is certain that Locke was not employed on the railway after his report was made though he played a part at the opening ceremony. In his stead, George Stephenson ordered Thomas Gooch to take charge of the tunnel.

Evidently rumours reached George Stephenson's partners in Newcastle that Locke's services had been lost to them, for Stephenson writes to Longridge on 8 February 1830 assuring him that "Locke has not withdrawn himself from me" and explaining that he had sent him to survey a line to Stockport to which neither he nor Robert could find time to attend.

One very odd episode which occurred while the Edgehill tunnel was building may be mentioned here because it adds a welcome note of comic relief to the depressing story of the clash of personalities which marred its history. George Stephenson was making an inspection of the tunnel one day when he was astounded to hear an echoing voice hailing him from the gloom of the arch above his head. Holding up his lantern, what should he see but the beaming face of an elderly gentleman peering down at him through a hole in the tunnel roof. It transpired that the interloper was an eccentric who lived nearby and who had become infected by the neighbouring works with such a mania for tunnelling that he had hired workmen to dig tunnels underneath his grounds. His enthusiasm upon thus unexpectedly encountering his more famous brother mole knew no bounds, but it is doubtful whether Stephenson was equally cordial.

Although operations had started on Chat Moss in June 1826 and on the tunnel in September, it was not until January 1827 that work was begun on the rest of the line, which included the great rock-cutting at Olive Mount and the Sankey Viaduct. According to the minutes of the directors' meetings, in addition to the capital raised by calls on the shareholders, a loan of £10,000 from the Exchequer had been arranged in May 1827 under the terms of the Exchequer Loan Bill, but towards the end of 1828 a further application was made. Before granting this, the Exchequer Loan Bill Commissioners requested their engineer, Thomas Telford, to carry out an inspection and to make a report. Telford sent his assistant, James Mills, to Liverpool in November with instructions to report to him weekly, and from these reports we can form an idea of the state of the works at this time and how they were organized.

George Stephenson's reaction to this investigation goes without saying. Telford's earlier and repeated requests for copies of the plans and sections had been ignored, and on his arrival James Mills discovered that the only plans and sections existing were those prepared by Vignoles for the Rennies. He made a copy of these for Telford by the grace of the only responsible man on the site who would give him any assistance—Tom Gooch. Stephenson was 'out' where the unfortunate Mills was concerned and he had to pick up

the information for his reports as best he could by talking to the
men on the works. He told Telford:

> There does not appear to be a single contract existing on the whole line.
> Stevenson [sic] seems to be contractor for the whole and to employ all
> the different people at such prices as he thinks proper to give them, the
> Company *finding all materials*, not only rails and waggons but even
> *wheelbarrows* and planks etc. There is some difficulty in making out the
> value of what is to do. . . . The first men I asked as to price said: 'I have
> no fixed price or specified distance to take the stuff (spoil); Mr. S. gives
> 8 pence, 10 pence or 13 pence as he thinks it deserves.' I asked him how
> far he was to do the cutting, he said nothing was fixed, he might go 20
> yards further or half a mile. It is the same with the masonry—the
> Company find every material and let it from 1s 6d to 6s per yard for
> labour.

In his next report to Telford, James Mills gives his chief some
more explicit information. Having explained how the thirty miles
of line were divided into three equal districts under Locke, Allcard,
and Dixon (he spells it Dyson) he goes on: "Each has 200 day men
employed and pay them every fortnight as *Company's* men for laying temporary roads, moving planks, making wheelbarrows,
driving piles and, in short, doing *every thing* but putting the stuff
into the carts and barrows which is done by a set of men which is
also under their direction and to whom they pay $3\frac{1}{2}$ per yard to 5s
as they think it deserves."

Telford must have raised his eyebrows when he received this
information. Here was a civil engineering work of the first magnitude being carried out by an organization utterly different from that
contract system which he had himself brought to perfection during
long years of experience as an engineer of canals and roads. An
arrangement whereby the Engineer-in-Chief of such an undertaking also acted as contractor for the whole work with the assistance of a body of the Company's employees paid at day rate,
would seem to Telford highly improper and fraught with opportunities for abuse. What seems even stranger to us is that this system
was also clean contrary to that which George Stephenson had
himself recommended and employed for the building of the
Stockton & Darlington Railway. In that case the Company had
actually invited him to be both Chief Engineer and contractor and

he had very properly explained to them why he should not act in both capacities. "Were I to contract for the whole line of road", he had written, "it would be necessary for me to do so at an advanced price upon the Sub-Contractors, and it would also be necessary for the Committee to have some person to superintend my undertaking. This would be attended with an extra expence, and the Committee would derive no advantage to compensate for it." Yet here was Stephenson, not only acting as engineer and contractor but strenuously resisting any move by the Company to appoint 'a person to superintend his undertaking'.

How can such a complete contradiction be explained? Michael Longridge and his Quaker associates Thomas Richardson and the Peases evidently had a low opinion of the two Stephensons as business men, but though he may have lacked their subtlety, George Stephenson showed himself a man of the highest principles in all his dealings with the Stockton & Darlington Company. Stephenson may have had grave faults. That he was obstinate, jealous and egotistical has already been made apparent, but such defects are not sufficient to explain that conduct of the affairs of the Liverpool & Manchester Railway which reveals him in so unfavourable a light. The inevitable conclusion must be that so far as George Stephenson was concerned the formation of 'George Stephenson & Son' was a most unholy alliance. It seems clear that in forming this Company in his name at the moment when the first short-lived wave of railway speculation was at its height, George Stephenson's shrewd Quaker partners were determined to exploit his talents to the full and did not scruple to play upon his own weaknesses to this end. The Company's indenture specifically states that its function should be to engage not merely in railway surveying and superintendence but in railway engineering also. This attempt to monopolize the whole business of railway construction in the interests of maximum profit, ignored all those ethical safeguards hitherto implicit in the relationship between engineer and contractor which Telford had defined and which Stephenson himself had hitherto upheld. It was bound to fail, and the dark cloud of criticism, ill-will and recrimination which surrounds George Stephenson's association with the Liverpool & Manchester Railway was undoubtedly caused by his efforts to carry out a mistaken policy laid down for him by his partners. In this we

should not be too hard upon him. He was not the first, and by no
means the last, eminent engineer to be beguiled by the sophistries
of so-called astute business men and to become the scapegoat of
their machinations. On the contrary, it is a measure of his greatness
that he was able to rise above all the faults and mistakes which
antagonized the entire engineering profession. Almost to a man his
fellow engineers dismissed him as an unprincipled and incompetent
schemer, but all their shafts broke against the armour of that stubborn determination to succeed which was to triumph over every
obstacle, including his own weaknesses.

Angered by the discourtesy shown to his assistants and alarmed
by the reports which Mills had sent him, Telford decided that he
must visit Liverpool himself. His arrival in January 1829 was an
occasion which even George Stephenson could not afford to ignore
however much he might resent it. He personally conducted Telford
and the assistant whom he had hitherto slighted over the whole
line. One would dearly like to know what passed between the two
men on this occasion, the one denounced and disowned by the
engineering profession, the other the acknowledged doyen of that
profession, first President of the Institution of Civil Engineers and
therefore king of that established order which Stephenson affected
to scorn.

For Telford, aged seventy-two and in failing health, the inspection
was an exhausting ordeal. "To accomplish [it]", he afterwards
wrote, "upon a line of thirty miles in the present unfinished and
complex state of the works was a tedious and laborious task."
Telford reported to the Commissioners that the tunnel at Edgehill,
2,250 yards long, 22ft wide and 16ft high was nearly complete but
that a great deal of excavation had still to be done between the
tunnel and Waverton Lane. He estimated that the 'great embankment' at Broad Green was unlikely to be finished before 1830 at the
present rate of progress. He found that the Sankey viaduct was
two-thirds finished and that nineteen bridges had been completed
'in a very perfect manner'. But there were thirty-nine still to build
which, again, were unlikely to be completed before 1830. He
estimated that over £200,000 would be required to complete the
railway. He was at a loss to know, Telford concluded, how the line
would be worked. He understood that the original intention was to

have four roads worked by horse traction, these to be free to the public on payment of tolls. In the present state of the works and the general uncertainty of aim he could not recommend a loan from public funds.

Telford's mystification was quite understandable. Even at this late hour the Company still had not made up their own minds as to how the line should be worked, but this did not prevent them issuing a printed circular bitterly critical of Telford's report. This provoked a stinging retort from the old engineer in which he declared that the works were being carried out without a proper survey and on no proper, businesslike system. His reason for making the first allegation was that to save earthworks Stephenson had introduced inclined planes at Whiston and Sutton in place of the level road surveyed by Vignoles for the Rennies. Whether it was intended to work the lines with horses or with locomotives, Telford insisted, it would have been better and more economical in working to stick to the level road. In this Telford was undoubtedly right and the compromise eventually reached, which involved the working of steam locomotives on steep gradients, was contrary to the policy of level roads that George Stephenson himself was later to advocate.

Because a capital loan was badly needed, neither the Company nor their engineer could afford to quarrel with Telford, who held the purse strings of the Loan Commissioners. They took steps to set their house in order and to settle once for all the vexed question of motive power. Alarmed by the way the works were dragging on, the Company persuaded a reluctant Stephenson, at the end of the year, to make an Affidavit by which he bound himself to complete the railway in 1830 at a cost which he estimated at £58,500. Telford on his side withdrew his disapproval, with the effect that altogether the sum of £100,000 was loaned to the Company by the Exchequer Loan Bill Commissioners.

Meanwhile the celebrated battle for the locomotive had been well and truly joined. Despite all George Stephenson's untiring advocacy of the locomotive there had grown up on the Liverpool & Manchester Board a strong body of opinion which was in favour of haulage, not by horses, but by fixed haulage engines. To this Stephenson was resolutely opposed. Now in view of Stephenson's use of inclined planes at this period this may seem inconsistent. He had built his first self-acting inclined plane on the Killingworth railway many years before; he had built planes with fixed-engine haulage on the Stockton & Darlington, had recommended them on the Canterbury & Whitstable line, and was now proposing to use them again. But it must be borne in mind that Stephenson, like other engineers of the period, followed the canal precedent when planning a line of railway. For the canal engineer's flight of locks he would substitute an inclined plane and for the level 'pound' of canal between locks he would have a length of railway which was either as nearly level as possible or falling with the load if, as on the Stockton & Darlington, the load was all one way. On such lengths of railway he championed locomotive haulage. What the dissidents on the Liverpool & Manchester board proposed to do was something quite different. They maintained that the whole thirty miles should be worked by a succession of fixed engines.

The first skirmish took place in November 1828 as a result of a visit paid to Darlington and Shildon in September by a deputation from the Liverpool & Manchester Board. "I am informed", wrote Edward Pease to Hackworth on the eve of this visitation, "that a deputation is coming from Liverpool to see our way, but more particularly to make enquiry about Locomotive power. Have the engines and men as neat and clean as can, and be ready with thy calculations, not only showing the saving, but how much more work they do in a given time. Have no doubt wilt do thy best to have all sided and in order in thy department."

Yet despite these efforts by Pease and Hackworth, the deputation, greatly to Stephenson's chagrin, reported in favour of fixed-haulage engines. Stephenson at once counter-attacked vigorously with a long and well reasoned report in favour of locomotives and pointing out the disadvantages of a chain of fixed engines. This document threw the directors into a fever of indecision in which they again put off the necessity to make up their minds by ordering yet another investigation. This time two experts, James Walker and J. U. Rastrick, were to be requested "to undertake a journey to Darlington, Newcastle and the neighbourhood to ascertain by actual inspection and investigation the comparative merits of Fixed Engines and Locomotives, as a moving power on Railways and

especially with reference to the Liverpool & Manchester Line. . . ."
To this end the co-operation of Benjamin Thompson of the Brunton
& Shields Railway was sought. Thompson, who was a confirmed
advocate of rope haulage, had previously carried on a heated newspaper controversy with Nicholas Wood, the latter, needless to say,
championing the locomotive.

When Walker and Rastrick presented their reports in March
1829, the Stephensons learned to their dismay that they had lost the
second round of the battle; Walker and Rastrick, like their predecessors, had reported in favour of fixed engines. Yet still the
Stephensons were not prepared to yield. "The report of Walker
and Rastrick has been received, but it is in favour of fixed engines",
wrote Robert Stephenson from Newcastle to an unnamed correspondent. "We are preparing for a counter-report in favour of
locomotives, which I believe still will ultimately get the day, but
from present appearances nothing decisive can be said: rely upon it,
locomotives shall not be cowardly given up. *I will fight for them until
the last*. They are worthy of a conflict."

Robert Stephenson also wrote a long letter to Hackworth asking
for his opinion on the outcome of the battle and received a heartening reply in which Hackworth said:

I hear the Liverpool Company have concluded to use fixed engines.
Some will look on with surprise. . . . Do not discompose yourself my
dear Sir; if you express your manly, firm, decided opinion, you have
done your part as their adviser. And if it happens to be read some day
in the newspapers—'Whereas the Liverpool and Manchester Railway
has been strangled by ropes', we shall not accuse you of guilt in
being accessory either before or after the fact.

Robert Stephenson and Joseph Locke prepared a further counterblast in favour of the locomotive which elaborated the substance of
George Stephenson's earlier report to the Board and was eventually
published in 1830 under the title of *Observations on the Comparative
Merits of Locomotive and Fixed Engines*. Apart from arguing the
superior economy of locomotives and making a number of valid
points which now seem too obvious to be worth repeating, the most
telling argument in the Stephensons' case against rope haulage
was that the failure of only one link in the chain of stationary

haulage engines would bring all the traffic on the line to a standstill.

Fortunately there was still a strong party on the Railway Board, led by the Treasurer, Henry Booth, which advocated the locomotive. They seized upon the admission in the Walker and Rastrick report that there were grounds 'for expecting improvements in the construction and work of locomotives' and made most effective play with it. Why should not the Company stimulate such improvements by offering a prize for the best locomotive? In this way an improved engine might be available in time for the opening of the line. This suggestion appealed strongly to the sporting instincts of the Board. Moreover, smarting under Telford's recent strictures, they were anxious to show the world that they meant business where this question of motive power was concerned. So it was that on 20 April 1829 the momentous resolution was carried which led to the famous Rainhill Locomotive Trials for a prize of £500. This was to be the third and decisive round in the battle. By this trial the locomotive, and with it the reputations of George and Robert Stephenson, must stand or fall.

Like all great dramas the Rainhill Trials did not lack comic relief. No sooner had the directors published abroad their historic challenge than it was eagerly taken up by every aspiring mechanic, every crack-pot inventor, every misunderstood genius. In the words of Henry Booth himself:

> communications were received from all classes of persons . . . from professors of philosophy, down to the humblest mechanic all were zealous in their proffers of assistance. England, America and Continental Europe were alike tributary. Every element and almost every substance were brought into requisition and made subservient to the great work. The friction of the carriages was to be reduced so low that a silk thread would draw them, and the power to be applied was to be so vast as to rend a cable asunder. Hydrogen gas and high-pressure steam—columns of water and columns of mercury—a hundred atmospheres and a perfect vacuum—machines working in a circle without fire or steam, generating power at one end of the process and giving it out at the other . . . —wheels within wheels, to multiply speed without diminishing power —with every complication of balancing and countervailing forces, to the *ne plus ultra* of perpetual motion. Every scheme which the restless ingenuity or prolific imagination of man could devise was liberally offered to the Company; the difficulty was to choose and to decide.

Bewildering though this cabinet of curiosities must have been to the promoters of the competition, we, with the advantage of historical perspective, could have told them that the issue was, in fact, a simple one; that there were then only three schools of locomotive design in the world capable of putting a serious challenger into the field. One was at Newcastle, the second was at Shildon, and the third was in London.

On the last day of August the Directors resolved "That the place of tryal for the Specimen Engines on the 1st October next be the level space between the two inclined planes at Rainhill; and that the Engineer prepare a double Railway for the two miles of level, and a single line from Rainhill down the plane to the Roby Embankment." So were the time and the place determined.

Elaborate conditions and stipulations of eligibility were issued, the more important of which may be summarized as follows. Locomotives must be mounted on springs and weigh not more than six tons with water if carried on six wheels or not more than $4\frac{1}{2}$ tons if carried on four wheels. They must consume their own smoke. A six-ton locomotive must show itself capable of drawing 'day by day' a gross load of twenty tons at ten miles an hour, a five-ton locomotive fifteen tons and so on in proportion to weight. Steam pressure was not to exceed 50lb per square inch, but the Company reserved the right to test the boiler up to 150lb hydraulic. J. U. Rastrick, Nicholas Wood and John Kennedy were appointed to judge the contest and to determine the form of the trial.

During the summer of 1829 all Robert Stephenson's thoughts and energies were bent upon the design and construction of what was called 'the Premium Engine' upon which so much depended. So far as mechanical layout was concerned he decided to follow the general lines of his *Lancashire Witch* since she had proved so satisfactory. Instead of coupled wheels, however, the inclined cylinders drove single driving wheels 4 ft. 8 ins. in diameter, the rear wheels of 2 ft. 6 ins. diameter being merely carriers. There were two reasons behind this change. The first was to obtain greater speed and freer running. The second was that Robert had observed that the rate of wear on some wrought-iron wheel tyres could be so rapid that the wheels on one engine might be of substantially different diameters. As he pointed out, on locomotives with all wheels coupled, this meant

Northumbrian, the ultimate development
of the *Rocket* type, L. & M. R.,
August, 1830.

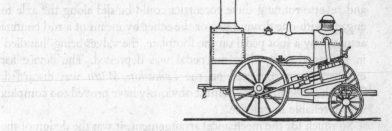

Planet, L. & M. R., October, 1830.

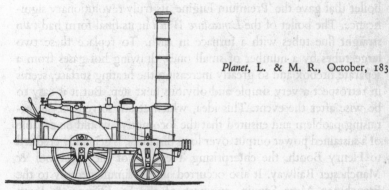

Harvey Combe, a refinement of
the *Patentee* of 1832 and the
first locomotive supplied to the
London & Birmingham Rail-
way, 1835.

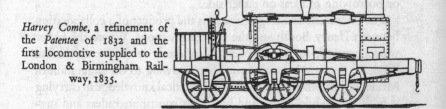

PROGRESS BY ROBERT STEPHENSON & CO., 1830–1835.
The locomotive finds definitive form.

a great deal of power loss and slipping which aggravated tyre wear.

Two loose eccentrics were mounted on the driving axle, these being driven by pegs screwed into the axle. To provide for forward and reverse running these eccentrics could be slid along the axle to engage with one driving peg or the other by means of a rod control actuated by a foot pedal on the footplate, the valves being 'handled' in the usual way while the pedal was depressed. The device for expansive working used on the *Lancashire Witch* was discarded. Though sound in theory it must obviously have proved too complex and unreliable in practice.

So much for the mechanical arrangement. It was the design of the boiler that gave the 'Premium Engine' its truly revolutionary significance. The boiler of the *Lancashire Witch* in its final form had two straight flue tubes with a furnace in each. To replace these two large tubes by a number of small ones, drawing hot gases from a separate firebox and so greatly increasing the heating surface, seems in retrospect a very simple and obvious next step. But it is easy to be wise after the event. This idea, which at last solved the steam-raising problem and ensured that the locomotive would be capable of a sustained power output over long distances, is generally credited to Henry Booth, the enterprising Treasurer of the Liverpool & Manchester Railway. It also occurred almost simultaneously to the Frenchman Marc Seguin, engineer of the St. Etienne & Lyon Railway to which Robert Stephenson & Co. supplied two loco-motives in 1828. Seguin had a multi-tubular boiler working before the Rainhill Trials, but he did not fit such a boiler to a locomotive until two months after and there is no evidence of any interchange or borrowing of ideas on either side.

The Newcastle challenger was thus the product of a collaboration between Henry Booth and the two Stephensons. Where the boiler was concerned, Robert Stephenson modestly wrote shortly before his death that it was 'more immediately owing to the suggestion of Mr. Henry Booth and to my father's practical knowledge in carrying it out'. But, while Booth and his father contributed ideas and sug-gestions from Liverpool, it was left to Robert and his staff at New-castle to give them practical shape. G. H. Phipps, a draughtsman at Forth Street, said in later life: "It must not be supposed that . . .

there were no difficulties to be overcome in the application of Mr. Booth's invention.... Having made the original drawings under Mr. Robert Stephenson, I can bear witness to the care and judgement bestowed by him upon every detail."

Twenty-five copper tubes three inches in diameter were used in this historic boiler. The water-jacketed firebox into which they fitted was a separate unit connected to the boiler barrel by copper pipes, while at the other end of the boiler there was not, properly speaking, any smoke-box, the base of the chimney being bellied out so that it covered the area of the tube-plate. In essentials, however, this was the prototype of the locomotive boiler used today. There was even a small steam dome on the top of the barrel from which the steam was drawn to ensure that it should be as dry as possible. The exhaust steam from the cylinders was led to two blast pipes in the chimney with $1\frac{1}{2}''$ orifices, only slightly smaller than the area of the exhaust ports. Robert Stephenson fitted a vacuum gauge to the expanded base of the chimney and found that this large opening produced quite satisfactory results. This point is important in view of allegations which were to be made later.

Robert Stephenson wrote to Henry Booth a series of letters reporting progress which are of the greatest interest but too lengthy to quote here verbatim. In the first, dated 3 August, he states that he hopes to have the engine working in the factory in three weeks. The firebox had not arrived, and as he hopes that Booth will despatch it as quickly as possible it was presumably made in or near Liverpool. He was naturally concerned to keep the locomotive within the weight limit and hopes the estimated weight of $2\frac{1}{2}$ tons on the driving axle which he considers desirable for adhesion will not be considered too high.

According to George and Robert Stephenson's biographers, Smiles and Jeaffreson, one of the greatest problems which had to be solved was how to secure the tubes in the tubeplates so that they would be steam-tight. They tell us that the ends of the tubes were at first threaded and secured by large nuts, an arrangement which proved a failure and reduced Robert almost to despair. His letters, however, make no reference to any such abortive scheme. His second letter, dated 21 August, reports that the tubes had all been 'clunk' (i.e. riveted) into the boiler, and that he hoped shortly to give the boiler an hydraulic test. The real trouble was that when pressure was put on the boiler the tube plates bulged outwards, breaking the caulked seals of the tube ends. In the interests of weight-saving the tube-plates were only $\frac{3}{8}''$ thick and were further weakened by the large holes made in them for the tubes. "The boiler end at 70 lb per sq. inch came out full $\frac{3}{16}$ of an inch", Robert told Booth on 26 August. "This you may easily conceive put a serious strain on the clinking at the tube ends." His answer to this was to put in a series of long stay rods between the two tube plates, and, after a further test, still more stays were put in before he was satisfied that the boiler would withstand the 150 lb test pressure which the Trial judges might require. Although he does not say so in his letters, later evidence suggests that wrought iron taper ferrules were driven into the ends of the tubes at the same time as an added precaution.

On 5 September Robert Stephenson was able to tell Booth that the new engine had had its first trial run.

I daresay you are getting anxious [he wrote], but I have delayed writing you until I tried the Engine on [the] Killingworth Railway. . . . The fire burns admirably and abundance of steam is raised when the fire is carefully attended to. This is an essential point because a coke fire when let down is bad to get up again; this rather prevented our experiment being so successful as it would have been throughout. We also found that from the construction of the working gear the Engine did not work so well in one direction as in the other, this will be remedied. . . . We started from Killingworth Pit, with five waggons each weighing four Tuns. Add to this the tender and 40 Men we proceeded up an ascent of 11 or 12 feet per Mile at 8 Miles per hour after we had fairly gained our speed.

We went three Miles on this Railway, the rate of ascents and descents my father knows—on a level part laid with Malleable Iron Rail, we attained a speed of 12 Miles per hour and without thinking that I deceived myself (I tried to avoid this), I believe the steam did not sink on this part. On the whole the Engine is capable of doing as much if not more than set forth in the stipulations. After a great deal of trouble and anxiety we have got the tubes perfectly tight. As requested by you in Mr. Locke's letter, I have not tried the boiler above 120 lb. The Mercurial Gauge and some other nick nacks are yet to be put on. On Friday next the Engine will leave by way of Carlisle and will arrive in L'pool on Wednesday week.

He adds the weight of the engine in a postscript—4T 5cwt 1qr with water.

A characteristic of Robert Stephenson in engineering matters was an extreme caution which amounted to pessimism. He was never given to premature jubilation or extravagant claims. This being so, we can judge from his letter that he was very well pleased with the result of this trial. It must have been an added pleasure to him to run his new and splendid machine for the first time over the very same track where, as an eager eleven-year-old school boy, he had watched his father's *Blucher* make her maiden trip fifteen years before.

After final alterations and adjustments had been made in the Forth Street Works, the locomotive was dismantled and hoisted into wagons which, on the afternoon of Saturday 12 September, lumbered off along the road to Carlisle. Exactly forty-eight hours later it was loaded into a lighter in the Carlisle Canal basin and thence conveyed to Bowness, where it was transhipped into the Cumberland steamer bound for Liverpool. On the 18th the precious cargo was safely landed and taken by wagons to the railway workshops at Crown Street for assembly. Here the engine met its tender, which had been made in Liverpool. Whether it was here or before it left Newcastle that the locomotive received the name *Rocket* is not known, nor do we know whose inspiration it was to bestow upon it a name so appropriate. It was intended to symbolize unexampled speed, yet with the passing of the years this significance of the name would be almost forgotten, so great would be the fame of the machine that bore it.

Meanwhile the other competitors had been equally busy. It is clear from Robert's letters to Booth that he regarded Timothy Hackworth as their most serious rival, and from the details he gives of the latter's progress it is evident that he was keeping a very watchful eye on Shildon shops where Hackworth's challenger, the *Sans Pareil*, was taking shape. But if Robert Stephenson was guilty of spying he was also spied upon by another competitor, Timothy Burstall, the steam-carriage builder of Leith.

Mr. Burstall Junior from Edinburgh is in N. Castle [he told Booth] I have little doubt for the purpose of getting information. I was extremely mistified to find that he walked into the manufactory this morning and examined the Engine with all the coolness imaginable before we discovered who he was. He has, however, scarcely time to take advantage of any hints he might catch during his transient visit. It would have been as well if he had not seen anything.

On the morning of Tuesday 6 October, a few days after the date first proposed, crowds began to converge upon Rainhill from Liverpool, St. Helens, Warrington, Manchester and all the country round. A large stand had been erected beside the middle of the course, flags and bunting flew, the inevitable brass band played "pleasing and favourite airs" and the neighbouring Rail-Road Tavern was packed out. A stranger from afar who had neglected to read his newspapers might have thought he had come upon a race meeting and have looked in vain for parading horses and jockeys, until he saw that the course consisted of two lines of iron rails which stretched away, straight and level, for nearly a mile upon either hand. Or supposing this ignorant and puzzled stranger had asked for a 'race card', he would have been given the following:

No. 1 Messrs. Braithwaite and Erickson of London, "The Novelty" Copper and Blue, Weight: 2 tons 15 cwt.

No. 2. Mr. Ackworth [sic] of Darlington, "The Sans Pareil" Green, Yellow and Black, Weight: 4 tons 8 cwt 2 qr.

No. 3. Mr. Robert Stephenson of Newcastle-upon-Tyne, "The Rocket" Yellow and Black, White Chimney, Weight: 4 tons 3 cwt.

No. 4. Mr. Brandreth of Liverpool, "The Cycloped" Weight: 3 tons, worked by a horse.

No. 5. Mr. Burstall of Edinburgh, "The Perseverance" Red Wheels, Weight: 2 tons 17 cwt.

Our stranger would then have realized that, along with the rest of the 10,000 spectators who jostled about him, he was to be privileged to witness a contest the like of which had never been seen before; a contest between new-fangled mechanical monsters the outcome of which might, in the words of the *Liverpool Courier*, "alter the whole system of our internal communications . . . substituting an agency whose ultimate effects can scarcely be anticipated".

In the distance, to the east and to the west of the grandstand, white posts exactly 1½ miles apart had been erected beside the line. These were known as the starting posts, although the course extended for an eighth of a mile beyond each of them to terminal points where fuel and water was available; also a blacksmith's shop and other repair facilities which the less fortunate competitors would put to good use before the Trials were over. There was also a weighbridge, for the Judges did not propose to take for granted the weights declared by the competitors. The Trial, or the 'Ordeal' as they called it, which the three judges decided upon was that each locomotive in turn, hauling a train three times its own weight, should make a total of twenty runs to and fro over the $1\frac{1}{2}$-mile course, an interval being allowed after ten runs had been made. This would be equivalent to a journey from Liverpool to Manchester and back. The course would be taken 'flying', the distance beyond the posts being used for braking and getting up speed. On the east to west run the competitors would have to propel in front of them the wagons of stone which formed the test loads. Timekeepers with 'second watches' would be stationed at each post to record not only the time taken to cover the $1\frac{1}{2}$-mile course on each run but also the time between runs, so that any precious minutes lost by the competitor in making feverish repairs or adjustments at the terminal depots would be duly noted down. The time and fuel consumed in raising a full head of steam from cold would also be recorded, likewise the fuel used and the water evaporated during the test runs.

Now for the competitors. Two of them need not be taken seriously. No. 4, Mr. Brandreth's *Cycloped*, was propelled by a horse trotting on a species of treadmill. This machine the Judges studiously ignored as it was quite outside the terms of the competition, but as Brandreth was a member of the Board his whimsies had to be indulged and he was presumably allowed to trundle up and down with his machine and so provide some light entertainment during the intervals which, owing to various mechanical derangements, were considerable.

The road wagon which was bringing No. 5, Mr. Burstall's *Perseverance*, to the trials, overturned with dire results, and it was not until the last day of the competition that the unfortunate owner was able to get it to the course. Having in the meantime seen his rivals perform, Burstall told the judges that he stood no chance and after making a short demonstration run the *Perseverance* was withdrawn.

It was not, commented Nicholas Wood briefly, 'adapted for the present celerity of Rail-road conveyance' having a boiler, which, to judge from Wood's description, was little more than a glorified domestic copper.

This meant that the honours lay between the first three competitors, and of these No. 1, Braithwaite & Erickson's *Novelty*, was easily the favourite not only with the ignorant populace but also with that company of scientific gentlemen and engineers which, claimed the local press, was the largest ever assembled on one spot. The *Novelty* represented the London steam-carriage tradition applied to the rails. Two vertical cylinders drove the cranked leading axle. Provision was made for the rear axle to be coupled by chain drive, but this was not used on the Trials. It had a very curious boiler consisting of a vertical unit mounted right at the back from which a long horizontal element extended to the full length of the frame. This was in communication with the vertical portion of the boiler and contained a long flue-tube which, having passed back and forth twice through the element, emerged in a small exhaust pipe at the front end. A forced draught was applied to the furnace under the vertical part of the boiler by mechanical bellows, and this drove the hot gases through the sinuous flue-tube. The exhaust steam from the engine passed straight to atmosphere. The proud sponsors of the *Novelty* were actively supported by Charles Vignoles, who doubtless hoped to see it run rings round the *Rocket*.

The Competitors were supposed to undergo their Ordeal in number order, and when the Judges arrived on the scene they found that the *Novelty* had already been showing her paces before an admiring crowd. In her royal blue livery with boiler, water tank and cylinders all clad in highly polished copper sheeting she certainly made a brave sight. The apparent absence of moving parts also deeply impressed the spectators, only the tops of the cylinders being visible. "The great lightness of this engine", wrote a rapturous reporter to the *Mechanics' Magazine*, "its compactness, and its beautiful workmanship, excited universal admiration; a sentiment speedily changed into perfect wonder, by its truly marvellous performance. . . . Almost at once it darted off at the amazing velocity of twenty eight miles an hour, and it actually did one mile in the incredibly short space of one minute and 53 seconds!"

Alas, pride had its speedy fall. A sudden dull explosion followed by a belch of smoke, flame and sparks from the nether regions of the *Novelty* brought consternation to the faces of Messrs. Braithwaite and Vignoles and a halt to their triumphal progress. A blowback from the furnace had burst the leather of the mechanical bellows. With No. 1 thus temporarily out of the running the Judges then turned their attention to the next on the list only to find a very hot and disgruntled Timothy Hackworth struggling with a leaking boiler on the *Sans Pareil*. He, like Braithwaite, begged for time in which to get his engine prepared, so, as the day was by now well advanced and it was raining heavily, the Judges ordered the Stephensons to present the *Rocket* for trial next morning and declared the proceedings closed.

The *Rocket* had also been demonstrated but was not popular with the crowd, who considered it cumbersome and 'unmechanical' by comparison with the *Novelty*, a verdict which was to some extent influenced by the fact that, with characteristic caution, the Stephensons made no attempt on this first appearance to vie with the speed of their glittering rival but conserved the powers of their steed for the trial proper.

On the morning of 8 October the *Rocket* was weighed in the presence of the Judges. This must have been an anxious moment for Robert Stephenson, but though the engine scaled 4T 5cwt—2cwt more than he had declared—it was well within the permitted maximum for a four-wheeled engine. Steam was then raised to 50lb from cold in 57 minutes using 142lb of coke, and two wagons loaded with stone were coupled up to make a train weight with the tender (which was considered part of the load) of 12Tons 15cwt. The two timekeepers, with their watches at the ready, then took up their stations, Rastrick at Post No. 1 at the western end of the course from which the first run was made, and Wood at the other.

It is nowhere positively stated who actually drove the *Rocket* on this famous occasion. Robert M'Cree of Killingworth was her regular driver, but the evidence suggests that George Stephenson himself drove her in the Trials accompanied by Robert and possibly employing M'Cree as fireman. The locomotive performed perfectly. The first eastbound run was covered in 6m. 15s. and speed continued around that figure until the last three runs when George Stephenson began to open up, finishing with a time of 4m. 12s. on the tenth eastward run. In between journeys the Stephensons put in some smart 'pitwork': 35 gallons of water were bucketted into the tender water butt in three minutes, while oiling round and 'greasing the pistons' occupied another three minutes. The Judges were completely mystified by the fact that the westbound times were invariably slower than the eastbound. Possibly George Stephenson drove more cautiously when he was propelling the loaded wagons in front of him, but it also seems likely that Robert Stephenson had not entirely succeeded in curing the defect he had mentioned to Booth when the engine was first tried at Killingworth and that in backward gear the valve events were not quite correct.

Having successfully completed the first half of the 'ordeal', a quarter of an hour was spent weighing-on a further supply of coke and filling the water butt. The Judges noted that all this time steam was blowing off from the safety valves. This could not have improved the overall consumption figures, but Robert Stephenson was obviously more concerned to avoid the mistake he had made on the Killingworth trial of letting the coke fire get too low. At all costs they must not get short of steam.

The second half of the trial went as smoothly and uneventfully as the first. As he approached the western post for the last time with success in sight, George Stephenson glanced quickly up at the long mercurial gauge beside the chimney, saw that steam pressure held steady at the 50lb mark and gave the *Rocket* full regulator. His long battle for the locomotive was almost won; now he would show the doubters and the mockers, those clever gentry from London who now clustered in the grand stand with their fine ladies, what new power he commanded. Flying a white pennant of steam from her tall chimney the *Rocket* thundered past the grandstand and away to the eastward post. Nicholas Wood looked at his watch; time: 3m. 44s., equal to a speed of a little over 29 miles an hour. "We wish", wrote the Judges in their report on the Trials, "to call the particular attention of the directors to the remarkable short time in which the last Eastward trip of one and a half mile was performed ... as demonstrating in a very eminent degree the practicability of attaining a very high velocity even with a load of considerable weight attached to the engine."

For the 60 miles the *Rocket* had averaged just under 14 miles an hour, nearly four miles an hour better than the speed stipulated. Water had been evaporated at the rate of 114 gallons per hour and 217lb of coke per hour had been burnt. It was a triumph for the Stephensons. By more than fulfilling all the conditions of the competition with consummate ease, they had at last most convincingly clinched their case for the locomotive. But they had not yet won the contest. Many spectators announced that they were not at all impressed by the performance of the *Rocket* and predicted that it would very soon be eclipsed by that of the *Novelty*. So strongly was the *Novelty* favoured, indeed, that even the Stephensons' supporters were alarmed, but George is alleged to have remarked to one doubter in his broadest Doric: "Eh mon, we needn't fear yon thing, her's got nae goots." Events proved him right.

At the conclusion of this day's experiment [wrote the Judges in their report] Mr. Hackworth requested he might be allowed a further time and declared he could not get his engine ready to start this week.

Messrs. Braithwaite & Erickson's Engine appeared to us not likely to be ready before Monday & it was agreed with a Friend of Mr. Braithwaite's (he not being present himself) that they should enter upon the trial of their Engine on Monday morning.

On Friday morning, however, Mr. Braithwaite waited upon us at Liverpool in company with his friend and declared that his engine would be all complete and perfectly ready for entering upon the task on Saturday morning, and insisted that his Engine should be put upon trial on that Day although we did every thing in our power to induce him to defer the trial until the Monday, being well aware that several joints were to be made which it would be almost impossible to get done in time to allow of their setting. . . .

This shows a most commendable desire on the part of the Judges to ensure fair play, but the impatient Braithwaite did not heed their good advice. On the Saturday the *Novelty* only managed one easterly run before the joints on the pipe from the feed pump to the boiler failed, "the water flying about in all directions". So that put a speedy end to the day's proceedings and it was not until the following Tuesday that they were officially resumed again, when Timothy Hackworth at last presented his *Sans Pareil* to the Judges for trial. The time taken to raise steam could not be checked because he had been working the engine during the night and the boiler was hot. The engine was then weighed and found to scale 4T 15cwt 2qr, 7cwt above the weight he had declared and 5cwt over the stipulated maximum for a four-wheeled engine. For the unfortunate Hackworth, who had been working night and day to get the *Sans Pareil* into shape, this must have been a bitter blow, for it excluded him from the contest. However, the sympathetic Judges determined to let him run and to leave it to the directors to decide the issue. They also appear to have obligingly ignored the fact that the *Sans Pareil* was completely unsprung. Hackworth had adopted his usual practice of mounting his cylinders vertically and this, combined with a direct drive by short connecting rods, prohibited the use of springs on the driving axle. He had also remained faithful to the return-flue boiler, his only modification being to extend the furnace end of the flue beyond the boiler proper in the form of a semi-circular water-jacketed canopy over the grate.

Having had her load attached, the *Sans Pareil* set off briskly and it was at once evident from the lumps of red-hot coke that shot from her chimney in true Shildon fashion that her designer's ideas on the blast pipe had undergone no modification. The time for this first run was 5m 9s, but it was never bettered. On the eighth eastbound journey, while his driver, 'Tammy Grey', manned the regulator, Hackworth could be seen fighting desperately to keep a reluctant boiler feed pump working. Five more runs along the course and there would be time to attend to it properly before the next half of the test began but alas for poor Timothy, it was not to be. The *Sans Pareil* was just in front of the grandstand on its return journey when it suddenly disappeared from view in a great cloud of steam. The lead fusible plug above the fire had melted owing to lack of water in the boiler, the most humiliating mishap that can befall an engine-man, and the *Sans Pareil* had to be pushed by a crowd of willing hands down to the blacksmith's shop at the end of the course. So ended the challenge of the Stephensons' most formidable rival. The *Sans Pareil* had averaged 14 miles an hour for the 22½ miles travelled with a load of 19 tons but, as we should expect, the consumption of coke had been fantastic, no less than 692lb per hour as against the *Rocket's* 217lb.

On the following day, Wednesday 14 October, the *Novelty*

1. Robert Stephenson as a young man. Engraved
from a portrait by George Richmond.

2. George Stephenson's birthplace, interior, Street House, Wylam.

3. The Stephensons' cottage at Killingworth as it appeared in 1881.

4. The opening of the Stockton & Darlington Railway, 1825. The inaugural train drawn by *Locomotion* crossing the Skerne Bridge. The coal drops at the end of the Darlington Branch can be seen in the background. This drawing by J. R. Brown is probably more authentic than Dobbin's better-known painting of the same scene.

5. The opening of the Canterbury & Whitstable Railway. *Invicta* and her train ascending the Church Street incline out of Whitstable.

6 and 7. Scenes on the Liverpool & Manchester Railway. Chat Moss and the Sankey Viaduct, both engravings by I. Shaw.

8. This drawing by Alexander Nasmyth was made shortly before the opening of the Liverpool & Manchester Railway. It shows the Stephensons with *Northumbrian*. Robert is firing up while his father oils the motion.

9. Opening day at Liverpool, L. & M.R. The Duke of Wellington's special train is on the left. An engraving by I. Shaw.

10, 11, and 12. Kilsby Tunnel, London & Birmingham Railway. The Pumps on Kilsby Hill, one of the working shafts, and the great ventilation shaft. All by J. C. Bourne.

13. The High Level Bridge, Newcastle, by J. Jackson,
engraved by T. A. Prior.

14. The Royal Border Bridge, Berwick-on-Tweed.
Engraved from a drawing by W. Banks.

15. George Stephenson in old age, from the portrait by John Lucas.

16. Conway Bridge, floating the second tube, lithograph by G. Hawkins.

17. The Britannia Bridge under construction, lithograph by G. Hawkins.

18. Robert Stephenson, a photograph taken shortly before his death.

made its final bid for the honours. What happened may be summed up in the words of the Judges' Report.

The Engine returning westwards the second trip, the Joints of the Boiler gave way, as indeed they might naturally be expected to do from being then so recently made, which put an effectual stop to the Experiment, so that the Engine and Train were obliged to be run up by hand. Mr. Erickson then declared to us that he would now withdraw his Engine from all further competition so far as regarded the Premium.

Timothy Hackworth then requested a second run, but this was refused. "Having considered", said the Judges, "the enormous consumption of fuel ... and the general construction of his Engine we found that we could not recommend it to the Directors' consideration as a perfect Engine & therefore as it was also overweight we did not think it necessary to expend further time in experimenting upon it. Mr. Hackworth then disputed the accuracy of the Weighing Machine, but as it has been since proved to be correct, this remonstrance in that head may be considered as fully answered." Having thus disposed of the *Sans Pareil* the Judges concluded by saying that 'Mr. Stephenson's engine' had alone fulfilled all the terms of the competition and was the best engine to be exhibited at Rainhill.

There is no doubt that the unlucky Hackworth was sorely disgruntled by his defeat and various allegations were, or have since been, made by his supporters, including that of deliberate sabotage by the Stephensons. It was said that the excessive coke consumption was due to the failure of a cylinder casting (cast by Robert Stephenson & Co. for Hackworth!) which cracked across the valve ports, causing live steam to blow straight up the chimney. Hackworth's biographer, Robert Young, stated categorically that this was the reason for the failure of the *Sans Pareil*, but there is no shred of evidence for this whatever. It is inconceivable that Hackworth would not mention such a failure to the Judges, even supposing they had failed to notice it, which is highly improbable. It is equally improbable that the Judges, in their scrupulously fair report, would fail to mention such a major disaster as a cracked cylinder. As for the high fuel consumption, Nicholas Wood, at least, had no doubts on this score, stating afterwards that the *Sans Pareil* threw most of its fire up the chimney because of the powerful blast. The engine could never have performed as it did with only one effective cylinder. Hackworth's supporters also sourly implied that with the Chief Engineer and the Treasurer of the railway company both concerned in the *Rocket*, only one result could be expected.

Whatever may have been alleged at the time or since, we, with the whole perspective of these past events before us, can say without hesitation that the great issue was fairly contested and fairly won by a locomotive which was far superior to any rival. The *Rocket* and the *Sans Pareil* are still to be seen in the Science Museum, where the superiority of the former both in design and workmanship is obvious. The fact was that Hackworth's design, though it had proved satisfactory for the slow-speed haulage of coal, was already obsolete and quite incapable of the high-speed performance which, as the Stephensons had realized, the Liverpool & Manchester Railway would demand. As for the *Novelty*, it was virtually a steam carriage on rails and, though spectacular when running light, as George Stephenson so shrewdly put it, it lacked guts. Its supporters declared that its failures were due only to hasty construction and bad workmanship, but they were proved wrong when the *William IV* and the *Queen Adelaide*, which Braithwaite & Erickson subsequently built for the railway on the same lines, proved equally unreliable and lacking in power.

Many and varied were the accounts written by eye-witnesses of the historic encounter, but by far the most graphic and entertaining was that given by John Dixon in a letter to his brother James at Darlington. It makes an appropriate postscript to this chapter.

Dear James,

We have finished the grand experiment on the Engines and G.S. or R.S. has come off triumphant and of course will take hold of the £500 so liberally offered by the Company: none of the others being able to come near them. The Rocket is by far the best Engine I have ever seen for Blood and Bone united. . . .

Timothy has been very sadly out of temper ever since he came for he has been grobbing on day and night and nothing our men did for him was right, we could not please him with the Tender or anything; he openly accused all G.S.'s people of conspiring to hinder him of which I do believe them innocent, however he got many trials but never got half of his 70 miles done without stopping. He burns nearly double the quantity of coke that the *Rocket* does and mumbles and roars and rolls about like an Empty Beer Butt on a rough Pavement and moreover weighs above 4½ Tons consequently should have had six wheels and as for being on Springs I must confess I cannot find them out. . . . She is very ugly and the Boiler runs out very much, he had to feed her with more Meal and Malt Sprouts than would fatten a pig. . . .

Dixon then goes on to describe the *Novelty*, "all covered with Copper like a new Tea Urn all which tended to give her a very Parlour like appearance", and deals with her failures. Then:

Burstall from Edinbro upset his in bringing from L'pool to Rainhill and spent a week in pretending to Remedy the injuries whereas he altered and amended some part every day till he was last of all to start and a sorrowful start it was; full 6 miles an hour creaking away like an old Wickerwork pair of Panniers on a cantering Cuddy Ass. Vox Populi was in favour of London from appearances but we showed them the way to do it for Messrs. Rastrig [sic] & Walker in their report as to Fixed and permt. Engines stated that the whole power of the Loco. Engines would be absorbed in taking their own bodies up the Rainhill Incline 1 in 96 consequently they could take no load. Now the first thing old George did was to bring a Coach with about 20 people up at a gallop and every day since has run up and down to let them see what they could do up such an ascent and has taken 40 folks up at 20 miles an hour.

After such a demonstration as this, a more striking display of the powers of the *Rocket* than the Rainhill 'Ordeal' itself, there could be no more talk of horses or fixed haulage engines. The battle for the locomotive had been most decisively won and it was as an exclusively locomotive-worked railway that the Liverpool & Manchester went forward to completion.

CHAPTER NINE

The Completion of the Liverpool & Manchester Railway

As a result of the Stephensons' victory at Rainhill the Liverpool & Manchester Company not only purchased the *Rocket* but also ordered four similar locomotives from Robert Stephenson & Company before the month of October was out. Yet there was still a dissident minority on the Board which was antagonistic towards George Stephenson. The ringleader appears to have been James Cropper. Having been the foremost advocate of the fixed haulage engine and found himself completely routed by Stephenson on that score, Cropper now became the champion of Braithwaite & Erickson and of Sir Goldsworthy Gurney, the steam-carriage builder, who offered to design a locomotive for the railway. The Gurney locomotive never materialized but, as mentioned in the last chapter, the Company did purchase two locomotives built by the former on the lines of the *Novelty* which proved utter failures notwithstanding the fact that their cost was almost double that of the *Rocket* and her sisters. But these successive defeats only served to increase Cropper's bitter enmity towards the two Stephensons and he missed no opportunity to bring about their discomfiture.

The excitement of the Rainhill Trials had hardly died down before, at Cropper's instigation, the Board agreed to appoint William Chapman to examine and report upon the state of the works. They must have known from past experience that this alone was asking for trouble where George Stephenson was concerned, but when it became obvious to Stephenson that Chapman's brief extended to positive interference with what he was doing, the fat was well and truly in the fire.

He protested against such interference in the following long letter to the Board, which is worth quoting at length not merely because it has never appeared in print before but also because it reveals so clearly Stephenson's character and the point of view which he proclaimed in such forthright and uncompromising terms throughout the whole of his stormy association with the Liverpool & Manchester project.

When you engaged Mr. Chapman [he writes] I understood that it was for the sole purpose of reporting to you on the progress made on the different works on the line. Whatever might be my private opinions as to the utility of such an officer I did not urge any objection to his election, especially as you informed me that his duty would in no way interfere with mine. Since his appointment I find that his attention has not merely been devoted to reporting on the progress of the works, but extended to things which I trust you will consider strictly within my department.

An engineman has been discharged from one of the Locomotive Engines because he did not give a satisfactory answer to some questions put to him by Mr. Chapman. The dismissal of this man from all I can learn is certainly injudicious. I brought him from the North where he bore a most excellent character. . . . His answers to Mr. C. may have been unsatisfactory, but it is doubtful whether he understood the import of the questions and it is still more doubtful if they were intelligible to any working Mechanic. I cannot but feel some reluctance to bringing Enginemen with their families from the North, who alone are capable of managing this class of engine . . . if they are to be interfered with by an individual unacquainted with the nature of the work.

A note also has been addressed by Mr. C. to Mr. Booth requesting him to give one of my assistants such directions as he might think fit respecting the Embankment at Newton, and that only two or three days after I had been on the spot myself. On the impropriety of such a step on the part of Mr. Chapman I shall make no comment as it is sufficiently obvious. It is a direct interference with my duty and by a person entirely ignorant of Engineering; nor can he be acquainted, when he views a piece of work on the line, what plans I intend adopting, why I am doing it, or what I intend to do afterwards.

To show you the bad effects which may be produced by persons reporting to you on subjects they are not equal to, I need only refer you to the accounts given by Mr. C. of the injury done to the Bolton & Leigh Railway by the *Lancashire Witch*, which induced almost every director in that concern to wish I had never recommended a travelling engine and some of them to express their opinions in a most unpleasant manner. I endeavoured by repeated journeys to Bolton to convince him that he was wrong but without avail. Experience I hope by this time has accomplished what I then failed in by argument.

This kind of interference with my duties as well as the doubts and suspicions which had been expressed regarding the opinions I have from time to time given on different subjects connected with this work has occasioned me much uneasiness. I have been accused of jealousy and a want of candour in the case of Mr. Brandreth's and Mr. Winan's waggons as well as in that of Mr. Erickson's engine, and even of worse than this in the case of Stationary v. Locomotive engines. In all these instances, instead of jealousy operating I confidently state that I have been only influenced by a disinterested zeal for the complete success of your work and by a laudable desire to support and establish my own credit.

May I now ask if I have supported your interests or not? Has Mr. Brandreth's carriage answered? Has Mr. Winan's saved 9/10 of the friction? Was not Walker & Rastrick's report wrong? Has the *Novelty* engine answered your expectations? Have the *Lancashire Witch* and the *Rocket* not performed more than I stated? These facts make me bold, but they also stimulate me to still further improvement. But I cannot believe that you will permit me to be thwarted in my proceedings by individuals who neither understand the work nor feel the interest which attaches me to this railway. Allow me therefore to ask if you intend Mr. C. to continue on the works.

Stephenson may have been unfair in his typically intolerant disparagement of Chapman, yet nobody, reading this spirited defence, can fail to sympathize with him and to admire the dogged courage with which he pursued his unswerving purpose in the face of every kind of difficulty. With a few honourable exceptions, led by Henry Booth, the Board of the Company he served were either actively hostile to their Engineer or weakly vacillating between one camp and another. Outside the Board the entire engineering profession continued to present a united front of jealous antagonism to Stephenson, missing no opportunity to criticize or to ridicule. That much of this was due to Stephenson's own provocation cannot be denied, but this should not in any way lessen our admiration for the way in which the great Northumbrian kept his enemies at bay with one hand while with the other he carried to a successful conclusion in 1830 an engineering work which set a pattern for the world to follow.

Notwithstanding all the feuds and arguments, all the mistakes in workmanship and organization, all the confident predictions of final failure and financial loss, the work went forward. Each day the sweating navvy gangs hacked and blasted their way a little farther through the great stone chasm of Olive Mount; each day raw embankments rose higher, and more huge blocks of stone, some of them two tons in weight, were bedded truly into place as the Sankey viaduct, arch by arch, advanced. And wherever a difficulty arose there would be seen the massive white-haired figure of the first railway engineer. Each morning early he would say goodbye to his wife Elizabeth at the little house in Upper Parliament Street, Liverpool, and ride off on his horse Bobby for another long day in the saddle along the thirty miles of route. At evening he would return tired and often plastered with mud, not to his home but for a conference with his chief draughtsman, Tom Gooch, at the Company's office in Clayton Square where all the drawings, the land plans and the charts of progress were kept. There he would explain his needs, illustrating them with crude little sketches which the faithful Gooch would translate into accurate drawings. Gooch, who lodged with the Stephensons, would then accompany Stephenson home where, after supper, he would take down letters and reports at his master's dictation.

Compared with the Stockton & Darlington Railway and the other mineral lines of the north-east which George Stephenson had previously built, the Liverpool & Manchester was a totally different and far more formidable engineering proposition. Bearing in mind Stephenson's lack of education and the fact that both he and his assistants had had no previous experience of civil engineering upon such a scale, the wonder is, not that he made mistakes, but that he did not make more. A mere thirty miles long, the Liverpool & Manchester was so soon eclipsed by the building of the great trunk lines that we are apt to forget that at the time of its completion there was only one other civil engineering work in England with which it could fairly be compared so far as the scale of the earthworks was concerned. This was Telford's Birmingham & Liverpool Junction Canal, a project which had defeated that premature scheme for a Birmingham and Liverpool railway which Stephenson and his assistants had surveyed in 1825. The main line of the canal was only eight miles longer than the Liverpool & Manchester Railway and the earthworks of both were begun at exactly the same time—January 1827. It is therefore worth noting that whereas Stephenson and his team of 'amateurs' completed their railway in September 1830, his professional rivals, undoubtedly the most experienced civil engineering team in the world at that time, ran into such trouble with slipping embankments and cuttings, that their canal was not completed until 1835, some months after Telford's death.

This parallel should not be stretched too far, because the canal engineers had to contend with more treacherous soils and rock strata, but it does help us to evaluate Stephenson's achievement. Moreover, the canal engineers certainly had nothing worse to contend with than the crossing of Chat Moss, that feat which so many engineers of repute had pronounced impossible. At the Manchester end of the Moss where the railway could not be 'floated' on the surface of the bog but must needs be raised on an embankment, so much spoil was tipped with no visible result that the Directors were thrown into a panic and all the wiseacres confidently predicted ruin. But Stephenson, undismayed, stubbornly went on tipping and by New Year's day 1830 a single line of rails had been laid which enabled the *Rocket* with a party of directors to cross the Moss for the first time. Francis Giles had estimated that if the Moss could be crossed at all the cost would be in the region of £270,000 whereas the actual cost was £28,000.

While George Stephenson was steering the railway through to its completion, Robert was making an equally great contribution to the locomotive department. By the spring of 1830 all four of the engines ordered in the previous October had been delivered from Newcastle and were named *Meteor*, *Comet*, *Dart*, and *Arrow*. These resembled the *Rocket* but weighed 1½ tons more and embodied important detail improvements which were obviously the fruit of the experience gained with the *Rocket*. The boiler tubes were reduced in diameter to two inches and their number increased to 88, while on the strength of this greater heating surface the cylinder diameter was enlarged from eight to ten inches. These cylinders were brought down from the 45° angle to a position nearly horizontal, a change which brought about far steadier running at high speed, and led to the similar alteration of the *Rocket*.

On 1 February 1830 the Company ordered two more locomotives, the *Phoenix* and the *North Star* which were delivered in June and August respectively—quick work. Cylinder diameter was again increased by one inch to eleven inches and the boilers were slightly longer, but the most significant development was that both these engines had smokeboxes instead of the bellied out chimneys of their predecessors. The *North Star* was accompanied by a third loco-motive, the *Northumbrian*, which represented the ultimate develop-ment of the *Rocket* type. The boiler of the *Northumbrian* contained 132 tubes of $1\frac{5}{8}''$ diameter which represented a tube-heating surface of 379 square feet as compared with the 117 square feet of the *Rocket*.[1] Most important of all, however, the separate, pipe-connected firebox was abandoned. Instead, the firebox was an inte-gral part of the boiler, which meant that in all essential particulars the boiler of the *Northumbrian* was the same as that fitted to every orthodox locomotive from that day to this. The *Northumbrian* also differed from her predecessors in having vertical plate instead of flat bar frames and also a true tender with iron water tank and railed bunker instead of the old wooden wagon and water cask which accompanied the previous engines.

At the time of the opening of the railway in September 1830 the *Northumbrian* was the last word in locomotives, yet only one more of her type, the *Majestic*, was built for the railway. So fantastically rapid was the pace of Robert Stephenson's design development that on the opening day there was already standing almost complete in the shops at Forth Street a locomotive which would make the *Northumbrian* and her sisters obsolete within two years. This was the famous *Planet*, which was delivered at Liverpool on 4 October, less than three weeks after the opening.

The *Planet* represented the complete fulfilment of that design policy which Robert Stephenson had explained in the letter he wrote to Longridge less than two months after his return from South America. In the *Lancashire Witch* he had taken the first step

[1] The famous *Rocket* was sold by the Company in March 1839 to a Mr. Thompson of Kirkhouse Colliery near Carlisle, where the engine worked for three years. After being laid up for some time, on 3 February 1851 she was sent by Thompson to Robert Stephenson & Company, his intention being that she should be overhauled and exhibited at the Great Exhibition of that year. But for some reason unknown to Thompson the locomotive re-mained at Newcastle until 1862 when, in a partly dismantled state, it was presented to the Science Museum.

of 'applying the engine on the side of the boiler' and now, in the *Planet*, he achieved the second step of placing it 'beneath it entirely'. The boiler dimensions of the *Planet* only slightly exceeded those of the *Northumbrian*, while the cylinder size was the same. The great improvement was in the mechanical lay-out. The cylinders were mounted directly under the smokebox and drove a cranked axle at the rear, the leading wheels now being carriers only. This reversal of the previous wheel arrangement placed more weight on the driving wheels and, combined with the new cylinder lay-out, gave still steadier running. In the *Planet* the locomotive can be said to have reached its definitive form, all subsequent development representing enlarged variations upon the *Planet* theme. Only one basic improvement was still lacking—a reversible valve-gear of modern type. The *Planet* still had the arrangement of single eccentrics used on the *Rocket*.

Like so many works of the Stephensons, the pre-eminence of the *Planet* has been disputed. Timothy Hackworth's *Globe* was under construction at Forth Street in 1830 and this, too, had inside cylinders and a cranked axle. It has been alleged that this design of Hackworth's inspired the *Planet* and that Robert Stephenson deliberately delayed completion of the *Globe* until two months after the *Planet* appeared. It has also been pointed out that Edward Bury of Liverpool, Robert Stephenson & Company's first great rival in the locomotive field, produced his *Liverpool* for the Liverpool & Manchester Railway in the same month and that this also had the same engine lay-out.

In the course of a discussion at the Institution of Civil Engineers which took place two years before his death, Robert Stephenson declared that the *Planet* was designed without any knowledge of the *Liverpool*, though he made no reference to the *Globe*. He said that his main reason for putting the cylinders in the bottom of the smokebox was to "prevent the condensation of the steam in the cylinders and consequent loss of power". "This had been resolved upon", he went on, "from information given to me by the late Mr. Trevithick who . . . had built a brick flue round the cylinder, and had applied the heat of a fire directly to the metal with very beneficial results. . . ." Of the cranked axle Robert Stephenson commented: "There was not anything new in its use in locomotives, for

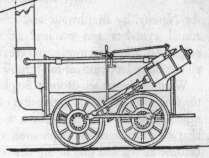

The *Rocket* prototype: Robert Stephenson's *Lancashire Witch* for the Bolton & Leigh Rly, 1828.

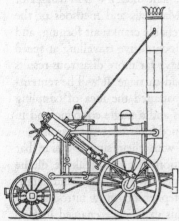

The Victor: Robert Stephenson's immortal *Rocket*, 1829

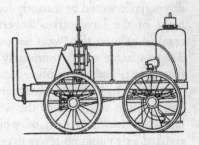

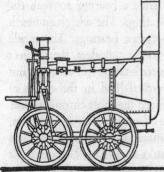

The *Rocket's* two challengers at Rainhill: Messrs. Braithwaite & Erickson's *Novelty* (above); Timothy Hackworth's *Sans Pareil* (left).

THE BATTLE FOR THE LOCOMOTIVE

the *Novelty*, by Braithwaite and Erickson, had one in 1829. Horizontal cylinders and cranked axles had also been commonly employed long previously, in Trevithick's, Gurney's, and almost all the other locomotives for turnpike roads."

What distinguished Robert Stephenson's *Planet* was that it was the first truly successful application of a design which he, along with other engineers, had long known to be feasible in theory. With his characteristic caution, Stephenson delayed using a cranked axle because he realized that in this department theory was in danger of running too far ahead of practice. Materials and methods of the day could not produce a completely reliable crankshaft forging, and the breakage of a cranked axle on a locomotive travelling at speed with a heavy train behind it would have far more disastrous results than any similar failure on a steam road-carriage. It will be remembered that George Stephenson had patented the idea of coupling the wheels by means of cranked axles and a single coupling-rod in his Killingworth days but had abandoned it for the same reason.

Both the *Globe* and the *Liverpool* with their simple inside bar frames were open to the fatal objection that the breakage of the driving axle would be instantly followed by the collapse and derailment of the locomotive. Robert Stephenson only introduced a cranked axle on the *Planet* because his experience enabled him to design a frame which completely eliminated this risk. This is why the *Planet* is justly remembered and its rivals for honours forgotten. The *Planet* had outside plate frames, which means that the main axle bearings were outside the wheels. There were also four inside bar frame members each of which carried a bearing so that the cranked axle ran in no fewer than six bearings. The wheels and each of the two crank throws were thus between bearings. The inside frame-members were rigidly anchored to the cylinders, their object being to relieve the crank from the horizontal power-stresses, but they were also capable of carrying vertical load in the event of crank-axle failure. Such failures were indeed the most chronic source of major trouble on locomotives of the *Planet* type for many years, until improved forging technique and materials less subject to flaws or fatigue conquered the evil, but thanks to Robert Stephenson's frame a broken crank-axle merely meant an engine failure and not a major disaster. As stronger crank-axles were produced, the two innermost bearings were dispensed with, leaving a double frame with bearings outside and inside the wheels which still ensured safety in the event of failure. Soon many designers, including Stephenson himself, would avoid this problem by reverting to outside cylinders once more, but it is one of the strange quirks of railway history that, through the medium of Daniel Gooch and his successors, the Stephenson double frame survived longest on the Great Western where, of all railways, the Stephenson writ never ran.

This matter of the *Planet*'s frame has been dealt with in some detail for two particular reasons. First, this elaborate design of Stephenson's has been contrasted disadvantageously by some writers with Edward Bury's far simpler bar frame which became the standard for American locomotives. This is another example of the errors of judgement which can so easily be made when the standards of the present are applied to the past. Secondly, it is important to establish the superiority of the Stephenson locomotives in view of the heavy fire of criticism to which both the Stephensons continued to be subjected before and after the opening of the railway.

Allegations inspired by envy and jealousy spread their poison through the engineering world and ultimately erupted like a boil in the form of a slashing attack by an anonymous writer in the *Edinburgh Review* in 1832. This declared that the directors of the Liverpool & Manchester Railway had become so 'fascinated' by George Stephenson that they had allowed him to gain a complete and unassailable monopoly whereby 'any part of the vast stock of national talent [was] excluded from the road'. Instead of local talent and labour, it was alleged, the directors employed a large body of strange men from the north who, from superintendent to gatekeeper, had become 'objects of favour and patronage'. Worse still, the Engineer-in-Chief, as the arbiter of policy, deliberately excluded from the road and condemned any engines or rolling stock which had not been produced by his son in his own works in Newcastle.

It transpired that the author of this attack was none other than Dr. Dionysius Lardner, and to the uninitiated reader it may seem strange that this same gentleman should, only four years later, deliver at Newcastle that extravagant eulogy of George Stephenson which provoked the wrath of William Hedley and others. To the student of the period, however, it will come as no surprise, for he finds

that this egregious ass keeps popping up to provide comic relief
to the dullest piece of research. Lardner was forever trying to sail
with the prevailing wind, but he was such a bad navigator that by
the time he got his sails up the wind had changed and he was invariably dismasted. So it was in this case when he received a withering
counterblast from Hardman Earle of the Liverpool and Manchester
Board.

Having pointed out that out of the 600 men employed on the
railway only sixty came from the counties of Durham and Northumberland, Earle asked: "Did it never occur to the Reviewer, that in a
novel and difficult undertaking, it may possibly be as wise a mode of
proceeding to employ 'workmen strangers to the soil' as labourers
strangers to the work?" In answer to the charge of a locomotive
monopoly, Earle stated that out of sympathy for Timothy Hackworth's misfortunes in the Rainhill Trials, his Board had purchased
the *Sans Pareil* for £500 but it had proved quite useless and had been
lately sold for £110. Earle also drew attention to the complete
failure of the *William IV* and *Queen Adelaide* for which the Board
had paid £1,000 a piece whereas the cost of the Stephensons'
Northumbrian had been £650. "What, permit me to ask, would you
have done had you been a Director?" he challenged. "Would you
not have ordered engines of that plan and construction which had
been found to succeed?" As for that galaxy of talents, which,
according to Lardner, was being so unjustly ignored, Earle asked:

> Are we, for the chance of their services, to relinquish the services of,
> beyond dispute, the soundest railway engineer in the kingdom, or to
> cease to employ the most successful engine builder, because to retain
> both is a violation of a mere theory? Railways, it is true, have long
> been in use, but it is to the genius and perseverence of Mr. Stephenson
> and his son that we are indebted for the present compact form of engine
> of the Planet class. . . . It is now two years since the Planet was laid
> down . . . and yet she comes nearer to what we consider perfection
> (relatively, of course) than any which have succeeded her. . . .

To such a crushing retort Lardner had no answer. Nor did the
Stephensons lack formidable defenders outside the Board. To the
Mechanics Magazine, which still championed Braithwaite &
Erickson and claimed that they had been unfairly ousted by George

Stephenson, the *Manchester Guardian* replied: "What the practical difficulties are which Mr. Stephenson has had to encounter, we do not know; but we understand the difficulty which Messrs. Braithwaite and Erickson had, and have still to encounter (and it is 'practical' enough) is that their engines will not work—at all events not to any useful purpose. . . ."

The indisputable fact was that for this brief period of railway history the two Stephensons possessed a monopoly, not of influence but of sheer talent which had been fairly won. This, in the locomotive department, created the situation where one small factory in Newcastle could not keep pace with the growing demands of the railway. It was for this reason that, in 1831, Robert Stephenson proposed to set up a second locomotive works near Liverpool and obtained the agreement of his partners to this step. The result was the foundation of the firm of Charles Tayleur, Junior & Co., Hey Foundry, near Warrington, soon to win fame under the name of the Vulcan Foundry of Newton-le-Willows. This new works, along with other firms of locomotive builders which rapidly sprang up, were soon building engines of the *Planet* class from drawings supplied by the parent firm in Newcastle.

It cannot be denied that through the agency of the two Stephensons the Liverpool & Manchester Company expended great sums of money on equipment and materials which soon became obsolete, but this was simply because their railway happened to be the 'guinea pig' in the fantastically rapid process of technical improvement which their genius dictated. The case of the *Rocket* class locomotives has already been mentioned. This speedy introduction of new and much heavier locomotives meant a great expense on the permanent way. The line was originally laid with wrought iron 'fish-bellied' rails weighing 35lb per yard (compared with 28lb on the Stockton & Darlington), but, writing in 1837, Peter Barlow tells us that this was soon found to be 'far too small' and was replaced by what he describes as 'Dublin 45lb parallel rail', which was better but still too light. At the time he wrote a 50lb 'T' section rail was being introduced with success. All these rails were laid on stone blocks except on Chat Moss or where embankments were liable to settlement.

Such outlay was inevitable where locomotive development was

so rapid, and for that development Robert Stephenson has never received his proper share of credit. That he has not seems to have been due in a great measure to his own reticence and modesty, characteristics which, in the opinion of this writer, represented a natural reaction to the attitude of his father, which was the precise opposite. Credit for the Liverpool & Manchester Railway is due entirely to the indomitable perseverance of George Stephenson, but without efficient and reliable locomotives all his labours would have proved vain. This was Robert Stephenson's great contribution. He had returned from South America to find the Newcastle factory insolvent and creatively stagnant, producing locomotives which were not markedly superior to those which his father had built at Killingworth fourteen years before. Yet the impact of his energy and far-sighted genius was such that in less than three years after his return the lumbering, unsprung coal haulier had been transformed as if by magic into the fleet, trim *Planet*, true prototype of the modern locomotive. When Walker and Rastrick made their report in 1829 they could be forgiven for doubting whether the crude machines they had seen would prove capable of pulling more than their own weight up the 1-in-96 gradients of the Whiston and Sutton inclined planes. The *Rocket* had first exploded this myth, albeit with a puny load, but early in 1831 Robert Stephenson delivered two locomotives, *Samson* and *Goliath* which had been built specially for service on these inclines and which give us the true measure of his extraordinary achievement. They were variants of the *Planet* design with bigger boilers and four coupled wheels, and on a test run in February 1831 *Samson* proved capable of hauling 80 tons up the inclines and 200 tons on the level. 'Locomotives shall not be cowardly given up. I will fight for them to the last', Robert Stephenson had said, and he proved true to his word. The victory was overwhelming. Mere words were no match for facts; when the *Planet* flew over Chat Moss and *Samson* stretched his iron thews on Sutton Plane, Dr. Dionysius Lardner and his crew received their answer.

During the period which elapsed between the conclusion of the Rainhill Trials and the public opening of the railway, George Stephenson and his directors appear to have been much concerned to win over public opinion by staging a number of 'private views'. As more line was laid and more locomotives were delivered from New-castle, these excursions became at once more ambitious and more frequent. The recorded impressions of those who were privileged to experience such preliminary canters make fascinating reading, revealing as they do the overwhelming impact of mechanical transport upon a world which had never known anything swifter than a galloping horse.

A participant in one of the first of these outings, on 14 November 1829, was Thomas Creevey, M.P., whose gossipy letters to his step-daughter, Elizabeth Ord, first published in 1903 as *The Creevey Papers*, throw such an entertaining light on the society of the Georgian Age. As an ally of Lord Sefton, Creevey had strongly opposed the Liverpool & Manchester Bill in 1825, and of a supporter of the railway he had written at that time: "Sefton and I have come to the conclusion that our Ferguson is *insane*. He quite foamed at the mouth with rage in our Railway Committee in support of this infernal nuisance—the loco-motive Monster . . ." But, his efforts having failed, Creevey's curiosity got the better of him when a visit to Knowsley gave him an unexpected opportunity to meet the Monster.

To-day [he informed Miss Ord] we have had a *lark* of a very high order. Lady Wilton sent over yesterday to say that the Loco Motive machine was to be upon the railway at such a place at 12 o'clock for the Knows-ley party to ride in if they liked and inviting this house to be of the party. So of course we were at our post in 3 carriages and some horse-men at the hour appointed. I had the satisfaction, for I can't call it pleasure, of taking a trip of five miles in it, which we did in just a quarter of an hour—that is 20 miles an hour. . . . But observe, during these five miles, the machine was occasionally made to put itself out or *go it* and then we went at the rate of 23 miles an hour, and just with the same ease as to motion or absence of friction as the other reduced pace. But the quickest motion is to me *frightful*; it is really flying, and it is impossible to divest yourself of the notion of instant death to all upon the least accident happening. It gave me a headache which has not left me yet. Sefton is convinced that some damnable thing must come of it; but he and I seem more struck with such apprehension than others. . . . The smoke is very inconsiderable indeed, but sparks of fire are abroad in some quantity: one burnt Miss de Ros's cheek, another a hole in Lady Maria's silk pelisse and a third a hole in someone else's gown. Altogether I am extremely glad indeed to have seen this miracle, and to have travelled in it. Had I thought worse of it than I do I should have had the curiosity to try it; but, having done so, I am quite satisfied with my *first* achievement being my *last*.

On 14 June 1830 a Board meeting was held in Manchester and for the first time the Liverpool directors were able to travel thither by train with George Stephenson driving the *Arrow*, then newly arrived from Newcastle, with Captain Scoresby, the circumpolar navigator, beside him on the footplate timing their progress. "The trip was a very delightful one to me", wrote Stephenson to Longridge, "as we took the Directors and a load along with us for the first time. . . . If I had slacked the Reins of our horse on that day they would have run over the ground in less time. Being as you know a very cautious man . . . we were much longer than we need have been." Even so, on the return journey the thirty miles were covered in $1\frac{1}{2}$ hours, the *Arrow* speeding across Chat Moss at 27 miles an hour.

The journey which was made on 25 August, most probably a preliminary trial of the *Northumbrian*, must have been much more delightful for George Stephenson. For on this occasion he had an appreciative and enthusiastic companion very different from the querulous Creevey with his prophecies of doom or the stolid sea captain. This was none other than the young and beautiful Fanny Kemble, who had lately achieved fame as Juliet on the stage at Covent Garden. She was playing in Liverpool at the time and was invited by the Directors to come for a trip, which she afterwards described to a friend in graphic and glowing terms.

What is so interesting and significant about Fanny's letter is its accurate and detailed description of the locomotive, a machine as novel and as formidable to the contemporary layman as a space rocket or an electronic brain seems to us. The action of the steam on the pistons, the connecting rods, safety valve and water gauge, all are lucidly described. Nowadays, when one of our most distinguished historians can boast of the fact that the mechanics of the bicycle are beyond him, such a display of intelligent interest on the part of a young actress seems to us astonishing, but we must remember that the arts and sciences were not then divorced from each other. To Fanny Kemble it would have seemed inconceivable that any intelligent man, let alone a historian, could ever turn a superior back upon inventions of such momentous consequence for all mankind.

Evidently those dark eyes which gaze at us so candidly from Fanny's portrait by Sir Thomas Lawrence so bewitched George Stephenson that he invited her to join him on the footplate—and remember that in those days it was literally a footplate and nothing more, there being no cab or even a spectacle plate. Whereas the terrified Creevey would have recoiled aghast at such a suggestion, the actress saw his fearful monster as "a snorting little animal which I felt rather inclined to pat" and needed no second bidding. Gathering her skirts together she climbed nimbly on board to stand beside Stephenson as he grasped 'the small steel handle' which was, as she put it, 'the reins, bit and bridle of this wonderful beast'. So they set off together through the deep Olive Mount cutting.

> You can't imagine [wrote the actress] how strange it seemed to be journeying on thus, without any visible cause of progress other than the magical machine, with its flying white breath and rhythmical, unvarying pace, between these rocky walls, which are already clothed with moss and ferns and grasses; and when I reflected that these great masses of stone had been cut asunder to allow our passage thus far below the surface of the earth, I felt that no fairy tale was ever half so wonderful as what I saw. Bridges were thrown from side to side across the top of these cliffs, and the people looking down upon us from them seemed like pigmies standing in the sky.

At the Sankey Viaduct Stephenson closed his regulator and brought the train to a standstill. They clambered together down the steep slope of the new embankment to the fields below where they stood, the tall, powerfully built engineer with his white hair and old-fashioned long black coat, the slim girl swinging her bonnet by its ribbons, gazing up in pride and wonder at the soaring stone piers that strode so boldly over field, river and canal. After suffering so much hostility and bitter criticism, the frank admiration of a beautiful woman must have been balm indeed to Stephenson. It made him feel twenty years younger; so much so that when they got back to the footplate of the *Northumbrian* he threw caution to the winds and opened the regulator wide. By doing so he unwittingly gave us the world's first description of the sheer exhilaration of speed, speed greater than any man had ever known before.

> The engine [wrote Fanny] . . . was set off at its utmost speed, 35 miles an hour, swifter than a bird flies. You cannot conceive what that sensation of cutting the air was; the motion as smooth as possible too. I could either have read or written; and as it was I stood up, and with my bonnet off drank the air before me. The wind, which was strong, or perhaps the force of our own thrusting against it, absolutely weighed my eyelids down. When I closed my eyes this sensation of flying was quite delightful, and strange beyond description; yet strange as it was, I had a perfect sense of security and not the slightest fear.

And what of her companion?

> Now [Fanny continues] for a word or two about the master of all these marvels, with whom I am most horribly in love. He is a man from fifty to fifty-five years of age; his face is fine, though careworn, and bears an expression of deep thoughtfulness; his mode of explaining his ideas is peculiar and very original, striking, and forcible; and although his accent indicates strongly his north country birth, his language has not the slightest touch of vulgarity or coarseness. He has certainly turned my head. . . .
>
> The railroad will be opened upon the fifteenth of next month [she concludes]. The Duke of Wellington is coming down to be present on the occasion, and, I suppose, that with the thousands of spectators and the novelty of the spectacle, there will never have been a scene of more striking interest. . . . The Directors have kindly offered us three places for the opening, which is a great favour, for people are bidding almost anything for a place. . . .

Fanny Kemble was indeed present at the opening but, alas, it was to be a far less happy occasion than her first visit.

As the opening day approached, public interest mounted and many of the less prejudiced figures in the engineering world made long journeys to see the new wonder. Among them was James Nasmyth who made a special trip from London on the outside seat of a coach and visited the Liverpool terminus on Monday 11 September, only four days before the opening. "There, for the first time, I saw the famous *Rocket*", he writes. "The interest with which I beheld this distinguished and celebrated engine was much enhanced by seeing it make several short trial trips under the personal management of George Stephenson, who acted as engineman, while his son Robert acted as stoker. During their trips along the line the '*Rocket*' attained the speed of thirty miles an hour—a speed then thought almost incredible! I eagerly availed myself of the opportunity of making a careful sketch of the engine which I still preserve", Nasmyth goes on. This charming drawing (Plate 8) shows that what the artist saw was not the *Rocket*, as he thought, but the very latest Stephenson achievement, the *Northumbrian* undergoing last-minute trials without nameplates.

Before dealing with the actual events which marked the opening of the railway, it is necessary to set the stage by describing the layout and traffic arrangements at the Liverpool end of the line. First of all it must be understood that the purpose of the long Edgehill tunnel was to pass goods traffic down to the Wapping docks by cable haulage. It was opened to public inspection from July 1829 and at once became one of the sights of the city, no visitor being allowed to escape before he had been conducted through it. This was no gloomy or perilous exploit but a popular subterranean promenade, for the tunnel was lit by gas-jets fifty yards apart, the walls were whitewashed, and the track formation was covered with sand levelled off to within an inch of the running surface of the rails. For the further edification of visitors, plates were fixed to the walls at intervals bearing the names of the streets passed under. The ends of the tunnel were protected by gates which were closed and locked at night.

Edgehill, the terminus for locomotives, lay in deep rock cutting, the lines disappearing into three tunnels, the tunnel down to Wapping being flanked by two smaller ones. One of these, 300 yards long, led on a rising gradient to the Company's Crown Street Yard where there were coal wharves and coach houses. The other tunnel merely led into a workshop and was contrived to 'balance the composition' at the suggesion of a local architect, John Foster, who was responsible for the architectural treatment in the Moorish style of the bridge linking the haulage engine houses. Here was housed the fixed engine for working the Edgehill incline. The engine was built by Robert Stephenson & Co. and in charge of it was Robert Weatherburn, who had been a fellow brakesman with George

Stephenson at West Moor pit twenty-five years before. The boilers which supplied this fixed engine were installed in a cavern hewn out of the rock, their flues being carried up through this rock and surmounted by two tall chimney stacks disguised as Grecian columns by the ingenious Mr. Foster. The complete picture, beetling walls of rock, dark tunnel mouths, Moorish arch, and the two mighty columns flaunting their dark banners of smoke, appealed strongly to the romantic imaginations of the period and was pronounced wondrously awe-inspiring.

Before, and for some time after, the opening of the railway, passengers for Manchester boarded their coaches in Crown Street Yard. The brakes were then released and the coaches ran by gravity down through the short tunnel on to the main line where a locomotive awaited them. Describing these coaches, a contemporary writer tells us that: "The most costly and elegant contain three apartments and resemble the body of a coach (in the middle) and two chaises, one at each end—the whole joined together. Another resembles an oblong square of church pews panelled at each end, and the rail which supports the back so contrived that it may be turned over so that the passengers may face either way." It is interesting to learn from this that the reversible seat which would later become so familiar on the upper decks of tramcars is of such respectable antiquity. Like their fellows on the roads which they so closely resembled, the "most elegant" of the Liverpool & Manchester coaches were named. The first to appear were christened the *Times*, *Experience*, the *Traveller* and the *Victory*.

The locomotive having been attached to these coaches, the same writer continues: "In a few moments . . . the engineer opens the valves, the hissing of the steam is suppressed, the engine moves and is heard as if to pant, not from exhaustion, but impatient of restraint, the blazing cinders fall from behind it and the train of carriages is dragged along with a sudden and agreeable velocity, becoming as it were, the tail of a comet." This description, like Creevey's account of the fate of Lady Maria's silk pelisse, suggests that Stephenson had taken a leaf out of Hackworth's book and sharpened up the blast.

It appears from this account that some traffic was allowed to descend the Whiston and Sutton planes by gravity. "Waggons let loose from the trammels of the break [sic] run down the plane like arrows from a bow nor stop till their impetus propels them far beyond the termination of the declivity". So writes the enthusiastic author with, one hopes, a certain amount of artistic licence. Such a proceeding sounds terrifying enough even if it applied only to goods traffic, especially when we realize that the only form of signalling on the line was provided by men with flags.

For the opening of the railway the most elaborate preparations were made and, through the agency of William Huskisson, M.P. for Liverpool, who, after a preliminary visit, had become an enthusiastic advocate of the railway, a most exalted company had promised to attend including, as Fanny Kemble had forecast, the Prime Minister of England, none other than the great Duke of Wellington himself. Yet no amount of careful planning could recreate the carefree atmosphere of gaiety, optimism and goodwill which had marked the opening of the Stockton & Darlington Railway only five years before. Then, the brief trade revival appeared to promise a bright future, but these hopes had not been fulfilled and now the times were not propitious. That the railway could not be completed without substantial Government loans is itself an indication of the state of trade. There was widespread unemployment and the vast weight of misery and discontent so caused expressed itself in the great movement for Parliamentary reform which was to bring England to the brink of revolution within the next two years. George IV had died in June, to be succeeded by 'Sailor William' who, though a good-natured and warm-hearted man, totally lacked the quality of statesmanship, with the consequence that the prestige of the monarchy was at a low ebb. The effect of the outbreak of revolution in France in July was to strengthen the reform movement and to exacerbate the fears of those who sought to repress it. Such were the heavy economic and political clouds that darkened the great day and which the presence of the Duke of Wellington certainly did not help to dispel.

As a resolute opponent of any measure of reform, no man in the England of 1830 was less popular with the rank and file than the Prime Minister. This was particularly true of the north-west, while in Manchester where, after ten years, the Peterloo massacre was still bitterly remembered, his appearance could have the effect of a spark to a powder barrel. Accordingly the most extraordinary precautions

were taken to ensure the Duke's safety. Not only was the whole line
heavily policed, but to guard against possible sabotage every point
and crossing between Liverpool and Manchester was removed by
the Company except those at the termini and at Huyton.

In view of all this and bearing in mind the Company's natural
anxiety for the popular success of their revolutionary venture, we
may wonder why the Duke was ever invited or agreed to attend
the opening. There were two reasons. In the first place the Company
had wittingly or unwittingly allowed themselves to become the
agents of a political manœuvre on the part of the Tory Party. The
more moderate Tories, who represented the majority, realized that
if Wellington maintained his implacable opposition to reform, his
Tory ministry was bound to fall. William Huskisson was the able
leader of the more liberal Tory group whose policies in high office
had, in his Liverpool constituency, won him the approval of both
Whig and Tory merchants. He had quarrelled with Wellington
and resigned from the Ministry. The Tories hoped to use the
occasion to bring about a reconciliation between the two men, the
effect of which would be to persuade Wellington to moderate his
policy and so avert his Party's defeat by the Whigs, who were
prepared to concede a considerable measure of reform. Secondly,
the Duke himself was totally unaware of the extent and depth of his
unpopularity, believing as he did that the movement for reform was
not a broad national one but merely the clamour of a minority of
radical agitators.

On the fateful morning of 15 September the Marquess of Salis-
bury's open carriage drawn by four splendid horses swept into the
Company's yard at Crown Street and from it there descended the
great Iron Duke, an austere, unsmiling, sombre figure, still clad in
deepest mourning for the late king and wrapped in a long Spanish
cloak. He was accompanied by Sir Robert Peel and together they
took their seats in the train reserved for eighty of the most distinguished guests which was to be hauled by the *Northumbrian*
driven by George Stephenson himself. This privileged trainload
included Prince Paul Esterhazy, the Austrian Ambassador, William
Huskisson, a number of other members of Parliament, the civic
dignitaries of the two cities, and the directors of the Company. The
rest of the guests to the total of six hundred were shepherded to their

seats in seven special trains by the Company's servants in their new blue liveries. To simplify this task the trains and the invitation tickets were distinguished by colours as follows: the *Phoenix*, green; the *North Star*, yellow; the *Rocket*, light blue; the *Dart*, purple; the *Comet*, deep red; the *Arrow*, pink; the *Meteor*, brown.

The first five of these trains were in charge of Robert Stephenson, George Stephenson's brother Robert, Joseph Locke, Thomas Gooch, and William Allcard, but it is most probable that they superintended operations from the footplates of their respective engines and did not actually drive them.

The procedure determined upon was that the Duke's train would depart first on the southern line while the other seven trains followed on the other line at close intervals. At Parkside, seventeen miles from Liverpool, all engines would stop for water at special watering places which had been installed along one and a half miles of line. It had then been agreed that the Duke's special would remain standing while the other seven trains passed by his state carriage in procession.

At first all went well. A single cannon boomed out as a signal to start and the *Northumbrian* moved away through the chasm of the Olive Mount cutting followed at a discreet distance by Robert Stephenson on the *Phoenix*. Every vantage point was thronged with a multitude of waving, cheering spectators, their grievances temporarily forgotten in the excitement and wonder of the moment. At Olive Mount they added an unbroken, many-coloured, swaying fringe to the high skyline of rock walls and bridge parapets; below the Sankey Viaduct, barges on the Sankey Canal, the towing path and the meadows beside it presented a sea of upturned faces and waving arms as the processional trains steamed proudly overhead. Parkside was reached in four minutes under the hour and it was here that fate took a hand and disrupted all the carefully laid plans.

While they were watching the passage of the other trains on the parallel track, a number of the passengers in the Duke's special, including William Huskisson and Prince Esterhazy, alighted to stretch their legs. It should be explained that here and throughout the line, the formation had been treated in the same way as in the Edgehill tunnel, being levelled off almost to rail level, thus making it fatally easy for these distinguished visitors to promenade on or between the tracks. The Duke of Wellington who, in order to watch the passing trains, was sitting in the corner seat of his state coach nearest the six-foot way, caught sight of Huskisson amongst the little group as they strolled past and acknowledged him by a slight nod and a motion of his right hand. This was the moment that the politicians in the party had been hoping for, and at once Huskisson and his friends hurried forward. The Duke opened the door of his coach and extended his hand. Huskisson grasped it and a few words had been exchanged when someone glanced up the line, saw the *Rocket* approaching with the third train, and shouted "Get in! Get in!" a cry which was quickly taken up by other spectators. Two of Huskisson's companions, Holmes and Birch, flattened themselves against the side of the Duke's train, another, Calcraft, scrambled up into one compartment, while Prince Esterhazy, a small, slight man, was hauled bodily into another. But poor Huskisson became fatally confused and was, moreover, far from agile. "Huskisson's long confinement in St. George's Chapel at the King's funeral", wrote Creevey afterwards, "brought on a complaint . . . the effect of which had been, according to what he told Calcraft, to paralyse, as it were, one leg and thigh." Moving clumsily, the unfortunate man attempted to get round the open door of the Duke's carriage, stumbled, lost his balance and fell with his leg doubled across the rail just as the *Rocket* bore down upon him. It must have been a terrible moment for Joseph Locke who was on the *Rocket* and for M'Cree who was presumably driving. Even had they commanded steam or vacuum brakes they would still have been powerless to avert disaster at such close range. The wheels passed over Huskisson's thigh, crushing it horribly and as frantic hands lifted him the luckless man was heard to murmur in his agony "I have met my death."

The truth of this must have been all too obvious, but amid the babel and confusion which ensued, one man took command and acted with promptitude and presence of mind. George Stephenson ordered the leading coach of the special to be uncoupled and the victim of the first railway accident to be placed in it. He then clambered back on to the footplate, opened the regulator of the *Northumbrian* and set off at full speed for Eccles. Whether or not he was driving before, all writers seem to agree that he was in charge now and this time it was not the attraction of a young actress but a dying man that made him throw caution to the winds. The *Northumbrian* covered the 15 miles to Eccles in 25 minutes, an average of 36 miles an hour. Anyone who had dared to claim five years before that such a speed was possible would have been called a lunatic, and the news of this feat created as big a sensation as the accident which provoked it. "This incredible speed burst upon the world", writes Smiles, "with the effect of a new and unlooked for phenomenon."

As the flying *Northumbrian* with her tragic freight dwindled to a steam-shrouded speck in the distance, a tragi-comic drama developed at Parkside. It was just as well that watering facilities had been laid on there because for an hour and a half the engines of the seven crowded trains stood and simmered while the great ones debated whether to go forward or to cancel the programme and go back to Liverpool. The Duke and Sir Robert Peel were in favour of a return and it was Sharpe, the Borough Reeve of Manchester, who finally managed to get this decision reversed. He pleaded desperately with the Duke and Peel. If they did not go on he could not be answerable for the peace of his city. Multitudes were waiting to witness their arrival and if they were disappointed, either exaggerated rumours of disaster would be believed or the mob would suspect that their Prime Minister feared to face them. "Something in that", the Duke is reported to have said tersely in answer to this plea, to which Peel added, "Where are these Directors? Let us see them."

The unhappy directors duly appeared and were informed that the Duke had decided to go forward. Yes, but how? The sickening realization dawned upon them that their elaborate precautions had recoiled against them. It was all very well for the great man to order the procession forward, but with the three remaining coaches of his special standing on the south line without motive power and with no means of crossing a relief engine from one line to the other, this was easier said than done. After more anxious debate, the two leading trains on the north line, drawn by the *Phoenix* and the *North Star* were coupled together and from their rear a chain was attached to the state carriages on the parallel line. In this extraordinary fashion the whole procession eventually reached Eccles, where the *Northumbrian* and the single coach were waiting, having left the unfortunate Huskisson in the vicarage there, where he died that evening. The trains then continued their advance in proper order, but what was the dismay of George and Robert Stephenson as they ran side by side on the footplates of *Northumbrian* and *Phoenix* to see the long cutting at the approach to Manchester blocked by a dense mass of people. The military had been called out in force to guard the Manchester terminus but, impatient of restraint and long delay, the mob had outflanked them. Forced to reduce speed to a crawl to avoid further bloodshed on the rails, it soon became obvious to the Stephensons and to everyone else on the trains that this crowd had not come to cheer. Instead there was heard that most terrifying of sounds, the sullen roar of an angry mob precariously poised on the brink of violence. Stones and brickbats hurled at the state coaches left no doubt as to the object of this demonstration, and above the heads of the struggling throng crudely painted banners and placards swayed to and fro declaiming the price of bread and labour or bearing such slogans as 'Remember Peterloo'.

Having run this frightening gauntlet, the trains rumbled slowly over the iron bridge at Water Street, with its massive Doric columns cast by Fairbairn, and drew to a belated halt in the Manchester station at 3.30 p.m. As they did so, the crowds rushed the station and the soldiery were unable to hold them back. Chaos prevailed. All communication between the different trains was cut off and only a few of the braver and hungrier souls in them clambered out to fight their way through to the belated lunch which was awaiting them in the new goods warehouse. The Duke refused to leave his carriage, which soon became the centre of such an uproar that ultimately Lavender, the Chief of Police for the city, struggled through the throng to urge an immediate departure; otherwise, he confessed that he could no longer answer for what might happen.

The *Northumbrian* was therefore brought round the train of state carriages and the Duke beat an orderly retreat, less sure, perhaps, than he had been that morning that his opponents were a mere handful of agitators. Alas, the wretched directors were again undone by their own precautions. In making the precipitate decision to return they had, in the general confusion, overlooked the fact that four of the engines from the other trains had already crossed over to the south line and gone out to Eccles to take on water. The

Duke's train had just got clear of the mob, and its distinguished occupants were breathing heartfelt sighs of relief at their safe deliverance, when these four engines were encountered, duly returning to Manchester to pick up their trains. What to do now? To go back into that lion's den was unthinkable, so there was only one thing for it, the four engines must run in front of the *Northumbrian* all the way to Huyton, leaving the seven crowded trains at Manchester to be dealt with by only three engines. the *Rocket*, the *North Star* and the *Arrow*. These three had still to get clear of their trains and run out to Eccles for water. This took some while and, by the time they returned, darkness was falling and it had begun to rain heavily. The already damped spirits of the passengers were not enlivened by the news of this drastic reduction in the available motive power.

At that moment Joseph Locke, old Robert Stephenson and Frank Swanwick of the *Arrow* may be said to have most worthily founded the slogan of the railway service: 'the trains must go through'. The honour of the new Company was at stake. Undismayed by the chaos and confusion all around them they succeeded in getting all the trains marshalled together and their engines coupled at the head. In the conditions of darkness and rain they wisely decided that this would be a safer proceeding than to run three separate trains. Slowly and laboriously the three locomotives managed to get their long train under way. It was a start made more difficult by the fact that owing to the way the formation had been levelled up, the mob had trampled sand and earth over the rails.

At Eccles, the long train stopped so that inquiries could be made about the injured Huskisson. In attempting to restart, two couplings at the head of the train parted under the unwonted strain, but the indomitable engine-crews lashed the train together with ropes and then continued, straining their eyes through the rain and the darkness on their open footplates, as three tall chimneys spouted fire. At the Parkside watering place there was welcome help awaiting them. A lantern waved on the line ahead; it proved to be three of the truant locomotives, *Dart*, *Comet* and *Meteor*, which had crossed over at Huyton and returned to their aid. The fourth absentee, Robert Stephenson's *Phoenix*, had gone ahead as pilot to the *Northumbrian*.

Two of these engines were coupled up to the rest, while the *Comet* ran as a pilot half a mile ahead of the train, looking out for obstructions, her fireman holding aloft flaming lengths of tarred rope to light the way. Her only unexpected encounter was with a wheel-barrow which splintered harmlessly under her driving wheels. Under the adverse conditions the climb up the Whiston plane was more than the combined efforts of five engines could manage with such a train, and all male passengers had to be ordered out of their seats to lighten the load. Once on the summit, however, it was all plain sailing. The five engines fairly got into their stride at last, bowling their long train over the Rainhill level, down the incline and finally, at 10 p.m., into the Liverpool terminus, where the weary passengers were heartened by the cheering of the crowds who had waited patiently, in rain and darkness, for their return.

The last act in the long day's drama followed as the carriages were attached to the incline rope and lowered down the long tunnel to Wapping. In the white-walled gaslit tunnel, out of the rain and in sight of home, the passengers, too, cheered lustily, and as the echo of their voices and the rumbling of the wheels grew louder, so the shouts were taken up by the waiting crowds at Wapping.

It was 11 o'clock before the last tired traveller left his carriage at Wapping and tottered home to bed. Despite all the unforeseen difficulties, with the exception of poor Huskisson the railway had brought all its passengers home safely, refuting the dire prophecies of disaster and the wild rumours which had spread abroad as a result of the delays. From George Stephenson downwards the day had subjected the new race of railwaymen to a crucial test, but they were learning fast the hard lessons of railway operation and came through with flying colours. Next morning the first booked train left Liverpool for Manchester with a complement of 140 passengers, and its successors have been steaming over Stephenson's road from city to city ever since. The age of railways as we know them had begun.

PART II

The Years of Fame
1830–1859

CHAPTER TEN

Rails to the South

THE Liverpool & Manchester Railway was not the first on which passenger trains were hauled by locomotives. It was narrowly robbed of that distinction by the Canterbury & Whitstable Railway which was opened on 3 May 1830. The latter's claim is more academic than real, however, for as originally laid out the first four miles of line at the Canterbury end were worked by fixed engines and a single locomotive was used only for the last two miles into Whitstable. When the Church Street incline out of Whitstable proved too much for its powers, yet another fixed engine was installed there and the locomotive confined to one mile of track. A detailed description of the construction of the line would not therefore be justified here even though the Stephensons and their associates were its authors.

After William James's retirement from the scene, first Joseph Locke and then John Dixon were engaged in surveying at Canterbury for George Stephenson, the final plans and sections being prepared by the latter. After his return, Robert Stephenson took over the superintendence of the works with Joshua Richardson as his resident engineer and Thomas Cabery as assistant, these two later becoming General Manager and Engineer to the Company respectively.

The single locomotive was built by Robert Stephenson & Co. and delivered by sea to Whitstable, being accompanied thither and driven at the opening by Edward Fletcher,[1] later to achieve railway fame as the Locomotive Superintendent of the North Eastern Railway. This engine, the *Invicta*, was of the Rocket type except that the cylinders were inclined towards the chimney end of the boiler and the wheels coupled. It has been preserved, and, as may be seen,

[1] Fletcher joined Robert Stephenson & Co. as an apprentice and assisted in the construction and trials of the *Rocket*.

for some reason unknown the tubular boiler was subsequently converted to the old single flue type.

Robert Stephenson attended the opening of the railway, and at the banquet at the King's Head in Canterbury which followed a local reporter commented: "On the health of Mr. Robert Stephenson, Civil Engineer, being given, that gentleman acknowledged the compliment, but spoke so low that the representatives of the Press could not hear distinctly what he said." This is an illustration of that diffidence or shyness in the presence of strangers which he never completely overcame even when he reached the peak of his career. He shared a distaste for public speaking with his great contemporary, I. K. Brunel, who, though by no means diffident, once remarked that it was like playing with a tiger. Like Brunel, however, and unlike his father, Robert became a most formidable witness before parliamentary committees, capable of parrying coolly and skilfully the most subtle and provoking onslaughts of opposition counsel.

Although the demands of the Newcastle factory were very pressing at that time, Robert Stephenson had a particular reason for securing for himself the position of engineer to the Canterbury & Whitstable. In March 1828 he wrote to a friend: "If I may judge from appearances I am to get the Canterbury Railway, which you know is no inconvenient distance from London. How strange! Nay, why say strange, that all my arrangements instinctively regard Broad Street as the pole?" The centre of attraction in Broad Street was Fanny Sanderson, the daughter of a City merchant, a girl he had met shortly before his departure for South America. The fact that he made Broad Street his first port of call in London after his return suggests a strong attachment which had stood the test of long absence. According to Robert Stephenson's biographer, Fanny "was not beautiful, but she had an elegant figure, a delicate and animated countenance, and a pair of singularly expressive dark eyes". She was also, we are told, "an unusually clever woman, and possessed of great tact in influencing others, without letting anyone see her power".

It was not until the end of 1828 that Robert Stephenson proposed marriage, and for the next few months his visits to Broad Street were so frequent that his implacable Quaker partners rebuked him for neglecting his business, a charge which his already recorded achievement during these months effectually refutes. However, after June 1829 there could have been no further cause for complaint for on the 17th of that month Robert and Fanny were married at Bishopsgate parish church and, after a brief honeymoon in North Wales, he took his bride to the home he had prepared for her at 5 Greenfield Place, Newcastle.

Because Robert Stephenson's great work at this period was the development of the steam locomotive it must not be supposed that this occupied him exclusively. On the contrary, in addition to the Canterbury & Whitstable he was responsible for three minor railway works which gave him civil engineering experience that he would very soon turn to much greater account. The first of these was the construction of a spur to connect the Bolton & Leigh line with the Liverpool & Manchester Railway at Kenyon. The second was the Warrington & Newton Railway, a branch line from the Liverpool & Manchester only five miles long which would soon become the first link in Britain's first trunk line. The third was the Leicester & Swannington Railway.

This last was the outcome of a visit by William Stenson, a partner in the Long Lane Colliery at Whitwick, to the Stockton & Darlington Railway in 1828. Like other coal owners in West Leicestershire, Stenson could not sell his coal in Leicester at a price which could compete with the Nottinghamshire owners who had the advantage of water transport. Stenson was much impressed by what he saw at Darlington and decided that a railway from the coalfield to Leicester was the answer to their problem. As a result of a discussion with his partners and John Ellis of Beaumont Leys, a local landowner, the latter undertook to go to Liverpool and see George Stephenson.

The two Stephensons came down to Leicester together and, having walked over the proposed route, George gave his opinion that the line was practicable and should prove a success. This preliminary survey was followed by a meeting at the Bell Hotel, Leicester on 12 February 1829 where a Committee was set up with Ellis as Chairman. This Committee appointed Robert Stephenson as engineer and commissioned a local man, Thomas Miles, to prepare a survey and estimate for the sixteen miles of line. The first section of the line from Leicester to Staunton Road was ceremonially opened on 17 July 1832 and the remaining portion a year later.

The only major engineering work on the line was the mile-long Glenfield Tunnel where an unexpected bed of sand was encountered, a difficulty which almost doubled the estimated cost of the work. The fact that the contractor, Daniel Jowett, fell down one of the working shafts and killed himself did not help matters either.

As at Canterbury, George Stephenson's assistants figure prominently on the Leicester & Swannington, though not always with conspicuous success. Robert Stephenson first transferred Joshua Richardson from Canterbury to act as his resident engineer, but he was succeeded by Gillespie when Richardson took the post of General Manager at Canterbury. Gillespie in turn was replaced by Birkinshaw when he proved dilatory and unsatisfactory. When the locomotives began to arrive from Newcastle, the Stephensons recommended Thomas Cabery's brother Henry to take charge of them, but he, too, failed to please for he was dismissed by the Company for insolence. Evidently Henry soon recovered from this setback for, as mentioned in the first chapter, he ultimately became engineer to the York & North Midland Railway.

The first locomotives supplied to the railway by the Stephensons were all either the coupled *Planet* type, or the larger *Patentee* type which had a third, trailing axle. They also supplied the fixed engines for the Swannington and Bagworth inclines. The Swannington engine, after a very long life, is now preserved in the York Railway Museum. The locomotives proved to be underpowered and in November 1833 Robert Stephenson undertook to supply a much more powerful machine. This was the *Atlas*, an enlarged and improved development of the *Patentee* type with six coupled wheels and equipped with the steam brake which the firm had just patented.

The Leicester & Swannington eventually became the oldest constituent of the Midland Railway and its Chairman, John Ellis, achieved celebrity for the way in which, as Chairman of the Midland, he steered that great Company through the difficult period which followed the fall of its creator, George Hudson. Primarily a mineral line, it was, from an engineering point of view, very small beer compared with the great works which the Stephensons were soon to undertake and its importance for the biographer is that it determined George Stephenson's course after he had completed the

Liverpool & Manchester. It also contributed greatly to his fortune. As a result of his work on the Leicester & Swannington, Robert Stephenson became convinced that the coalfield which the new line served was capable of great development. The existing workings were very shallow and he was sure that richer seams would be tapped by sinking deeper pits. Having satisfied his father that such a venture was worth while, the latter persuaded two of his Liverpool friends, Joseph Sandars and Sir Joshua Walmsley, to join him and together the three partners purchased an estate at Snibston, near to Coalville and adjoining the new railway. At the same time, George Stephenson bought Alton Grange, a house midway between Coalville and Ashby-de-la-Zouch, so that he could superintend operations on the spot. So it came about that in 1831 the engineer closed the front door of the little house in Upper Parliament Street, Liverpool, for the last time, clambered into a high gig drawn by the faithful Bobby, and, with his wife Elizabeth by his side, set off to drive by easy stages down to their new home in Leicestershire.

The sinking of the new pit at Snibston proved a difficult operation. First there was the Keuper marl where water was present in such quantity that it had defeated the Leicestershire miners, who shook their heads and pronounced that Stephenson was attempting an impossible task. Below this treacherous formation the coal measures were overlaid by a bed of extremely hard volcanic greenstone twenty-two feet thick. But mining methods in Northumberland and Durham were at this time far in advance of the Midlands and George Stephenson reinforced his sceptical local labour with men summoned from the Killingworth district, Caldwells, Blackburns and Parkers, friends and associates of his youth and the most skilled miners in the world. To Snibston, too, came his brother James Stephenson and Henry Boag, the son of one of his most intimate friends of West Moor days. The Leicestershire men had failed to master the Keuper marl because they attempted to line their shafts with bricks, but the men from the north knew better and used segments of cast-iron, a system known as 'tubbing' which the midlanders had never seen before. Driving through the hard greenstone below was a desperately slow and costly task, but the faith of the two Stephensons was justified for below it, sure enough, there was a rich seam of excellent coal.

Three shafts in all were sunk at Snibston, and to superintend the winding engines George Stephenson brought from Liverpool a young man named James Campbell, who had entered his employ as a youth soon after the construction of the Liverpool & Manchester railway began. Campbell later became resident engineer on a number of new railways, including the difficult Matlock and Buxton line, and was described by George Stephenson in his old age as 'the best working engineer I ever had'. He was also wont to refer to Snibston Colliery as the most profitable enterprise he had ever undertaken.

While all this activity was going on at Snibston a major campaign was being planned on the railway front; no less than a long-range assault from the north upon the capital. The schemes which had been so eagerly mooted in 1824-5 had lain dormant, partly because of trade depression and the unsettled state of the country, but also because even the most enthusiastic railway advocates deemed it prudent to lie low and await the outcome of the Liverpool & Manchester experiment. The triumph of the Stephensons in the battle for the locomotive at Rainhill led to the revival of the schemes, while the immediate success of the completed railway a year later encouraged speculators to subscribe the necessary capital. Finally, the more settled conditions and the mood of optimism which followed the passage of the Reform Bill and the election of the first reformed parliament in 1832 helped to translate paper plans into hard facts of iron and stone. By creating a great demand for labour, not only on construction work but also in the coal and iron industries, these first great railway projects helped further to ease a tension which, in 1831, had almost reached the breaking point of revolution.

Foremost among these schemes were the plans to connect Liverpool with Birmingham and Birmingham with London. Flying surveys for both these lines had been made in 1825, but now there was great argument over rival routes. In the autumn of 1829 the directors of the Warrington & Newton requested their engineer, Robert Stephenson, to survey an extension of their railway to Sandbach which they envisaged prolonging to Birmingham. Political difficulties then arose, for it appeared that a line through Sandbach would be opposed by the Marquis of Stafford whom, for reasons which are somewhat obscure, both the Liverpool &

Manchester Company and George Stephenson were pledged to support. This placed Robert Stephenson in a serious dilemma for it meant that if he went to Parliament as engineer for this Sandbach scheme he would find his father on the opposition side.

With the support of the Liverpool & Manchester Board, George Stephenson instructed Joseph Locke to survey an alternative route to be known as the Grand Junction which would also be linked to the Warrington & Newton but avoided the disputed territory, passing well to the west of Sandbach by Crewe Hall where the first of the great railway towns would presently grow. This plan naturally appealed to the Liverpool & Manchester directors because it meant that, from the junction at Newton, Birmingham traffic would pass in both directions over their metals, but in Liverpool there was a strong feeling in favour of some more direct route. Charles Vignoles surveyed a line to Runcorn, crossing the Mersey there by what Robert Stephenson described as an 'enormously costly' bridge. Yet another proposal was for a tunnel under the Mersey nearer Liverpool and a line thence to Chester, where it would join up with the route to Birmingham which had been surveyed under George Stephenson's direction in 1825.

These rival Liverpool schemes were too grandiose to succeed at this date; it was Locke's route which won the day, and the Grand Junction Railway, Britain's first trunk line, was authorized by Parliament on 6 May 1833. This Act was remarkable for the curious clause that no Parson was to be a director of the Company.

Although the relationship between George Stephenson and Joseph Locke had been strained since the episode of the Edgehill Tunnel, there had been no break in their association, for Locke was by far the most talented of his assistants and much too valuable a man to lose. As late as February 1832 they had visited Dublin together to report upon plans for the railway from Dublin to Kingstown. But now, over the Grand Junction Railway, differences arose between the two men which rapidly widened into a permanent breach. The root of the trouble was again that disastrous organization, 'George Stephenson & Son', to which Stephenson had been committed by his Quaker partners in 1824. Its defects had already become evident and had been rightly criticized by Telford on the Liverpool & Manchester Railway. Applied to construction schemes of greater magnitude it was bound to fail. In the nation-wide extension of railways which now seemed probable, an ambitious young civil engineer like Locke could see before him a field of almost limitless opportunity in which his services would be eagerly sought after and handsomely rewarded by railway promoters. A system by which George Stephenson had enriched himself and his partners by delegating responsibility to young and inexperienced pupils or to miserably underpaid assistants could not hope to survive in such circumstances. The more talented assistants must inevitably kick over the traces as Robert Stephenson himself had done in 1824, leaving behind only incompetents or new and unfledged apprentices. Evidently the 'Father of Railways' was unable to accept the fact that such a process was inevitable; that he could not hope to maintain indefinitely an undisputed sway over so rapidly expanding an empire; that sooner or later his one-time pupils must become his equals if not his superiors. On the contrary there was never a more jealous parent when, like Locke, one of his railway children grew up, spread his wings and left the Stephenson nest.

Although Locke had been directed by Stephenson when he carried out his Grand Junction survey, it is clear that he hoped to secure the post of Engineer-in-Chief on his own account and considered himself free to do so, his agreement with Stephenson having expired. He had carried out the work so competently that the Grand Junction Board also hoped to appoint him to that high office. George Stephenson, however, thought otherwise and a protracted wrangle ensued which so disgusted Locke that he informed the Company that he would withdraw altogether and have nothing more to do with the railway. This placed the directors in a serious dilemma. They were most anxious not to lose the services of Locke, but on the other hand they were equally anxious not to offend George Stephenson. Their solution was a compromise; they would divide the line into two equal halves, giving Locke the northern and Stephenson the southern division. The boundary between these divisions fell in the little parish of Chapel and Hill Chorlton between Market Drayton and Stone in Staffordshire. This solution was accepted by both sides, though doubtless with some chagrin by Stephenson and his partners.

Locke agreed to the proposal with alacrity, appreciating that even half so large a loaf represented a splendid opportunity for a young and ambitious engineer. He determined to make the most of this great chance, devoting the greatest care to the preparation of minutely detailed estimates and specifications before tenders were invited from contractors. When the line was put out to tender it was, on Locke's insistence, divided into specific contract lengths not exceeding ten miles. By the end of September 1834 all these contracts had been let at prices which agreed with Locke's estimate within very narrow limits.

To this display of businesslike efficiency the southern division presented a sorry contrast. Samuel Smiles, in his biography of George Stephenson, draws a discreet veil of silence over this unhappy episode in his hero's career, while even Locke's biographer, Joseph Devey, though more outspoken, exercised considerable discretion since he was writing only two years after the death of Robert Stephenson. It is evident that Stephenson repeated the mistake he had made on his survey of the Liverpool & Manchester Railway by delegating the work to untrained or incompetent assistants. Drawings and specifications were so inaccurate that prospective contractors wishing to tender were completely baffled by them. The outcome of this was that two months after Locke's last contract was signed only one contract on the southern division had been let. The estimates, too, were as vague as those which Stephenson had made for the Liverpool & Manchester. For example, Devey makes the almost incredible statement that only £6,000 was allowed for the Penkridge viaduct, for which the most favourable tender received was £26,000.

No matter how great the fame of George Stephenson might be in the new railway world, no board of directors could possibly allow such a state of affairs to continue. In their difficulty they appealed to Locke and, still unwilling to offend Stephenson, suggested that the two should become joint engineers for the whole project. With relations between the two men already strained to breaking point, however, such an arrangement could never have worked—as Locke, from his long experience of Stephenson, was probably the first to point out. The end was inevitable. In August 1835 George Stephenson withdrew and Joseph Locke became Chief Engineer for the whole of the Grand Junction Railway. In his summing up of the affair Joseph Devey says of George Stephenson: "The systematic organization of public work where every part has to be foreseen and described was alien to the mind which regarded discipline and method as trammels to fetter its free action, and could not be brought home to it late in a life whose early experience had not been tempered by vigorous education."

From an engineering point of view, the route surveyed by Locke was a relatively easy one, the only major works being the great Dutton viaduct over the Vale Royal near Northwich consisting of twenty 60ft spans 60ft high, and the lesser viaduct over the valley of the River Penk at Penkridge. Smiles describes Dutton as 'perhaps the finest of George Stephenson's viaducts', but as he also makes the erroneous statement that Stephenson was in charge of the northern and Rastrick of the southern divisions of the railway, he was evidently labouring under a misapprehension.

The building of the Grand Junction marked the début of Thomas Brassey, a Cheshire land agent and surveyor, who was soon to become the greatest of railway contractors. He had earlier worked as an assistant surveyor on Telford's Holyhead road and had first made the acquaintance of Stephenson and Locke by supplying stone for the Sankey viaduct. Now, he tendered for both Dutton and Penkridge viaducts, losing the first but securing the second. He soon proved that in the management and control of large labour forces he was a genius without rival, possessing as he did the rare gift of inspiring the most dogged loyalty and devotion in the toughest of navvy gangs. When he died, Brassey had built nearly 4,500 miles of railway in all parts of the world, including no less than 1,700 miles in Britain. For much of his railway work in Britain and on the Continent, Joseph Locke was Engineer-in-Chief, for, in association, the two men formed a team second to none in the railway world and comparable only with that of Telford and his contractors in the earlier canal age. Locke combined engineering genius with level-headed virtues which were rare during the years of the 'railway mania'.

Ironically enough, the work which occasioned most difficulty on the Grand Junction was not the viaducts but a modest cast-iron aqueduct in the Black Country which the Company had to build to carry the Bentley Canal over the line. So persistently did it leak that it was the last structure on the line to be successfully completed, a circumstance which would have amused that master of the iron aqueduct, Thomas Telford, had he still lived. The Grand Junction was opened in 1837 without the customary pomp and ceremony. The locomotive *Wildfire* drew the first train into Birmingham, distinguished only by two small flags bearing the Royal Arms and ciphers. It consisted of the *Triumph*, *Greyhound* and *Swallow* coaches from Liverpool and the *Celerity*, *Umpire* and *Statesman* from Manchester with the addition of a mail coach from each city, these two portions having been united at Newton Junction. Onwards to London His Majesty's mails could not yet travel by rail for the next link, the London & Birmingham Railway, was proving a much tougher proposition and was not then completed.

As in the case of the Grand Junction there was, in the first place, much argument as to the best route to adopt for the London and Birmingham line. One group favoured a route surveyed by Francis Giles through Coventry and Rugby, while another advocated a line through Banbury and Oxford for which Sir John Rennie was responsible. In the summer of 1830 the Stephensons were asked to report on the merits of the two routes and pronounced in favour of the Coventry line, whereupon both groups wisely decided to accept this decision and join forces. The next step was to carry out a detailed survey so that parliamentary powers could be obtained, and the Stephensons undertook to do this by an Agreement signed in Birmingham on 18 September 1830. Because this document was drawn up between the Railway Committee and 'George Stephenson & Son' and was signed by father and son, some subsequent writers, including Samuel Smiles, have wrongly concluded that George Stephenson was responsible not only for surveying but also for constructing the London & Birmingham Railway and that Robert acted as his subordinate or resident engineer. In fact, this agreement applied only to the survey, and even so this preliminary work was carried out under Robert Stephenson's sole command. Exactly what passed between father and son will probably never be known, but it is clear that with the memory of past mistakes in mind and with so much at stake, Robert was taking no chances. Like Locke, he realized that success depended on his breaking the shackles of

"George Stephenson & Son" and tackling this great work as a free agent. Events on the Grand Junction would soon show how right he was. So far his great contribution had been the development of the locomotive, but now he had just joined the Institution of Civil Engineers and was concerned to establish his reputation in the field of railway construction where, until now, he had played only a minor part.

Having been responsible for the preliminary surveys it was not to be expected that either Francis Giles or Sir John Rennie would stand passively aside and allow Robert Stephenson to invade so rich a field unchallenged. Both these engineers had allies on the Railway's London Committee who criticized the agreement which their Birmingham colleagues had reached with the Stephensons. They proposed that Francis Giles should be appointed to act jointly with Robert Stephenson, a suggestion which the latter flatly refused to accept. At the same time Thomas Tooke, one of the London Directors and the Solicitor to the Company, was campaigning on behalf of the Rennie brothers. "Mr. Rennie is stirring up as much interest as possible to get part of the London line", wrote George Stephenson to Michael Longridge on 11 October 1830. "I hope you will do all you can with your friends to counteract this. Tooke the Solicitor is I think Rennie's principal man. You are quite aware that Rennie will be very much in the way and will most likely spoil the job." Obviously George Stephenson had neither forgotten nor forgiven George Rennie's contemptuous refusal to act with him on the Liverpool & Manchester, while Robert Stephenson's repudiation of Giles may not have been entirely free from personal antagonism. Yet, in the case of Giles, events would soon prove that his exclusion was in the best interests of the Company, for Giles later secured the post of Engineer-in-Chief of the London & Southampton Railway, where he showed himself so incompetent that the directors of that Company were compelled to dismiss him and call in Joseph Locke. The truth was that Giles, a middle-aged canal engineer, was not equal to the demands of the railway age. The post of Engineer-in-Chief to a great trunk line of railway called for abilities of quite a new order; for outstanding technical skill allied with a capacity for organization and powers of sheer physical and mental endurance that must be almost superhuman. In such an exacting race the spoils went to the young and the swift, to Robert Stephenson, Joseph Locke, Charles Vignoles and Isambard Brunel, while an older generation of engineers, including George Stephenson himself, lost ground.

That an engineer so young and relatively inexperienced as Robert Stephenson was able to snatch the coveted prize of the London & Birmingham Railway from men of such established reputation as Francis Giles and the Rennies requires further explanation. It is partly explained by the tenor of George Stephenson's letter to Longridge. The majority of England's engineers might still be hostile to the Stephensons, but the new railways needed money before they could employ engineers, and among many of the men who held the purse-strings the name of Stephenson now acted like a charm. The Stephensons wielded this power in two ways: through the close connection between their Quaker partners and the great City bankers such as the Gurneys, and through the backing of the Liverpool merchants. The Liverpool & Manchester Railway had been the particular child of the Liverpool speculators and as the result of its success they were always prepared to back Stephenson's schemes with hard cash. They were also willing to extend this backing to railways with which George Stephenson's name was not directly associated, provided the works were executed in accordance with the Stephenson canon, preferably by an engineer of his school. In the case of the Leicester & Swannington, George Stephenson had little difficulty in raising over a third of the necessary capital in Liverpool, and later and greater schemes met with an equally ready response. But he who pays the piper calls the tune, and so it comes about that over and over again we find, when studying the history of the early railways, an influential 'Liverpool Party' making its presence felt at Company meetings, and almost invariably prevailing. Only on the Great Western where they found themselves confronted by a rebel engineer of quite exceptional calibre did the Liverpudlians fail. Yet it was only after a most heroic struggle with them that Brunel was able to throw the sacred Stephenson rules overboard and adopt his broad gauge.

It was with such formidable support as this that Robert Stephenson was able to prevail on the London & Birmingham and to embark upon a detailed survey with Tom Gooch as his chief assistant. This work was undertaken in the autumn of 1830 when the Company hoped to be ready to promote a Bill in the next parliamentary session, but it was soon obvious that time was too short. Robert Stephenson carried out a second survey in 1831 and the London & Birmingham Railway Bill was read for the first time on 20 February 1832. The route determined by Stephenson, which was that actually built, differed materially from that originally recommended by Francis Giles, who had proposed leaving London by Islington, Chipping Barnet, South Mimms, Leverstock Green, and Hemel Hempstead.

Although in the industrial midlands and north-west the strength of the opposition to railways was already weakening, in the home counties where Tory landowners and farmers still held undisputed sway the opposition to the railway monster was still implacable. The little surveying parties encountered fierce antagonism which gave Robert Stephenson a foretaste of the coming struggle in Parliament and must have carried his mind back to that first eventful survey of the Liverpool & Manchester railway with William James. The furtive Sunday-morning survey through the property of a hostile clergyman while he was delivering his sermon was typical of the stratagems which Stephenson and Gooch were forced to employ, for while Parliament insisted upon the presentation of detailed plans, it did not give the unfortunate surveyors any rights of entry in order to prepare them.

To the support of the opposing landowners rallied those whose profits or livelihood depended on roads or canals. To these existing transport interests which had for so long enjoyed an undisturbed monopoly the Stockton & Darlington and the Liverpool & Manchester railways had seemed purely local threats which wishful thinking outside the area refused to take seriously. But the London & Birmingham was a very different matter. This insolent newcomer threatened to march for mile after mile beside the Grand Junction Canal, that great water link between the Midlands and London where, in addition to the slow-moving bulk carriers, an average of twenty-six fly-boats a day passed through in each direction carrying the lighter and more perishable traffic which would surely be lost to a swifter competitor. No less grave was the threat to the teeming traffic of Watling Street: to the coach proprietors who despatched sixteen coaches each way daily between London and Birmingham alone; to the owners of post horses; to the wagoners and to the drovers of the great herds of sheep and cattle, 8,000 head or more each week, that travelled to London on the hoof. This new fire-breathing monster threatened to ruin all. Moreover, the fact that the builders of this new iron road proposed to enjoy a monopoly of the traffic upon it sharpened antagonism. It seemed a flagrant repudiation of the time-honoured principle that any highway should be open to all upon payment of tolls. Both the canal and the early tramway proprietors had accepted this principle without question, but now it had been lightly cast aside. The fact was, of course, that the Stockton & Darlington Company had, for the benefit of its successors, proved by bitter practical experience that this old principle and the steam locomotive simply did not mix. Hence the railway's only sop to the old tradition was the private-owner wagon.

When we try to assess the weight of opposition which the first railway engineers encountered, we tend grossly to underestimate the extent and magnitude of the road-coach industry that so suddenly found itself threatened with extinction. The efforts of generations of Christmas-card artists have made the road coach the supreme romantic symbol of the 'good old days' when the world moved at a leisurely and stately pace. In fact it was only the work of the great road engineers, Telford and Macadam, that made a reliable all-the-year-round and nation-wide network of coach services possible. Hence it was a young and virile industry which had scarcely reached the peak of its development when the unexpected iron bolt fell out of a clear sky. It was, moreover, very far from leisurely. Man's desire to get from place to place as quickly as possible is much older than mechanical transport and the coach industry did its best to satisfy it.

We are all familiar with the artist's scene at the coaching inn where the travellers are welcomed by a jovial landlord who fortifies them with liquor while an old ostler leads out the change horses. In fact, the real scene at such an inn when one of the crack coaches came in can only be compared with a pit stop during a Grand Prix motor race where every second is vital. It was in this way that England's coaches achieved a unique reputation for speed and the

Hirondelle (nicknamed the 'Iron Devil'), the *Hibernia* and the *Shrewsbury Wonder* were able to dispute the title of 'fastest coach in the world'. When the *Shrewsbury Wonder*, which was reputed to cover one eight-mile stage in half-an-hour, stopped to change horses, the wheelers were standing ready-harnessed to a spare pole so that the change only involved coupling the pole pin and attaching the traces of the leaders. Benton, the famous whip of the *Hirondelle*, however, scorned such devices, yet could boast that with the change horses precisely positioned at each side of the road and every move perfectly drilled, he could complete a change in thirty seconds.

In their campaign against their iron enemy, the coach proprietors painted dire pictures of the fearful disasters in store for those who were foolhardy enough to travel by rail. Yet travel by the fast road-coaches was by no means without risk, as we read in a letter from George Stephenson to Longridge dated at Alton Grange in June 1835. "I left London last night and arrived here this morning," he writes, "without the repetition of the upset I had in going up by the 'Hope' which I daresay you would see by the papers. I *saw* she was *going to upset* and being inside made use of a little science which brought me off safe. I never saw such a sight before, passengers like dead pigs in every direction and the road a sheet of blood. Two, I apprehend, will die."

Yet notwithstanding such hazards as this and the discomforts of an outside seat in bad weather, even a railway engineer like F. R. Conder could look back in later life with nostalgic regret to that brief heyday of road-coach travel which the railways so speedily extinguished. "No mode of getting over the ground has yet been discovered," he wrote, "to equal, in the physical enjoyment it conveyed, that of the old first-class coaches. ...." He then goes on:

The stage between Cheltenham and Tewkesbury was one of the most rapid and agreeable run over by any of the fast coaches. As the hand of the Town clock reached the quarter before 6 am, the two opposition coaches, on each of which its coachman had been seated for 4 or 5 minutes with elbows squared and whip advanced, while the guard stood behind with one foot on the step, would begin to move, rather with the gentle motion of machinery than the ordinary jerk of starting horses. Steadily and rapidly the pace quickened to a flight, without a touch, with scarcely a sound to the horses. Then the bugle began to ring out a cheery tune, not the classical double note of the mail horn, but the merry strains of 'Jim Crow'. The bugle of the opposition coach, at some fifty yards distance, would re-echo. The fresh morning air, the fragrance of the wide, hedgeless beanfields, the distant rugged outline of the great Malvern range, clear in the early morn before you; the purple glory of the sunshine bursting over the Cotswolds behind; the steady, unswerving, rapid motion, all combined to give a sense of exhilarating power for which the greater speed of the dusty, noisy, uninteresting train can afford no substitute.

The author of this eloquent tribute was an articled pupil under Robert Stephenson on the London & Birmingham who later worked on the Birmingham & Gloucester Railway which soon silenced the coach horns on the Tewkesbury road. That a railway engineer could write like this helps us to understand the weight of feeling, disinterested as well as interested, that was ranged against the new railways. In these days of supersonic flight we may feel a certain sympathy for that opposition which attempted in vain to stay the progress of steam power. For it is at least arguable that with every increase in speed, travel has become less pleasurable, and that as we are all bound for the same ultimate destination we might profitably enjoy such pleasure as we may upon our journey.

The road-coach proprietors, like their amphibious brethren the owners of canal 'fly-boats' and 'swift packets', realized that the challenge of the London & Birmingham Railway Bill was their Waterloo. If Parliament sanctioned it their day was done, for other great trunk lines would surely follow. Consequently there took place a parliamentary struggle which made the battle for the Liverpool & Manchester Bill seem a mere skirmish. And the great target for the skilful sorties of opposition counsel was Robert Stephenson. They made great play with his youth and inexperience and used every artifice in their efforts to fault his plans and estimates and to trap him into some contradictory statement. But these weapons, which they had employed against the elder Stephenson with such devastating and humiliating results, never got past the son's guard. Whatever hesitancy and diffidence Robert Stephenson may have displayed before, it certainly was not evident now as hour after hour he coolly and skilfully parried their onslaughts to emerge from the long ordeal quite unscathed.

One subject of attack was his estimate for the great cutting through the chalk at Tring, where the opposition maintained that his angles of slope were far too steep. If the excavation was not to fall in upon itself, Counsel maintained, the sides would have to be cut back at a cost far greater than that shown in the estimate. Robert Stephenson could do no more than deny this, but after the Committee rose he recalled that when his greater predecessor, Thomas Telford, had been working on the Holyhead road improvements he had made a cutting through the same Chiltern chalk at Dunstable. Robert had already been under examination for three days and for the four preceding nights he had worked continuously without sleep, but he determined to visit Dunstable before the next day's session. He worked in his rooms until midnight, had a quick meal and a nap, and then set off for Dunstable in a post chaise with Tom Gooch. They arrived at Dunstable at dawn, found to their intense satisfaction that the angle of Telford's cutting was exactly the same as theirs, and drove back in triumph to London armed with an invincible defence.

On 1 June 1832 the Bill passed the Commons by a large majority, but on 8 July it was thrown out by the Lords. "By God!" an opposing peer was heard to remark, "it is one of the damnedest, rascally things I ever saw in my political existence!" "Why", exclaimed Sir Astley Cooper, one of the affected landowners, "if this sort of thing be permitted to go on, you will in a very few years destroy the *noblesse*!" On this sally Robert Stephenson had commented wryly to Gooch afterwards: "It is really provoking to find one who has been made a 'Sir' for cutting that wen out of George the Fourth's neck, charging us with contemplating the destruction of the *noblesse*!"

Always easily cast down, Robert Stephenson was almost heartbroken by the thought that all his labours, his sleepless nights and the interminable hard-fought battle in the Committee Room had been in vain. But he was greatly encouraged when the Chairman of the Lords' Committee, Lord Wharncliffe of the 'Grand Allies', took him aside and consoled him with the words: "My young friend, don't take this to heart. The decision is against you; but you have made such a display of power that your fortune is made for life." Robert Stephenson had indeed made a profound impression upon all who heard him, and this, coupled with the success of the Bill in the Commons, led to the Company's refusal to accept defeat notwithstanding the fact that they had already expended £32,000 in legal and parliamentary expenses.

Five days after the rejection of the Bill, Lord Warncliffe presided over a meeting of the Lords and Commons favourable to the railway, at which the following resolution was carried unanimously: 'That this meeting see no parliamentary or other grounds for abandoning this great undertaking, convinced as they are that by timely explanations and a continuance of judicious management, the difficulties which occurred in the progress of the Bill may be removed in the ensuing Session of Parliament.'

Removed they certainly were, for in the next session the Bill speedily passed both Houses almost without opposition. In the meantime Robert Stephenson had carried out a third survey by which some of the landowners' objections had been met, but for the most part the 'timely explanations and judicious management' consisted simply in buying off the opposition. The Company learnt that if the landowners were shown blank cheques the impending destruction of the *noblesse* miraculously ceased to be a matter of concern to them, and by paying out £750,000 for land originally valued at £250,000 the most strenuous objectors were silenced.

With the London & Birmingham Bill safely passed at last, the great question for Robert Stephenson was whether he would secure the post of engineer to the Company. On 28 May 1833 he received an encouraging letter from Richard Creed, the London Secretary, who wrote: "Nothing is said as to the appointment of engineer or solicitor, but I think *you* may be easy on that head. You have friends here and in Birmingham who appreciate your merits and services." As Lord Wharncliffe had said, he had scored a great personal triumph in Parliament which had silenced the claims of rival engineers and won over the London directors to his side. Yet four more anxious months went by before he was able to write in his notebook: "Signed contract with the London and Birmingham directors, before Mr. Barker, at the Hummums, Covent Garden." The date was 20 September 1833, and this time the signature was Robert Stephenson's alone. There was no more talk of 'Messrs. George Stephenson & Son'. That unhappy association was ended so far as he was concerned. He was now, as Engineer-in-Chief, solely responsible for building through difficult country 112 miles of railway. He had not yet passed his thirtieth birthday, but he now confronted, not without secret misgivings, the greatest task that any civil engineer had ever undertaken.

CHAPTER ELEVEN

Building the London & Birmingham Railway

A T THE TIME the London & Birmingham Bill passed into law the Company's directors requested two engineers, H. R. Palmer and J. U. Rastrick, to report upon Robert Stephenson's plans. At the conclusion of his long and favourable report Rastrick wrote:

> Let nothing deter you from executing the work in the most substantial manner and on the most scientific principles so that it may serve as a model for all future railways and become the wonder and admiration of Posterity. There is not anything but what a Large Spirited Company like yours can accomplish. Remember that faint heart never won fair lady. Therefore let me conclude with the advice of Queen Elizabeth to one of her courtiers: *Climb Boldly Then*.

It was with such heartening support from a fellow engineer who had once opposed him in the battle for the locomotive that Robert Stephenson set about his colossal undertaking. Today, when we look at his London & Birmingham Railway, at the massive masonry work of bridge or tunnel portal or towering viaduct, at the lofty embankments or the chasm-like cuttings at Tring or Blisworth, and appreciate that these were the works of human hands unaided by mechanical equipment, we can surely agree that Stephenson did indeed build to the wonder and admiration of succeeding generations.

Hitherto, notwithstanding the constant travelling which it entailed, Robert had kept his home in Newcastle, but now, not without regret, he was compelled to move to London. He and his young wife took a furnished cottage in St. John's Wood until they were able to move into the house he had bought on Haverstock Hill. To him as to Joseph Locke, the difficulties which had arisen during the building of the Liverpool & Manchester Railway had been a salutary lesson and he devoted the greatest care and thought to the preliminary planning and to the choice of Assistant Engineers.

The line was already divided for administrative purposes into Birmingham and London divisions, the boundary being near Roade. For engineering purposes Robert Stephenson divided each of these divisions into two districts and appointed to each an Assistant Engineer with three sub-assistants under him. These Districts and their engineers were as follows (the place names are inclusive):

    I   Camden Town-Aldbury,[1] John Birkinshaw;
   II   Tring-Castlethorpe, John Crossley;
  III Blisworth-Kilsby Tunnel, Frank Forster;
  IV Rugby-Birmingham, Thomas Gooch.

Later, while the work was in progress, Forster was transferred to District IV when Gooch was promoted to the Manchester & Leeds Railway, and Forster's place was taken by G. H. Phipps whom Robert Stephenson brought from the Newcastle works.

For contract purposes, Robert Stephenson split each district into lengths which averaged approximately six miles of line. In addition, certain of the major works, such as the Kilsby tunnel and the viaducts over the rivers Avon and Rea, were the subject of special contracts, making twenty-nine in all. The contracts in each district were separately numbered, these numbers being distinguished by the addition of the initial letter of the name of the engineer responsible. Thus, for example, the contract numbers in Gooch's district bore the suffix 'G'. By later standards these contract lots were small but, as Robert Stephenson realized, no civil engineering contractors existed in 1834 with the capital resources which would enable them to undertake more than a small portion of a work of such magnitude. Even as it was, many of the contractors would soon discover that they had bitten off more than they could chew. The era was still to come when a great railway contractor such as Thomas Brassey could tender for a whole trunk line of railway and, by the flux of his own picked labour force, weld an army of small sub-contractors into one efficient and disciplined team. Such an organization to a

[1] Jeaffreson states that the London Division was split into three districts, the first, from the terminus to the Brent river bridge being under Robert Stephenson's own supervision with Birkinshaw as his assistant. This may have been an original plan which was abandoned at an early stage, since the contract lists in the Company's records show four divisions as stated above.

very great extent relieved that burden which, on the London & Birmingham, fell so heavily and squarely upon the shoulders of the Engineer-in-Chief and his senior staff. The only men who did not profit by the rise of the great contractors were the small sub-contractors who found themselves so shrewdly and efficiently organized. On the London & Birmingham they too frequently contrived to profit at the expense of an inexperienced main contractor, and the more work the unfortunate man let out to them the greater his risk of failure. "The more you dissects it [the work]", a cynical sub-contractor once remarked, "the better it cuts up."

An abuse which was freely indulged on the London & Birmingham and which the large contractor stamped out was the truck system whereby the contractor paid his men with credit tickets which could be exchanged for provisions and other stores in a 'tommy shop' owned by himself. Robert Stephenson's pupil, F. R. Conder, maintains that the unscrupulous contractor who ran a tommy shop could raise the profit on his contract from the normal 8 to 12 per cent to as much as 30 or 40 per cent. This pernicious system, which was responsible for many a dark chapter in the history of the Industrial Revolution, had long been prohibited by the Truck Acts, but this did not prevent it flourishing on the London & Birmingham. Here is Tom Gooch reporting a typical case to Robert Stephenson: "Ellison, one of the sub-contractors on No. 2, has a shop at his own dwelling near Lea Hall which is kept by himself and supplies his men with shoes, bacon, bread and groceries. There is occasional grumbling amongst the men against the high prices they pay, but I cannot tell how far they are justified."

Although these tommy shops were illegal, in calling for such reports as this Robert Stephenson was more concerned to check too flagrant an abuse of the system than to stamp it out. From his point of view the advantage of tommy shops like Ellison's which did not sell liquor was that they reduced the number of man-hours lost through drunkenness. When the navvies were paid in cash they at once went 'off on the randy', as they put it, spending most of their wages on a drinking spree which frequently put them out of action for several days. In order to limit this lost time, Robert Stephenson ruled that cash wages should not be paid weekly but monthly.

Yet the ex London & Birmingham navvy whom Henry Mayhew

found penniless and starving in a refuge at Cripplegate one bitter winter's night in 1849 presented a very different picture of the tommy shop.

> The first work that I done was on the Manchester and Liverpool [he told Mayhew]. I was a lad then. I used to grease the railway wagons, and got about 1s 6d a day. . . . The next place I had after that was on the London and Brummagen. There I went as a horse-driver, and had 2s 6d a day. Things was dear then, and at the tommy shops they was much dearer; for there was tommy shops on every line then; and indeed every contractor and sub-contractor had his shop that he forced his men to deal at or else he wouldn't have them in his employ. . . . Well, sir, I worked on that line through all the different contracts till it was finished: sometimes I was digging, sometimes shovelling. I was mostly at work on open cuttings. All this time I was getting from 2s 6d to 3s and 3s 6d a day; that was the top price; and if I'd had the ready money to lay out myself, I could have done pretty well, and maybe put a penny or two by against a rainy day; but the tommy shop and the lodging house took it all out of us. You see, the tommy shop found us in beer and they would let us drink away all our earnings there if we pleased, and when pay time came we should have nothing to take. If we didn't eat and drink at the tommy shop we should have no work. Of an evening we went to the tommy shop after the drink and they'd keep drawing beer for us there as long as we'd have anything coming to us next pay-day . . . and when we had drunk away all that would be coming to us, why they'd turn us out. . . . Well, with such goings on, in course there wasn't no chance in the world for us to save a halfpenny . . . and now half of us walk about and starve, or beg, or go to the union.

It is clear that this young giant in his blue smock and high lace-up boots, burst now and almost soleless, was 'telling the tale' to the credulous Mayhew. He was understandably bitter, for he was looking back from a day when the great railway boom had collapsed and the navvy had fallen on hard times. The reports which Stephenson received from his staff on the tommy shops reveal how close an eye he kept on their activities. That the system was pernicious and exploited the navvies by overcharging them for food is certain, but liquor they usually obtained elsewhere. It was no more in the interest of the contractors than the engineers to let their men drink themselves senseless in their tommy shops, since by so doing they would lose on the contract what they won in the tommy shop. The main concern of both was how to stop the navvies drinking, and the tommy shop system was certainly used to this end.

Having completed his advance planning and engaged his staff, Robert Stephenson's next task was to stake out the line. This work was begun in November 1833, and despite appalling winter weather conditions it was completed in the following February. That the Engineer-in-Chief shared with his staff the rigours of the English winter is clear from a letter he despatched to Captain Moorsom, the Birmingham Committee Secretary, from the Cock Inn at Stony Stratford in January. "I have been over the whole of Forster's length with him. . . . The weather is past endurance. I am nearly laid up having been thoroughly drenched for the last few days." Such work was a severe ordeal for a man whose health was never robust. Altogether, by the time the railway was completed, Robert Stephenson reckoned that he had walked its entire length no fewer than fifteen times, apart from the journeys made on horseback.

As the staking-out proceeded, so the contract drawings and specifications were prepared and this alone was a major undertaking. Three copies of each drawing were made, one for Robert Stephenson, one for his District Engineer, one for the Managing Committee, and for eighteen months thirty drawings a week were produced, each representing two days' work by one draughtsman. This work was begun in a cottage at a point where the Edgware Road crossed the route, but as this was far too small the Company bought the Eyre Arms Hotel at Swiss Cottage, in what was then open country, and turned its large dining room into a drawing office. Here, among others, Robert Stephenson's Edinburgh friend, G. P. Bidder, was employed.

Work was to proceed simultaneously over the whole line. By the autumn of 1835 every contract had been let, while those which had been let the previous year were already in progress. Among the names of contractors were several which are familiar to the engineering historian: Daniel Pritchard, who drove the new Harecastle canal tunnel for Telford; the brothers Cubitt; John Chapman and John Burge, who later built the greater part of Box tunnel for Brunel. With all these contractors engaged, as many as 20,000 men were at work and the labour force never fell below 12,000 until the task was completed. Never since the building of the Pyramids had the world witnessed an undertaking upon so gigantic a scale and the master of it was one young man. That it never mastered him was due in great measure to Robert Stephenson's care in the preliminary planning of his organization and in the choice of his assistant engineers. The result was that although he kept a finger on the pulse of the whole enterprise and was always to be found on the spot wherever trouble threatened, he was able to delegate a great deal of responsibility to his District Engineers. In this respect he differed both from his father and from his famous rival, I. K. Brunel, whose star was then just rising in the railway firmament. George Stephenson's attempts to delegate were usually disastrous because he lacked administrative capacity and often relied too much on young and untrained assistants. Brunel's powers of organization were outstanding and he chose able assistants, but, because of what Conder called his "extreme and unprecedented insistence on excellence of work", he was unable to delegate and so retained a degree of personal control that was almost superhuman. Conder, speaking from personal experience, puts the contrast between the two great engineers in this way: "The order of his [Robert Stephenson's] office was not such as to over-burden the Engineer-in-Chief with details that fell properly within the competence of Residents, or even of the sub-assistants. But the engineers on the Broad Gauge lines appeared to regard themselves less as the officers of the Company than as the channel of the will of Mr. Brunel." In other words Robert Stephenson developed and extended to suit his greater purposes that organization which had first been evolved by his famous predecessor, Thomas Telford, and by so doing he, like Joseph Locke, set a pattern for posterity. Brunel, on the other hand, neither followed nor set any precedent, because it was only his unique genius that made his system workable at all.

No matter how successfully he might delegate, Robert Stephenson's task was still extremely exacting. His pupil describes the man and his work as he saw him at that time. 'In earlier days', says Conder, 'he charmed all who came in contact with him', but he 'showed something of his father's determined and autocratic temper when in the saddle on the London & Birmingham.' Conder particularly recalled his eyes, which he describes as 'piercing and very direct'. 'It is rare', he says, 'that a civilian has so free and almost martial an address, it is still more rare for such features to be seen in any man who has not inherited them from a line of gently nurtured ancestors.' 'He knew how to attach people to him; he also knew how to be a firm and persistent hater' and there were 'occasional outbursts of fierce northern passion'. He spoke rapidly, incisively and always to the point. 'He was,' Conder recalled, 'very jealous of opposition or self-assertion and could be very unjust at times on suspecting it.' Frankness and honesty on the part of his opponent would speedily disarm him, however. Conder remembered an occasion when an errant contractor was subjected to a withering dressing-down from the Chief which ended by Stephenson calling him 'a most infernal scoundrel'. 'Well, sir, I know I am', the unfortunate man replied meekly, whereupon Stephenson's anger at once evaporated and peace was restored.

Despite his youth, Robert Stephenson had obviously become a formidable personality by this time, as indeed the commander-in-chief of such a vast, tough and unruly army had to be. His lieutenants, the District Engineers and their assistants, had to be equally hard-boiled, and Conder recalls one of them, whom he does not name, whose every sentence was punctuated with unprintable swear words. He records a Sunday-morning conversation between a contractor and this engineer which ran as follows: "Been to church?" asked the contractor. "No" replied the engineer, "I've such a —— headache that I said I'll be —— if I go to the —— church, so I took a little walk and what the —— —— do you think I met? Why three of your —— men. I never heard fellows swear in such a —— way in all my —— life. I was —— shocked. I said 'Hello you ——s, is this the way you go on coming from a —— church?'"

Yet beneath Robert Stephenson's autocratic façade lurked that self-doubt and lack of confidence in his own powers which haunted him all his life. To an old and intimate friend who at this time congratulated him on his rise to fame and fortune he confessed: "I sometimes feel very uneasy about my position. My courage at times almost fails me and I fear that some fine morning my reputation may break under me like an eggshell." Consequently he lived in such a state of anxiety and acute nervous tension that he not only became, like Brunel, a heavy cigar-smoker, but also, according to

Conder, resorted to 'the fatal aid' of drugs. When we add to this an
output of physical and mental energy so unsparing that it left little
time for sleep, it is no wonder that the London & Birmingham
undermined Stephenson's health and shortened his life. When he
felt his presence was needed somewhere up the line, it was no
uncommon thing, says Conder, to see him jump to the outside seat
of a northbound coach on a winter's night without pausing to put
on an overcoat or otherwise equip himself for such a rigorous
journey.

Robert Stephenson's anxieties were not lessened by the knowledge
that he and his father had many jealous and bitter enemies who
would miss no opportunity to attack him and who would be delighted to see him fail and fall from his high position. He realized,
too, that the most formidable of these enemies were within the
gates, being James Cropper and his faction, who formed the dissident minority within that same 'Liverpool Party' which had helped
both him and his father to fame. It was at the beginning of 1835,
when many of the contracts had still to be let, that these enemies
found a pretext for attack.

To assist in the construction work the new Company ordered its
first locomotive[1] from Robert Stephenson & Company and at once
James Cropper raised again the cry of monopoly. In great distress
Robert Stephenson wrote for advice to Michael Longridge on 26
January:

> Our enemies, viz, Rathbone and Cropper, are raising a hue and cry
> about our having an Engine to build at Newcastle—they say another
> article will be brought out by Lardner on the subject. They half intimate
> that I shall withdraw either from the Railway or the Engine building.
> The revenge of these people is quite insatiable. This distresses me very
> much. Can I withdraw temporarily from the engine building? I wish
> you would think this over for the above named parties are annoying
> me all they can by advancing Vignoles and his opposite opinions. The
> Directors support me, but it makes it sad uphill work.

To this the philosophical Longridge replied:

> I have maturely considered what you say concerning dispensing *pro*

[1] This was the *Harvey Combe*, and when delivered for work on the Cubitt Brothers'
contract it represented the highest development of the six-wheeled *Patentee* type. It was
fitted with a form of gab valve-gear using four eccentrics.

tempore of your shares in the Engine Building concern—this can easily be accomplished by your Father taking them on his own account with an understanding that he is to transfer them again to you upon your having finished your Agreement with the Directors of the London & Birmingham Rail Way.

I feel very solicitous that you should devote the whole of your faculties *undividedly* to this magnificent undertaking; this being once *well accomplished*, your name and future are built upon a Rock, and you may afterwards smile at the malice of your enemies. The only reason which induces me to approve of this arrangement is that it will leave your *mind quite at ease*. Were you as case-hardened in these matters as myself I would set Messrs. Cropper, Rathbone, Dr. Lardner and all such at defiance—but you have not yet attained sufficient philosophy to say 'None of these things move me',—when you arrive at the sober age of Fifty you will bear these rubs better.

James Cropper pressed home his attack, for in February Robert Stephenson again wrote to Longridge:

My Liverpool friends are annoying me more than I anticipated even when I wrote you last. They have passed a resolution in the shape of a recommendation to our Directors, 'that no Director or Engineer shall have any Contract with the Company, more particularly for locomotive Engines'.

The Liverpool people do not disguise that this recommendation to our Directors is aimed especially at me. *The Directors will be compelled to act upon it.* This has all sprung from the Quakers and Bury our Liverpool Rival.

In reply, Longridge urged him on no account to resign from the Railway ("you will suffer in your Fortune—and still more in your Fame—and your enemies will mightily triumph over you") but to transfer his shares in the Engine Company. In the event the hostile resolution was passed, but Robert Stephenson did not part with his shares and for ten years thereafter the Newcastle Works received no orders for locomotives from the London & Birmingham Company.

James Cropper's principle that if you sling mud sufficiently copiously and vigorously some of it is bound to stick was certainly well founded, for the view that the Stephensons held a tightly exclusive railway monopoly remained widely current long after this decision was taken. Thus Colonel Sir Charles Dance, the steam-carriage builder, writing to the Duke of Wellington in 1837 could say: "The monopoly on the rail-roads is such that however objectionable the present engines may be, no invention has a chance of being tried if it is likely to interfere with Mr. Stephenson's arrangements. . . ." There is no doubt that George Stephenson's attitude contributed to this view. He considered himself, and was regarded by many, as the great oracle where railway matters were concerned, and was usually sceptical if not contemptuous of the ideas and inventions of others. The fact that he was often right did not make him more popular. Yet the pessimistic Robert's attitude was the precise opposite of his father's. So far from claiming any monopoly of knowledge or skill, he could not foresee any prosperous future for the firm which bore his name because of the number of rival locomotive builders who were entering the field.

Robert Stephenson's gloomy forecast was proved wrong, and his decision against the temporary transfer of his shares in the firm to his father was a wise one. Such an obvious ruse would certainly have been detected, exposed, and bitterly attacked by Cropper. Furthermore, although the resolution which prevented Robert Stephenson & Co. from supplying locomotives to the railway was moved by jealousy, it was nevertheless ethically correct and in accordance with that code of conduct governing engineers and contractors which Thomas Telford had laid down. In the event, too, it was the railway company which suffered from the decision. Ironically, Edward Bury obtained a far more effective monopoly of London & Birmingham motive power than the Stephensons would ever have done, and exercised it to the company's great disadvantage. For Bury was appointed Locomotive Superintendent with full responsibility both for supplying and maintaining the necessary locomotive power. All these locomotives were built at his own works in Liverpool and such was his devotion to the little four-wheeled engine, which he originally designed to compete with Robert Stephenson's *Planet*, that it was still the standard type on the London & Birmingham long after other companies were using the far more powerful engines built by Robert Stephenson & Co. and other makers. That Edward Bury 'got away with it' so long was thanks to the superbly level road that Robert Stephenson laid down for his little engines; but even so, in the later days of his monopoly, it was no uncommon sight to see three or more of them harnessed to one train.

Meanwhile the Newcastle firm took the loss of the London & Birmingham Company's custom in its stride. Indeed, having been responsible for developing locomotives of such outstanding quality and performance it is very hard to understand why Robert Stephenson should ever have entertained any doubt as to the success of his firm or taken so seriously the loss of one Company's orders. By 1840, quite apart from satisfactory sales at home, the Newcastle factory had sent locomotives all over Europe; to France for the Alais & Beaucaire, the Havre de Grace and the St. Etienne Railways; to the State Railways of Belgium; to Austria for the Kaiser Ferdinand Northern Railway; to Germany for the Berlin & Potsdam, Berlin & Saxony, Leipzig & Dresden and Nuremberg & Furth Railways; to Italy for the Milan & Como Railway and to Russia for the St. Petersburg & Pavlovsk Railway. In America the list of new railways which ordered Stephenson locomotives was no less impressive, including as it did the Mohawk & Hudson, the Newcastle & French-town, the Baltimore & Susquehanna, the Saratoga & Schenectady, the Charlestown & Columbia and the Camden & Amboy.

So, in a few years, the genius of the two Stephensons sent the fire which old Robert Metcalf had kindled with his burning glass in the belly of *Locomotion* flaming across the world like an Olympic torch to herald a new world-order. Admittedly, no pioneers can ever hope to maintain for long a national, let alone a world-wide, supremacy in a development of such overwhelming importance. In the United States Matthias Baldwin was soon building loco-motives better suited to local operating conditions than the im-ported product, and the same was true in the Continental countries, but the spread of railways was so rapid and so great that Robert Stephenson & Company had no reason to fear any lack of orders. This, then, was one anxiety which Robert Stephenson might have spared himself at a time when his work on the London & Birming-ham was extending him to the utmost limit of his powers.

The original Act of the Company laid down that the London terminus of the railway should be 'in a field on the west side of the high road leading from London to Hampstead'. This had been chosen because the land beyond the road belonged to Lord Southampton, one of the most resolute opponents of the railway in the Lords. But Robert Stephenson soon learned from the Agent for the Southampton Estate that his lordship had had second thoughts as a result of the increasing prosperity of the Liverpool & Manchester Company. On the strength of this information, therefore, Robert Stephenson, after some hesitation, suggested to his directors that the line should be extended to Lancaster Place, Strand, a site with direct access to London River. He was apparently told to mind his own business, but notwithstanding this rebuff the Board soon accepted his proposal to extend, though not as far as he had suggested. Parliamentary powers were obtained to extend the railway to a terminus on 'a vacant piece of ground in a place called Euston Square', and the contract for the extension was let to the Cubitt brothers in December 1835. Unlike the rest of the line, the Euston extension involved a steep gradient, falling to the terminus, which it was decided to work by fixed engines at Camden Town.

In order to appreciate the immense impetus which railways gave to the transformation of England from a rural to an urban and industrial society it is only necessary to picture London as it was at this moment. The total population of London was slightly less than one and a half millions and on this north-western side the arc of the Regent's Canal bounded the city like a moat. From Kilburn to Camden Town the line of way lay through open country, while the area between Park Street and the Hampstead Road bridge was occupied by market gardens and, curiously, by the huts of a small colony of firework makers. The latter combined with the market gardeners to put up a stubborn but ineffectual resistance to the railway surveyors. Their leader, Bunyan by name, who was something of an orator, inveighed against "you who clamber over folkses walls with your ladders and your hammers, your levels and your bevels and your devils". That 'vacant piece of ground' at Euston Square where the railway would terminate consisted of the fields and buildings of a great milk purveyor. Legend had it that this man was always trying to build up a herd of a thousand cows but that owing to losses he could never exceed 999. His vast herd was fed on brewer's grains, and Conder remarked caustically that 'a visit to the abode of the 1000 cows was not calculated to give one an appetite for milk'. This, then, was a typical cross-section of London's perimeter as it was before the railways made it possible to import milk and perishable foods from a distance so that the capital could grow and cover miles of fields with bricks and mortar.

The building of the line from Camden Town to Euston Square was a difficult operation. The Regent's Canal had to be crossed without interrupting traffic; sewers had to be avoided; it was stipulated that the levels of existing roads must not be altered and that many additional bridges should be built to allow for future urban development. The works were made wide enough to allow for four lines of railway because at this time it was anticipated that the new Great Western Railway would form a junction and use the same Euston Square terminus. This proposed junction never materialized, but the provision of a four-track formation saved Robert Stephenson's successors a great deal of work later.

On this extension the lines ran in cutting between high retaining walls. These walls gave a great deal of trouble because Stephenson did not appreciate the treacherous behaviour of the blue clay when exposed to air and moisture. The walls persistently gave way until inverts had to be built from wall to wall under the road bed. The same mistake cost the Company dear on the first major work on the line—the Primrose Hill tunnel. Robert Stephenson had assumed that the tunnel could be built without an invert and on this assumption the contract was let for £120,000. Not only did an invert prove necessary, but to resist the pressure of the clay the thickness of brickwork in the arch had to be increased and Roman cement instead of mortar used for jointing. Primrose Hill was the first contract to be started, in June 1834, and by November the contractors, Jackson & Sheddon, had already been defeated by the difficulties. Robert Stephenson then took over direct control of the works, which were completed at a cost of £280,000, more than double the estimate.

The same sorry story was to be repeated elsewhere on the line. Indeed the Watford tunnel was the only major engineering work which the original contractor was able to complete without the direct intervention of the Company. Only at Watford did the chalk enable Robert Stephenson to dispense with an invert as he planned to do at Primrose Hill, and this was the reason for the contractor's success. Even here, however, there was a disaster. A pilot-heading was incautiously opened out to full height beneath the mouth of a working shaft which had not been adequately secured, and a sudden run of sand overwhelmed nine men who were working below.

At Wolverton in December 1834 Robert Stephenson ran into trouble of quite a different kind. To form the long embankment across the Ouse Valley north of Wolverton he proposed carrying spoil from the deep cuttings at Blue Bridge and Loughton to the south, but to do this meant building a temporary timber bridge over the Grand Junction Canal. The canal company, who, for obvious reasons, were not disposed to be co-operative, disputed his right to construct such a bridge, which involved driving piles into the canal banks. Acting on the principle that possession is nine points of the law, Robert decided to take advantage of the approaching Christmas festivities to catch his enemy unawares. On the night of 23 December he concentrated a strong force of engineers and navvies at Wolverton and began building the bridge by torch light. All through Christmas eve the work went on until, at noon on Christmas day, the bridge was finished. The infuriated canal company, however, were not prepared to take this defeat lying down. On 30 December their engineer, Lake, marched on Wolverton at the head of an even stronger body of canal employees who proceeded to pull up the piles and demolish the bridge completely. The third and last round in the drama was fought out in January in the Court of Chancery where the railway company sought an injunction to restrain the canal company from 'putting down, taking up or destroying' any of their works. Robert Stephenson sat through the long hearing and was highly delighted when the injunction was granted. For the canal company it was the final defeat in a long and costly campaign to stay their new and deadly rival.

This was not the end of the trouble at Wolverton. There was a serious slip on the embankment on the south side of the Ouse Viaduct, while another long section of the same embankment caught fire. These mishaps involved months of work before they were remedied. The fire was an extraordinary disaster which could not have been foreseen, being due to the presence of alum shale containing sulphuret of iron which ignited spontaneously. The astonished locals, however, had a different explanation; they were convinced that the fire was the result of some new and subtle roguery on the part of the canal company.

By far the most troublesome earthwork on the whole line was the tremendous cutting through oolite and clay between Roade and Blisworth. The great defile through the chalk at Tring defeated Townsend the contractor, but this was due to the sheer magnitude of the job proving too much for his resources and not to any unexpected difficulty. At Blisworth, on the other hand, William Hughes had to battle against treacherous, crumbling rock and powerful springs of water, troubles which had previously beset the engineers who drove the Blisworth canal tunnel. Pumping engines had to be installed, walls and revetments had to be constructed to underpin the rocks, and the sides of the cutting had to be cut back. Robert Stephenson had planned to use the material excavated from this cutting to form the Blisworth and Ashton embankments to the north and south, but so much of it proved unsuitable that the embankments had to be raised by side-cutting.[1] Here, as elsewhere, Robert Stephenson was forced to take over the works by the failure of the contractor, but the tremendous efforts made to recover lost time were handicapped by the fact that there was only room for a limited number of men to work in the bottom of the chasm. Consequently, with the sole exception of Kilsby tunnel, Blisworth cutting was the last work on the line to be completed.

All the difficulties so far mentioned become insignificant beside the engineering saga of Kilsby tunnel, where for four long years Robert Stephenson fought his famous battle against subterranean quicksands. The story is one of the great epics of engineering history and has often been told, not always correctly. It was stated by Jeaffreson and repeated by later writers that Robert Stephenson was forced to drive the Kilsby tunnel because the townsfolk of Northampton refused to allow the railway to pass through their town As Miss Joan Wake proved in her booklet *Northampton Vindicated*, this story is incorrect. The town of Northampton wanted the railway but were thwarted by the opposition of local landowners.

---

[1] "Side-cutting" meant scooping up the ground on each side of the line to build the embankment. Barrow-runs were used for this purpose. The decision to side-cut usually involved purchasing extra land or paying heavy compensation to the landowners concerned.

Moreover, so far from forcing Stephenson to take his line away from the town it had been a question of persuading him to bring it nearer until the landowners intervened. Concerned always to maintain a level road, the problem of carrying the line down into the valley of the Nene where Northampton lies was one which Robert Stephenson was happy to avoid. Behind this level-road policy of his was his father's axiom that it was best to eliminate gradients even at a greatly increased first cost in tunnelling or earthworks, so that all the power of the locomotive could be economically applied to draw a maximum load instead of to surmounting inclines. Joseph Locke became the great exponent of the opposite school of thought, which favoured going up and over natural obstacles which the Stephensons would either go round or tunnel through.

Robert Stephenson did indeed make a deviation from his original line to placate the most determined of the local landowners, Squire Thornton of Brockhall, but this had nothing to do with the decision to drive Kilsby tunnel. It is at this point, the Watford Gap as it is called, that the oolite uplands which extend across England from the south-west to the north-east contract to a narrow ridge linking the North Oxfordshire with the Leicestershire Wolds. This ridge may be conveniently pierced—the canal engineers had already done so at Braunston and Crick—but it cannot be avoided. Indeed the fallacy of the story is illustrated by the fact that the engineers who later accommodated Northampton by building the Roade-Rugby loop line were forced to tunnel through this same ridge.

Another misleading statement which has often been repeated is that the presence of quicksands under the Kilsby Ridge was totally unsuspected by Stephenson until they were encountered. It is quite true that by a most unfortunate mischance the trial borings failed to disclose the magnitude of the fault, but that Stephenson was aware of the hazard beforehand is clear from a letter which he wrote to Captain Moorsom in October 1835 when the sand was first encountered. "The best line through the Kilsby Ridge", he writes, "is undoubtedly that which I originally examined by Crick, but the Union Canal having abandoned it on account of the quicksand I considered it prudent to take that which we have adopted. . . ."

In 1809 the Grand Union Canal Company planned a tunnel through the ridge on a line between the Watford valley and a point to the west of Crick village, but after trial borings had disclosed a quicksand it was abandoned in favour of the line to the east of Crick. It is clear from his letter to Moorsom that by carrying his line still farther to the west towards Kilsby, Robert Stephenson hoped to avoid the hazard which the canal engineers had encountered. "I understand you carry your line through those hills", said the great Dr. Arnold of Rugby when Robert called on him in the course of his survey. "I confess I shall be much surprised if they do not give you some trouble." Arnold owned property at Kilsby and it may have been the recollection of the past difficulties of the canal engineers which prompted his warning.

Kilsby tunnel is a little over 2,400 yards long and at the time it was projected no tunnel of such magnitude had been contemplated for locomotive haulage. The opponents of railways and the apostles of woe predicted that foolhardy passengers would inevitably be suffocated in the dark depths. Even the engineers were doubtful, and an ingenious person named Thorold proposed that all locomotives should be fitted with a diaphragm, stiffened with whalebone, to promote ventilation in tunnels. It was because of these doubts and fears that Robert Stephenson planned Kilsby's two huge ventilation shafts, each 60ft in diameter and more than 100ft deep. Crowned by castellated towers, squat and sinister, they have fumed their steam and smoke on Kilsby Hill from that day to this.

In addition to these two great shafts, Robert Stephenson planned to sink sixteen working shafts[1] from the bottom of which the headings would be driven towards each other. When the second shaft from the southern end had been sunk 35ft, sand and water was encountered in such volume that work had to be abandoned. No. 3 shaft was driven 71ft through rock before it was similarly drowned out; Nos. 4 and 5 were sunk successfully to tunnel level and No. 6 encountered water at the same depth as No. 3. It was at this point that James Nowell, the unfortunate contractor, driven almost to despair, was taken mortally ill, while his two sons shortly afterwards threw up the contract. This was at the end of December 1835 and Forster, the District Engineer, reported: "There appears

[1] When the original estimates were prepared, Stephenson proposed only eight shafts but the number was increased with the object of speeding completion. This was one source of additional expense to which he later referred. The effect of the encounter with the quicksand was that a total of 25 shafts were sunk.

a sort of fatality among our Contractors. Nowell has been dangerously ill and is still very weak. Chapman [Bugbrooke and Stowe
Hill Contracts] is very ill of an inflammation in the region of the
heart and poor Hughes [Blisworth] is lying in almost a helpless state
at Northampton of a paralysis of the limbs." It was indeed a black
moment, and to make matters worse the whole countryside lay
under deep snow.

The final attempt on the part of the contractors to retrieve the
situation at Kilsby was to excavate a driftway into the south-eastern
side of the hill parallel with the line of the tunnel with the object
of draining off the water, but the sand suddenly swept into this
drift, blocking it completely for a distance of 90 yards. Although the
drift was subsequently reopened and extended, the same thing
happened repeatedly until the plan had to be abandoned. It was at
this juncture that the directors panicked. They sent Captain Moorsom to Kilsby to interview Robert Stephenson on the site and to
propose that the help of other engineers should be sought. James
Cropper and his faction instigated this move by implying that the
Company's difficulty at Kilsby was the logical result of employing an
engineer so young and inexperienced. Robert informed Moorsom
that he needed no outside assistance, and Moorsom was so impressed by his air of assurance and the cool, incisive way he outlined
his plans for dealing with the situation, that on his return to Birmingham he convinced the directors that their Engineer-in-Chief
merited their entire confidence.

Robert Stephenson then proceeded to put his plans into action.
Charles Lean, one of the sub-assistant engineers for the District was
placed in command of the tunnel works and of the force of 1,250
men and 200 horses which was concentrated at Kilsby. A temporary
line of railway was laid over the hill and a series of new shafts lined
with wooden tubbing were sunk a little to one side of the line of the
tunnel and linked to the drowned workings by cross headings. At
each of these new shafts a steam pumping engine was erected, for
their purpose was to act as sumps, draining the water away from the
working shafts so that the latter could be driven down to tunnel
level. Each week Charles Lean submitted a report to Stephenson on
the water levels in the shafts and the progress made. At first these
made depressing reading, for it soon became evident that the quick-

sand must amount to a great underground reservoir of unknown
extent, doubtless the same as that encountered earlier by the canal
engineers which Stephenson had hoped to avoid. The first steam
engines appeared to make no impression at all on the waters; then
for several weeks Lean would report a steady fall and hopes would
rise proportionately, only to be dashed again by a sudden fresh
influx. The only resort in this long and stubborn battle with the
waters was more pumps and it was not until Robert Stephenson had
mustered thirteen pumping engines on Kilsby hill that, slowly but
surely, he began to prevail. But it was a slow and costly task.
Pumping at the rate of 1,800 gallons a minute, the thirteen engines
laboured for nineteen months before the quicksand was finally
mastered and it became possible to drive the tunnel beneath it.

By this time the work was so far behind schedule that herculean
efforts were made to complete the tunnel by shifts of navvies toiling
incessantly, night and day. Describing these efforts, Francis, in his
History of the English Railway, writes: "Robert Stephenson infused
into the workmen so much of his own energy that when either of
their companions were killed by their side they merely threw the
body out of sight and forgot his death in their own exertions."
Though victory at Kilsby was undoubtedly won at a terrible cost
in human life and the navvies were a hard-bitten crew, this statement should be taken with a large pinch of salt.

The overwhelming impact of these events upon the quiet little
village of Kilsby was recorded by Charles Bracebridge, the Lord
of the Manor. Nothing like it had been witnessed since the forces of
King and Parliament had converged upon the district before their
last decisive battle on Naseby wold. A thousand men were quartered
in Kilsby alone, some in barns and outbuildings but the great
majority in crazy turf-thatched huts which they built themselves.
The Ox Green at Kilsby became the stage for wild saturnalia with
which the villagers dared not interfere. Barrels of beer were rolled
out of the inn on to the green, where the navvies danced and fought
each other or wagered their money on dog fights and cock fights.
When a gang felt hungry they would buy a beast from a local
farmer, slaughter it, cut it up on the green, and bear away on forks
or shovels carried over the shoulder great joints of meat to be roasted
over their encampment fires. On one occasion the long-suffering

villagers were goaded into a counter-attack. Banding together they seized and imprisoned two of the most notorious bruisers. The men's mates rallied to their aid, however, broke open the lock-up, released the prisoners and created such a dangerous tumult that troops had to be called to the rescue. Fourteen men were arrested in this affray and marched off to Daventry gaol roped together in pairs.

An orgy of a much more polite and orderly variety but no less impressive in its way than the nightly scenes upon the green at Kilsby, took place at the 'Dun Cow' at Dunchurch on 23 December 1837. Realizing that, with the end of the great work in sight, they would soon be disbanded, Robert Stephenson's staff decided to present him with a silver soup tureen at a dinner to which both father and son would be invited. It was a tremendous occasion. The entire engineering staff rallied to the 'Dun Cow', while some guests, notably Tom Gooch, who was working on the Manchester & Leeds line, drove 140 miles to be present. Robert Stephenson arrived at the inn in a carriage and four at 5.30 p.m. and took his place at the table on the right of the Chairman, Francis Forster, who had George Stephenson on his left. "I think", wrote the *Railway Times* correspondent, "I never saw on any occasion a more fixed determination in the faces of all the party to be completely happy." "One thing was of universal remark," the writer goes on, "this was the great alteration for the better in the appearance of the latter gentleman [George Stephenson], he looked at least half-a-dozen years younger. . . . There is the making of a hundred railways in him yet." The truth was that George Stephenson, at the age of fifty-six, was already well on the way to becoming a Grand Old Man, pioneer of railways and a 'Character' whose very faults and prejudices could now be regarded with amusement and affection by the younger generation of engineers.

"It would have done any man's heart good", the same writer continues, "to have heard the deafening applause which followed when the healths of the father and son were drunk; everyone felt they came warm from the heart and spoke of feelings that could not be uttered." Many of those present, including the two Stephensons, were moved to tears. "The youngest man who sat down to dinner on this occasion", the correspondent concludes, "will never live to see such another day", and we may well believe him. It was 2 a.m.

before Robert Stephenson left the table with Francis Forster, but even so the party was by no means over. George Stephenson was then voted into the Chair, which he occupied until 4 a.m., when, possibly from *force majeure*, he made way for Tom Gooch. It was six o'clock when Gooch rose and tottered away, while 'some few choice spirits', we are told, 'heard the clock strike eight'. Truly there were giants in those days, but there must have been some aching heads and disordered livers among the engineering staff of the London & Birmingham Railway for some days after.

Although the engineers were unanimous in their tributes to their Chief, the directors of the railway company were not so happy, for on every contract the cost had far exceeded Robert Stephenson's original estimates. So much so that whereas the total estimate was £2,400,456 the actual cost was £5,500,000, representing, in terms of cost per mile, £50,000 as against an estimated £21,736. This may be compared with the cost-per-mile figure of £18,846 for Joseph Locke's Grand Junction, but it must be remembered that the works on the London & Birmingham were far heavier. There were three reasons for the vast expenditure on the London & Birmingham: the unexpected difficulties encountered, a great increase in the cost of labour and materials, and the additional outlay incurred in the effort to recover lost time at Kilsby and on other troublesome contracts. Notwithstanding such efforts, Robert Stephenson was unable to fulfil his promise to have the line opened by the end of January 1838 between Birmingham and Rugby and from London to a temporary terminus at Denbigh Hall, where the railway crossed the Watling Street north of Bletchley. Until Blisworth cutting and Kilsby tunnel could be completed the intention was that coaches should ply between Denbigh Hall and Rugby to maintain a through service, but it was not until the spring that this came into operation. Stephenson explained the reason for the delay in a Report to Moorsom and Creed dated 17 February. At the beginning of January a severe frost had set in which held for six weeks and brought permanent-way laying and all masonry work to a complete standstill. In answer to the complaints of excessive expenditure Stephenson wrote:

> Important works have been abandoned by the contractors and left to be executed by the Company under circumstances calling for extraordinary exertions and costly expedients to regain lost time. This has

unquestionably been one of the most fruitful sources of increased expenditure. Indeed, in cases where the Company have been compelled to take up works the task to be performed has required means hitherto without precedent in engineering and consequently involving expenses which no experience could indicate. These are: Tring, Wolverton, Blisworth, Kilsby, Rugby and Coventry. In the execution of three of these contracts, which individually equal, if they do not surpass, in expense and difficulty, besides differing in character from, every other work at present executed in this country, I had no guide—I was thrown entirely upon my own resources and those of my Assistants to devise means for accomplishing that which was not only deemed precarious but nearly impracticable in point of time.

Under such circumstances I must without hesitation admit that my calculations have not been borne out but on the contrary far exceeded. Throughout the course of these works I have in vain indulged a hope that the expenditure might be lessened by establishing a system and adopting suitable plans for procedure pointed out by experience—but, unfortunately the advantages accruing from the employment of proper methods have been counteracted by the pressing necessity for an early completion of all the works. . . .

"This report", he concludes, "places me in a position from which I cannot by possibility retreat, except through the aid of the Directors, without a slur amounting to a stain upon my character as an engineer and for which I am persuaded there are no just grounds."

The directors' dismay at the colossal cost of their railway, a cost far surpassing that of any public work which had ever been undertaken, is understandable, but we may sympathize with Robert Stephenson's feelings after four years of superhuman effort and anxiety. Yet the end of the struggle was at long last in sight. On 21 June 1838, just over four years since the first sod had been cut at Chalk Farm, the two Stephensons, with a crowd of directors, engineers and workmen, assembled beneath the great south ventilation shaft of Kilsby tunnel to watch Charles Lean insert the last brick with a silver trowel. When he had done so the inevitable band struck up 'God Save the Queen', for the Victorian Age had by this time begun. Then the whole company marched through to the north end of the tunnel where the customary repast awaited them. The victory was won and the marauding army which had invested Kilsby for so long melted away as swiftly as it had come, leaving the village to resume, with infinite relief, its rudely interrupted slumber.

On the following Sunday, 24 June, the 9.30 a.m. train from Euston to Denbigh Hall ran through to Birmingham, while a new up train, leaving Birmingham at 10 a.m. was also booked through to Euston. These two trains were advertised as Sunday workings, but may have run through on other days at the discretion of the engineers, the works being still incomplete and, very probably, only one line available. All other trains continued to terminate at Denbigh Hall or Rugby until 17 September when the line was officially opened. On that day Robert Stephenson travelled on the footplate of the special train which conveyed the London directors to Birmingham where they dined with their fellow directors at Dee's Royal Hotel. "I rejoice to see it", was the great Doctor Arnold's comment on the completed line, "and to think that feudality is gone forever; it is so great a blessing to think that any one evil is really extinct."

Robert Stephenson's main task was done, but the Company retained him as their Consultant, and his remaining anxiety became the settlement of the new embankments, and earth-slips in the deep cuttings. Knowledge of soil mechanics was limited at this time, nor was there any chemical or mechanical means of consolidation. Only the weight of traffic could consolidate the embankments and this meant constant watchfulness lest a sudden subsidence should cause derailment and disaster. It also meant frequent lifting and packing of the permanent way. For this reason Stephenson ruled that at the outset no passenger traffic should move after dark and that as much remedial work as possible should be carried out during the night. He also imposed a speed restriction of 15 m.p.h. on the section between Denbigh Hall and Rugby until such time as he was satisfied that the earthworks were secure. Yet as late as July 1844 we find him writing to Creed on the subject of slips at Wolverton, Weedon and Bugbrooke.

If any aspect of Stephenson's work on the London & Birmingham is open to criticism it is his choice of permanent way. He specified 15ft malleable iron 'fish-bellied' rails weighing 50lb to the yard. The rail ends were not fishplated but rested in a common joint chair where they were secured by an iron key. On ground liable to settlement he called for cross sleepers of oak or larch, but elsewhere for stone-block sleepers 2ft square by 1ft thick as used on the Liverpool & Manchester. These blocks were extremely costly, and to save expense Robert Stephenson tried placing them at 4ft centres and diagonally instead of square and at 3ft centres as on the older railway. He was compelled to reduce this to 3ft 9in centres, but even so there were continual reports of the rails spreading out of gauge. On the Leeds & Selby line, where stone blocks were also used, iron tie-bars were introduced to prevent them creeping apart. It is difficult to understand or to justify this addiction to stone blocks which the two Stephensons displayed. As already explained, the use of individual blocks on a railway intended for horse traffic is understandable, but those days were over and their use on the London & Birmingham is indefensible. On the Grand Junction, Locke introduced the chaired 'bull-head' rail on cross sleepers which was to become the British standard. Vignoles designed the flat-bottomed rail which has now superseded it, while on the Great Western Brunel was laying down his famous road of bridge rail on longitudinal timbers.

On the credit side, Robert Stephenson's most original contribution to civil engineering on the London & Birmingham was his construction of skew bridges in masonry. Each arch stone or brick course formed, as it were, the thread of a large screw, the pitch determined by the angle made by the intersecting centre lines of road and rail and by the radius of the arch. A wooden model of each skew bridge was made and the measurements for the worked stones and courses were determined from these. On the site, the centering for the arches was covered with sheeting on which the lines for the courses were marked out with a flexible straight edge. "Then", writes Conder, "the great screws twisted themselves into place without a check and without an error."

When they had completed their contract for the Euston extension, the Cubitt brothers went on to raise, from titanic blocks of Bramley Fell stone, that huge Doric portico which Philip Hardwicke the elder had designed for the entrance to the new terminus. Augustus Welby Pugin scorned it as a senseless, pretentious extravagance, contrasting it with the modest train sheds within. But Pugin failed to appreciate its significance. It was not merely the entrance to a station; it was the gateway to the first great railway to storm England's capital city, a triumphal arch celebrating the engineer's victory over the treacherous clays of Blisworth and the quicksands of Kilsby. This great soot-blackened portico at Euston epitomizes the simple, sombre yet monumental grandeur of every bridge, viaduct and tunnel portal on this high road to the north; works which express the spirit of the great Northumbrian who designed them, as surely as the works on the Great Western typify the Gallic virtuosity of Brunel.

CHAPTER TWELVE

Fame without Fortune

DURING THE years that accompanied and immediately followed the building of the London & Birmingham Railway the fame of the two Stephensons became world-wide, but so far as Robert was concerned a capricious fate took away with one hand what she gave with the other. Devey, in his biography of Joseph Locke, gives the misleading impression that after the Grand Junction Railway débâcle, George Stephenson went into a retirement from which he was only recalled during the years of the Railway mania. This is quite untrue. The success of his Liverpool & Manchester Railway had brought him a reputation as the foremost railway engineer in the kingdom which neither the efforts of his detractors nor his own mistakes could shake. So much so that when a new railway scheme was launched the appearance of George Stephenson's name on the prospectus as principal or consulting engineer was sufficient to ensure a full subscription list.

I. K. Brunel always refused to allow his name to appear as engineer of a railway unless he took full responsibility for the work and he acidly defined the term 'Consulting Engineer' as meaning 'a man who, for a consideration, sells his name but nothing more'. No other engineer was ever more sorely or persistently tempted than George Stephenson to do precisely this, and although he may have lacked Brunel's high scruples, it stands to his everlasting credit that he resisted the bribes and blandishments of railway speculators so effectually as he did. He was far too canny and far-sighted to become involved in any of the impracticable 'bubble' schemes which un-scrupulous promoters dangled before a gullible public. Also, though he may not have exercised that full responsibility upon which Brunel insisted, he was never a mere figurehead. While the detailed survey, organization and execution of a great railway project may have been beyond him, his grasp of broad essentials amounted to genius. In preliminary reconnaissance he was brilliant; that is to say, after one ride or drive through a strange tract of country, he would propose a line for a railway which was not only the best from an engineering point of view but also from the standpoint of traffic potential, grasping as he did the local resources which the new railway might exploit and the part it might play in the future as a link in some through-route. In this last respect George Stephenson had no rival. Whereas other railway promoters and engineers, Brunel not excepted, were still thinking of railways in local or, at best, regional terms, Stephenson, influenced to some extent perhaps by William James, had from the outset visualized the railway becoming a great nation-wide system. Although he did not live to see the completion of that system, George Stephenson was without doubt its supreme architect, drawing the first bold lines across the map which others would elaborate.

Even if we concede to George Stephenson only the minimum responsibility for the railways with which his name is associated as engineer, the work involved must have been prodigious and Samuel Smiles was probably correct in saying that this was the busiest period of his whole life. In the three years 1835-1837 alone he is said to have covered 20,000 miles by postchaise, usually accompanied by his personal assistant, Frank Swanwick, who had succeeded Tom Gooch as his amanuensis. Although these journeys took him far and wide, the railways with which he was most directly concerned at this time were all in the north midlands and with one exception they eventually became, like the earlier Leicester & Swannington, part of the Midland Railway. They were: the Birmingham & Derby, the North Midland[1] (Derby to Rotherham, Normanton and Leeds), the Sheffield & Rotherham and the York & North Midland (Normanton to York). These lines together formed a through route from Birmingham to Leeds and York with a branch to Sheffield. As a route between London and the north, the Midland Counties Railway engineered by Charles Vignoles from Rugby through Leicester to Derby was more direct than Stephenson's Birmingham & Derby and it was the bitter competition for London traffic

[1] George and Robert Stephenson were appointed Engineers of the North Midland on 16 July 1836 at a joint salary of £2,000 a year, but this was subject to Robert Stephenson's agreement with the London & Birmingham. Until that railway was completed he could act only in a consulting capacity for other railway companies.

between these two companies that led eventually to the Midland amalgamation. Such intricacies of railway politics, however, have no place here.

The railway outside this Midland group for which George Stephenson was responsible was the Manchester & Leeds, a formidable work which involved the first rail-crossing of the Pennines. This was yet another railway which was first proposed in the optimism of 1824 but had since lain dormant. Construction began in August 1837 and, as previously mentioned, T. L. Gooch was transferred from the northern district of the London & Birmingham to take charge of the work. Instead of running directly to Leeds as originally planned, the line was altered to join the North Midland Railway at Normanton. It ultimately became a part of the Lancashire & Yorkshire Railway system, the change of name taking place in 1847.

The major work on the Manchester & Leeds was the great summit tunnel at Littleborough, near Rochdale, a quarter of a mile longer than Kilsby and only exceeded in length by Brunel's tunnel at Box. Box tunnel was begun a year earlier but not completed until three months after Littleborough was opened to traffic. It was hoped that this first trans-Pennine railway tunnel would be finished by the end of 1840, but in December of that year there were alarmist rumours that part of the tunnel had collapsed. George Stephenson made a personal inspection and he and Gooch subsequently issued a joint report in which they made clear what had in fact happened. Between Nos. 2 and 3 shafts there was a treacherous belt of blue shale which had given way under the invert, causing the latter to be thrust upwards by the weight of the arch above for a distance of 80 yards. The two engineers estimated that six weeks work would be required to strengthen the invert, but stated that in the meantime the eastern section of the line could be opened as far as Hebden Bridge. The western side was already open.

There was evidently some spirited running on the Manchester & Leeds from the outset to judge from a warning sent by Stephenson to Gooch on 21 February 1841: "I should advise you to cause the Locomotive Engines to go slower," he wrote, "certainly not to exceed 26 or 28 miles an hour until the road is consolidated. At the rate you are now running you will destroy both rails and engines.

I believe I came along the other day at the rate of 50 miles an hour."
This is characteristic of Stephenson's habitual caution, but if he did
not exaggerate it was certainly justified in this instance. Fifty miles
an hour in a little four-wheeled carriage on a stone sleepered road
must have been as uncomfortable as it was exciting and it is safe to
say that Stephenson's comments to the driver afterwards were
considerably stronger than those he later expressed to Gooch.

Notwithstanding the drama of the first railway over the Pennines,
it was the North Midland Railway which afforded George Stephenson the greatest satisfaction, for two reasons. First, he considered it
the finest piece of railway engineering associated with his name, and
secondly he looked upon it as a most important part of a great
trunk route between the south and north of England. Years before,
in his Killingworth days, he had prophesied that he would live to
see the mails carried by steam power from London to his native
Newcastle. It had seemed a wild dream then, but with the opening
of the North Midland on 11 May 1840 an unbroken line of metals
stretched from London to Leeds and to York and the translation of
his vision into fact became simply a question of time. Would he live
long enough? He was now fifty-nine.

The North Midland railway is an excellent example of the
Stephensons' insistence upon easy gradients even at the cost of
circuitous routes. George Stephenson considered that the country
between Chesterfield and Sheffield was unsuitable for a railway, and
he therefore curved his line eastwards to skirt the fringe of these
central highlands, thus missing Sheffield altogether. Hence the
necessity for the Sheffield & Rotherham Railway. The industrialists
of Sheffield, however, did not long rest content with their situation
at the end of a branch line, with the result that the present heavily-
graded direct line from Chesterfield to Sheffield through Dronfield
and Bradway tunnel was built later. Although they were inspired by
different motives, a parallel may be drawn between James Brindley's
first circuitous canals and the first railways. In both cases a later
generation of engineers supplemented them by building more direct
'cut off' routes. Any policy can become unsound if it is pushed too
far and the plethora of 'Direct Railways' which were projected
during the Railway mania illustrate the policy of Joseph Locke
carried to unwise and even absurd lengths. It became associated with

the ludicrous 'undulating railway' theory which enjoyed quite a vogue among projectors who insisted that such a line could be worked as economically as a level one because what you lost on the 'ups' you gained on the 'downs'.

The Stephensons' championship of easy gradients rested on the sound argument that the power of the steam locomotive should be used for hauling maximum loads and not dissipated in climbing steep gradients. Yet they also erred by carrying their policy too far. The classic example of this is the west coast route to Scotland. In the 1830s two railways had been projected in Lancashire, the Liverpool & Preston and the Preston & Wyre, the former now a part of this trunk route. The Preston & Wyre directors were already considering the projection of a line northwards to Carlisle and they consulted George Stephenson on the matter. In his report dated 5 June 1839 he recommended a route via Whitehaven and Maryport and proposed to carry this line from Lancashire into Cumberland over a great embankment which would reclaim a large part of Morecambe Bay from the sea. This, he concluded "is the only practicable line from Liverpool to Carlisle. The making of a railway across Shap Fell is out of the question." As a glance at the map will show, this line proposed by Stephenson was impossibly circuitous for a trunk route to Scotland and it is not surprising that his rival, Joseph Locke, stepped in to build the line over Shap Fell which he had repudiated. The severe climb to Shap Summit remains one of the classic tests of locomotive performance, yet in this case Locke was undoubtedly right and Stephenson's Maryport & Carlisle Railway, though it did eventually form part of the coastwise route which he envisaged, has never had more than a local importance.

Earlier, in 1836, the Stephensons suffered a similar defeat in the south of England at the hands of an old and bitter rival, Sir John Rennie. In this case no fewer than four companies came forward with rival plans for a railway from London to Brighton, and a battle royal ensued in Westminster. Their respective engineer advocates were Robert Stephenson, Rennie, Joseph Gibbs and a certain Mr. Cundy who, it transpired, had saved himself a great deal of labour and discomfort by preparing his plans at home with the aid of a map. Unfortunately this method of planning railways by the fireside produced results so wildly inaccurate that 'Cundy's line' became a stock joke among civil engineers for years afterwards. Rennie and Robert Stephenson were the chief contenders, the former favouring a direct line which involved very heavy engineering works in crossing the north and south Downs and the latter a longer but less costly route by way of the valleys of the Mole and the Adur.

Robert Stephenson was very distressed by his defeat because he was greatly concerned at this time to consolidate his reputation as a civil engineer in London circles, and felt he had suffered a major setback. As usual, he was unduly pessimistic, but his feelings are understandable because it is arguable that the route surveyed by G. P. Bidder under his direction was in fact the best. Compared with Rennie's line it was very little longer and would have saved four million cubic yards of earthwork including the long tunnels at Balcombe and Clayton. Reading the transcript of the evidence given before the Lords' Committee, it is difficult to escape the conclusion that Robert Stephenson made a serious tactical error by admitting his father as an engineer witness in support of his scheme. The older man, as his son should have realized, was no match for skilled opposition Counsel, and fell heavily into every trap they laid for him. To survive such cross-examinations an engineer had to be the master of every detail of his project whereas mastery of broad principle, not detail, was George Stephenson's strong suit. He had carried out one of his flying surveys by postchaise from London to Brighton, and of Rennie's line he said he was 'surprised that any person living should have projected a railway through that country'. Yet Counsel succeeded in making him a laughingstock when, in answer to further questions, he was unable to remember the name of any of the places he had visited. To those unfamiliar with George Stephenson it must have seemed that, like Cundy, who stayed at home with a map, he was not to be taken seriously.

Although, under the terms of his agreement with that company, Robert Stephenson could not undertake any other engineering work while the London & Birmingham Railway was building, he was free to practise as a consultant, to direct surveys or to undertake parliamentary business. At first those seeking his advice would call to see him at his London & Birmingham office at Camden Town, but by 1836 his services were so much in demand that he realized the time had come to open an office of his own, preferably in West-minster. His first office was in Duke Street, but after twelve months he moved to 24, Great George Street, which became the business headquarters of the two Stephensons for the remainder of their lives. Both the Stephensons and their staff of assistants had profited by experience and learned the lessons of past mistakes. They had become an efficient team and there was no repetition of the Grand Junction Railway fiasco. An intuitive, rule-of-thumb genius like George Stephenson had always needed an efficient business manager at his heels to look after his detail planning and staff organization. Hitherto, by his pride and obstinacy, his jealousy and mistrust of others, he had forfeited this essential support even from his own son, with results which in any lesser man might have brought him to complete personal disaster. Now, however, the combined effect of wealth, advancing years and public recognition and acclaim was not to spoil George Stephenson but to make him mellower, more amenable and altogether more likeable. No longer could he feel that every man's hand was against him, or see a potential rival in every pro-mising assistant. The effect of this was that he allowed Robert to become the directing brain of the partnership, accepting the younger man's advice and guidance both in the choice of staff and on tech-nical questions. This was the secret of his success in his great railway-building programme in the north midlands.

In the civil as well as in the mechanical engineering field the activities of the Stephensons now ranged across the Channel. In May 1835 father and son paid a flying visit to Belgium at the in-vitation of King Leopold to advise him on the construction of the Belgian State Railway system. On this occasion the King decorated George Stephenson with the Order of Leopold and two years later when the Stephensons returned to attend the opening of the railway from Brussels to Ghent they dined with the King and Queen at Laaken. In 1841, when Robert Stephenson paid a third visit to Belgium, King Leopold conferred upon him the same honour as he had given his father six years before. Later, for his contributions to railway development in Norway and France, Robert was created a Knight Grand Cross of the order of St. Olaf and a Chevalier de la Legion d'Honneur. On the other hand he refused an English knight-hood, nor would he allow these foreign honours to be recognized in his own country. In this context it may be recalled that Telford refused to allow his Swedish knighthood to be recognized in England and that when it was suggested to Brunel that his French honour should be similarly recognized it provoked a typically scathing retort on the subject of civil honours. This common characteristic of three of the greatest engineers of all time, that they scorned at home the recognition they accepted abroad, is not without interest.

All this intense civil engineering activity gave the Stephensons few opportunities to visit the locomotive works in Newcastle. This was a source of great disappointment to Robert. Although his own ambition as well as the pressure of outside circumstances had drawn him into the civil engineering field which was to remain his major concern for the rest of his life, there is no doubt that the development of the locomotive was the work nearest his heart and that the time he spent at Newcastle between 1827 and 1831, which yielded such splendid results, was the happiest in his career. That he never lost touch with the affairs of Robert Stephenson & Company is revealed by the frequent correspondence which passed between London and Newcastle.

So far as the design and technical side of the Newcastle business was concerned Robert Stephenson could rest easy. The gap left by his removal to London was ably filled by the Works Manager, William Hutchinson, who, after twenty-four years' service with the firm, was eventually admitted to partnership on Robert's recommendation in 1845. Under Hutchinson was a most capable team of designers and craftsmen: Ralph Whyte and William Weallens in the drawing office and George Crow, who was to succeed Hutchinson as Works Manager, as head foreman in the shops. There was also John Starbuck who acted as outside technical representative and salesman for the firm in Europe and who followed up, on the locomotive side, the associations which the Stephensons formed as civil engineering consultants.

Where business administration and finance was concerned, however, it is clear that Robert Stephenson was dissatisfied with the policies pursued by his Quaker partners. He was disconcerted when, in 1836, Michael Longridge announced that he could no longer act as managing partner and that he proposed building locomotives himself at his Bedlington ironworks. More disquieting still, Longridge procured the services of Starbuck to act as his Continental agent. However, the firm won back Starbuck in 1840. Robert Stephenson's answer to this announcement by Michael Longridge was to recommend to Joseph Pease the appointment of Edward Cooke as Chief Clerk at Newcastle. In fact, whether Joseph Pease realized it or not, Edward Cooke was very much more than a clerk, as the correspondence between him and Robert Stephenson reveals. Cooke was uncle to Robert's wife. The two men were on intimate christian-name terms, and Cooke was Robert's confidential agent, charged to watch over his financial and business interests in the north of England generally and, particularly, within the firm which bore his name. That Robert had some serious cause for concern about the direction of the business is disclosed in a letter he despatched to Cooke in February 1840 in which he writes:

> I shall read Longridge and Pease a lesson by post in a day or two; they shall either rescind the £200 resolution or else I shall go out of the thing altogether. Indeed there is scarcely one thing that they have done that I will not undo—the resolutions are conceived and phrased in a style which I will not put up with from those who have done nothing for the concern for many years past and only began to show an interest in our proceedings after I had succeeded by my own resources and those of my father in establishing a character for the firm. The impudence of a Quaker is beyond estimate by Heavens!

Unfortunately the precise cause of this indictment, in common with the other sources of Robert's concern, is not revealed either in the firm's records or by Warren's exhaustive history of the Company. But whatever the immediate causes of dissatisfaction may have been, it is clear that Robert resented the amount of influence on policy which was wielded by men whose only interest in the business was the amount of profit they could draw from it. He endeavoured to counteract this by getting more men with technical qualifications admitted to the partnership. In the case of William Hutchinson he succeeded, but he failed with Starbuck and one other nominee. It was true, as Robert must have realized, that it was the financial backing of the Quakers which had set his father on the road to fame, but it was also true that they had made his father the instrument of a greedy policy with which he had disagreed and which had nearly proved disastrous to the older man's career as a civil engineer. Now, by turning from the mechanical to the civil side of railway engineering, he had most successfully retrieved that situation, but feared that his earlier good work at Newcastle might be undone. In short, Robert Stephenson had an extraordinarily difficult role to play and succeeded in acting it out with great skill. Whereas Brunel, Locke and other great engineers of the day could at this time concentrate the whole of their formidable talents on railway building, Robert had to keep a wary eye on the locomotive business also.

Another important milestone in locomotive history was passed by Robert Stephenson & Company during these years. This was the perfection of the famous 'Stephenson Link' valve-motion which is still in use on many locomotives at the present time. By virtue of the name, it is often popularly supposed to have been a Stephenson invention, whereas in fact it was evolved by the Company as an inspired simplification of the complex gab valve-gear introduced on the *Harvey Combe* of 1835 and used in varying forms by the Stephensons and other makers up to 1842. Who first thought of the idea was subsequently the subject of much controversy between William Williams, at the material time an apprentice draughtsman at Newcastle, and William Howe a pattern maker. It seems most likely that Williams had the idea and that Howe worked out some of the practical details which made it workable. Edward Cooke sent Robert Stephenson a small model of the gear and on 31 August 1842 the latter wrote: "On the first blush it is very satisfactory and I sincerely hope on a more mature investigation will prove really so. My impression is that at certain parts of the stroke the motion of the slide valve will be backwards instead of forwards." But he confesses that he found the model too small to test accurately and he instructs Cooke to have a full size model made. "If it answers", Robert concludes, "it will be worth a Jew's eye and the contriver of it should be rewarded."

As Edward Cooke was one of the family, Robert Stephenson's letters to Newcastle often included news from his home at Haverstock Hill and personal commissions: a new picture to be purchased for him; a roll of Northumbrian plaid to be sent down to London. That Robert Stephenson had little time for home life hardly needs

saying. When he was in London and engaged on the London &
Birmingham Railway he always tried to keep his Sundays clear,
apart from letter writing, but on weekdays he worked early and
late. His only relaxation was reading, poetry for him being the
equivalent of the 'whodunit' which is so popular an escape for men
in his position today. Occasionally he gave a small dinner party,
his guests being usually business associates and fellow engineers:
Tom Gooch, G. P. Bidder, Francis Forster, Joseph Bramah, Budden,
his secretary, or Charles Parker of Binfield, Berkshire, his solicitor.
Another frequent visitor was Professor Wheatstone, joint inventor
with William Cooke of the electric telegraph. Their invention was
first tried out successfully between Euston and Camden Town
stations in the presence of Robert Stephenson. Curiously enough,
however, it did not supersede the peculiar compressed air whistle
which was used for signalling between Euston and the fixed engine
house at Camden Town. It was Brunel who first adopted the electric
telegraph as a permanent installation for railway communication.

Though Robert Stephenson's home life in London was limited, it
was at first happy enough except for one private grief—he had
dearly hoped for a son who might carry on the Stephenson tradition
but he was disappointed; Fanny Stephenson was unable to bear him
a child. To this sorrow there was added another cruel blow when
it was made known to him by his wife's doctors in 1840 that she was
suffering from an incurable cancer. For the next two years he had
to meet calls upon his time, ability and energy which were as un-
remitting as ever, and it must have been hard indeed to fulfil them
while he knew that the wife to whom he was devoted stood condemned to slow and agonizing death. The end came on 4 October
1842, when he wrote in his diary: "My dear Fanny died this morning
at five o'clock. God grant that I may close my life as she has done,
in the true faith, and in charity with all men. Her last moments
were perfect calmness."

Almost until her last breath, Fanny had begged Robert to marry
again, aware as she was of that desire for children which she had
failed to satisfy. He never did so. The house at Haverstock Hill became repugnant to him, and since the London & Birmingham
Railway had been completed only Fanny's liking for it had held him
there. Now he resolved to move nearer his office in Westminster

and to make his work his whole life. He therefore took the lease of a house in Cambridge Square and sold Haverstock Hill. He had only just moved in to his new home when fire broke out in the middle of the night and nearly all his furniture and possessions were destroyed.

This catalogue of Robert Stephenson's misfortunes which, in his own words, took away 'half of his power of enjoying success' is still incomplete. On his appointment as Engineer-in-Chief to the London & Birmingham Railway he had felt himself free for ever from financial anxiety, no matter what other worries he might have. His salary of £1,500 a year was later raised to £2,000. In addition there were his fees as a consultant and his income from the Newcastle business, so that, because he continued to live simply, he soon became a wealthy man. Yet during that melancholy two years when he knew that his wife was slowly dying, he suddenly found himself facing the prospect of complete financial ruin. This was through no fault of his own and the threatened catastrophe took him completely unawares.

Nothing reveals more clearly the calibre of Robert Stephenson than the way in which he maintained so indomitable a public front despite such a crushing burden of private grief and anxiety. The financial thunderbolt which fell so suddenly upon him out of an apparently clear sky was the outcome of his past association with a relatively obscure and unimportant mineral line in the north of England—the Stanhope & Tyne. The story of this extraordinary and ill-starred railway and of Robert Stephenson's moves to extricate himself from the disaster with which it threatened him is closely connected with the realization of his father's dream—the completion of the iron road from London to Newcastle.

CHAPTER THIRTEEN

The Stanhope & Tyne Fiasco

THE TRAVELLER bound north for Newcastle, Corbridge or Hexham who climbs the steep hill out of Stanhope with the heights of Weather Law on his right hand finds himself in a landscape reminiscent of certain inland parts of Cornwall. Here, above the 1,000ft contour, is a vast expanse of open moorland made lonelier and more desolate by the evidence of bygone activity: ruined engine-houses and chimney stacks; the road bed of a long forsaken railway climbing steeply beside the road. These traces of lost endeavour, given over now to the sheep and the buzzards are all that remain of the westernmost extension of what was once described as "one of the most wonderful railway rarities in existence" —the Stanhope & Tyne.

There is limestone at Stanhope and in 1831 two brothers, William and Walter Harrison, with Thomas Barnard, launched a scheme to build a limeworks there and connect these works by railway with a colliery at Medomsley which lies a few miles north of Consett on the slopes of the Derwent valley. It was at first proposed that this new railway should be linked near Medomsley with the ancient Pontop and Tanfield wagonways which together provided a route to the Tyne above bridge at Dunston Staithes. This plan was soon dropped, however, in favour of a much more ambitious scheme of carrying the line twenty-four miles farther to new deep-water staithes at South Shields. Crushed limestone was, of course, in demand as a blast-furnace flux, and as one effect of the new railways was a great expansion of the iron industry the Stanhope & Tyne prospectus must have looked very promising on paper. Yet any potential investor with knowledge of the country between Stanhope and Medomsley should have been wise enough to keep his money in his pocket, for in order to connect these two places the line would have to be carried over a moorland summit 1,445ft above sea-level at Whiteleahead, between Collier Law and Bolt's Law. On the western side of Whiteleahead, too, there lay across the path of the proposed line Hownes Gill, a dry ravine 150ft deep and 800ft wide.

Undeterred by these formidable obstacles, the projectors went ahead. Robert Stephenson agreed to act as consulting engineer while T. E. Harrison, an ex-pupil of William Chapman, who became one of Stephenson's most able assistants,[1] was appointed resident engineer. This was in 1832. With the commercial prospects of the railway and its business management Robert Stephenson did not concern himself at all. He was at that time far too preoccupied with the London & Birmingham and so he confined himself to giving the promoters his advice on the best way to execute their fantastic project. This would have been well enough had he not, in a fatal moment, yielded to their persuasion to accept five £100 shares in the Company's stock in lieu of his agreed fee of £1000. He should never have consented to this without the most careful inquiry, but, preoccupied as he was, he accepted the proposal on trust. He was to pay dearly for his misplaced confidence.

When completed in 1834 the Stanhope & Tyne Railway combined every form of motive power then known. Ten and a half miles were worked by horses, nine and a quarter miles by locomotives; there were three miles of self-acting inclined plane and no less than eleven miles which were worked by fixed haulage engines. There were nine of the latter totalling 375hp. From Stanhope the Crawley and Weatherhill inclines lifted the line up to the Whiteleahead summit level, one and a half miles long, which was worked by horses. Then followed Meeting Slacks, the first of three descending inclines, the third, which was self-acting, becoming known as 'Nanny Mayer's' after the proprietress of a nearby public house. Here a solitary Stephenson *Patentee* type locomotive driven by one William Craggs took charge for the next two and a half miles, which brought the line to the lip of the Hownes Gill ravine. A most remarkable device enabled the railway to negotiate this obstacle. A single fixed engine at the bottom of the gorge worked two vertiginous inclines down each side, the gradients being 1 in 3 and 1 in 2½. Special incline carriages, on which the wagons travelled

[1] Finally T. E. Harrison became first General Manager of the North Eastern Railway, a post he held from 1854 to 1888.

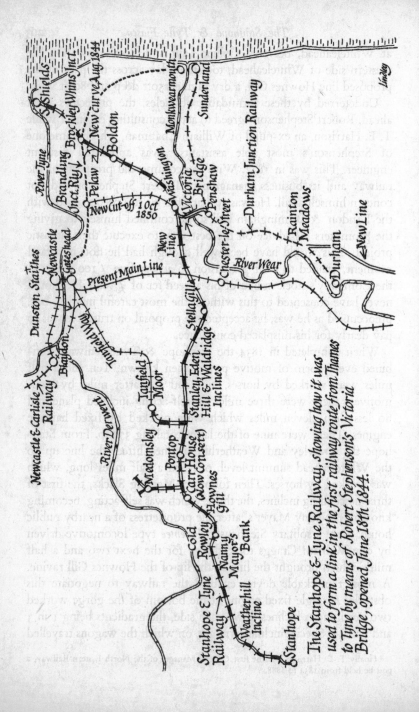

Lindley

The Stanhope & Tyne Railway, showing how it was used to form a link in the first railway route from Thames to Tyne by means of Robert Stephenson's Victoria Bridge, opened June 18th 1844.

S.Shields

River Tyne

New curve Aug 1844

Brockley Whins Junct

Branding Junct Rly

Pelaw

New cut-off 10 Oct 1850

Boldon

Newcastle

Gateshead

Monkwearmouth

Sunderland

Washington

Victoria Bridge

Penshaw

Durham Junction Railway

Rainton Meadows

New Line

Chester-le-Street

River Wear

Durham

New Line

Present Main Line

Dunston Staithes

Blaydon

Newcastle & Carlisle Railway

River Derwent

Tanfield Moor

Tanfield Way

Stella Gill

Stanley, Eden, Hill & Waldridge Inclines

Medomsley

Pontop

Carr House (now Consett)

Hownes Gill

Cold Rowley

Nanny Mayor's Bank

Weatherhill Incline

Stanhope & Tyne Railway

Stanhope

sideways, were used here. These ran on two sets of rails, the outer ones being of 7ft gauge. The fixed engine worked both inclines simultaneously, but even so it could not pass more than twelve wagons in an hour.[1] Two engine-worked inclines then carried the railway over the Pontop ridge and these were followed by four descending planes, Stanley, Twizell, Eden and Waldridge. From the foot of Waldridge Bank to South Shields the line was worked by locomotives.

In operation, the Stanhope & Tyne Railway gave an excellent practical demonstration of the weakness of the fixed-engine system of haulage. As Ralph Robinson, the Traffic Manager, once remarked ruefully to Joseph Pease: "It was like a lot of fiddlers playing at a concert; if one made a mistake it spoiled all the rest." "Mistakes" there certainly were; even the opening day in 1834 was marred by a breakaway on the Weatherhill incline in which two lives were lost. In view of Robert Stephenson's championship of the loco-motive against the fixed engine, the fact that he was responsible for the Stanhope & Tyne may appear contradictory, but there was no other way of carrying a mineral line economically through such an impossible line of country.

The Stanhope & Tyne might have overcome its practical draw-backs had the financial background been sound, but this was far from the case. On the contrary the whole project was a monument of rash speculation and commercial folly which seems scarcely credible in retrospect. When the original plan of a railway from Stanhope to the Pontop wagonway was launched, it was decided to proceed by obtaining wayleaves from the landowners through whose property the line would pass instead of applying to Parliament for an Act of Incorporation. Since time out of mind the Tyneside wagonways had been constructed under this system of wayleave agreement, so there was nothing novel in the proposal and the necessary wayleaves were obtained at the average rental of £40 to £50 per mile, which was reasonable. So far so good. But when the decision was made to extend the line to South Shields the Company should have applied for an Act of Incorporation. Instead they set about obtaining more wayleaves for this extension. Now the rosy prospects which the promoters of the scheme had painted took effect

[1] These Hownes Gill inclines were replaced by a viaduct in 1858.

in a way they had not anticipated. The landowners determined upon getting a rich share of this promised prosperity. So keenly did they bargain, that wayleave rentals on this eastern half averaged £280 to £300 per mile with the addition of £100 per mile as compensation for surface damage. "It is enough to make a horse sick", complained Russell Bowlby, the Company's solicitor, "to see parties, instead of blessing providence for such a godsend, treating as if one was taking a road through a gentleman's pleasure ground." Nor was this all. The terms were for twenty-one years only with no option of renewal.

Although these ruinous agreements were made in 1832, no Deed of Settlement was made until 1834. This deed fixed the capital at £150,000 but permitted the Company to raise further capital by shares or loans up to a total of £290,000. £50,000 worth of the original shares and half the profits in the undertaking were allotted to the Harrison brothers, who then sold their interest on very favourable terms, leaving others to hold their ugly baby. Their shares were never paid up, and the Company then began to raise money by bills of exchange and mortgages negotiated on the most extravagant terms, the average interest payable on them being 11%. In this way the Company's liability rose to the staggering figure of £440,000 quite regardless of the ceiling fixed by the Deed of Settlement. Out of this sum £40,000 was invested in the Durham Junction Railway project of 1835. In 1835 and again in 1836 a dividend of 5% was paid to stockholders out of this borrowed money, these being the only dividends the company ever yielded.

On the revenue side the picture was just as disastrous. The western section of the line proved so costly to work that in 1839 the lime-works at Stanhope and eleven miles of railway from Stanhope to Carrhouse (Consett) were closed to traffic, notwithstanding the fact that the Company still had to pay out wayleave rentals on this section. At the same time the Company had to face the prospect of the early loss of all traffic from the Tanfield Moor Colliery, which was yielding them a revenue of £5,000 a year. This had come about through the agency of the Brandling Junction Railway with which, ironically enough, both George and Robert Stephenson had been concerned.

The Brandling Junction Railway had been promoted in May

1835 by the brothers Charles and Robert Brandling to connect
Gateshead with South Shields and Monkwearmouth. Seldom has a
modest mineral line attracted such a galaxy of famous names. In
addition to the two Stephensons, Nicholas Wood was associated
with the project, while I. K. Brunel also comes into its story through
his connection with the Monkwearmouth dock improvements. In
fulfilment of an agreement made with the Marquis of Bute, owner
of Tanfield Lea Colliery, the Brandling Junction Company began,
in 1839, to relay as an iron railway the ancient wooden wagonway,
reputedly the oldest in the world, from Tanfield Lea to the Tyne at
Dunston Staithes. They proposed extending this line to Tanfield
Moor, an action which would, and eventually did, draw all the
Tanfield Moor traffic away from the unhappy Stanhope & Tyne.

In the light of this situation in the north, the reason for Edward
Cooke's appointment as Robert Stephenson's confidential agent in
Newcastle becomes the more apparent. Yet although Robert was
made aware of the parlous state of the Stanhope & Tyne, he did
not realize what ruinous implications it held for him, believing that
he could not lose more than the amount of his fee. So matters stood
until December 1839, when he was suddenly presented with a large
bill from one of the Stanhope & Tyne creditors which that Company was unable to meet. Mystified, Robert Stephenson hurried off
to his solicitor, Charles Parker, who explained to him the horrid
truth. As the Stanhope & Tyne Company had not been incorporated
there was no limit to the sums which individual shareholders might
find themselves called upon to meet in the event of the failure of
that Company to meet its liabilities. Moreover, as Robert Stephenson
was a public figure and his enjoyment of a handsome income was
well known, he was naturally the first person to whom the disgruntled creditors would turn. Having so lately won through to
success and prosperity as a civil engineer, Robert Stephenson now
suddenly found himself facing, through no fault of his own, the
prospect of utter financial ruin.

> I hope you will be able to make a dividend soon [he wrote to Cooke just
> after this blow fell]. I wish this for two reasons—firstly, because I want
> money, and secondly because I don't like your bankers. If they are not
> speculating beyond what is prudent I am deceived. . . . That prince of
> rogues has, I am sorry to say, involved all parties connected with the

Stanhope & Tyne and almost all the banks of Newcastle and Sunderland. When I first became acquainted with the awful responsibilities which the Stanhope & Tyne had incurred, and the utter inability of the concern to meet them, I was perfectly stunned, and your bank has lent them on bills £51,000, which are at this moment floating. Some become due next Saturday, on which day, I have no doubt, the Stanhope & Tyne Company must stop payment. . . .

Acting on Charles Parker's advice, Robert Stephenson called an extraordinary meeting of the Stanhope & Tyne shareholders on 29 December 1840, and after an adjournment it was decided to form a new Company with a capital of £400,000 to take over the old Company's property and debts and to apply to Parliament for incorporation. This seemed to be the only slender hope of staving off complete disaster.

The Company's affairs are awfully deranged [Robert told Cooke], and the precise consequences no one can venture to predict. We may possibly struggle through, but this hope may prove fallacious. . . . The History of the Stanhope & Tyne is most instructive, and *one miss* of this kind ought to be, as it shall be, a lesson deeply stamped. If the matter gets through, I promise you I shall never be similarly placed again. Ordinary rascality bears no relation to that which has been brought into play in this affair. . . .

The capital for the new venture, entitled the Pontop & South Shields Railway Company, was eventually raised and Robert Stephenson agreed to pay in £20,000 as his contribution. To do this meant scraping the bottom of his financial barrel, including the sale to his father of half his interest in Robert Stephenson & Company. To this end he wrote to Cooke on 4 January as follows:

Dear Edward,
    Your view as to my wishes respecting one half of my interest in the factory is exactly what I wish. The transaction is not intended to be otherwise than *bona fide* between my father and myself. The fact is, I owe him nearly £4,000, and I have not now the means of paying him as I expected I should have a month or two ago. All my available means must now be applied to the Stanhope & Tyne. On the 15th of this month I have £5,000 to pay into their coffers. The swamping of all my labours for years past does not now press heavily upon my mind. It did so for a few days, but I feel now master of myself; and though I may

become poor in purse, I shall still have a treasure of satisfaction amongst friends in my prosperity. The worst feature in the case is the all-absorbing character of my attention to the rectification of its embarrassments, which if produced by legitimate misfortune would have been tolerable, but when produced by —— men who are indebted to me, they become doubly afflicting. . . .

It is at this juncture that the Stanhope & Tyne—or rather the Pontop & South Shields as we must now call it—begins to figure in railway events of much wider importance through the agency of that extraordinary character George Hudson, 'the Railway King', and in order to appreciate how this came about it is necessary to go back a few years.

The extraordinary career and remarkable personality of George Hudson has been most ably described by Richard S. Lambert in his biography *The Railway King* (1934). Here it is only necessary to deal briefly with those of his activities which most directly affected the two Stephensons. Hudson had an immense and perfectly honest admiration for the Stephensons and once, when he was singing their praises in the course of a speech, he described himself as "only a tool in the hands of genius". This was a characteristic piece of unctuous mock-modesty on Hudson's part, for, as he very well knew, he was a law unto himself in the new railway world, and his enemies could say with more show of truth that the Stephensons had allowed themselves to become the tools of George Hudson.

For all his faults—and they were certainly grievous ones—the figure of Hudson, like those of his engineer contemporaries, looms larger than life-size out of the shadows of history. Like the engineers, he was of humble stock, the son of a yeoman farmer at Howsham on the Derwent, and he brought to the field of railway administration and finance the same tremendous energy. It was of him that a rhymster in the *Railway Times* wrote:

> George in his chair
> Of railways Lord Mayor,
> With his nods
> Men and Gods
> Keeps in awe;
> When he winks
> Heaven shrinks;

When he speaks,
Hell squeaks,
Earth's globe is but his taw.

He was, indeed, a phenomenon for which there was then no precedent, a tycoon accustomed to think coolly in millions when his contemporaries hesitated over thousands. Thomas Carlyle called him 'a big swollen gambler', which was true. In the pursuit of his vast ambitions Hudson was utterly unprincipled, committing crimes any one of which would have landed him in gaol had not Company law been in its infancy. He manipulated accounts, issued false balance-sheets, misappropriated shares and paid dividends out of new or borrowed capital. He did this by appointing his own stool-pigeons to the offices of Secretary and Treasurer in the Companies he controlled. He would also corner huge stocks of rails and other materials and then sell them to his own railway companies at great personal profit. Yet despite all this, W. E. Gladstone could say of Hudson that he was "no mere speculator but a projector of great discernment, courage and rich enterprise", and, in a sense, Gladstone, too, was right. For beneath all the knavery, the bombast and the exhibitionism there was vision, enthusiasm and a sense of purpose. Unlike some later financiers, Hudson was not impelled solely by his lust for power and wealth; he did not exploit railways as his successors would exploit oil or matches, only as a means to serve selfish ends. On the contrary he believed passionately in their future and in this sense he was as devoted a railwayman as George Stephenson. Like Stephenson, Hudson foresaw the creation of a great national railway system at a time when most men were still thinking locally. The practical expression of George Stephenson's foresight was his insistence upon uniformity of gauge, but his mind could never grasp the implications of his vision in terms of administration and finance. Just as he favoured the small contractor, so he believed that railways should be sponsored, financed and administered locally by those most immediately concerned.[1] George Hudson, like Joseph Locke, saw that the future lay with the big battalions. In construction, Locke favoured the large contractor; in operation,

[1] In the year of his death George Stephenson wrote to T. R. Cobb of Warwick urging him to ensure that money for the proposed Leamington and Banbury Railway was raised locally so that none of the great Companies could secure control of the project.

Hudson favoured the big company and did not believe that a national railway system could be effectually worked by a multiplicity of small undertakings. Hence he directed all his energies towards unification with such effect that at the height of his power he controlled 1,450 route miles of line out of the total of 5,000 miles then built.

Hudson's activities engendered the Railway Mania and when he fell that crazy speculative bubble soon burst. His trickeries exposed, his financial empire fell in ruins and those who had cheered and flattered him were the first to pull him down. Those in charge of the Companies he had controlled, such as John Ellis of the Midland, were left to fight their way back to solvency as best they could. Nevertheless, George Hudson left an indelible mark upon Britain's railway system. The great Midland Railway Company was his creation, while most of the lines which later formed the North Eastern Railway, with headquarters in Hudson's own stronghold of York, were built at his inspiration.

When George Stephenson was building the Liverpool & Manchester Railway, George Hudson was running a draper's shop at the corner of Goodramgate and College Street in York. There he might have remained had he not received an unexpected legacy of £30,000 from a great-uncle in 1827. "It was the very worst thing that had ever happened to me", declared Hudson in his old age. "It led me on to railways and to all my misfortunes since." With his new wealth, Hudson started a joint-stock bank in York and this led him easily into railway speculation. Railways were the talk of the hour in financial circles, and being a great local patriot Hudson determined that his city of York should figure prominently on the new railway map. To this end he roused local interest in a scheme for a railway from York to Leeds and commissioned the Rennies to make a survey. This was early in 1834, but that summer an historic meeting took place which induced Hudson to change his plans. At this time Hudson cherished another scheme for developing the village of Whitby as a coast resort and connecting it with York by railway. It was in connection with this idea that he met George Stephenson at Whitby. The two men took an immediate liking to each other. It was of this meeting that Joseph Devey wrote: "Unfortunately he [Stephenson] was introduced to George Hudson; still more unfortunately, Faust was not inattentive to Mephistopheles." The comparison is over-dramatic and scarcely fair to either man. Hudson was not all black, while although Stephenson showed himself willing to march some of the way under Hudson's banner, he was by no means one of Hudson's puppets.

Stephenson confided to Hudson his dream of an east-coast route to Newcastle and the Border, and Hudson returned the compliment by unfolding his plan to make York a great railway centre. "Mak' all t'railways come to York", he is said to have urged, and in this way he persuaded Stephenson to make York and not Leeds the pivot of his great north road. It was as a result of this momentous meeting that Hudson dropped his Leeds-York scheme and promoted instead the York & North Midland to join Stephenson's North Midland line at Normanton. In this he was opposed unsuccessfully by a formidable figure from Doncaster named Edmund Beckett Denison, who urged a more direct eastern route from London to York. Later, Denison would prevail against Hudson's might and father the Great Northern Railway, but that epic conflict is no part of this story. For the present, Hudson and Stephenson prevailed and the York & North Midland formed the next vital link of the northern route. It had not been staked out before another link, the Great North of England Railway from York to Newcastle, was under discussion.

At the outset the Pease family and their Quaker associates in Darlington were the prime movers in the Great North of England Railway scheme; in fact it could be called the child of the Stockton & Darlington Railway Company. Construction had not proceeded far before the Great North of England Railway ran into both engineering and financial difficulties and this situation coincided with the crisis in the affairs of the Stanhope & Tyne and its re-organization as the Pontop & South Shields. Robert Stephenson saw in the Great North of England project a possible way of financial salvation for himself and his fellow shareholders of the Stanhope & Tyne but not, unfortunately, as it had been projected by Joseph Pease and his fellow promoters. As luck would have it, however, their difficulty was his opportunity, for they sought his advice. Robert Stephenson urged them to concentrate their resources on completing the easier southern part of the railway between York and Darlington so that the Company could begin earning revenue and to abandon work on the section between Darlington and Gateshead. In the circumstances the advice was sound, and apparently Joseph Pease and his colleagues did not suspect that Robert Stephenson had any ulterior motive in giving it. His recommendations were accepted; land which had been acquired for the railway north of Darlington was sold back to the original owners; all work was concentrated on the York-Darlington section, and in this truncated form the Great North of England Railway was completed and opened for traffic in the spring of 1841.

Meanwhile George Hudson's power had been growing rapidly as the iron rails crept northward. The first section of the York & North Midland line had been opened to traffic on 29 April 1839 with great pomp and circumstance. Then, on 30 June 1840, the whole of the North Midland Railway was opened, George Stephenson and Hudson travelling in state by special train from York to Derby and from Derby back to Leeds. This meant that a continuous though roundabout line of metals stretched from London to York over a distance of 217 miles. It also meant that when the Great North of England Railway was opened in the following spring, Darlington was linked by rail to London and George Stephenson's dream was a stage nearer realization. The next extension must be from Darlington to the south bank of the Tyne at Gateshead, and for this Robert Stephenson had a plan ready for which he had secured George Hudson's powerful backing. This was a scheme which would absorb the Durham Junction (in which, be it remembered, the old Stanhope & Tyne Company had taken a substantial holding), the Pontop & South Shields, and the Brandling Junction Railways. This was launched by George Hudson with a great flourish of trumpets as the Newcastle & Darlington Junction Railway. Joseph Pease and his colleagues on the Stockton & Darlington Railway Board were furious when they found that Hudson had stretched out his arm to grasp the power which they had hoped to wield north of Darlington and, not unreasonably, they felt they had been tricked and betrayed by Robert Stephenson. They bitterly opposed the Newcastle & Darlington Junction scheme, which their chief spokesman, Captain Watts, denounced as "an abortion with a crooked back and a crooked snout, conceived in cupidity and begotten in fraud". Yet such fulminations did not prevail against the might of George Hudson, and the Newcastle & Darlington Junction Railway was duly incorporated. The new Company made use of the Durham Junction, a portion of the Pontop & South Shields between Washington and Brockley Whins, and finally the Brandling Junction railway from Brockley Whins to Gateshead. The terms of this arrangement relieved Robert Stephenson and his fellow shareholders of all future anxiety. At the same time, through Hudson's influence, Robert secured the post of Engineer-in-Chief of this last link in the line of rails between Thames and Tyne.

The first act of the Pontop & South Shields Company had been to sell to the Derwent Ironworks at Consett both the Stanhope Lime works and the mountainous western section of the Stanhope & Tyne which that Company had closed in 1839. Thus the skeleton of the old Stanhope & Tyne which had rattled so ominously in Robert Stephenson's cupboard was dismembered and laid to rest.[1]

Having described the manœuvres of Robert Stephenson and George Hudson over the Newcastle & Darlington Junction Railway, Hudson's biographer, Richard Lambert, writes: "Robert Stephenson had little of the geniality and unpretentious simplicity of his father; he belonged to a harsher, more selfish type which despised the very class from which it had sprung; but, like his father, he could not avoid falling under the influence of his domineering and self-confident friend Hudson." There is no contemporary evidence to support so unflattering a characterization, but, presented in this particular context, it might appear to possess an element of truth. Yet the picture which Lambert presents is misleading because he says nothing whatever about the disastrous affair of the Stanhope & Tyne which determined Robert's course of action and drove him, under pressure of necessity, to seek Hudson's powerful aid. He was never, as Lambert implies, a free and willing partner in Hudson's unprincipled speculations, but was forced by the threat of ruin to play Hudson's game for a while, a situation which suited Hudson very well since it placed within his power the most celebrated railway engineer in the country. In the letter already quoted, Robert promised Edward Cooke that if he managed to extricate himself from

[1] For the later history of the railway see "The Stanhope & Tyne Railway" by A. F. Snaith and Charles E. Lee, *Railway Magazine*, Vol. 88, 1942.

his financial difficulties he would see to it that he was never similarly placed again and he was true to his word. As his biographer Jeaffreson tells us, he never indulged in railway speculation although there was every temptation to do so. He died a very rich man, but his wealth was derived from professional fees, from the Newcastle business, and from the fortune he inherited from his father.

In denouncing the Newcastle & Darlington Junction Railway, Captain Watts had used the word 'crooked' in a double sense, for a most circuitous course was necessary in order to make use of portions of the three existing lines for part of the route. Yet despite the ulterior motive behind this plan of Robert Stephenson's, it was not without justification on purely practical grounds, although it was later to be superseded, first, in 1850, by a "cut-off" from Washington to Pelaw and finally by the present main route through Chester-le-Street. Including a short branch to Durham, Stephenson's line involved only 24¼ miles of new construction and only one major engineering work—the splendid stone viaduct at Penshaw, then known as the Victoria Bridge, by which Stephenson spanned the valley of the Wear to join the Pontop & South Shields line at Washington. Consequently the work went forward rapidly and in the early summer of 1844 George Stephenson's long-cherished dream became a reality; Tyne and Thames were united by rail.

George Hudson made the opening of the line on 18 June the occasion for a display of that showmanship in which he gloried. Flags flew, cannon fired, church bells rang, and the employees of Robert Stephenson & Company paraded through the streets of Newcastle with banners to welcome 'Wylam Geordie' and 'Young Bobbie' as they returned to their native Tyneside in triumph on the special 'Grand Opening Train' organized by Hudson. They were greeted at the Gateshead terminus by the Mayor of Newcastle and other notables, who escorted the passengers to the Newcastle Assembly Rooms where a company of 500 sat down to a fabulous banquet which lasted from 5 p.m. until midnight. The occasion was also marked by the arrival from Euston of a special 'Flying Train' which brought copies of the London morning papers to Gateshead in the remarkable running-time of eight hours eleven minutes for the 303 miles. This represents an average speed of 37 miles an hour, no mean feat on the narrow gauge in 1844, and a measure of the progress which had been made in the fifteen years which had elapsed since the Rainhill Trials. In 1829 the momentary achievement of such a speed had been considered quite fantastic; its maintenance over a distance of 300 miles would have been dismissed as beyond the bounds of possibility.

The Newcastle banquet was distinguished by an extraordinary statement which was made in a speech by the Hon. H. T. Liddell. In proposing the health of George Stephenson he saluted him as the man who had 'constructed the first locomotive that ever went by its own spontaneous movement along iron rails'. This claim was greeted with loud applause although many of those present including the speaker himself, whose father, Lord Ravensworth, had financed the building of the *Blucher*, ought surely to have known that it was completely false. Tyneside, the cradle of the locomotive, was the last place in the world to choose for the perpetration of such a crashing blunder and it is saddening to record that George Stephenson himself was not great enough to disclaim there and then a credit to which he had no title. That he did not do so explains at once the growth of the popular Stephenson legend and also the enmity which he aroused in other, less successful pioneers. The matter passed off. In that convivial atmosphere of mutual congratulation no one had a thought to spare for Richard Trevithick, cold in a forgotten grave at Dartford.

The rails had reached the Tyne but there was now a greater ambition: to unite the capitals of England and Scotland. Already George Hudson had taken the first step by promoting the North British Railway from Edinburgh to the Border at Berwick and a month after the Newcastle banquet this Company was incorporated. It remained to bridge the formidable, smoky gulf of the Tyne valley between Gateshead and Newcastle and then to drive the lines north to the Border. This was to be the Stephensons' next task and it brought them into direct conflict with their greatest rival, I. K. Brunel.

CHAPTER FOURTEEN

George Stephenson—the Closing Years

IN AUGUST 1837, after three hectic years, George Stephenson wrote to Michael Longridge: "I intend giving up business in the course of the next two or three years when I shall be able to devote more time to my friends. I have had a most delightful trip among the Cumberland Lakes; I should like to have remained a month to fish. . . . I want to take 30 or 40,000 acres of land on the West Coast of England. I think it will be a good scheme."

As is evident from this letter, George Stephenson was now a very wealthy man to whom railway work was no longer a necessity, and to an increasing extent he began to hand over responsibility to his son. To the end of his days he continued to act as a consultant more for pleasure than profit, but he was true to his word and after 1840 he concerned himself seriously with only two railways in Britain, the Norfolk Railways and the Manchester, Buxton, Matlock & Midland Junction Railway. This last, which joined his beloved North Midland at Ambergate, was, as he confessed, the favourite child of his old age, and his last work was to see an amending Act for the line safely through Parliament. But in 1837 there was still much to do. Not only did the Chester & Crewe, Birkenhead & Chester and Trent Valley lines all claim a share of his attention, but in 1838 he carried out two preliminary surveys of the greatest significance. One of these was for the Chester & Holyhead and the other for the Newcastle & Berwick. Both these lines would eventually be carried out by his son and would include some of the finest monuments to Robert Stephenson's genius as a civil engineer.

George Stephenson began by examining two possible routes for a line from Newcastle to Edinburgh. One was a direct but hilly route which followed the valley of the North Tyne through the Cheviots and that of the Gala Water between the Lammermuirs and the Moorfoots. Needless to say, Stephenson greatly preferred the longer but much easier line which skirted the coast via Morpeth, Alnmouth and Berwick. On 10 November 1838 he writes from Berwick to Robert Brandling at Gosforth: "I have arrived at this place this evening and have again traversed the line—more particularly than I did before, and I believe you will find when accurate levels have been taken that my report will be found very near the truth as to the merits of the line between Newcastle and this place." The previous night he had been the guest of Earl Grey at Howick. Here the ladies of the company, like Fanny Kemble before them, evidently found the tall, burly figure of the engineer with his white hair, ruddy cheeks and clear grey eyes quite irresistible. "You may imagine the predicament I was in," he told Brandling in the same letter, "when all the Ladies seized me at dinner. I wanted your assistance very much to help me through as you have done on former occasions."

Had Stephenson but known it, he had strayed into an enemy camp. He was never to be received again with such favour at Howick Park. For five years the Newcastle & Berwick scheme lay dormant, but in 1843 when the railway army was advancing to the Tyne it was revived under the banner of George Hudson. It then became speedily apparent that the Newcastle & Berwick had a most formidable foe in the person of Lord Howick, Earl Grey's eldest son, who acted as his father's lieutenant.

As the projected line would pass close to his Bedlington Ironworks, Michael Longridge was deeply interested in the scheme, and at the beginning of December 1843 he received this characteristic letter from George Stephenson on the subject of Lord Howick's opposition:

I am rather astonished [he wrote] at Lord Howick's observations about the line passing Howick. It does not go through any of their pleasure grounds, it passes over one of the drives which run down a dingle to the coast. . . . There is a turnpike road between the house and the intended railway. . . . My senses are puzzled in judging how these people can set about making such paltry objections! It is compensation they want, nothing else. The line can not be moved to the place Lord Howick alludes to, west of the house; it would require a tunnel a mile long. It would do very well for Lord Howick as it would pass through their Limestone quarries. . . . This species of objection is a genteel way of picking the subscribers' pockets; there cannot be a doubt but it is meant to do so.

I have never taken any part in politics, but I think I now will and become a Tory, and I shall buy a piece of land in Northumberland to oppose Lord Howick. I do not like this double-dealing work; we shall not fear Lord Howick's opposition.

Is the great thoroughfare through England and Scotland to be turned aside injuriously for the frivolous remarks made by Lord Howick? No! the times are changed. The legislators must look to the comforts and conveniences of the Public. Are hundreds and thousands of people to be turned through a tunnel merely to please two or three individuals? I wonder the pulse does not cease to beat when such imaginations enter their brains! I can have no patience with them. . . .

Spurred on by such forthright and uncompromising pronounce-ments as this from the 'Father of Railways', the Newcastle & Berwick promoters refused to make any deviation in their proposed line at Howick and war to the knife was declared. Lord Howick retaliated by promoting a rival line from Newcastle to Edinburgh by the direct route which George Stephenson had examined and rejected more than five years before. This 'Northumberland Railway', as it was called, won considerable support. The Newcastle & Carlisle Company declared in its favour because if, as they hoped, the route was diverted westwards along the south bank of the Tyne from a junction with the Newcastle & Darlington Junction at Redheugh to Blaydon, it would bring the Anglo-Scottish traffic on to their metals between Blaydon and Hexham. Great play, too, was made with the argument that by this route the Tyne could be crossed much more simply and cheaply at low level. The Stephen-sons threw all the weight of their influence against the Northumber-land Railway. "If the line is diverted from the East Coast both England and Scotland will hereafter regret it", declared George Stephenson in a letter to George Hudson. But Lord Howick would not yield an inch and he secured the services of I. K. Brunel as engineer for his railway.

So far as the Stephensons were concerned, Lord Howick could not have taken any more provocative step, for they looked upon Brunel as their greatest rival. An often repeated story relates that when Brunel first visited Newcastle on Northumberland Railway business, George Stephenson encountered him and, seizing him playfully by the collar, asked him how he dared to venture north of the Tyne. If the action and the words were indeed playful, then they masked a very real bitterness, according to the judgement of contemporaries. "If in anything Stephenson showed a littleness of feeling it was about Brunel", commented a writer in the *Civil Engineer and Architect's Journal* for December 1848. Stephenson, the same writer continues, "was too much given to do as others did about him, to look upon railways and engines as belonging to himself alone and that no one else had a right to meddle with them. Forgetting that he himself was the follower of Trevithick, Jessop and Chapman, the helpmate of James, Birkenshaw, Booth and others, he could not bear coolly anything which was not of his school. He never forgave Brunel for taking another gauge."

This is strong criticism, but the honest biographer must admit that it is valid. Two characters more sharply contrasted and more antipathetic to each other both in their natures and in their approach to engineering problems than George Stephenson and Brunel imagination could not conceive. Although, in his fight for the locomotive railway, George Stephenson had battled almost single-handed against an overwhelming weight of prejudice and established precedent, he was, paradoxically, himself one of the most prejudiced of men. With that caution and conservatism which is characteristic of the clever but ill-educated craftsman who solves problems empirically, having once arrived at a solution which satisfied him Stephenson clung to it as though it was some eternal and universal truth, valid for all time. Consequently, as fast as he destroyed the old precedents of pre-railway days he erected new ones of his own. For him railway construction was a mystery to which he alone held the key and over which he presided with papal infallibility. Engineers who pursued a contrary course were heretics to be denounced either as fools or rogues. Even so did he pour contempt upon the efforts of the steam-carriage builders and on Jacob Perkins's experiments with ultra high-pressure steam. If, like Joseph Locke, the rebel engineer had once been a member of Stephenson's own school, then he stood twice condemned.

Two classic examples of the precedents which George Stephenson established and clung to were the use of stone-block sleepers and the rail gauge of 4ft 8ins. He recommended this gauge for the Stockton & Darlington and the Liverpool & Manchester Railways for no better reason than that it was the gauge of the Killingworth wagonway. When the iron rails pushed south from the Liverpool & Manchester to Birmingham and on to London this fortuitous dimension became a part of the sacred Stephenson dogma which could no longer be challenged. Yet one man did have the temerity to challenge it—Brunel the dynamic perfectionist who owed nothing to Stephenson and accepted nothing from him. Whereas Stephenson spent his life establishing technical precedents, Brunel dedicated himself to their demolition. Brunel's approach to any engineering dogma was to question its right to exist, and for him safe precedents were like so many sandbags holding down the balloon of the mind; if you wanted to rise to the heights you must throw them overboard, and that is precisely what Brunel did throughout his spectacular career. The first item of ballast to go overboard was Stephenson's so-called 'standard' gauge.

That Tyneside coal-wagon gauge would never do for the main line of the Great Western Railway where Brunel's restless genius envisaged speeds in excess of a mile-a-minute, and so he adopted the princely gauge of no less than 7ft. Brunel argued that speed was a saleable commodity; that, other things being equal, the travelling public would always choose the fastest form of transport. Although the true pleasure of travel does not consist in getting from A to B in the shortest possible time, the subsequent history of mechanical transport has proved that, as a social psychologist, Brunel was absolutely right. George Stephenson, however, roundly denounced Brunel's ideas of high-speed rail travel, unmindful of the fact that, not so many years earlier, his own more modest estimates of railway speed had been repudiated in almost precisely the same terms.

Unfortunately, in the matter of the broad gauge, Brunel was less far-sighted than George Stephenson. Technically it was a *tour de force* and completely successful, but it came too late to prevail against a standard gauge which was already too securely established. Brunel looked forward to a complete broad gauge monopoly of the south and west of England, but, even if he had achieved this aim, such an arbitrary and mutually exclusive partition of the railway system would have been disastrous. This the Stephensons rightly foresaw. At first Brunel and the two Stephensons had pursued their separate courses in comparative isolation, but such was the pace of railway development that direct conflict became inevitable as the rival systems began to invade each other's territory, and the east-coast route to Edinburgh was only one of several bones of contention.

As if the broad gauge were not provocation enough, by this time Brunel was enthusiastically advocating another innovation which George Stephenson found even more exasperating. This was the atmospheric system of traction which had been developed by Messrs. Clegg and Samuda and which would, Brunel announced, supersede the steam locomotive, that darling child of the Stephensons. Moreover, to add insult to injury, this impudent young man was proposing to introduce this new-fangled system on Stephenson's own native heath where it would, so Brunel assured Lord Howick, make light of the heavy gradients on the proposed Northumberland Railway.

Briefly, the principle of the atmospheric railway was this. Between the rails was laid a large-diameter pipe which could be exhausted by a series of pumping engines placed at three-mile intervals beside the line. A special carriage at the head of the train carried a piston which travelled through the pipe, propelling the train by atmospheric pressure. The arm connecting the piston to the carriage passed through a slot in the pipe which was sealed by a continuous flap valve. This valve was momentarily opened by the passage of the carriage. When everything was in perfect order the system worked so well that many reputable railway engineers besides Brunel were attracted to it, but the continuous valve proved to be the Achilles heel of the invention.

The full story of the development of the atmospheric system and of its subsequent disastrous failure on Brunel's South Devon Railway has been told elsewhere.[1] It is entirely typical of the Stephensons that whereas George at once denounced it as 'humbug from beginning to end', Robert did not venture an opinion until he had carried out a most exhaustive investigation. Because the Chester & Holyhead Company were bitten with the atmospheric idea, he sent assistants over to Ireland to carry out practical experiments on the

[1] See this writer's *Isambard Kingdom Brunel*, pp. 162-175.

Kingstown & Dalkey atmospheric line and compared the results
with those of similar experiments made on the cable-worked incline
between Euston and Camden Town. His report on these experiments
and the conclusions he drew from them were all the more damning
because, unlike his father's sweeping dismissal, they were so obviously fair-minded and so carefully considered. Robert foresaw many
of the technical difficulties which would later prove insurmountable,
but over and above all such criticisms of detail he saw the whole
controversy over the merits of the atmospheric system as another
round in the battle for the steam locomotive against those advocates
of fixed-haulage engines whom he and his father had defeated so
decisively at Rainhill years before. Except that it used 'a rope of air'
he saw no fundamental distinction in the atmospheric system. Even
if it functioned perfectly it was still open to the same fatal objection
as rope haulage in that the failure of only one of a chain of lineside
engines could bring traffic to a standstill over a whole route.

By launching an ambitious scheme for the development of
Sunderland Docks, George Hudson had secured his election as
Member of Parliament for Sunderland and so greatly increased his
influence on Tyneside. The 'Railway King' was now at the height
of his fame and power and in the great parliamentary struggle of
1845 over the route to Edinburgh he committed all his formidable
resources to the Newcastle & Berwick, inducing the Newcastle
& Darlington Junction proprietors to subscribe heavily to the
scheme. As a result, Lord Howick and Brunel were defeated, the
Newcastle & Berwick was incorporated on 31 July 1845, and no
more was heard of the atmospheric Northumberland Railway.

The Newcastle & Berwick Act included sanction to construct the
great bridge over the Tyne between Gateshead and Newcastle,
although this work was carried out by a separate undertaking known
as the High Level Bridge Company to which both the interested
railway companies subscribed. The idea of a high-level road-bridge
on the site is said to have originated in a proposal made by Telford
in 1825. Later, plans for the bridge were prepared by John Green,
the Newcastle architect who, in addition to much architectural
work in Northumberland, was responsible for the Scotswood
suspension bridge over the Tyne, the Tees suspension bridge at
Whorlton near Barnard Castle, and the Ouseburn and Willington

Dean viaducts. For the last-named work, Green used a very interesting and ingenious form of laminated timber construction. A company was formed under the chairmanship of John Hodgson Hinde to execute Green's plan, but it failed to raise the necessary capital and the scheme had lain dormant until the coming of the railway. Hinde remained chairman of the revived company and Green's plans and estimates were used to obtain parliamentary sanction upon the understanding that Robert Stephenson would subsequently revise them. Green's original plan had been for a road-bridge, whereas it was now proposed to carry both road and rail traffic on one structure.

The total length of the High Level bridge and its approaches is 1,372ft and it is carried across the Tyne upon five great piers of local sandstone of which the tallest is 146ft high. These piers rest upon massive timber piles encased in concrete, this foundation work being carried out within piled coffer dams which were left *in situ* as a protection for the pier bases. By this date James Nasmyth had invented the steam hammer and his machine was adapted to drive these piles, this being the first major bridge-building work on which a power-driven pile-driver was used. By its aid, piles 13in square and 40ft long were driven through the sand and gravel of the river bed down to a rock base, Robert Stephenson personally supervising the driving of the first pile on 24 April 1846.

On the design of the superstructure for the bridge, Robert Stephenson devoted great care and forethought. Had he been asked to design such a bridge a few years later he might have used wrought-iron girders, but at this date he still pinned his faith to cast-iron and it was his rival Brunel, a profound pessimist where cast-iron was concerned, who evolved by experiment the first large wrought-iron bridge girders. Thinking in terms of cast-iron, therefore, there were three possibilities for Stephenson to consider, each of which he had already used on earlier railway works. One was the so-called compound trussed girder which consists of a straight cast-iron beam strengthened by a truss of wrought-iron tie rods. As any civil engineer will appreciate, this is a most undesirable combination and it must be recorded as a serious technical fault on the part of both the Stephensons that they made extensive use of large compound girders of this kind until a serious disaster, to be recorded later, showed Robert Stephenson the error of his ways. Fortunately, for the two-deck high-level bridge the compound girder was rejected as unsuitable. The second possibility was the simple cast-iron arch, but this also was rejected because Robert Stephenson decided that the tall piers must not be subjected to the thrust which the simple arch exerts and which would at once come into play in the event of pier settlement. There remained the bow-and-string girder, a form of construction which Robert had first used in 1835 for his bridge carrying the London & Birmingham Railway over the canal at Weedon. The name explains the form and principle. A cast-iron arch forms the bow, but it does not exert any thrust on piers or abutments because its ends are tied by the horizontal wrought iron member which is the 'string'. This was Robert Stephenson's choice and it was in this form that the bridge was constructed. It was particularly suited to the bridge's dual function, for a deck carrying three lines of railway was supported on the crowns of the girders, 120ft above the Tyne, while the horizontal strings below carried a 20ft roadway flanked by two 6ft footpaths.

All the ironwork, which weighed over 5,000 tons, was produced locally by Hawkes, Crawshay & Co. of Newcastle, and it is characteristic of Robert Stephenson's extreme care and caution that he carried out exhaustive experiments to determine the best mix of iron to use for the cast girder work. As a result, the furnace mix prescribed by Stephenson and used by Crawshay consisted of a proportion of selected scrap iron plus no less than five varieties of pig-iron, some cold and some hot blast, from Resdale, South Wales, and Coalbrookdale. Notwithstanding all this preliminary care, each span was temporarily erected and tested at the foundry before being conveyed to the site. The calculated load on the pier foundations is exceptionally high, no less than 70 tons on the head of single 13in square timber pile, but the soundness of Robert Stephenson's design has been proved by time under a steadily increasing weight of traffic, and his high-level bridge stands today in splendid tribute to his engineering skill and foresight. How long such achievements of the engineer pioneers can continue to defy not only the effects of time and decay but loads undreamed of by their creators is a question of great concern.

While the high-level bridge was building at Newcastle, farther north a second great work was going forward under Robert Stephenson's superintendence. This was the splendid stone viaduct known as the Royal Border Bridge which Robert Stephenson designed to carry the railway over the Tweed at Berwick. It consists of 28 arches each of 61ft 6in span and carries the rails 126ft above the bed of the river. Here again the Nasmyth steam pile-driver was used to construct the coffer dams and pier foundations. Although there is nothing unique about it from an engineering point of view, there is no more romantic and evocative railway structure in the world than the Royal Border Bridge. He who would measure imaginatively the magnitude of the Stephensons' achievement and seek to recapture something of the triumph and the wonder of that heroic age of engineering, should stand upon the ruined castle keep at Berwick and gaze down that long, proud perspective of slender stone piers as the Flying Scotsman thunders across the water.

These two great bridges over Tyne and Tweed were the last links to be closed on the east-coast route to Scotland and George Stephenson did not live to see them completed. Thanks to the efforts of his rival and ex-pupil Joseph Locke in driving the rails over Shap and Beattock summits, the west-coast route was completed first.

The first train from the south was able to enter Newcastle at the end of August 1848 over a temporary timber bridge which had been erected beside the scaffolding upon which ran the large traverser used to lower the girder segments of the permanent bridge into place. The last arch was closed on 7 June 1849, the bridge was examined and passed by the Board of Trade inspector in August, and in September it was formally opened by Queen Victoria. So pleased was Her Majesty by the enthusiastic reception she received from her northern subjects that she agreed to return a year later to open the Royal Border Bridge, which completed the east-coast route to Edinburgh. On 28 August 1850 the Queen was the guest of the Earl of Carlisle at Castle Howard and on the following day, having opened the Border bridge, the royal train, its locomotive elaborately decorated with Royal Stuart tartan, drew the Sovereign to her palace of Holyrood. It was upon this occasion that Robert Stephenson was offered but refused a knighthood. A month earlier he had been the guest of honour at a grand banquet in Newcastle station to celebrate the completion of the line.

The railway company had determined that their conquest of the capital of the north should be worthily celebrated and had commissioned John Dobson, who had succeeded Ignatius Bonomi as the leading architect in the north of England, to design their Newcastle Central Station. Dobson was without doubt the greatest of railway architects, a man of rare talent and vision who combined architectural with engineering skill of the highest order. Had his original design for the Central Station been executed it would have been unquestionably the finest work of its kind in the world. Unfortunately he was compelled to modify it on the score of expense and to accommodate the headquarters offices of the railway company, while the great portico he had planned was added later by another hand. Yet, even so, it remained a unique achievement, including as it did the first large vaulted roof of iron ribs and glass ever constructed. The success of this splendid architectural adventure, the precursor of all great station roofs, was largely due to Dobson's own invention of special rolls for producing the curved wrought-iron ribs. Most appropriately it was on the platform of this station, under the high vault of Dobson's iron roof, that the banquet in honour of Robert Stephenson was held.

Perhaps when Robert Stephenson rose to speak he remembered his embarrassment on the previous occasion when he had heard such extravagant claims made on behalf of his father, for now he did his best to disclaim the credit given to him.

If you would read [he said] the biographies of all your old distinguished engineers, you would be struck with the excessive detail into which they were drawn; when intelligence was not so widely diffused as at present, an engineer like Smeaton or Brindley had not only to conceive the design, but had to invent the machine and carry out every detail of the conception; but since then a change has taken place, and no change is more complete. The principal engineer now has only to say 'let this be done' and it is speedily accomplished, such is the immense capital, and such the resources of mind which are immediately brought into play. I have myself, within the last ten or twelve years, done little more than exercise a general superintendence and there are many other persons here to whom the works referred to by the chairman ought to be almost entirely attributed. I have had little or nothing to do with many of them beyond giving my name, and exercising a gentle control in some of the principal works. In this particular district, especially, I have been most fortunate in being associated with Mr. Thomas Harrison. Beyond drawing the outline I have no right to claim any credit for the works above where we now sit. Upon Mr. Harrison the whole responsibility of their execution has fallen, and I believe they have been executed without a single flaw.

So multifarious were Robert Stephenson's railway concerns during the 1840s that he was probably paying the resident engineer, T. E. Harrison, who had worked for him in the old Stanhope & Tyne days, no more than his due. Yet nothing reveals more clearly than his speech how a reaction to the attitude of omniscience which his father too often adopted, drove Robert Stephenson to the opposite extreme of self-depreciation and diffidence.

In September 1845, George Stephenson, accompanied by Sir Joshua Walmsley, left England to examine the route of a proposed Royal North of Spain Railway. They were joined in Paris by Mackenzie, the contractor for the Orleans & Tours Railway, whereupon the little party then headed south and crossed the Pyrenees. Having reached the course of the proposed railway, they proceeded to follow it through Irun, St. Sebastian, St. Andero, Bilbao and across the province of Old Castile towards Madrid, surveying as they went. They also visited the Escorial and the Guadarama mountains, where Stephenson realized that most formidable tunnelling operations would be unavoidable. Such physical difficulties combined with lack of potential traffic led him to advise against the scheme and the party turned for home. The rigours of the long journey, much of which had to be made on mule-back over rough mountain-passes, had been too much for a man of sixty-five, and by the time they reached Paris George Stephenson was obviously ill. He insisted upon proceeding, however, but as soon as they had boarded the Southampton packet at Havre he retired to his cabin with a severe attack of pleurisy. This was a danger signal which even the restless and indomitable Stephenson could not ignore. He had but three more years to live, and these he spent in almost complete retirement at Tapton House, Chesterfield.

George Stephenson leased Tapton House, standing upon a hill

overlooking the tracks of the North Midland Railway, on 25 May 1843.[1] The motive for this move was exactly the same as that which had dictated his earlier removal from Liverpool to Alton Grange— the presence in the locality of coal and other natural resources which could be exploited with the aid of the new railway. Joseph Sandars of Liverpool, who, it will be remembered, was his partner in the Snibston Colliery enterprise, joined him in this new venture and so did George Hudson and William Claxton. The four partners developed coal mines and ironworks at Clay Cross, near Chester-field, purchased the Crich limestone quarries and built a large lime-works beside the railway near Ambergate, their venture proving almost as successful as the earlier one in Leicestershire.

Limestone had been quarried and burnt at Crich since 1734, but with transport restricted to pack-horses loading two hundredweights each, the output was very small. Now, with rail transport at hand, George Stephenson developed the industry upon an enormous scale. Twenty lime-kilns were built at Ambergate which yielded an output of 25,000 tons a year. On one occasion 2,200 tons were burnt in eleven days and the output of unburnt limestone from the quarries was almost as great. Charles Binns, who had succeeded Frank Swanwick as George Stephenson's secretary, was appointed manager of the lime-works, while James Campbell was transferred from Snibston to act as engineer. Thomas Summerside was another old associate of George Stephenson's who joined the staff at Crich along with others who had served him at Snibston or on the con-struction of the North Midland Railway.

The lime-kilns at Ambergate were linked with Crich quarry by two miles of tramway which included two formidable self-acting inclines, that leading down to the kilns having a gradient of one in five. This little railway was the favourite toy of George Stephenson's old age and the many distinguished guests whom he entertained at Tapton House were invariably taken along to see it at work, such tours of inspection usually ending with a tankard of beer and a grilled chop at the 'Wheatsheaf' at Crich.

On one such occasion George Stephenson brought over a party

---

[1] This is the date which appears on the lease indenture which exists in the library of the Institution of Mechanical Engineers. Some letters of Stephenson's, addressed from Tapton House, bear dates earlier than this which indicate that he must have rented the place on a short-term basis before negotiating the lease.

which included Robert Stephenson and George Carr Glyn,[1] only to find that there had been a breakdown on the steep incline. "What a thing it is, Summerside," he complained, "I have brought these gentlemen to see the working of the incline and you have had an accident." The party began to scramble up the incline, leaving Summerside below to put matters to rights and to hang a rake of empty wagons on to the rope to be drawn up. It was old George's intention that the company should ride down the incline on the loaded wagons, but, fortunately for them, there was more delay until a sorely disgruntled Stephenson began to lead them down again on foot. They had scarcely reached the bottom when the loaded wagons at the top broke away. With a roar they rushed down upon the party at frightening speed, hurling out blocks of limestone to right and left as they came. With equal rapidity the distinguished guests took to their heels and sprinted for cover, while the wagons dashed themselves to pieces at the foot of the gradient. As the dust subsided, Robert Stephenson and Glyn stepped from the shelter of a wall to be greeted by the spectacle of George Stephenson's face peering round the bole of a tree and wearing an expression of blank amazement. The sight struck them as so comic that both men burst into a roar of laughter. "Ye dinna need to laugh," shouted the old engineer, furiously, "'tis a hundred pounds out of my way!"

George Stephenson's wealth was such that the loss of a few trams was nothing to him, but this little story is typical of the unpredictable blend of generosity and parsimony which distinguished him throughout his life. He was ever generous over large things and mean over trifles. He would often, says Summerside, bring to Ambergate from his gardens at Tapton House, boxes of fruit, grapes, apricots and peaches, which he would present to Summerside and other members of the staff to take home to their wives and children. Such presentations were invariably accompanied by the injunction, "Mind! fetch the box back", and the precious boxes worth a few coppers would be carefully transported back to Chesterfield by rail in a first-class carriage.

The gardens at Tapton House were the other great interest of George Stephenson's old age. In the far off days when he was a

---

[1] Banker and first Chairman of the Railway Clearing House and of the London & North Western Railway.

brakesman at Killingworth, one of his keenest pleasures had been to grow larger cabbages and cauliflowers than his neighbours, and now his wealth enabled him to indulge this pleasure again on a far greater and more lavish scale. He built a whole range of hot-houses where he grew grapes, melons, pineapples and other exotic fruits, his great rival in this art being old Paxton, the Duke of Devonshire's gardener at Chatsworth and the father of Joseph Paxton, the designer of the Crystal Palace. To his huge satisfaction he succeeded in defeating Paxton by producing a straight cucumber, but he did not live to see his 'Queen' pineapple win first prize in competition with the Chatsworth strain.

Happily occupied with his garden and his works at Ambergate and Clay Cross, George Stephenson followed but took little active part in the turbulent events which were taking place in the great railway world which he and his son had created. The activities of his friend George Hudson culminated in the fantastic railway mania of 1845. On Sunday 30 November in that year, the last day on which railway plans for consideration in the next session of Parliament could be deposited at the Board of Trade, there were fantastic scenes. Riots between groups of rival speculators broke out in Preston and Mansfield; roads and railways leading to London were blocked with coaches and special trains as 800 groups of eager promoters joined the race to Whitehall. In one case this goal could only be reached in time over the metals of a railway company bitterly hostile to the scheme in question. The resourceful promoters triumphantly overcame this difficulty by putting their plans into a coffin, whereupon, disguised as mutes in sombre black, they were readily given the necessary special transport. Robert Stephenson's office in Great George Street was described as resembling a levee of a Minister of State as hordes of railway promoters endeavoured to obtain his blessing on their schemes. In vain would tempting bribes be offered, for the association of the name of Stephenson with any project was enough to set its shares at a premium. A testimonial[1] was launched for George Hudson who, of all men at this time, did not need it, and in no time at all £30,000 had been subscribed by grateful shareholders, including such unlikely people as Emily and Anne Brontë, who contributed a pound

---

[1] It is said that Hudson drafted the testimonial advertisement himself.

apiece. Only their sister Charlotte held back and advised them to sell their shares in the York & North Midland while the going was good. Unfortunately they did not take her advice.

From all this turmoil George Stephenson held aloof. Once he had fought for the railway almost alone against a sceptical world, and now that same world had rushed to the opposite pole, becoming railway mad, ready to swallow any wild-cat scheme that was put before it. "What a Railway World this is!" he exclaimed in a letter to Joseph Pease, "When will the bustle be over?" And in another letter, to his solicitor, Thomas Morris of Warwick, he wrote: "I hope you have kept clear of the mania of wild railway schemes—thousands of people will be ruined as I have learned that many have mortgaged their little properties to get money; of course their property will be lost up to the amount of money they have got."

And what did he think of his friend George Hudson, now living like some eastern potentate in the huge house at Albert Gate, Hyde Park, which he had purchased from Thomas Cubitt for £15,000? "Hudson has become too great a man for me now", wrote the old engineer, "I am not at all satisfied at the way the Newcastle & Berwick has been carried on and I do not intend to take any more active part in it. I have made Hudson a rich man, but he will very soon care for nobody except he can get money by them."

George Mitchison, the manager of the Clay Cross ironworks, recalled to Thomas Summerside an occasion when George Hudson arrived at Tapton House at a time when George Stephenson and Mitchison were in conversation. The 'Railway King' imperiously demanded an interview in private. "Oh no, Hudson," replied Stephenson, "this is an old friend of mine, if you have anything to say you can say it here." Hudson then explained a scheme of his which involved selling out shares from one railway and buying in another and declared that Stephenson would be the richer by several thousand pounds if he would agree to it. No one knew better than Hudson the cash value of George Stephenson's name, for years he had flattered and beguiled him, producing him like a trump card at an endless round of banquets, opening celebrations and Company meetings. But those days were over now. The engineer had dis-covered the rottenness at the heart of Hudson's business genius which turned his gold to dross. Stephenson was very indignant, told Hudson roundly that he would not be a party to his schemes, and when the financier had retired discomfited he spoke very vehemently, said Mitchison, against Hudson's doings.

Another railway drama which the ageing Stephenson watched from his hilltop eyrie at Chesterfield was the epic battle of the gauges,[1] with his son and Isambard Brunel in command of the contending forces as the broad- and narrow-gauge metals advanced upon each other along a wide front in the southern Midlands. The highlight of this hard fought campaign was Brunel's dramatic challenge to put the respective merits of the two systems to practical test in a series of locomotive trials. The courses selected were York to Darlington and Paddington to Didcot, and the choice of locomotives was somewhat ironical. The locomotives picked by Robert Stephenson to uphold the honour of the narrow gauge were one named *Stephenson* from the North Midland Railway and another, known as Engine A, which was specially built at Newcastle for the occasion. These were both of the latest 'long-boiler' type constructed according to Robert Stephenson's patent of 1841. On the other hand, Brunel's broad-gauge champion *Ixion* was no more than Daniel Gooch's development of the much earlier Stephenson *Patentee* type.

The long-boiler locomotive represented another development in Robert Stephenson's quest for greater heating-surface and therefore greater economy. In six-coupled form as a heavy freight engine the long-boiler type proved most successful and was the prototype of the standard British goods engine. But for sustained high speed running the long-boiler type was a failure. Not only was it very unstable at speed, but under such conditions steam-raising power was inadequate. Consequently the Stephenson locomotives were soundly trounced by their broad-gauge rival of earlier design. The *Stephenson* could not match the performance of *Ixion*. 'Engine A' from which so much had been hoped, left the rails when travelling at 48 m.p.h. and turned over on her side, much to the alarm of the judge, Professor Airey, the Astronomer Royal, who was riding the footplate at the time but very luckily escaped serious injury.

Not content with this success, there appeared from Swindon in

[1] For a fuller account of the 'Battle of the Gauges' see this writer's *Isambard Kingdom Brunel*, pp. 150-161.

1846 the *Great Western*, the first of Gooch's great 8ft single express engines which put broad-gauge locomotive performance far ahead of anything the narrow gauge could accomplish. Such achievements must have been very galling to old George Stephenson but, as he was probably shrewd enough to realize, they were pyrrhic victories. The brilliant sorties of Brunel and Gooch may be compared with Prince Rupert's cavalry charges in the war between king and parliament, or with that famous charge of the Light Brigade in the war soon to come which called forth the classic comment: *C'est magnifique mais ce n'est pas la guerre*. They were certainly magnificent but they could not hope to stem the relentless advance of the Stephenson gauge.

Although George Stephenson had felt in his younger days, unreasonably at times, that every man's hand was against him, yet he was one of those few fortunate pioneers who lived to enjoy both wealth and honour. At the end of December 1844 the directors of the Liverpool & Manchester Railway resolved to commission a marble statue of their engineer, "Father of the improved railway of modern times", and this was placed in St. George's Hall, Liverpool, shortly after his death. Two further statues of George Stephenson were executed posthumously by John Lough and E. H. Baily and erected in Newcastle and at the foot of the staircase in P. C. Hardwick's noble hall at Euston. Between 1841 and 1845 the Boards of practically every railway with which George Stephenson's name had been associated voted him a free pass for life over their lines as a mark of their respect.

It was the old engineer's great delight that while he remained plain George Stephenson with no handles to his name and never tempered his broad Northumbrian brogue, no door in the country was closed to him. More than once he returned to Killingworth, visiting again the scenes of his youth and yarning with old friends in cottage parlours. He would go the rounds of the pitmen's cottages, tapping on the thresholds with his stick and calling out "Well, and how's all here today?" Yet he was equally at home at Drayton Manor, near Tamworth, as the guest of Sir Robert Peel, at whose house-parties he met many of the most distinguished figures of the day in the spheres of politics, science and the arts. A few months before his death he visited Whittington House, near Chesterfield, the home of his former assistant, Frank Swanwick, where he met the famous American, Emerson, who said afterwards that to have talked with George Stephenson was alone worth crossing the Atlantic.

He remained to the last a simple man, hating only the pompous and pretentious. On his frequent journeys between Chesterfield and Ambergate he took a childish pleasure in flourishing his free pass and being ushered deferentially to a first-class compartment. Yet Thomas Summerside recalls how, when no passenger train was due, he would cheerfully clamber into one of a train of empty coal-wagons bound from Ambergate to Clay Cross and be trundled away perched quite contentedly on an extemporized plank seat. Summerside also recalls an occasion when the old engineer was waiting for a train on Derby station. The driver of a train which had stopped at the platform was unable to get it on the move, the locomotive having stopped on dead centre. Such a display of incompetence made George Stephenson's fingers itch, and in a moment he was up on the footplate to grasp regulator and reversing lever in practised hands. A few seconds of skilful humouring was followed by a reassuring snort from the smoke stack and as the engine started to move Stephenson hopped nimbly back on to the platform beaming with pleasure.

In earlier editions of Samuel Smiles's biography of George Stephenson there occurs a passage which has been the subject of much controversy. This is to the effect that late in life, apparently in 1846, only two years before his death, George Stephenson applied for membership of the Institution of Civil Engineers but was informed by the Council of that body that he must comply with the regulations governing admission by submitting details of his professional experience and by obtaining the supporting signatures of several members of the Institution. Stephenson, the story goes on, was mortally offended by this slight and it was largely as a result of this cavalier treatment that a number of his railway associates formed in Birmingham the Institution of Mechanical Engineers and invited George Stephenson to be their first President, an honour which he accepted.[1]

In later editions of Smiles's book this story was omitted, and today

[1] The Institution was founded at a meeting held at the Queen's Hotel, Birmingham, on 27 January 1847. Robert Stephenson succeeded his father as President in 1849, an office he held until 1853. The headquarters of the Institution were transferred from Birmingham to London in 1877.

documentary evidence which would establish the truth of the matter beyond question seems to be impossible to find. On 27 February 1847 George Stephenson wrote in a letter to J. T. W. Bell: "I have had the honour of Knighthood of my own country made to me several times, but would not have it. I have been invited to become a Fellow of the Royal Society; and also of the Civil Engineers Society, but I objected to these empty additions to my name. I have, however, now consented to become President of a highly respectable mechanics' Institute at Birmingham."

It has been made abundantly clear in earlier chapters of this book that during George Stephenson's active career there was no love lost between him and the engineers who at that time formed the influential caucus of the Institution of Civil Engineers. They had made their reputation in the sphere of canal and turnpike-road engineering, and on both sides there was jealousy and prejudice which left lasting bitterness behind it. The London engineers for long regarded Stephenson as an impostor and it must be acknowledged that by their professional standards he never possessed any technical qualifications as a civil engineer. Telford, though he too was of humble birth, took immense pains to educate himself in the theory of his profession, whereas George Stephenson did not, relying instead upon his great natural gifts and the help of his son. Had George Stephenson applied for membership of the Institution in his early days he would certainly have received a dusty answer. That he received such an answer at the end of his life when he was world famous and when his son was a member of the Council of the Institution seems scarcely credible. It also seems unlikely that Stephenson was invited to become a member of the Institution as his reference to the 'Civil Engineers Society' in his letter of 1847 seems to imply. In the light of all the events which have been chronicled in this book, the most credible explanation would seem to be that, notwithstanding the mediating influence of Robert Stephenson, a legacy of bitterness remained and there was no *rapprochement* upon either side.

Prejudiced as he was where his fellow engineers were concerned, in politics and religion George Stephenson had a sceptical and open mind. He was never wedded to any political party or religious denomination. Thomas Summerside, a devout nonconformist, was evidently very concerned about his great master's apparent lack of belief, and during these last years at Tapton House there were several passages of arms between them on the subject. "I wish you were a Christian of the real sort", said Summerside one day. "I am a Christian, Summerside", Stephenson insisted. "No Sir, you are not", declared Summerside boldly. "I am a far better Christian than many of those priests", retorted Stephenson hotly, and then he added enigmatically, "When I was a brakesman I believe I would have been a man of one book but for one inconsistency of a professor of religion." Like other men of his generation, George Stephenson had a faith in material progress which was unbounded, unquestioning and, in relation to his own contribution, almost messianic. "I will send the locomotive as the great Missionary over the World", he once declared when Summerside had expatiated upon the virtues of foreign religious missions.

In 1845, to George Stephenson's great sorrow, Elizabeth, his faithful wife of so many years, died, and early in 1848 he took as his third wife his housekeeper, Miss Gregory, the daughter of a farmer near Bakewell. Though his health was now more delicate and his hand was unsteady, Stephenson was still active. That summer he visited the Royal Agricultural Society's show at York, where he was the guest of George Hudson at Newby Park. He read a paper at the "Mechanic's Institute" in Birmingham and attended meetings in connection with the railway to Matlock and Buxton. At the beginning of August, however, only six months after his third marriage, he had a second serious attack of pleurisy and, although his wife and Dr Condell of Baslow nursed him night and day, on 12 August 1848 George Stephenson died. He was in his sixty-seventh year. The enginemen on the North Midland line no longer saw the familiar figure with the white hair and the old-fashioned square-tailed frock coat who had so often stood on the slopes of Tapton hill watching the trains go by. "That railway", he had once said proudly as he gazed down at the gleaming rails, "will be there a hundred years from now." Time has proved him right. Northbound from Bristol to his native Newcastle, expresses still thunder by Tapton hill and past the crooked spire of Chesterfield where he lies buried in Trinity churchyard.

From near and far the friends of a lifetime converged upon

Tapton House to say farewell to the 'Father of Railways' and to follow him on his final journey. Among them was the man whose confidence in him had first set George Stephenson on the road to fame so many years before—Edward Pease, now over eighty years of age. The old Quaker recorded the event in his diary in his own inimitable style:

Wednesday, Aug. 16. Left home in company with John Dixon to attend the interment of George Stephenson at Chesterfield, and arrived there in the evening. When I reflect on my first acquaintance with him and the resulting consequences my mind seems almost lost in doubt as to the beneficial results—that humanity has been benefited in the diminished use of horses and by the lessened cruelty to them, that much ease, safety, speed and lessened expense in travelling is obtained, but as to the results and effects of all that Railways have led my dear family into, being in any sense beneficial is uncertain.

Thurs. Aug. 17. Went in the forenoon to Tapton House, late G. Stephenson's residence, and received from Robert a welcome reception; had a serious friendly conference with him, under a feeling expressed to him of my belief that it was a kindness to him his father was taken, his habits were approaching to inebriety; his end was one that one seemed painfully to feel no ground, almost, for hope. I fear he died an unbeliever—the attendance of his funeral appeared to me to be a right step due to my association with him and his son. I do not feel condemned in doing so, yet gloomy and unconsolatory was the day. In the church I sat a spectacle with my hat on, and not comforted by the funeral service.

Of the many obituaries of George Stephenson which appeared in the press, Thomas Summerside, who had known him for so many years, most favoured that which appeared in the *Derby and Chesterfield Reporter*. "He was too truly great to be ashamed of the beginning out of which he sprung . . .", said the writer, and went on:

He seemed the impersonation of the moving, active spirit of the age; and though mechanical agencies had raised him to so high a reputation, it was not the successful engineer, but the thinking man before whom one bent as to a superior.

What faults he had (and who will pretend that he was without them), cease to be remembered, now that he is no more. Take him for all in all, we shall not look upon his like again. Nay, we *cannot*, for in his sphere of invention and discovery, there cannot again be a *beginning*. . . .

CHAPTER FIFTEEN

The Great Tubular Bridges

W HILE THE east-coast route to Edinburgh was under
construction, work was proceeding simultaneously on
the rail route from London to Dublin. When George
Stephenson, at the suggestion of the Chester & Crewe Company,
made his first survey for this line in 1838, two alternative railheads
on the Welsh coast were under consideration, the existing port of
Holyhead in Anglesey or a new harbour at Porthdynlleyn on the
Lleyn Peninsular. Having examined both routes, George Stephenson
had pronounced in favour of Holyhead as promising the better and
more level line, notwithstanding the fact that it involved crossing
the Menai Straits. At a public meeting at Chester in January 1839
he proposed overcoming this difficulty by laying a single line of
rails along one carriage way of Thomas Telford's famous Menai
suspension bridge and using horses to draw the trains across. To say
it was fortunate that this plan was soon abandoned implies no
criticism of Telford's bridge. The unsuitability of a suspension
bridge of this type for railway purposes had been demonstrated
practically by the failure of Captain Brown's bridge over the Tees
at Stockton.

When the Act for the Chester & Holyhead Railway was finally
passed at the end of June 1845 and Robert Stephenson was appointed
Engineer-in-Chief, he found himself confronting the same problem
of bridging the Conway and the Menai which Telford had solved
so brilliantly when building his roads to Holyhead. Although nearly
twenty years had passed since Telford's two great bridges had been
completed, the suspension principle was still the only known method
of constructing a bridge of great span. Telford had originally
planned to span the Menai straits with a rigid cast-iron bridge, but
the Admiralty stipulations regarding headroom and width of
channel for navigation forced him to abandon this design and to
adopt the suspension principle which had not then been applied

upon such a scale. Now history repeated itself. Robert Stephenson also prepared a design for a cast-iron bridge, but was forced for the same reason to abandon it and, since a suspension bridge of the Telford type was out of the question, to evolve instead a bridge design which was without precedent. The result was his greatest civil engineering achievement, yet by an ironical twist of fortune the Chester & Holyhead Railway was first the scene of his most disconcerting professional failure.

The first section of the new railway to be completed was at the Chester end, and this included a bridge over the river Dee just outside the city. Here Robert originally planned a five-span brick bridge but, when piling had actually begun, doubts about the pier foundations induced him to abandon the design and to substitute a three-span structure consisting of masonry piers and compound trussed girders of the type described in the last chapter. The river was crossed on the skew and the girders had a clear span of 98ft, there being four to each span, making twelve in all. This was the greatest span which Stephenson had bridged in this way, but as he had used 87ft compound girders for his replacement bridge at Stockton he had complete confidence in their suitability. In fact, however, their design was open to grave criticism, as Robert should have realized. Each girder consisted of a single casting of I-section 3ft 9in deep. This was reinforced by two wrought-iron truss-rods placed on either side, each consisting of three linked portions of equal length. The centre sections of these truss-rods were horizontal, and supported the middle of the lower flange of the girders by means of jack screws. The two end-sections were inclined and were secured at their extremities to two massive bosses or shoulders cast on the ends of the upper flanges of the girders and rising four feet above the level of these flanges.

This Dee Bridge was completed by the end of September 1846 and on 20 October it was inspected and passed for traffic by Major-General C. W. Pasley, the Board of Trade Inspector-General of Railways. Now, so far as the owning Company was concerned, this traffic consisted only of construction trains, but the recently completed Shrewsbury & Chester Railway had secured running powers over the Chester & Holyhead between Saltney Junction and Chester, with the effect that their passenger trains began to use the new bridge as soon as it was opened. So things continued until 24 May 1847. On that fateful day a passenger train bound from Chester to Shrewsbury met with disaster. It had reached the last of the three spans when the outer of the two girders directly beneath it broke into three pieces. The driver of the train had a miraculous escape from almost certain death. He stated afterwards that because he heard a peculiar noise and felt an unusual amount of vibration as his train ran on to the third span, he sensed that something was wrong and opened his regulator wide in an effort to get clear. His locomotive had just reached firm ground when the girder collapsed. The tender-coupling parted, with the result that his unfortunate fireman, who was breaking coal on the tender at the time, fell to his death as, with a noise like a clap of thunder, the whole train plunged into the river. In addition to the unlucky fireman, a guard and two coachmen who were travelling in the leading van were killed instantly, one passenger died later and sixteen were injured. In the circumstances it is remarkable that anyone should have escaped alive.

The accident caused a tremendous furore in engineering circles; all the more so because it implicated the most eminent railway engineer of the day, and the inquest at Chester became a *cause célèbre*. One happy outcome of the disaster, however, was that it brought about a reconciliation between Robert Stephenson and Joseph Locke. The estrangement dated from George Stephenson's ignominious defeat by Locke on the Grand Junction Railway, though whether it was due simply to the fact that Robert took his father's part in the affair or whether he had some private quarrel we do not know. Some engineers held that the Stephensons were jealous of Locke's success in France where, among other lines, he had engineered the railway from Paris to Rouen. When Robert Stephenson was invited to act as consultant for the line from Rouen to Havre he refused in these terms:

> You are very likely aware that there is an unfriendly feeling between ourselves and Mr. Locke. We think he has used us ill; whether we are right or wrong is not the point. But, under that impression I feel it due to myself to avoid giving him any possible ground for complaint against me. . . . The line to Havre is so necessary a prolongation of the line to Rouen that he might say I was interfering with his district if I went there while all the Continent was open to me. . . .

The use of the plural 'we' suggests that so far as Robert was concerned the quarrel was not a personal one but that his actions was governed by loyalty to his father. However this may be, adversity forged once again the ties of youth and the two great engineers remained fast friends for the rest of their lives.

Joseph Locke, like Brunel, distrusted cast iron in railway bridges and while Brunel made extensive use of timber and carried out experiments with wrought iron girders, Locke used masonry wherever possible. Nevertheless, despite his own personal judgement he came forward to give expert testimony on behalf of Robert Stephenson. Charles Vignoles, Tom Gooch and John Kennedy, the locomotive engineer, did likewise. To this formidable array of engineering talent there was opposed only Robertson, the engineer of the Shrewsbury & Chester Railway, who roundly declared that the bridge had been badly designed and that, so far from strengthening the girders, the wrought-iron truss-rods actually weakened them by imposing severe local stresses.

F. R. Conder attended the inquest at Chester and afterwards described an occasion heavily charged with drama. Although Robertson had such a galaxy of engineering talent ranged against him, it is obvious now, even if it was not so apparent then, that his condemnation was perfectly correct. Moreover, so widely and so outspokenly had he proclaimed his views that by the time the inquest took place he had roused strong and bitter local feeling against Robert Stephenson. So much so that Conder declares that Sir Edward Walker, the foreman of the Coroner's jury, was determined to get a verdict of manslaughter or of possible murder against him. The latter suggestion is, of course, absurd, but a charge of manslaughter was a very real possibility.

Major-General Pasley, who had passed the bridge for traffic, was so agitated that when he was called upon to give his evidence he could scarcely speak and what he said was inaudible to the body of the court. As for Robert Stephenson, Conder had never seen him look so pale and haggard and he betrayed, he said, 'the most intense vexation and inquietude'. Well he might, for he was terribly aware of the fact that despite all that extreme care and caution which characterized him throughout his career he had committed a serious blunder. Never before had he found himself in such a profoundly false and unhappy position, torn as he was between personal honesty and loyalty to the Company he was serving. He had been prepared to make an honest admission but had been vehemently dissuaded from doing so by the Solicitor to the Chester & Holyhead Company who conducted the defence and who insisted that any admission of liability would be fatal not only to himself but to the Company. Yielding to such persuasions he agreed to accept the prepared line of defence which was that the girder could only have failed as a result of its receiving a heavy blow. It was alleged that this blow had been caused by the derailment of the locomotive tender due to the breakage of a wheel. Supported as it was by such an array of expert witnesses and by the fact that the similar bridge over the Tees at Stockton had proved quite satisfactory, this argument prevailed to the extent that the jury evidently regarded the issue as 'not proven'. They returned a verdict of accidental death, but they added that they considered the bridge unsafe and recommended a government inquiry into the safety of such bridges generally.

In the particular case of the Dee Bridge a careful examination of the broken girder, which was retrieved from the river, proved that the fracture had begun in the top flange, which had failed in compression due to the stresses imposed by the method of fixing the ends of the truss-rods to shoulders four feet above this flange. To distribute these stresses over the length of the girder, wedge-shaped compression pieces were inserted in the angles formed between the vertical shoulders and the girders, while the latter were also supported from below by inclined struts which butted against the masonry of the piers and abutments. Other cast-iron bridges were similarly strengthened, while the cast-iron girders of 96ft span supplied to Robert Stephenson's design for the bridge carrying the Florence & Leghorn Railway over the Arno were modified in similar fashion before the bridge was erected later in the same year. This Arno bridge was the last on which cast-iron girders of large span were used, for Robert Stephenson had learnt his lesson. He acknowledged his error fully and frankly in the last year of his life when, after a detailed explanation of the defects of the compound girder, he concluded:

> The objection to this girder is common to all girders in which two independent systems are attempted to be blended; and, as a general principle, all such arrangements should be avoided.

It is useless to say more on the subject of this form of girder, as since the adoption of wrought-iron for girders they have been entirely superseded; they were designed when no other means existed of obtaining iron girders of great span, and the melancholy accident which occurred at Chester is the only existing instance of their failure.

The Dee Bridge disaster had far-reaching effects on the whole railway world. The Railway Commissioners circularized every railway company, calling for detailed information about all cast-iron bridges in use or under construction on their lines. Later, too, the government set up a Royal Commission to inquire into the use of iron in railway structures. All this activity undoubtedly stimulated the development of wrought-iron construction, but where the Royal Commission was concerned Robert Stephenson feared that government caution and control might go too far by restricting the enterprise and initiative of civil engineers. "I think a collection of facts and observations would be most valuable," he wrote; "but if you attempt to draw conclusions from those facts, and confine engineers, even in a limited way, to those conclusions, I am quite sure that it will tend to hamper the profession very much." Brunel expressed precisely the same view to the Commissioners in a much more forcible manner.

Although Robert Stephenson escaped a criminal charge which might have ruined him professionally and would certainly have left an indelible stain on the Stephenson name, nevertheless the Dee Bridge disaster cast a temporary shadow over his reputation which he was most anxious to dispel. That anxiety was all the greater because, only a few months before the collapse of the Dee Bridge, he had, after most exhaustive experiments and intense thought, determined to build a bridge which would be quite without precedent both in size and in form of construction. Needless to say, the scene of this great operation was to be the Menai Straits. "I stood", Stephenson admitted afterwards, "on the verge of a responsibility from which, I confess, I had nearly shrunk." It was indeed an immense responsibility and it had to be accepted by a man who could not now afford the slightest suspicion of failure.

When his father's suggestion of utilizing Telford's bridge for the crossing had been abandoned, Robert Stephenson selected as a site for a new bridge a point about a mile to the west of the suspension bridge where the Britannia Rock offered a convenient foundation for a pier in the centre of the strait. It was here that he at first proposed to erect a bridge of two cast-iron arches each of 350ft span with a roadway height of 105ft above high water. When this plan was rejected by the Admiralty, Stephenson then considered a new type of suspension bridge in which, instead of a mere platform, the suspension chains would support some form of deep trussed-girder construction. Trellis work of wood or wrought iron was the first thought, but this was rejected in favour of solid vertical members made up of wrought-iron plates. In section, the proposed bridge-platform which Stephenson envisaged now resembled a box without a lid and this naturally led him on to consider the effect of putting a lid on it. It was obvious to him that the result would be a great increase in strength. It was in this way, by progressive stages, that the idea of a great wrought-iron tube was born, a tube so large that the trains would pass through it.

Stephenson's deliberations had reached this point when a mishap occurred during the launching of the new iron steamship *Prince of Wales* at Blackwall. Owing to a failure of the launching tackle the ship stuck in such a way that her hull was left quite unsupported over a length of 110ft, yet it was not strained in any way. The news of this episode greatly impressed and encouraged Stephenson by demonstrating the strength of a wrought-iron structure, so much so that he was won over to the belief that a wrought-iron tubular bridge could be built strongly enough to dispense with suspension chains. He now sought the assistance of two experts, one practical and the other theoretical. The former was his father's old associate, William Fairbairn, now a famous engineer and ship-builder, while the latter was Professor Eaton Hodgkinson, F.R.S., who was described as 'the first scientific authority on iron beams'.

When these two men submitted their reports to Stephenson they differed as experts so frequently do. "If it be determined to erect a bridge of tubes", wrote the scientist, "I would beg to recommend that suspension chains be employed as an auxiliary, otherwise great thickness of metal would be required to produce adequate stiffness and strength." "Provided the parts are well proportioned and the plates properly rivetted," declared the practical engineer confidently, "you may strip off the chains and have it as a useful Monument of

the enterprise and energy of the age in which it was constructed."
Faced with such divided counsels, the ultimate choice and responsibility remained with Robert Stephenson. "It was a most anxious
and harassing time with me", he admitted to Tom Gooch afterwards. "Often at night I would lie tossing about seeking sleep in
vain. The tubes filled my head. I went to bed with them and got up
with them. In the grey of the morning when I looked across the
square it seemed an immense distance across to the houses on the
opposite side. It was nearly the same length as the span of my
bridge!"

Notwithstanding his habitual caution and the headshakings of
Professor Hodgkinson, whose views were shared by a large body
of professional opinion, Stephenson finally decided against the use of
suspension chains and threw in his lot with William Fairbairn. A
most elaborate series of calculations and practical experiments were
made at Fairbairn's shipyard at Millwall which culminated in the
construction of a large model of the proposed bridge-tube 75ft
long between bearings, 4ft 6ins deep and 2ft 8ins wide. This was
progressively loaded in the centre until the bottom plates tore apart
under a load of $30\frac{1}{4}$ tons. Stronger plates were then fitted, after
which the side plates of the tube gave way at 43 tons. Improvements
were made in this way until, for an addition of only one ton of
material, the model bore a load of 86 tons.

It was upon the results of these experiments that the design of the
actual tubes was based. Cellular construction was used for the roof
and floor of the tubes and single plates with stiffening ribs of 'T'
section for the sides. The strength of materials was nicely proportioned to the load, each tube being progressively strengthened and
stiffened towards its extremities. It was a suggestion made by
Robert Stephenson, however, which made the greatest contribution
to the strength of the bridge and finally disposed of the idea of using
suspension chains. As originally conceived, each of the two lines of
railway would be carried over the Menai through two tubular
girders each of 460ft clear span. These would extend from the great
central pier on the Britannia Rock to piers built on the Caernarvon
and Anglesey shores, which would be linked to the land by masonry
approach-viaducts similar to those built by Telford for his suspension
bridge. Robert Stephenson's new proposal was to use additional

230ft lengths of tube instead of these approach-viaducts and to unite the whole into a continuous tube, 1,511ft long, stretching from land to land. This would be rigidly mounted in the central pier but free to move over bearings on the shore piers and abutments to allow for expansion. It will be appreciated that in this way Robert Stephenson introduced the cantilever principle and by so doing vastly increased the strength of the structure. He realized, however, that each of the main sections of the tube must still be self-sustaining, because they could not be united to each other and to the two end sections until they had been lifted into position on the piers.

Stephenson proposed the same tubular construction for the smaller bridge over the Conway, which would consist of a single 400ft span of two tubes. Having settled upon the design, the next great problem was how to build the two bridges. The first idea was to prefabricate the tubes in small sections at the ironworks, but this presented almost insuperable transport and handling difficulties. It was Evans, the contractor for Conway, who first proposed building the tubes on a staging near the site, floating them into position between the piers on pontoons, and then lifting them by means of powerful hydraulic presses housed in the pier towers. This was the method used subsequently with such success by Brunel at Chepstow and Saltash, but at this date such an operation had never been attempted upon so grand a scale. It is true that Telford had floated out the chains for his Menai suspension bridge, but whereas each of these chains weighed $23\frac{1}{2}$ tons, each of the main tubes for the Britannia Bridge scaled more than 1,500 tons, while each of the two Conway tubes exceeded 1,000 tons in weight. However, Evans backed his plan by pluckily volunteering to complete the whole operation at Conway himself. This sporting offer was accepted and Conway thus became the scene of a dress rehearsal for the larger and more difficult undertaking at the Menai. It taught Robert Stephenson at least one very valuable lesson by which certain disaster was later avoided on the Britannia Bridge.

Stephenson appointed Edwin Clark his resident engineer for both bridges and just as Telford's resident William Provis recorded the building of the suspension bridges, so Clark wrote a definitive account of the two tubular bridges in a book from which most of the facts in this chapter have been drawn. The contract for one main section of the Britannia tubes was let to Messrs. Garforth of Manchester, but the other seven sections were contracted for by C. J. Mare of Ditchburn & Mare, whose shipbuilding yard at Millwall would later be acquired by John Scott Russell and used for the building of the *Great Eastern*. At this date only ship-builders had any extensive experience of large-scale wrought-iron construction; hence the association of the names of Fairbairn and Mare with the first large wrought-iron bridges.

The masonry work on both bridges was begun in the spring of 1846 and to house the workmen villages of wooden huts sprang up on the shores of Conway and Menai. Little ships landed their freights of Anglesey marble and sandstone from Runcorn whenever weather and tide served, and in June 1847 the first shipments of iron began to arrive from Liverpool. For the construction of the great Britannia tubes a massive timber platform was built which stretched for a thousand yards along the Caernarvon shore from a stone wharf near the Caernarvon pier to a pontoon dock. Altogether there were 3¼ acres of timber staging.

The technique of producing wrought iron plate and angle or tee sections was then in its infancy, and practically every plate and rib received had to be laboriously flattened or straightened before it could be punched for riveting and passed to the erectors. Some of this work was done by means of cold rollers, but the larger and heavier plates were laid upon huge cast-iron blocks called 'stretching beds' where they were flattened by hand with 40lb sledge-hammers. As a 16lb sledge is considered a heavy hammer today, this detail gives us some conception of the muscle of the men who built the Britannia Bridge. By such means massive bedplates 3½ inches thick were flattened out and for months on end the clangour of these mighty hammers carried far over the waters.

As the first great tube began to take shape, a new and most awkward difficulty arose when the timber staging yielded under its immense weight. Robert Stephenson had designed the main sections of the tube with a nine inch camber, but when the timbers settled under the heavy bedplates this camber was lost. It was essential to restore it before the sides of the tube could be erected and in order to do so the staging had to be lowered under the extremities of the tube and the centre raised by driving in wedges, a most laborious and difficult task. Elsewhere the platform had to be strengthened to prevent a recurrence of the same trouble and this too was a slow and awkward job.

Anyone looking out across the strait from Anglesey after darkness fell beheld a fantastic and unforgettable spectacle when the works were in full swing. Forty-eight rivet-hearths pricked the length of the opposite shore line with flickering points of flame, and from them, all the night long, a golden rain of dazzling sparks shot upwards, describing graceful arcs of light to be caught and reflected in the moving seas. This dramatic effect was produced by the rivet boys who, drawing in their tongs the white-hot rivets from the hearths, hurled them forty feet into the air to be dexterously caught by the riveting gangs at work on the tops of the tubes. Edwin Clark remarks upon the extraordinary accuracy and skill with which this feat was continuously performed. Altogether, 900 tons of rivet iron was consumed in building the Britannia tubes and nearly every rivet was closed by hand.

By the end of February the first of the two Conway tubes was ready for floating. It had been planned to float on the spring tide of 20 February, but arrangements could not be completed in time and the event was postponed until the next favourable tide on 6 March. The six pontoons which would float the tube on the rising tide were moved into position, the tube being temporarily strutted internally with timbers over the bearing points to guard against any distortion. In charge of the pontoons and tackles was Brunel's old friend, Captain Claxton, just returned from refloating the unfortunate *Great Britain* at Dundrum Bay, while beside Robert Stephenson on the top of the tube, hands in pockets and cigar in mouth, stood Brunel himself. Edwin Clark would have been with them, but during a rehearsal three days previously he had had the misfortune to get his foot caught under a capstan which severed his big toe. He therefore described the scene as he saw it while looking up the Conway valley from his seat in an open carriage drawn up on Telford's suspension bridge.

The weather was beautifully serene [he wrote]. The magnificence of the spectacle can scarcely be conceived. As the mass crept along the heavy guide chains, the beautiful valley of the Conway was imperceptibly veiled and like a dissolving view the hills disappeared, the estuary closed gradually and the wide lake with all its mountain scenery was permanently obliterated from the magic scene.

Unfortunately, one set of pontoons slewed slightly until they fouled a rock at the Conway end and the situation could not be retrieved before the tide began to ebb. Consequently the tube, slightly out of position, had to be blocked up where it lay, with the intention of completing the operation the following day. But the exceptionally favourable weather and tide conditions did not hold and during the next four days repeated attempts to get the pontoons back into their positions under the tube all failed. There were several serious accidents; pontoons were swept out to sea or stranded on sandbanks, until Robert Stephenson, says Clark, 'quite despaired'. However, on 11 March the tube was successfully manœuvred into its position and on 8 April the hydraulic presses began to lift it. The lift required was not very great, but even so the work was now completed with extraordinary speed. The first locomotive, with Stephenson on the footplate, passed through the tube ten days later and the bridge was opened to single-line traffic on 1 May.

The second Conway tube was floated into place without a hitch on 12 October, but in lifting it a most alarming mishap occurred. The tube had been raised to within 2ft 3ins of its correct height and Robert Stephenson was standing with a party of visiting engineers on the tube deck, when a crack several inches long appeared in the crosshead of one of the lifting presses. The tube was hastily underpinned with timber packing and this was closely followed up as, with infinite care and in an atmosphere tense with anxiety, lifting was continued. Luckily the fractured crosshead held, though by the time the tube had reached its place the crack had spread a further three inches.

Evans having thus completed his contract and proved the feasibility of his method, the pontoons and tackle were towed round to the Menai straits, where the far more formidable task of floating and raising the Britannia tubes was to be carried out under Robert Stephenson's direct supervision. Here, of course, there were four great tubes to be floated out across the treacherous waters of the Menai, raised to a height of over 100ft above high water and then connected to each other and to the landward portions of the tubes. The latter were already completed, having been built *in situ* on timber stagings. Every detail of the floating operation was pondered and rehearsed with most minute care, a model being made for this purpose to the scale of 1in to 6ft.

Sheer from the Britannia Rock the great central pier now towered to a height of 230ft, the two side-piers being slightly lower for the sake of proportion. This additional height was necessary in order to house the hydraulic gear for lifting the tubes. Arrangements were made to float the first tube, that destined for the up line on the Anglesey side of the Britannia tower, on 19 June 1849. No civil engineering undertaking of such magnitude had ever been attempted and the occasion was reminiscent of the scenes which had marked the raising of the first chain of Telford's bridge twenty-four years before; the same crowds thronged both shores; the same cannon stood ready to thunder a salute to the victorious engineers. The decks of the three great tubes remaining along the Caernarvon shore had been converted into a grandstand which was packed with spectators, while on the Anglesey side a special stand had been erected for the Chester & Holyhead Company directors. Once again Brunel stood beside Robert Stephenson as he controlled the operation, and this time the other member of the great triumvirate, Joseph Locke, was with him as well. With breathless anxiety everyone awaited the signal to start.

As the afternoon lengthened into evening the pontoons lifted the tube on the tide and at six o'clock Stephenson gave the long-awaited signal: 'Cut away!'. The result was an anti-climax. Owing to over enthusiasm on the part of its crew, the capstan on one of the pontoons gave way and there was no alternative but to bring the tube home and postpone operations until the following day. The disappointed crowds melted away, but those who returned on the morrow had their fill of drama and excitement.

A strong breeze was blowing in the morning and the tide was running through the strait so swiftly that it defeated all the efforts of Captain Claxton and his crew of Liverpool sailormen to get the hauling lines laid out. Buoy moorings were uprooted; heavy cables tore themselves free from the buoys and either drifted away on the tide or lashed violently to and fro shooting clouds of spray into the air and creating such a tension that they tended to drag the pontoons from their positions; small boats moored to buoys with spare lines were sunk or dashed to pieces. All day the battle against wind and sea went on until by 7.30 p.m. order had been restored. There was still a stiff south-westerly breeze and a strong tide but Robert Stephenson decided to float and once more gave the signal to cut away. At last the patient spectactors were rewarded by the sight of the great tube gliding smoothly out into the tideway. As it felt the pull of wind and current it began to gather momentum with alarming rapidity. Stephenson ordered the screw cable-stoppers to be applied to check the speed, but one of these stoppers failed to grip and then an 8-in. checking-cable snapped like a thread. For several tense minutes it seemed to the silent crowds that the engineers were losing their precarious hold over their monster and that 1,500 tons of iron would be swept away to irretrievable disaster.

The success of the whole operation depended upon guiding the Anglesey end of the tube so that it would butt against the base of the Anglesey pier. Once safely lodged there it could be swung on this fixed bearing until its other end went home beneath the Britannia tower. But it looked as though the end of the tube was going to miss the pier and drift too near the Anglesey shore. The crucial task of guiding the end of the tube into its correct position had been allotted to Foreman Rolfe, who was in charge of a capstan at Plas Llanfair on the Anglesey shore. From this capstan a 12-in. cable ran to a block on the end of the tube and from this to a carefully positioned fixed mark. At the critical moment there was a disaster. As the end of the tube swung too far and Rolfe's men tried to check it, the coils of cable over-rode and jammed the capstan. At once the capstan was torn from its foundations, all the men were thrown down, and some of them were flung by the capstan-bars into the sea.

Fortunately Foreman Rolfe did not lose his head. Somehow he contrived to get the rope clear of the useless capstan. Seizing the free end, he staggered up the shore, dragging the heavy cable behind him and shouting as he did so for help from the watching crowds. At once his call was answered. Men, women and children alike seized the cable and pulled as they had never pulled before. Never was there so dramatic a tug-of-war. It must have seemed to those who witnessed it that puny human muscles alone could not hope to regain control over the huge iron hulk which was swinging so relentlessly on the tide. Yet sheer weight of numbers prevailed. At first the struggling, shouting snake of humanity was dragged irresistibly forward towards the sea. Then it checked, held fast on the sea's edge. Finally, amid deafening cheers and cries of encouragement, slowly, slowly, fighting for each heel-hold, it began to move back. Obediently the great tube checked its career, drew back also and then began to swing majestically towards its appointed place. At last, with a thunderous reverberation, it struck the base of the Anglesey pier and the battle was over. At once the Caernarvon capstans spun into action and in a few more minutes the other end of the tube was drawn safely home under the Britannia tower. The cannon fired their salutes; the bands struck up; the crowds cheered. "Now," remarked Robert Stephenson to Brunel, "I shall go to bed."

The excitements of this long June day were not yet over, however. With the tube safely secured it still remained to get the pontoons with their crews safely away on the ebb tide and back into their dock by the Caernarvon staging. Night was falling, the wind had risen and the ebb was running very swiftly. The men on board were terrified as the violence of the wind and current tore timberheads out of the decks of the pontoons and they found themselves drifting helplessly. Some managed to anchor, some were picked up by small steamboats, others were swept away on the tide and were brought with difficulty into the safety of Velin Hele harbour. It was midnight before all the pontoons were clear, yet, in spite of the darkness and confusion, when a roll-call was held it was found that there had been no casualties.

Early next morning, Sir Francis Head, one of the many distinguished visitors, strolled down from Llanfair village to survey the scene of the previous day's drama only to find that someone else had got there before him. Upon a precarious perch on the high staging of the Anglesey pier Robert Stephenson sat alone, gazing down at the great tube below and contentedly puffing a cigar in the bright June sunshine. To a friend who had said to him the previous night: "This great work has made you ten years older", he had admitted that he had not slept sound for three weeks, but now the tension was relaxed he felt certain of success, a success which, after the failure of the Dee Bridge, meant so much to him.

Throughout the rest of June and July the tube lay low over the water while the lifting tackle in the towers was prepared. The two hydraulic presses from Conway were installed in the Britannia tower and a single new and larger press in the Anglesey tower. Edwin Clark and his assistants declared enthusiastically that they could raise the tube to full height in two days, but after the mishap at Conway Robert Stephenson insisted that the lift must be closely followed up with masonry in case of accidents. Well it was that he did so, for when the tube had been raised 24ft the cylinder of the new large press broke. The cylinder cover, crosshead and chain tackle, weighing altogether more than 50 tons hurtled from the tower to land with a tremendous crash on the deck of the tube, sweeping one man to his death like a fly as it fell. But for Stephenson's proper caution all would have been lost; as it was, the tube only fell a few inches on to the supporting masonry, although this, with so great a weight, was enough to cause additional damage. Six weeks were lost in repairing the tube and in waiting for a new press-cylinder to arrive from the Bank Quay Foundry at Warrington, so it was not until 13 October that the tube reached its full height.

The second tube was floated on 6 December and had been raised to its place by 7 January 1850. It was placed in line with the first so that when it had been connected to its fellows it was possible to open a single line of way across the strait. On 5 March Robert Stephenson and C. J. Mare, the contractor, drove the last rivet. Then, accompanied by G. P. Bidder, Francis Trevithick, Edwin Clark and other engineers, they boarded a train of prodigious length which was drawn slowly through the tube by three locomotives. Consisting of carriages seating seven hundred people followed by forty-five loaded coal wagons, it weighed over 500 tons. On 18 March the bridge was opened for public traffic.

The work of floating and raising the two tubes for the down line was carried on throughout the following summer, and on 19 October both lines of the iron road to Holyhead were finally completed. To commemorate this engineering triumph and to symbolize the strength of the bridge, four huge couchant lions executed by the Victorian sculptor John Thomas were placed at the bridge approaches. It was also intended to crown the central tower with a colossal figure of Britannia, but happily this idea was abandoned on the score of expense. As it is, the faces of the lions faintly resemble those of be-whiskered Victorian politicians. Unlike Telford's suspension bridge, the Britannia Bridge is not a thing of grace and beauty, but Robert Stephenson's design has a simple power and grandeur which is eloquent enough without the embellishments of Victorian sculptors. According to Samuel Smiles the cost of the bridge was £234,450, but in fact the ironwork alone cost over £300,000 and the total was double this figure. Capital, however, had not been lacking when the Chester & Holyhead Railway was launched. The London & Birmingham Company alone had backed the enterprise to the tune of a million pounds, the largest single investment ever made by one railway company in another. But by the time Stephenson's mighty bridge over the Menai had been completed, his first and latest achievements as a civil engineer had been linked with his father's Liverpool & Manchester Railway and Locke's Grand Junction to form one great Company—the London & North Western Railway.

The success of the Conway and Menai bridges encouraged Robert Stephenson to design other tubular bridges. Two of these were built for the Alexandria & Cairo Railway, one to span the Damietta branch of the Nile at Benha and the other the Karrineen Canal at Birket-el-Saba. Both included a swinging span over the navigation channel and in each case the railway was laid on the tops of the tubes instead of within them. All the materials were manufactured in England under the supervision of Robert's cousin, George Robert Stephenson,[1] and both bridges were opened for traffic in October 1855.

These two Egyptian bridges and even the Britannia Bridge were eclipsed in size by the last great engineering work with which Robert Stephenson was associated. This was the Victoria tubular bridge over the River St. Lawrence at Montreal. The idea of bridging the St. Lawrence first occurred to a Canadian, John Young, who engaged

[1] George Robert Stephenson was the only son of George Stephenson's younger brother Robert. His father died while he was in his teens and his uncle George then placed him in the drawing office of the Manchester & Leeds Railway, where he remained until 1843. George Stephenson then appointed him engineer at Tapton Colliery, Chesterfield. When the works and collieries at Ambergate and Clay Cross were sold to Samuel Morton Peto in 1851, Robert Stephenson appointed his cousin one of his Assistant Engineers and he worked under his superintendence on the South Eastern Railway. Robert Stephenson also left to his cousin in his will his share in Robert Stephenson & Company, with the effect that George Robert Stephenson became the Managing Partner of the Newcastle works in 1859. His two sons, George and Robert, later became Joint Managing Directors.

to make a survey and plan an engineer named Alexander McKenzie Ross. Ross had prepared the plans and estimates for the Chester & Holyhead Railway and assisted in the building of the Conway bridge. Young realized the immense value of such a bridge to Montreal, for although the St. Lawrence, linked to the Great Lakes, made a magnificent trade highway during the summer months, it was frozen up in winter and completely impassable by any form of transport in early spring when the ice began to break up. Yet to call the idea of the bridge a bold one is an understatement, for the St. Lawrence at Montreal is nearly two miles wide. However, Ross prepared a tentative plan for a tubular bridge which the Grand Trunk Railway of Canada accepted and he was sent back to England to confer with Robert Stephenson. This was in the spring of 1852 and in the following August Stephenson himself visited Montreal, inspected the site, and pronounced the scheme practicable. He was appointed Engineer-in-Chief with Alexander Ross as resident, while the work was undertaken by two of the greatest British civil engineering contractors of the day, Thomas Brassey and Messrs. Peto & Betts.

On Stephenson's return to England the detailed design of the bridge was prepared at Great George Street. It consisted of a single line of tube 6,588ft long, built in the same way as those used for the Britannia Bridge. The tube would be made in twenty-five sections and rest on twenty-four stone piers. Stone-faced approach embankments made up a total length of 8,600ft. Headway above high (summer) water level was 30ft rising to 60ft under the two large navigation spans. All this iron work, amounting to more than 9,000 tons, was supplied from England drilled and marked ready for assembly, this being done at the Canada Ironworks at Birkenhead under George Robert Stephenson's supervision.

The St. Lawrence at Montreal is comparatively shallow and it has a rock bottom, two factors greatly in favour of the engineers. But these two advantages were offset by the icing of the river (which meant that work on pier-foundations could only be carried on for six months out of twelve) and by the swift currents—up to eight knots in summer. To enable masonry work to continue under extreme frost, felt covered with a layer of asphalt was used instead of mortar for jointing the ashlar but, even so, work on the great bridge proceeded extremely slowly. The first stone was laid on 22

April 1854, but the first train did not cross it until 24 November 1859, six weeks after Robert Stephenson's death. It was formally opened in August of the following year by Edward VII, then Prince of Wales.

Stephenson's great bridge, the ultimate development of his tubular principle, did duty for forty years before it was completely rebuilt using steel lattice trusses. More than a single line of way had become essential, while, despite the introduction of smoke-vents in the top deck, the long tube became extremely foul, so that to travel through it was a suffocating experience. Robert Stephenson designed the piers with massive cutwaters of iron-bonded stone projecting on the upstream side the better to resist pack ice and to prevent it piling up against the bridge. By building up these cutwaters and by cantilevering the bridge platform a deck width of 66ft was obtained for the rebuilt bridge. This was used to carry a central double track flanked on one side by a roadway and on the other by the two electrified lines of the Montreal & Southern Counties Railway. The latter were removed in 1956 and a dual-track highway now flanks the lines of the Canadian National Railways.

By 1942, after resisting extreme weather conditions and the annual assault of pack ice for over eighty years, the massive stone-work of the piers at last began to show signs of decay and disintegration. Thanks to modern techniques undreamed of in Stephenson's day, including the intrusion of cement grout under pressure, they have now been completely restored and should still stand a century hence as a memorial to the British engineers who designed and built them.

By the time the Victoria Bridge was completed it was already obsolete in design, so rapid was the development of technique. In his splendid Royal Albert Bridge over the Tamar at Saltash, which was opened in May 1859, Brunel demonstrated an altogether lighter, more scientific and economical form of wrought-iron construction for bridges of large span than the great rectangular tube. Yet this should not lessen our admiration for Robert Stephenson's achievement at the Menai. He led where others followed. Pre-dating Brunel's work at Saltash by nine years, the Britannia was the first great wrought-iron bridge and today, when the bridge still stands fast after more than a century, we can affirm that if its creator erred in his design it was on the side of excessive strength which has so far proved impervious to time.

CHAPTER SIXTEEN

The End of an Era

SO FAR AS the personal supervision of great engineering works was concerned, Robert Stephenson's engineering career in Britain can be said to have ended with the completion of the Royal Border and Britannia bridges in 1850. In only one other work in England did he take an active interest. This was the reconstruction and strengthening of the famous cast-iron arch over the Wear at Sunderland, the second large cast-iron bridge in the world, the first being at Coalbrookdale. In charge of this work at Sunderland was G. H. Phipps who, it may be recalled, was one of Stephenson's right-hand men at Forth Street when the *Rocket* was building, but was transferred to civil engineering work on the London & Birmingham Railway. He afterwards remained a member of Stephenson's staff at Great George Street. The reconstruction of this bridge was a difficult and delicate task; Stephenson last visited the works in 1857 and they were not completed until after his death.

In 1850 Robert Stephenson was only forty-seven, yet the stresses, anxieties and sorrows of the past ten crowded years had aged him prematurely and left him broken in health. Not only had he grossly overdriven himself, achieving more in a decade than many an engineer would accomplish in a lifetime, but at the same time he had had his fill of sorrow and anxiety. He had lost his wife and his father and had had to contend with the Stanhope & Tyne and the Dee Bridge disasters, the one threatening his fortune and the other his fame. Both were now secure. When his inherited wealth from his father was added to his own very considerable professional earnings, his annual income totalled, according to Jeaffreson, £30,000, a very high figure considering the value of money in those days. No engineer before him had achieved such wealth, while, judged in terms of purchasing power, he can have had very few richer successors in his profession. As for his fame, the completion of the two great railways to Edinburgh and Holyhead set an un-breakable seal upon it and made him the undisputed peer of his profession. Though he refused a knighthood, the eminence of 'the Chief', as he was always affectionately called by his staff of engineers at Great George Street, was acknowledged in other ways. He became Vice-President of the Institution of Civil Engineers in 1847 and President in 1856. He was elected a Fellow of the Royal Society in 1849 and in 1857 received an Honorary Doctorate of Civil Law at Oxford in company with Brunel and Dr. Livingstone the explorer.

Yet only he realized how heavy a price he had paid for his wealth and fame. Since the death of his wife he had devoted his life to his work in the same single-minded and unsparing fashion as did Brunel, and although, unlike Brunel, he began to ease his pace while he was still to outward appearance in the prime of life, this relaxa-tion came too late for a constitution which had never been robust, and was by 1850 fatally undermined. With no wife and no children to live for and with the knowledge that not many years remained to him, he was at heart a sad and lonely man though his friends did not suspect it. Before them he always appeared to be the soul of good humour and good fellowship. Friends were, in fact, his great solace. He was a member of the Athenaeum and Carlton Clubs, where he was frequently to be found, and he regularly attended the dinners given by the Geographical Society, the Royal Society Club and other similar bodies. "At these dinners," his biographer Jeaffreson tells us, "Robert Stephenson was one of the principal attractions and causes of enjoyment. He thoroughly enjoyed them, always stopping late for 'a little more talk and just another cigar'."

Such was his life in London during these last years. The truth was that he hated returning to the solitude of that large house at 34 Gloucester Square, whither he had moved in 1847, and he would always postpone that return as long as possible. He employed a large staff there; he had filled its spacious drawing-rooms with rare and curious clocks, with microscopes, electrical instruments and other expensive toys; the walls were hung with paintings by Danby, Lucas and Landseer, while the marbles which he purchased from the Great Exhibition of 1851 glimmered like ghosts in the corridors. But no amount of wealth could make Gloucester Square a home, and when a lady visitor once complimented him upon it he recalled his first small house in Newcastle and answered sadly: "It is the Robert Stephenson of Greenfield Place that I am most proud to think of." He looked back to those few years he had spent with his young wife in Newcastle, before he was drawn into the frenzied maelstrom of railway promotion and construction, as the happiest and most fruitful of his life. Not only did he possess a true home then, but he was doing the work that he loved best. For Robert Stephenson's true vocation was mechanical engineering, and despite his mighty accomplishments as a civil engineer the development of the steam locomotive was his greatest achievement and his pride. That the public should applaud his spectacular feats of tunnelling or bridge-building and either take the locomotive for granted or award his father credit for it which was properly due to himself mattered not at all. For the man whose heart is engaged, the satisfaction of the work is all.

It is fortunate for us that Robert Stephenson, like Brunel, lived into the age of photography. With slick technical competence the Victorian portrait painter produced what he considered the sitter and the public expected to see—the public man, smooth, imperturbable, dignified but as far removed from life as a tailor's dummy. Today, the fashionable photographer can, by clever lighting and skilful retouching, produce a more subtle yet equally misleading result; in the 1850s there was no such artifice. In the long exposure under simple, direct lighting the camera's eye was true and pitiless. So it is with the photograph taken of Robert Stephenson late in life. Here there is no concealing the furrows which the years of strain and anxiety have carved in harsh diagonals from the corners of eyes, nose and mouth. The expression in the eyes is poles apart from that confident, self-satisfied gaze with which we so wrongly suppose the great ones of the Victorian age regarded their world. There is not only sadness and suffering in these eyes, but a profound disillusionment. The picture tells us more about Robert Stephenson in his last years than all the pages of Smiles or Jeaffreson.

To portray Robert Stephenson's declining years as altogether sombre and tragic would be misleading. If they had the melancholy they also had the calm and the brightness of a fine autumn that follows a stormy spring and summer. Indeed, the contrast between

these years and the atmosphere of hostility, the bitter rivalries and
jealousies which had accompanied his father's rise to fame and in
which he had become inescapably involved, could not be more
profound. "No man of such eminence", writes Jeaffreson, "has ever
had less of jealousy and detraction embittering success." This was
true. The legacy which Robert inherited from his famous father had
its debit as well as its credit side. Though George Stephenson's
vision and single-minded determination had begotten the world of
railways in which his son had won such fame and fortune, his
obstinacy, his egotism and his intransigent temper had shadowed the
Stephenson name with dissension and enmity. It is perhaps the
brightest revelation of Robert Stephenson's quality as a man that he
should have succeeded so triumphantly and so completely in dis-
pelling this unhappy atmosphere. He did so by a scrupulous avoid-
ance of his father's mistakes. Though he might, as Conder says,
occasionally betray passion or arrogance in his dealings with subordinates, he remained essentially a humble man. His habitual
caution and conservatism was a mark of this humility, for he totally
lacked the proud man's abundant self-confidence. He never hesitated
to seek help and advice from others whom he considered better
qualified than himself and he was scrupulous in his acknowledge-
ment of such help when given. Though the ultimate responsibility
rested with him and was never shirked, he was always the first to
acclaim the part played by his resident engineers and to deprecate
his own contribution. Unlike his father, to whom a professional
rival was necessarily a personal enemy, he was able to combine public
rivalry with private friendship to a degree that set an example to his
profession. By such patient, unassertive and tolerant means did
Stephenson charm away prejudice and reconcile old differences to
win his reward in universal affection.

Stephenson's reconciliation with Locke was mentioned in the
last chapter. He was also reconciled to the Pease family with whom
he had once been at odds over the conduct of the Newcastle factory
and the Newcastle & Darlington Junction Railway. In October 1854
he spent several days with Edward Pease and the old man wrote in
his diary:

"*Mon. Oct. 23.* My friend, Robert Stephenson the engineer, to
spend two or three days with me—a man of most highly gifted and

talented power of mind, of benevolent, liberal, kindly, just, generous dispositions, in company most interesting." But on the next day
he wrote: "The evening pleasantly spent nearly alone, expressing
to Robert Stephenson my anxious desire that smoking and taking
wine might be carefully limited. Free, open converse. Oh my soul,
be upon the watch."

In the course of this visit to Darlington, Stephenson renewed his
friendship with Edward Pease's sons, Joseph, John and Henry, with
John Dixon and Francis Mewburn. He last visited Edward Pease in
April 1857, when the whole Pease family were gathered to meet
him. "The evening was gratifyingly spent in converse", wrote Pease.
"But oh, my leanness in feeling at home in the body." Edward
Pease died at the end of July 1858, aged ninety-one.

Even more revealing was Stephenson's friendship with Brunel,
and nothing does the two greatest engineers of the day more credit.
Totally unlike in character and background and pursuing engineering policies which were diametrically opposed, the two men
formed a friendship based on mutual esteem and respect which
deepened as their deaths drew near. "It is very delightful," wrote
Brunel in his diary after an evening spent with Stephenson in 1846,
"in the midst of our incessant personal professional contests, carried
to the extreme limit of fair opposition, to meet him on a perfectly
friendly footing and discuss engineering points." To illustrate this
friendship of opposites, F. R. Conder relates the following revealing
anecdote. One winter's day Robert Stephenson, Brunel and Locke
were travelling together in a first-class compartment. Train heating
then being primitive or non-existent, Stephenson wrapped himself in
his Northumbrian plaid, observing as he did so that Brunel was
watching the operation with keen interest. "I'll bet you ten pounds
you can't put it on properly first time", he challenged. "Done,"
replied Brunel promptly, "but I won't take your money. If I put it
on right when we get out, it's mine." He then appeared to fall into
a brown study, leaving Stephenson and Locke to carry on an
animated conversation while he covertly studied the folds of the
plaid. As they approached their destination, Stephenson took it off
and tossed it on the seat beside Brunel. To his dismay and greatly
to Locke's amusement Brunel picked it up, calmly flung it about his
shoulders as to the manner born and strode off down the platform,

remarking over his shoulder: "First attempt, but I think it's mine."

Brunel waived all other engagements to be at Stephenson's side during the floating of the Conway and Menai tubes, when his boundless vitality and self-confidence gave the pessimistic and easily discouraged Stephenson just the moral support he needed. Stephenson was able to repay this debt at the end of his life when Brunel, who had by then, like the ailing Stephenson, driven himself almost to death, was fighting his last epic battle to launch his huge steamship *Great Eastern*. An appeal from Brunel for help and advice was handed in to Gloucester Place late one winter's evening in 1857. Weak and ill though he was, Stephenson responded immediately and by 6 o'clock the next morning he was at his friend's side at Millwall. At midday while the two engineers were superintending the hydraulic presses which were pitting their strength against the towering hull, Stephenson stepped on a baulk of timber which upended and landed him up to his waist in Thames mud. He was urged to go away and change, or at least to dry himself, but he waved such solicitude aside. "Oh, never mind me", he insisted impatiently, "I'm quite used to this sort of thing" and although it was bitterly cold and he was wearing no overcoat he continued to paddle about on the muddy Thames shore, advising and encouraging Brunel as they smoked cigar after cigar until darkness fell and put an end to the day's efforts. He was laid up for a fortnight with bronchitis as a result of this escapade, but he continued to send messages of advice and encouragement to Brunel from his sick-bed. At a time when press and public alike ridiculed Brunel and prophesied failure, Stephenson repeatedly expressed his complete confidence in the ultimate success of the launch, and such loyalty on the part of his old antagonist warmed Brunel's heart.

Notwithstanding his ill-health and his ample means, Robert Stephenson never retired from his profession. By declining personal responsibility for engineering works in Britain he lightened his burden and secured for himself much greater freedom of action and movement. He could now work or not as he chose, but in practice his last years were still full of activity, for the world would not let him go. His staff of engineers at the Great George Street office, notably Tom Gooch, G. P. Bidder, Edwin Clark and G. H. Phipps, would not dream of embarking upon any project of importance without consulting 'the Chief'; while over certain works abroad Stephenson exercised a very close personal supervision. In addition to the Egyptian and Canadian tubular bridges, these overseas works included the construction of a railway in Norway from Christiania to Lake Miosen. Stephenson's association with this project originated from a holiday trip which he and G. P. Bidder paid to Norway in the summer of 1845, but it was not until 1850 that a survey was undertaken. Construction was subsequently begun with Stephenson as Engineer-in-Chief and Bidder as his resident engineer. In 1851, 1852 and again in 1854 Robert returned to Norway to superintend the operations. It was for this work that he received the Order of St. Olaf.

As a consultant, Stephenson's business continued to be very great, and as he was now the most distinguished civil engineer in the country this practice was by no means wholly confined to railways. He made a report on Liverpool's water supply in 1850; he was joint engineer with Sir John Rennie to the Norfolk Estuary Company, while until his death he acted as engineer to the committee set up to improve the course of the River Nene between Peterborough and Wisbech.

In addition to all this there was his parliamentary business to attend to. Stephenson was returned unopposed as the Member for Whitby in 1847, contested the seat successfully in a subsequent election, and continued to represent the constituency until his death. Unlike the Member for Cricklade, his fellow-engineer Daniel Gooch, who in twenty years never spoke a word in the House, Stephenson was an active parliamentarian though never a distinguished one. While his father, though a conservative by inclination, remained politically uncommitted, Robert was a staunch and uncompromising Tory, insisting that by Tory he meant Tory and not merely conservative. An ardent protectionist, he was one of the small group who fought the free-traders to the last ditch, yet he was never the slave of the Whips. If the views of his party ran counter to his own judgement he would unhesitatingly speak and vote against them. His maiden speech in 1850 was a defence of the Great Exhibition proposal against the attack launched upon it by his fellow Tory, Colonel Sibthorp. He was one of the Exhibition Commissioners and a member of the Building Committee with his friend

Brunel. He was forthright in his condemnation of the government's mishandling of the disastrous campaign in the Crimea. "It is distressing, execrable and contemptible", he wrote. "There is not one redeeming feature in the whole thing", and he supported the motion introduced by the radical, Roebuck, which brought down the government.

Some idea of Robert Stephenson's religious opinions may be gained from the views he expressed during the storm which arose in the winter of 1850 as a consequence of the Pope's action in creating Bishop Wiseman the first English Cardinal since the Reformation. In a pastoral letter addressed from Rome immediately after his creation, Wiseman spoke of the "restoration of Catholic England to its orbit in the ecclesiastical firmament", words which provoked an outcry in English protestant circles, where Wiseman's creation was condemned as a flagrant act of papal aggression. Stephenson was away in Malta at the time this storm blew up, but in a letter to Starbuck he wrote:

I am now very anxious about getting home as I feel I am deserting my colours in the matter of papal interference. It is a sad exhibition of the worldly character of religion—a battle as to the mere *form* in which the creator shall be worshipped—the true spirit of Christianity is never allowed to appear. The step which the pope has taken is nothing but an ostentatious aggression upon a country where he must have known that it would be incompatible. He must be a fool as I always considered him. Wiseman, on the other hand, is a cunning, designing, talented rogue; it is from him and not the pope that I consider this movement has emanated, if so, then I say to him 'who sows the wind reaps the whirlwind'. Will the Cardinal's scarlet robes make one better or sincerer papist in England than there was before?—no, not one . . . it will never add to his flock one Christian in the true sense of the word.

On the subject of education, Robert Stephenson also held strong views and opposed Lord John Russell's educational reforms. "It is all nonsense Lord John preaching and preaching education for the working classes", he declared. "What the artisan wants is special education for his own particular speciality. And the more he leaves everything else alone the better." Brunel went even further than this by declaring on one occasion that he preferred his enginemen to remain illiterate, as formal education only caused their minds to wander from the responsible job in hand. So provocative a remark was typical of Brunel, but such views on education come strangely from Stephenson, who had himself risen from the ranks and received an intensive education through the help of his father. Possibly, however, he had his father's example in mind, believing, not that the world was full of 'mute inglorious Miltons', but that, come what may, talent will find its way to the top. Nevertheless, in this case Stephenson's precepts and practice did not agree. By 1859, when he uttered this forthright statement he had already made liberal donations to several educational bodies and drawn up his will in which he left a legacy of £7,000 to the Newcastle Literary and Philosophical Institution where he had studied as a boy.

This was by no means his only substantial contribution to his native city, where he had spent the happiest years of his life. To the end, the now famous Newcastle locomotive works was always his first consideration, communications passing to and fro continually between Stephenson's office in Great George Street and his staff at Newcastle: William Hutchinson the managing partner, William Weallens, who was now chief draughtsman and was admitted to the partnership in 1855, or George Crow the Works Manager. Stephenson's railway undertakings at home and abroad almost invariably produced locomotive orders for Robert Stephenson & Co. The Victoria Bridge contract brought orders for engines for the 5ft 6in gauge Grand Trunk Railway of Canada in 1856, while the Alexandria & Cairo Railway was equally productive. In this case the orders included a most richly decorated locomotive and special saloon for the Egyptian Viceroy, Mohammed Said, who was a warm friend to Stephenson.

It was in connection with the Alexandria & Cairo Railway that Robert Stephenson's professional conservatism and caution led him to make a serious error of judgement. In 1847 he had accompanied the French engineer, Paulin Talabot, and the Austrian, Negrelli, on a survey of the isthmus of Suez in order to determine the possibility of cutting a canal from the Mediterranean to the Red Sea. He decided against the canal and in favour of an extension of the Alexandria & Cairo Railway across the isthmus. When, undeterred by this adverse report, the great Ferdinand de Lesseps at last procured the backing of the French government and of Mohammed Said which enabled him to translate his dream into a reality, Robert Stephenson opposed him. He supported Lord Palmerston's refusal of British participation in the canal scheme by vigorous speeches of denunciation which he delivered in the House of Commons in 1857 and 1858. He agreed with Palmerston in calling it a 'bubble scheme' and declared that from an engineering point of view the canal was impossible. The sands, he said, would quickly fill the channel and the result would not be a canal but a useless ditch. That this was an honest opinion uninfluenced by any political considerations is clear from a letter which Stephenson wrote to Tom Gooch in 1858.

You see [he said] I have been pitching into my dear friend Lesseps again about the Suez Canal. . . . Roebuck was determined to bring the matter again before the House. . . . I tried to get him to withdraw the motion, as I knew any fresh discussion upon it could only engender bad feeling on the part of the French. He was perfectly resolute and would not listen to any course but the one he had proposed for himself. I had therefore no alternative but to repeat what I had formerly said, and to stop, as far as I could, the English people from spending the money on an abortive scheme.

It has been said that British opposition to the Suez Canal scheme was wholly political, being guided by the fear that it would result in a great increase in French power and influence in the Middle and Far East. No doubt power politics did enter into the matter, but the condemnation of Britain's foremost civil engineer, who had himself been over the ground, undoubtedly carried very great weight in the House of Commons. Britain subsequently acquired her interest in the Suez Canal through Lord Beaconsfield's purchase from the Khedive, Ismail Pasha, of Egypt's shares in the undertaking, but Robert Stephenson did not live to see de Lesseps prove him wrong.

During and after the railway mania Robert Stephenson frequently inveighed against the profligate waste of capital on innumerable conflicting railway projects, many of them barefaced 'bubble schemes' such as he wrongly suspected the Suez canal to be. He strongly advocated the appointment of an independent tribunal of engineers to sit in judgement upon all new railway schemes before their submission to Parliament. He claimed that by thus separating the sheep from the goats, reputable promoters would no longer have to expend enormous sums in legal and parliamentary expenses solely in order to defeat rival schemes concocted by unscrupulous share-pushers. This suggestion was never acted upon, for although sound in theory it would have been difficult to carry out. It would have been almost impossible to select a panel of engineers at once sufficiently expert and unprejudiced to carry out so invidious a task with complete fairness.

Robert Stephenson saw the downfall of George Hudson in 1849, a downfall largely brought about by that influential 'Liverpool Party' of railway shareholders whom even Hudson could not offend with impunity. They never forgave him for an over-subtle stroke by which he scooped the Leeds & Bradford line out of their clutches and into his own empire. The fall of Hudson pricked the railway bubble and the resulting slump was followed by a slow and painful recovery. This situation undoubtedly helped Robert Stephenson's resolve to play a less prominent part in railway affairs, but, slump or no slump, he was still besieged by enthusiastic promoters or optimistic inventors. Even when ill-health kept him away from his office at Great George Street they would invade his house in Gloucester Square. "Swarms of talkative, and for the most part profitless clients intruded on the privacy of the man whose too pliant temper laid him open to their annoyance", writes Jeaffreson. He continues by relating how a personal friend of Stephenson once called at Gloucester Square and, finding every downstairs room crowded with people, was forced to take refuge in a bedroom until Stephenson could see him. Such importunate visitors were kept at bay by Robert's brother-in-law, John Sanderson, who acted as his business manager and lived at Gloucester Square until his death in 1853. Stephenson felt the loss of Sanderson very keenly, and it was after this that he found the solitude of Gloucester Square at night so unendurable.

During these last years of his life Robert Stephenson had one infallible way of escape from the two evils of unwelcome clients and loneliness. It was also his greatest pleasure and the medicine which alone enabled him to keep his mortal sickness at bay for as long as he did. This was his yacht *Titania*, 'the house that has no knocker' as he sometimes called her affectionately. There were, in fact, two *Titania*s, both built for him by John Scott Russell, the builder of the *Great Eastern*. The first *Titania* was a hundred-tonner, launched for him in 1850. His first long voyage in her was to Alexandria, where she lay during the 1850-51 winter. She was evidently a fast but somewhat wet and uncomfortable sailer, to judge from a letter which Stephenson wrote to a friend in May 1850 when she was running her trials.

We have had a sail or two in *Titania* in very rough weather, in fact in the late very boisterous and fatal gales [he wrote]. She behaved very well, beating anything we could find to sail with—she is certainly very fast, say 11 knots or 12½ miles an hour, and as a necessary consequence *rather wet*. I suppose it is in navigation as in Mechanics, you cannot have both [comfort] and speed at the same time; we must therefore not expect velocity and dryness in a vessel in a boisterous sea and beating to windward. When nature makes a law, how consistently she sticks to it! How much valuable time man wastes in resisting her; his chief wisdom consists in first determining her laws and then by his ingenuity making use of them.

In 1852 the overheated flue of a cabin stove set fire to the *Titania* while she was anchored at Cowes and she was burned to the water line. Undismayed by the news of this disaster, Stephenson immediately instructed Scott Russell to build him a second, larger and better, *Titania*, which was launched, appropriately, on midsummer day 1853. She was a slower ship than her unlucky predecessor but was much more roomy and comfortable. She was 184 tons burden, 90ft long, 21ft beam and drew 13ft of water. She was most luxuriously equipped and in her Stephenson made many long and happy voyages. The spacious saloon, 16ft by 15ft, contained a large library of books, for he had become a voracious reader, and the ship was always well stocked with wines and cases of cigars. It was her proud owner's greatest delight to invite a few choice friends to join him on board and escape with them to the inviolable sanctuary of the open sea. According to these fortunate friends, as soon as *Titania* had put to sea, 'the Chief' seemed quite transformed both in health and spirits. The years seemed to fall away from him and he would behave like an excited schoolboy.

In the early autumn of 1857 Stephenson set out in *Titania* with G. P. Bidder and two other friends to revisit, first, the place of his boyhood and then the scene of his greatest engineering triumph. It is almost certain that he knew by this date that his time was running out and that this was to be a voyage of farewell, but of this his friends had no inkling for 'the Chief' seemed as cheerful as ever. The *Titania* first put in to Sunderland so that Stephenson could visit West Moor, Killingworth and make a pilgrimage to his father's birthplace at Wylam. On the threshold of the old cottage at West Moor he stood for a few moments gazing up at the sundial which he and his father had fixed there so many years ago. Then he went inside to find that the bookcase and writing-desk which his father had made was still in its old place, its cunningly contrived secret drawer undiscovered by subsequent tenants. He spent some time gossiping in the little parlour, and when he left his companions noticed that he was weeping. They tramped off down the familiar road to Long Benton which Robert had trodden so many times on his way to Tommy Rutter's school, and as they went he pointed out the smithy where he used to bring the pitmen's picks to be sharpened. Robert was again deeply moved to find that some of the old cronies of his Killingworth days could no longer recognize in his careworn face the slim, dark-haired youth whom they had once known. "What, don't you know me, old friend?" he exclaimed to one who gazed blankly at him. "Why," said the other after long scrutiny, "it must be Bobbie Stephenson!" "Ay, my lad", he answered sadly, "it's all that's left of him."

Such encounters as this, such memories of a past that seemed a world away, were too poignant to be borne. Better to forget. Better to be at sea again with canvas crowded, with good wine and good books; with good companions who could not recall those old Killingworth days. So the *Titania* soon put out from Sunderland, sailed north to Clachnaharry, passed through Telford's Caledonian Canal and then turned south again down the west coast bound for Holyhead.

While the *Titania* lay in Holyhead harbour, Stephenson and his three companions visited the Britannia Bridge. One of them afterwards described the scene. They climbed on to the upper deck of the great tube and from this splendid vantage point 'the Chief' gave them a graphic description of the floating of the tubes, living the battle over again. It was a perfect autumn morning, brilliant, clear and almost windless. Below them the straits of Menai were calm and of an almost Mediterranean blue while along the eastern horizon the mountains of North Wales, the Glyders, Snowdon, Carnedd Llewelyn, rose sharp and majestic, dark against the morning light. Wrote Stephenson's companion: "We smoked a cigar in silent contemplation before we left the spot, none of the party being disposed to speak. . . ."

Almost exactly a year later, on 14 October 1858, the *Titania*, with Stephenson and a small party of friends on board, sailed from Southampton Water bound for Alexandria. After touching at Malaga, Algiers and Malta the yacht dropped anchor opposite the Pasha's palace at Alexandria on 3 November and throughout the winter Stephenson divided his time between *Titania* and Shepheard's Hotel in Cairo. On 5 December, in a letter to Tom Gooch, he wrote: "I shall stay quietly in Cairo and enjoy daily a drive into the desert, which I have always found most invigorating. By the last post I had a message from Brunel, inviting me to dine with him at Cairo on Christmas day."

On 20 December, Brunel, accompanied by his wife and younger son Henry, arrived at the Hotel d'Orient and there, on Christmas Day, the two greatest engineers of the century met and dined together for the last time. In that warm climate the health and spirits of both men speedily revived. Brunel had been seen riding round the streets of Cairo on a donkey, enjoying himself hugely, yet in fact the long ordeal of the launching of the *Great Eastern* had left him in no better case than Stephenson. Like him, Brunel was now suffering from chronic nephritis, or Bright's disease as it was then called, and the shadow of approaching death hung over them both. Perhaps both may have realized that it was unlikely that they would ever meet again.

Stephenson arrived back in London on 9 February 1859. His health seemed to be restored and for the next few months it was a case of 'business as usual' accompanied by his customary round of political and social activities. But in June he suffered a relapse and at the last dinner of the Royal Society Club which he attended on 11 August his companions noticed that he ate scarcely at all; that he looked wretchedly ill and quite lacked his usual cheerfulness. Three days later he boarded the *Titania* once more for his last voyage.

Robert Stephenson and G. P. Bidder had been invited to attend a banquet at Christiania to celebrate the completion of the new railway which they had engineered. Bidder had his own yacht, the *Mayfly*, and the two little ships sailed from Harwich together, arriving in Christiania f jord on 21 August. Among those who sailed on the *Titania* were Tom Gooch and G. H. Phipps. Stephenson was well enough to enjoy a journey over the new railway and then the party returned to their quarters on the yachts until the banquet took place on 3 September. As Stephenson sat, with the Order of St. Olaf pinned to his breast, listening to the long eulogy which preceded the proposal of his health, a sudden attack of nausea and faintness seized him and it was with the utmost difficulty that he managed to struggle to his feet to acknowledge the toast. This he managed to do, though much more briefly than he had intended, insisting merely that the credit should be given to Bidder and not to himself.

Back on board *Titania* he at once retired to his cabin. The next day he was so ill with an acute attack of jaundice that an immediate return to England was ordered. Early the following morning, 5 September, the two yachts weighed anchor and dropped down the f jord, but just before they reached open sea Tom Gooch came alongside the *Mayfly* in one of *Titania*'s boats betraying great anxiety. The condition of 'the Chief' was so grave that they feared he might die before they could reach the English coast. He asked whether one of Bidder's guests, who was a doctor, could, with his wife, come to the *Titania* in exchange for two of their passengers. This was agreed, and with great difficulty, in a rising wind and sea, the exchange was effected. No sooner had the two yachts reached the open sea than they ran into very heavy weather and when darkness fell they lost contact with each other. For seven long days and nights of storm *Titania* battled her way towards the English coast with the dying engineer. Darkness had fallen by the time she made a landfall off the Suffolk coast on 13 September. She was forced to beat about till daybreak, and while she was doing so she encountered the *Mayfly* close beside her, the two yachts entering Lowestoft harbour together at dawn. Leaning upon the arms of two of his companions, Stephenson insisted upon walking from *Titania* to the railway station, whence the train took him back to London and to Gloucester Square.

It was a sad homecoming. Unknown to him, on the very morning the *Titania* had left Christiania, Brunel had collapsed with a stroke on the deck of his great ship and had been carried, partially paralysed, back to his home in Duke Street, Westminster. Now, as Stephenson lay on his death-bed at Gloucester Square he learnt that his great rival and loyal friend had gone before him. Stricken by the news of the disaster which had befallen his *Great Eastern* on her maiden voyage, Brunel had died on the evening after Stephenson's return to London. Although for a brief spell Robert Stephenson rallied, he had now resigned himself to the fact that his own end was very near. He died shortly before noon on 12 October 1859. He was fifty-six, three years older than Brunel.

Seldom has the death of a commoner been more widely mourned or marked by such tokens of respect. It was arranged that Stephenson's body should lie beside that of his great predecessor, Thomas Telford, in the nave of Westminster, and with the Queen's permission the funeral cortége passed through Hyde Park on its way to the Abbey. The whole route of the procession was lined by silent crowds; on Thames and Tyne, Wear and Tees, all shipping lay silent with flags at half-mast. In the Tyneside towns all business ceased at noon on the day of the funeral, and in Newcastle, at their own request, the employees of Robert Stephenson & Company, fifteen-hundred strong, marched through the silent streets to a memorial service in the church of St. Nicholas. Within the walls of the Abbey, everyone of note in the engineering and scientific world had assembled to pay their last respects to Robert Stephenson. But because he himself had remained a humble man for all his wealth and renown the humble also came. One of them was an engineman on the South Eastern Railway who sent in an urgent request for a card of admission. He was Henry Weatherburn, the son of George Stephenson's old workmate at West Moor, Robert Weatherburn, and the driver of the *Harvey Coombe*, the first engine to work on Stephenson's London & Birmingham Railway.

One of the pall-bearers at the Abbey ceremony was Joseph Locke, who had succeeded his old friend as President of the Institution of Civil Engineers. Yet within six months Locke, too, had joined Brunel and Stephenson in the grave. So, in the space of a few short weeks, did England lose prematurely her great triumvirate of engineers; three men for whose mighty achievements history holds no parallel. That they died while they were still comparatively young men was due to more than the simple fact that they grossly overworked themselves. As such great movements are apt to do, the railway revolution proceeded much more rapidly and was far more profound in its effects than its instigators had ever thought possible. Even George Stephenson, for all his vision, was dumbfounded by the rapidity and the scale of the economic and social changes which his railways brought about. As early as December 1830 he wrote in a letter to Longridge: "It is really shameful the way the country is going to be cut up by Railways; we have no less than eight Acts for Parliament this session." What then must his feelings have been during the years 1845-7 when Parliament sanctioned the expenditure of over £138,000,000 on more than 7,500 miles of new railways? Like the Sorcerer's apprentice he had pronounced a spell that loosed titanic forces which he was quite unable to control. Old and bewildered, he made little attempt to do so. It was Robert Stephenson and the engineers of his generation who had to ride the steam-driven whirlwind. Unlike their successors, Robert Stephenson, Brunel and Locke grew to manhood in a world whose affairs had been governed since the beginning of recorded history by the pace of the horse. Yet they had to adapt themselves to a new world in which the whole rhythm of life was changed by the speed of mechanical traction. It is almost impossible for us to conceive the strain which such an adaptation imposed upon body and mind, but to attempt to do so is to understand why they died before their time; why their triumph was also their tragedy.

"No individual intellect", declared William Harle in 1866, "in so short a space of time, ever produced such great and lasting effects as George Stephenson." Robert Stephenson experienced those effects. He saw great industries develop upon a scale impossible before and a new, swollen industrial population transform small towns into great smoking cities, and villages into new black townships whose existence depended upon the new mobility. He may, like old Edward Pease, have wondered uneasily sometimes whether this great revolution which he and his father had brought about was for good or for evil. Yet his refuge, if ever such doubts assailed him, was his faith in the ultimate betterment of mankind through material progress. Like his father he believed that the triumphal progress of their locomotive across the world must ultimately lead to an era of universal peace and prosperity when men would 'beat their spears into pruning hooks and learn war no more'.

We know now that this faith is a pathetic fallacy; that its exclusive service can too easily become a fatal obsession. Yet because the successors of the Stephensons have fallen a prey to that obsession and sown the world with dragon's teeth, we should not on that account fail to honour them for what they achieved and what they believed. They were the pioneers, and with their deaths a great era of heroic endeavour drew to a close. For good or ill, they laid the foundations of the modern world and all our subsequent achievements.

Some of those who watched, fearful yet fascinated, as the *Rocket* swept past the stands at Rainhill on her triumphal run realized that this was a unique moment in the story of mankind; that the world would soon be utterly changed. "The chariots shall rage in the streets," one of them quoted, "they shall jostle one against another in the broad ways; they shall seem like torches, they shall run like lightning." We have seen this biblical prophecy even more accurately fulfilled. Yet the conquests of man over space and time have followed the flying wheels of the *Rocket* as surely as night follows day. As was so truly said, there could never again be a beginning.

A Note on Sources and Acknowledgements

ALTHOUGH THE works of Samuel Smiles and J. C. Jeaffreson are the only authoritative biographies of George and Robert Stephenson respectively, the body of railway literature in which they figure more or less prominently is very considerable. The following bibliography, though it includes only the works actually consulted when writing this book, will give some idea of its extent. Of these other sources perhaps the most valuable is J. G. H. Warren's monumental and scholarly centenary history of Robert Stephenson & Company, *A Century of Locomotive Building* (1923) upon which I have drawn very freely. F. R. Conder's *Personal Recollections of English Engineers*, which he published anonymously in 1868, and Thomas Summerside's little book of personal recollections of George Stephenson were both useful to me because they present the Stephensons in a more personal and intimate light than their official biographers.

The stories of the more dramatic achievements of the two Stephensons have often been told in railway histories, but I have tried to present them afresh in more graphic detail by ignoring later and sometimes conflicting accounts and going back to contemporary sources and the descriptions of eye witnesses. In the case of the famous Rainhill Locomotive Trials I was fortunate in having access to the actual Report of the Judges, of which no copy was thought to exist until 1939 when the late Captain E. W. Swan, O.B.E., discovered one in Newcastle in a manuscript Report Book of Nicholas Wood's. Although Wood gives an account of the trials which is obviously based on the Report in the second edition of his *Treatise on Rail Roads*, the Report itself adds valuable details which helped me to reconstruct the scene of this historic encounter—the first contest between machines that the world had ever seen.

Other original documents, collections of letters, reports, minute books and so on which I have consulted are so numerous that I have listed them at the end of the bibliography. It is tantalizingly evident that both Smiles and, to a greater extent, Jeaffreson, had access to certain material which has since disappeared. On the other hand this loss is to some extent compensated by private collections of letters which have been presented to libraries in recent years, some of which the original biographers do not appear to have seen. No doubt further research would yield much more interesting original material, but work of this kind is enormously time-consuming and unless such a research programme is subsidized in some way, which this one was not, it must of necessity be strictly limited.

For their unfailing courtesy and help to me in carrying out the research for this book I am deeply grateful to the Librarians of the Institution of Civil Engineers and of the Institution of Mechanical Engineers; also to Messrs. L. C. Johnson and E. H. Fowkes, British Transport Commission Archivists at London and York respectively.

My thanks go to the many friends who gave me help and advice and who so trustingly lent me precious books for a long period which I would otherwise have had to consult in reference libraries. Among them I would especially mention Messrs. C. R. Clinker, Charles Hadfield, J. Hollingworth, J. F. Parker, John Rapley, John Shearman, David Swan and P. B. Whitehouse. Mr. C. R. Clinker not only placed his splendid collection of railway literature at my disposal but patiently answered a number of tiresome queries which involved research on his part. My friends Charles Hadfield and John Shearman also carried out research work for me, while Mr. David Swan most generously allowed me to borrow and to hold far too long a number of rare items from the library formed by his late father.

I acknowledge the help of the Science Museum in supplying me with a photograph copy of the Rainhill Report and express my thanks to officials of the Canadian National Railways in London and Montreal for their help in supplying me with information regarding the Victoria Tubular Bridge.

In conclusion, I could not bring this biographical trilogy to an end without paying tribute to the kindness, the help and the co-operation I have received throughout from my Publishers and from Mr. John Guest in particular. In this happy association I have felt that we were maintaining a long tradition for, as a glance through my bibliography will show, a high proportion of the nineteenth-century books on Engineers and Engineering were published under the Longman imprint.

L. T. C. R.

Bibliography

ANON. *A Chapter in the History of Railway Locomotion and a Memoir of Timothy Hackworth, the Father of Locomotives.* Leamington: T. Hamblen, 1875

ANON. *Joseph Pease, a Memoir.* Reprinted from the *Northern Echo.* Darlington: Harrison Penney, 1872

ANON. *Observations on the Proposed Rail-Way or Tram-Road from Stockton to the Collieries.* Durham: Francis Humble, 1818

ARCHER, M. *William Hedley, the Inventor of Railway Locomotion.* Newcastle: J. M. Carr, 1882

BARLOW, PETER. *Report on the Weight of Rails, the Description of Chairs and Fastenings, and Distance of Supports & the Size of the Blocks on the Liverpool & Manchester Railway.* London: John Weale, 1837

BOOTH, HENRY. *An Account of the Liverpool & Manchester Railway.* Liverpool: Wailes & Baines, 1828

CLARK, EDWIN. *The Britannia and Conway Tubular Bridges* (2 vols.) London: Day & Son, 1850

CLINKER, C. R. 'The Leicester & Swannington Railway.' Leicester: Leicestershire Archaeological Society, *Transactions*, 1954

COLVIN, H. M. *Biographical Dictionary of English Architects, 1660–1840* London: John Murray, 1954

CONDER, F. R. *Personal Recollections of English Engineers and of the Introduction of the Railway System in the United Kingdom.* London: Hodder & Stoughton, 1868 (This book was published anonymously, but on the copy in the Library of the Institution of Civil Engineers the author's name has been inscribed in manuscript on the title page)

CORDEROY, EDWARD. *Progress, the Life of George Stephenson.* London: James Nisbet, 1857

DANCE, COL. SIR C. W. *A Letter to His Grace the Duke of Wellington on the Application of Steam Power to Carriages.* London: James Ridgway, 1837

DEVEY, JOSEPH. *Life of Joseph Locke.* London: Richard Bentley, 1862

DICKINSON, H. W., and TITLEY, A. *Richard Trevithick Memorial Volume*, Cambridge: University Press, 1934

"E.M.S.P." *The Two James's and the Two Stephensons*. London: G. Phipps, 1861

Extracts from the Minutes of Evidence, Committee of the Lords, London & Birmingham Railway Bill. London: Privately Printed, 1832 (the copy consulted signed and annotated by I. K. Brunel)

FELLOWS, REV. R. B. *The Romance of a Railway, the History of the Canterbury & Whitstable Railway*. Canterbury: J. A. Jennings, 1930

FORWARD, E. A. 'The Stephenson Locomotives at Springwell Colliery.' London: The Newcomen Society, *Transactions*, 1943

—— 'Chapman's Locomotives, Some Facts and Some Speculations.' London: The Newcomen Society, *Transactions*, 1951

—— 'Report on Railways in England in 1826-27, A Translation and Review.' London: The Newcomen Society, *Transactions*, 1953

FRANCIS, JOHN. *History of the English Railway*. London: Longman, Brown, Green & Longman, 1851

GALLOWAY, ROBERT L. *The Steam Engine and its Inventors*. London: Macmillan, 1881

HARLE, WILLIAM LOCKEY, *George Stephenson or Memorials to Genius*, A lecture (c. 1866). Newcastle: J. M. Carr, Rep. 1881

HATTON, JOSEPH. 'Memoir of George Stephenson.' London: *Illustrated London News*, 1881

JEAFFRESON, J. C., with POLE, WILLIAM. *The Life of Robert Stephenson* (2 vols). London: Longman, Green, Longman, Roberts & Green, 1864

JEANS, J. S. *Jubilee Memorial of the Railway System, a History of The Stockton & Darlington Railway*. London: Longmans, Green & Co. 1875

LAMBERT, RICHARD S. *The Railway King, 1800-1871, A Biography of George Hudson*. London: Allen & Unwin, 1934

Larchfield Diary, The. Extracts from the Diary of the Late Francis Mewburn, First Railway Solicitor. London: Simpkin, Marshall, 1876

LAYSON, JOHN F. *Robert Stephenson and Railway Enterprise*. London: Tyne Pub. Co. N.D.

LEE, CHARLES E. *Narrow Gauge Railways in North Wales.* London: Railway Pub. Co., 1945

—— 'The World's Oldest Railway'. London: The Newcomen Society, *Transactions,* 1946

MACNAY, CHARLES. *George Stephenson and the Progress of Railway Enterprise.* Newcastle: Andrew Reid, 1881

MAXWELL, SIR HERBERT (Ed.) *The Creevey Papers,* A Selection. London: John Murray, 1923.

'Memoir of Robert Stephenson.' Institution of Civil Engineers, *Proceedings,* Vol. XIX

NASMYTH, JAMES. *Autobiography,* Ed. Samuel Smiles. London: John Murray, 1883

NOCK, O. S. *The Railway Engineers.* London: B. T. Batsford, 1955

Northern Echo Railway Centenary Supplement. Darlington: North of England Newspaper Co., 1925

PARSONS, R. H. *History of the Institution of Mechanical Engineers.* London: I. Mech. E., 1947

PEASE, SIR ALFRED E., BART. (Ed.) *The Diaries of Edward Pease.* London: Headley Bros., 1907

PRIESTLEY, JOSEPH. *Historical Account of the Navigable Rivers, Canals and Railways Throughout Great Britain.* London: Longman, Rees, Orme, Brown & Green, 1831

ROSCOE, THOMAS. *The London & Birmingham Railway.* London: Charles Tilt, n.d. (c. 1838)

—— *The Book of the Grand Junction Railway.* London: Charles Tilt, 1839

SMILES, SAMUEL. *Life of George Stephenson.* London: John Murray, 1864 (and 1904 edn.)

STEEL, WILFRED L. *A History of the London & North Western Railway.* London: Railway & Travel Monthly, 1914

Stephenson Centenary, The. Official Report. London: E. W. Allen, 1881

STEVENSON, ROBERT LOUIS. *Records of a Family of Engineers.* London: Chatto & Windus, 1912

SUMMERSIDE, THOMAS. *Anecdotes, Reminiscences and Conversations of and with the Late George Stephenson, Father of Railways.* London: Bemrose & Sons, 1878

TOMLINSON, WILLIAM WEAVER. *The North Eastern Railway, its Rise and Development.* Newcastle: Andrew Reid. London: Longmans, Green, 1914

TREVITHICK, FRANCIS E. *Life of Richard Trevithick*. London: E. F. & N. Spon, 1872

VIGNOLES, OLINTHUS C. *Life of Charles Blacker Vignoles*. London: Longmans, Green, 1889

WAKE, JOAN. *Northampton Vindicated*. Northampton: Joan Wake, 1935

WALKER, JAMES SCOTT. *An Accurate Description of the Liverpool & Manchester Railway*. Liverpool: J. F. Camell, 1831

WARREN, J. G. H. *A Century of Locomotive Building by Robert Stephenson & Company, 1823-1923*. Newcastle: Andrew Reid, 1923

WILLIAMS, FREDERICK S. *The Midland Railway, its Rise and Development*. Nottingham: F. S. Williams.

WOOD, NICHOLAS. *A Practical Treatise on Rail-Roads*. London: Hurst, Chance, 1825 (1st edn.) Also revised edn, 1831

YOUNG, ROBERT. *Timothy Hackworth and the Locomotive*. London: Locomotive Pub. Co., 1923

Original Material

In the Library of the Institution of Civil Engineers:

Reports to and from Thomas Telford on the progress of the works of the Liverpool & Manchester Railway.

In the Library of the Institution of Mechanical Engineers:

The following collections of original letters and documents:

The Brandling Papers.
The Crow Collection.
The Phillimore Collection (part only).
The Longridge Collection.
The Thompson Collection.
The Austin Wright Letters.

In the Liverpool City Reference Library & Record Office:

Letters from George and Robert Stephenson to various correspondents, including the letters found at 5, Rochester Road, Coventry, 13.9.30.

In the British Transport Commission Archives, London:

Liverpool & Manchester Railway: Prospectus, Company and Committee Minutes. Minutes of Evidence in Committee, L. & M. Bill, 1825.

London & Birmingham Railway. The Rastrick Report, 13.5.33. Engineers Reports and correspondence, 1833-1844.

The Brighton Railway. Minutes of Evidence, Lords' Committee, 1836.

Preston & Wyre Railway. George Stephenson's Report on Extension.

Manchester & Leeds Railway. George Stephenson's Report on Littleborough Tunnel and speeds.

Chester & Holyhead Railway. Engineers' Reports and sundry letters.

London, Midland & Scottish Railway. Secretary's File of notes on George Stephenson.

In the British Transport Commission Archives, York:

Stockton & Darlington Railway. Company and Committee Minutes Engineers' Estimates, Reports, Expense Accounts and sundry correspondence. Manuscript reminiscences of George Graham.

Index

Note: *The two Stephensons are referred to throughout the Index by their initials,*
G. S. *and* R. S.

FOR THE BEST IN PAPERBACKS, LOOK FOR THE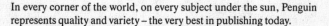

In every corner of the world, on every subject under the sun, Penguin represents quality and variety – the very best in publishing today.

For complete information about books available from Penguin – including Pelicans, Puffins, Peregrines and Penguin Classics – and how to order them, write to us at the appropriate address below. Please note that for copyright reasons the selection of books varies from country to country.

In the United Kingdom: For a complete list of books available from Penguin in the U.K., please write to *Dept E.P., Penguin Books Ltd, Harmondsworth, Middlesex, UB7 0DA*

In the United States: For a complete list of books available from Penguin in the U.S., please write to *Dept BA, Penguin, 299 Murray Hill Parkway, East Rutherford, New Jersey 07073*

In Canada: For a complete list of books available from Penguin in Canada, please write to *Penguin Books Canada Ltd, 2801 John Street, Markham, Ontario L3R 1B4*

In Australia: For a complete list of books available from Penguin in Australia, please write to the *Marketing Department, Penguin Books Australia Ltd, P.O. Box 257, Ringwood, Victoria 3134*

In New Zealand: For a complete list of books available from Penguin in New Zealand, please write to the *Marketing Department, Penguin Books (NZ) Ltd, Private Bag, Takapuna, Auckland 9*

In India: For a complete list of books available from Penguin, please write to *Penguin Overseas Ltd, 706 Eros Apartments, 56 Nehru Place, New Delhi, 110019*

In Holland: For a complete list of books available from Penguin in Holland, please write to *Penguin Books Nederland B.V., Postbus 195, NL–1380AD Weesp, Netherlands*

In Germany: For a complete list of books available from Penguin, please write to *Penguin Books Ltd, Friedrichstrasse 10 – 12, D–6000 Frankfurt Main 1, Federal Republic of Germany*

In Spain: For a complete list of books available from Penguin in Spain, please write to *Longman Penguin España, Calle San Nicolas 15, E–28013 Madrid, Spain*

LIVES AND LETTERS

THE DAUGHTERS OF KARL MARX
Family Correspondence 1866–98
Commentary and notes by Olga Meier
Translated and adapted by Faith Evans
Introduced by Sheila Rowbotham

The letters of Jenny, Laura and Eleanor Marx form a unique and intimate family portrait.

'Excellently translated and edited . . . an enlightening introduction to the preoccupations, political and personal, of the Marx family' – Lionel Kochan

'The daughters' letters express a passionate attachment to their father, passionately returned. They revelled in family jokes and gossip; they lived and breathed the same political passions' – Judith Chernaik in *New Society*

'The tale they tell is riveting – an Ibsen domestic tragedy in the making' – Kay Dick in the *Standard*

THE PASTONS
The letters of a family in the Wars of the Roses
Edited by Richard Barber

Spanning several generations of the redoubtable Paston family, these letters form a unique record of their rise to eminence in their native Norfolk, and of life during the upheavals of the civil war between Yorkists and Lancastrians.

Speaking to us across the centuries, the Pastons work, woo, plot, quarrel and travel, keeping in touch with these letters that all reflect the individual personalities with a fresh, unforgettable immediacy.

For this edition the language has been modernized for easy reading and the editor has provided an invaluable linking text.

A Penguin Book

ISAMBARD KINGDOM BRUNEL
L. T. C. Rolt

'As Brunel's biographer, Mr Rolt is almost too accomplished. He has every admirable quality. He is an excellent writer in love with his subject' – A. J. P. Taylor in the *New Statesman*

'Mr Rolt has the rare gift of making the technical problems of engineering interesting and comprehensible to the layman. He combines this with an appreciation of Brunel's forthright, vigorous and humorous character' – John Betjeman in the *Daily Telegraph*

'Mr Rolt has written an exceptional book, based on original research, temperate, imaginative, truthful, and one in which the influence of family – for Brunel's father, Marc, was of a stature not far short of his son – is given proper weight. Moreover, he has been able to convey the effect of Brunel's force and charm' – *The Times*

A Penguin Book

THOMAS TELFORD
L. T. C. Rolt

The son of a shepherd from the Scottish borders, Thomas Telford rose to be the greatest engineer in Victorian Britain, whose bridges, aqueducts, roads and canals were the wonder of the world, combining aesthetic grace with brilliant engineering. His life spanned one of the most dynamic periods in British history, the decades of the industrial revolution, and no one contributed more to making Britain the 'workshop of the world'.

'A most readable and enjoyable book, for Mr Rolt manages to bring and keep Telford alive . . . a feat which has hitherto defeated his biographers' – *Listener*

'Mr Rolt writes faithfully and thoroughly of Telford's work and achievements. He brings to their interpretation the outlook of an engineer, something from which his book benefits greatly' – Sir Arthur Elton in the *Sunday Times*

'Mr Rolt realizes from the start that what makes Telford important is what he did, not what he was . . . an original writer on fresh themes; he knows his subject inside out' – *The Times Literary Supplement*

A CHOICE OF PENGUINS

☐ *The Complete Penguin Stereo Record and Cassette Guide*
Greenfield, Layton and March

A new edition, now including information on compact discs. 'One of the few indispensables on the record collector's bookshelf' – *Gramophone*

☐ *Selected Letters of Malcolm Lowry*
Edited by Harvey Breit and Margerie Bonner Lowry

'Lowry emerges from these letters not only as an extremely interesting man, but also a lovable one' – Philip Toynbee

☐ *The First Day on the Somme*
Martin Middlebrook

1 July 1916 was the blackest day of slaughter in the history of the British Army. 'The soldiers receive the best service a historian can provide: their story told in their own words' – *Guardian*

☐ *A Better Class of Person* **John Osborne**

The playwright's autobiography, 1929–56. 'Splendidly enjoyable' – John Mortimer. 'One of the best, richest and most bitterly truthful autobiographies that I have ever read' – Melvyn Bragg

☐ *The Winning Streak* **Goldsmith and Clutterbuck**

Marks & Spencer, Saatchi & Saatchi, United Biscuits, GEC ... The UK's top companies reveal their formulas for success, in an important and stimulating book that no British manager can afford to ignore.

☐ *The First World War* **A. J. P. Taylor**

'He manages in some 200 illustrated pages to say almost everything that is important ... A special text ... a remarkable collection of photographs' – *Observer*

A CHOICE OF PENGUINS

☐ *Man and the Natural World* **Keith Thomas**

Changing attitudes in England, 1500–1800. 'An encyclopedic study of man's relationship to animals and plants . . . a book to read again and again' – Paul Theroux, *Sunday Times* Books of the Year

☐ *Jean Rhys: Letters 1931–66*
Edited by Francis Wyndham and Liana Melly

'Eloquent and invaluable . . . her life emerges, and with it a portrait of an unexpectedly indomitable figure' – Marina Warner in the *Sunday Times*

☐ *The French Revolution* **Christopher Hibbert**

'One of the best accounts of the Revolution that I know . . . Mr Hibbert is outstanding' – J. H. Plumb in the *Sunday Telegraph*

☐ *Isak Dinesen* **Judith Thurman**

The acclaimed life of Karen Blixen, 'beautiful bride, disappointed wife, radiant lover, bereft and widowed woman, writer, sibyl, Scheherazade, child of Lucifer, Baroness; always a unique human being . . . an assiduously researched and finely narrated biography' – *Books & Bookmen*

☐ *The Amateur Naturalist*
Gerald Durrell with Lee Durrell

'Delight . . . on every page . . . packed with authoritative writing, learning without pomposity . . . it represents a real bargain' – *The Times Educational Supplement*. 'What treats are in store for the average British household' – *Daily Express*

☐ *When the Wind Blows* **Raymond Briggs**

'A visual parable against nuclear war: all the more chilling for being in the form of a strip cartoon' – *Sunday Times*. 'The most eloquent anti-Bomb statement you are likely to read' – *Daily Mail*

A CHOICE OF PENGUINS

☐ *The Diary of Virginia Woolf*
Edited by Quentin Bell and Anne Olivier Bell

'As an account of the intellectual and cultural life of our century, Virginia Woolf's diaries are invaluable; as the record of one bruised and unquiet mind, they are unique' – Peter Ackroyd in the *Sunday Times*

☐ Volume One
☐ Volume Two
☐ Volume Three
☐ Volume Four
☐ Volume Five